Education in Bruton, Somerset c.1400-c.1914.

Vol. 2   Schools for All.

by

P. W. Randell

Grosvenor House
Publishing Limited

This book is published by
Grosvenor House Publishing Ltd
Link House
140 The Broadway, Tolworth, Surrey, KT6 7HT.
www.grosvenorhousepublishing.co.uk

A CIP record for this book
is available from the British Library

ISBN 978-1-78623-233-5

Contents

CONTENTS

Books by the same author.

Stones We Cannot Eat: Poverty, the Poor Law, Philanthropy and Self-help in Bruton, Somerset, c1500-c1900,
Pen Press, 2009.

Life in a Rural Workhouse, Wincanton Workhouse, Somerset, 1834-1900,
Pen Press, 2010.

Crime, Law and Order in a Somersetshire Market Town: Bruton, c1500-c1900,
Pen Press, 2011.

Alcohol, Violence, Feasts and Fairs: Leisure Pursuits in Bruton, Somersetshire, c1500-c1900,
Pen Press, 2012.

Death Comes to Bruton, a market town in Somerset c1400-c1900,
Grosvenor House, 2014.

The Life and Times of Hugh Sexey of Bruton, Auditor to James I,
Grosvenor House, 2015.

Education in Bruton, Somerset c1400-c1914: vol. I, The Free Grammar School,
Grosvenor House, 2018.

Acknowledgements.

As for my previous books, I must thank the staff of the National Archives and Somerset Heritage Centre for their assistance. Several years ago Dr. Colin Clark drew my attention to the fact that two of the Log Books of Bruton National School had been deposited in Bruton Museum and for that information I am very grateful as they have proved invaluable in this study. Similarly I must express my thanks to Douglas Learmond, one time Chairman of Bruton Museum, for granting me access to the material on the Sunday and National Schools which is not usually on display. I also wish to thank Mrs Sarah Stallion of Sexey's School, Bruton, for arranging access for me to examine some of the very limited archives of the School, particularly the school magazines.

My wife Anne has once again been very supportive and undertaken her accustomed role of proof-reading this material. For that I am very grateful - any errors which remain are my responsibility alone.

Tables.

Illustrations.

Explanation of Terms.

A Tenement	the land held by a tenant which may have common rights attached to it. It could include a house and garden.
Nail	a medieval measure of cloth, 2¼ inches in length.
Perch	a linear measure of land, usually 5½ yards.
	a square measure of area, 30¼ square yards or 160th of an acre.
Rod	a square measure of area, usually 30 square feet.
Offices	toilets.
Pattens	protective overshoes worn outdoors, often had a wooden sole to raise the shoe above wet or muddy ground.

Money.

2 halfpennies, ½d	=	1d, one penny
12 pennies	=	1s, one shilling (equivalent to 5p)
20 shillings	=	£1
21 shillings	=	One Guinea
1 mark	=	13s 4d.

In the earlier part of the period under consideration the £ sign was often written as *li* and followed by the figure and it was not unusual for these figures themselves to be in Roman numerals until the last small *i* which was written as a *j* to indicate the end of the figure, for example,

v *li*	=	£5
vj *li*	=	£6
xjs viijd	=	11s 8d.

Relative value of money.

The Table gives the approximate purchasing power of £1 in the years indicated compared with 2017.

Year	Value of £1 in 2017 in £s.
1750	149
1800	77
1810	68
1820	76
1830	85
1840	86
1850	102
1860	90
1870	91
1880	95
1890	105
1900	103
1910	97
1914	91

For £10 the above figures would need to be multiplied by 10 and for £50 by 50 etc.

Introduction: Setting the scene.

For much of its existence Bruton was a small market town that developed from an Anglo Saxon settlement in which a Royal Mint had been based before the Norman Conquest in 1066. The overwhelming majority of its medieval inhabitants lived in narrow long-established streets which radiated from its market place on the sloping northern side of the River Brue. The southern side of the river was occupied by at least one Church and an Augustinian Priory founded in the early twelfth century and which was raised to the status of an Abbey in 1510.

Away from the bounds of Selwood Forest to the east, agriculture flourished with many inhabitants leasing land, first in the Open Fields and later in the enclosed fields, often referred to as 'Closes'. Some labourers found employment on this land that was extensively used for pastoral purposes. As late as 1798 one survey indicated that in the Manor of Bruton just under 50% of land was pastoral, 11% meadow, 20% arable, 17% coppice and the remainder occupied by houses, gardens and orchards.

For centuries rural industries, especially the woollen trade, flourished in the town and its immediate neighbourhood. In 1542 John Leland found that the town was "much occupied with the making of clothe." The Accounts of John Smythe, a Bristol merchant, revealed that he received substantial amounts of woollen cloth in the 1540s from John Yerbury of Bruton. In the middle of the eighteenth century there were "manufactures of Broad Cloth, Serges and knit Stockings." Families such as the Yerburys, Whiteheads and Goldesbroughs monopolized production, sometimes for generations.

As the woollen industry in the West County declined in the eighteenth century the Ward family became a major employer with their silk factories. By 1823 John Sharrer Ward estimated that he employed "From eight to nine hundred, or perhaps one thousand, the children often working at their own houses with their parents." Faced with foreign competition it too declined and there developed greater diversity in the nineteenth century with other smaller industries such as horsehair seating operated by the Boyds and the Whites and brewing with the Jones family. (1)

The possibility of regular employment meant that Bruton acted as a magnet for labourers and their families. While population growth was far from continuous or uniform there was nearly a ten-fold increase in some nine hundred years. At the time of the Domesday Survey in 1086 there was estimated to be about 250 inhabitants, a figure which increased steadily until the fourteenth century when it was, like the rest of the country, decimated first by harvest failure between 1315 and 1317 and then by the Black Death in 1347-8. Nationally the population was reduced by between one third and one half, and there is no reason to believe that Bruton was in any way different. A slow decline in the population continued until the 1520s when a recovery occurred and various Subsidy Rolls suggest that by the late sixteenth century the town had a population of about 900. A century later, having been checked once again by plague it was just over 1,100. The real explosion which doubled the population started in the late eighteenth century and continued into the nineteenth so that the Census of 1861 recorded a peak of 2,232. (2)

Until the nineteenth century for the overwhelming majority of this population the education facilities in the town were extremely limited. For a very small number of boys there was the possibility of attending the Free Grammar School. (For an account of the history of this school, see volume 1) For the rest there were mainly just the fee-paying alternatives which many labouring families could not afford. The names of a number of the men and women involved in such activities appeared in a range of documents but few details were ever given. Each year from the 1660s four boys a year were elected to Sexey's Hospital where they were educated for three years before being apprenticed. The children of the really poor of the parish, especially orphans, had few opportunities with most being apprenticed by the Overseers of the Poor as soon as possible, as a batch of surviving Apprenticeship Indentures from 1660 to 1832 reveal and in 1733-4 the Overseers paid for "a Warrant in order to send the wenches of ye Parish to service." It cost them 1s 6d. (3)

It has been estimated that at the time of the Civil War in the 1640s about 30% of men and 10% of women were able to sign their own names. Yet the vast majority of these men and women functioned perfectly well even though they were illiterate or semi-literate. Many were able to learn a trade or occupation through experience and practice - common sense was important and they were of course in most cases able to function orally. Much of what was around them was visual, such as picture signs on inns and alehouses and virtually every shop had a picture to advertise its wares, whether it was a fish or a loaf of bread. As Bruton had a weekly market much of the produce could actually be seen on the various stalls.

Children learned a great deal from observation and instruction at home whether it was the fancy needlework of the upper classes or basic housekeeping and cookery for the other classes. For those in rural areas they soon had to learn how to help in the fields and in their own garden, and it was not unusual for young children to be put in charge of even younger brothers or sisters. There were often local rhymes which were associated with the farming year or the weather which guided the very young, such as "Red sky at night, shepherd's delight. Red sky in the morning shepherd's warning." They quickly had to learn the difference between wild plants that were beneficial or good for food and those which were harmful.

So much started to change in the eighteenth century with the Agricultural, Industrial and Transport Revolutions and by the nineteenth century it had become clear that the old ways were no longer enough as a vastly different range of skills were required. Bruton provided one example of what was happening to small towns and villages through the centuries, especially as it population grew and life became more complex.

1

Within Sexey's Hospital.

a) The Boys.

On 14th June 1616 Hugh Sexey, who had risen from obscurity in his native Bruton to become one of the Auditors of James I, sealed an Indenture to appoint twelve Trustees who were to administer his large and valuable estate as he and then his heirs directed. At the time of his death on 19th August 1619 he had no such heirs and as his Will did not contain any instructions for the Trustees they were required to act as they saw fit to fulfil "good and charitable uses."

By the late Elizabethan and early Stuart periods such charitable activities were considered to be almost an obligation by the wealthy. Examples of such action may be found throughout Somerset, such as the almshouses of Nicholas Wadham at Ilton near Ilminster established in 1606, of Edward Hext in Somerton in 1626 and Robert Graye in Taunton in 1635; Blue Schools were founded in towns such as Frome, Wells and Bath; and one of Sexey's own Trustees, John Whitson, left money to Bristol Corporation which resulted in the Red Maids' School in 1634. A study of philanthropy in Somerset between 1480 and 1660 discovered that some £116,531was donated, of which £30,158 (26%) went to the education of the poor and £29,413 (25%) to almshouses. (1) It was a pattern repeated the length and breadth of the country but such actions were of course not entirely philanthropic as many believed that if the children of the poor were educated, or

4

at least taught a trade, then in later life they would be able to support themselves and their families and so would not be a burden on the parish.

By 1623 Sexey's Trustees reported that "they have made diligent search and inquiry both by viewing of the said Hugh Sexey's writing and evidence and papers, and by conference with his most inward and familiar friends." They came to the conclusion that he had intended to erect a new almshouse or hospital in Bruton, particularly as the existing one "is a rotten unfytt buildinge."

As well as a new almshouse for the poor the Trustees also agreed "that a Workinge howse should be erected for ye maintenance & the setting to worke of poore Children and orphans betweene the ages of seaven yeares and Thirteen, and then to be bound Apprentices.... The worckinge house to be as well for gyrles as boyes and to be founded in Bruton." The poor children were to come from Bruton and parishes within a six-mile radius. (2) Given the subsequent history of education in the Hospital it is important to stress that the original intention was to include girls as well as boys.

It soon became clear that the cost involved in constructing the new, large and architecturally striking almshouse, along with on-going commitments, such as payments to the poor, meant that the Trustees faced severe financial pressures. In 1642 one of the original Trustees, Edward Biss of Spargrove, wrote to another one, Edward Wykes of Wells, "I know what with money which must be given to Bancks his children and other occasions which will arise by the Addition of Twelve Children to be maintained in the Almes house money will ill be spared." (3) The result was that once the new Almshouse was built the Trustees or Visitors as they became known, were cautious: in the Deed of Incorporation in December 1638, they included the commitment that revenue from the estates was to be used "for the new buildings of a Working House there for breeding [*that is educating or training*] of children and setting them to work.... and for raising of money to bind children apprentice." They did however add the proviso, "if it shall be so thought fit hereafter." (4)

5

The exact date on which boys were first elected has not survived. Similarly there was no explanation recorded for the Visitors' decision to shorten the period during which they were educated compared with their proposals in 1623, or for their decision not to elect girls. Initially the financial situation may have been part of the reason for the latter but when this improved still no further action was taken. It may have reflected the attitude of men towards females in seventeenth century England, especially as the Visitors were exclusively male. Earlier accounts of the development of the Hospital have tended to be vague about the date when boys were first elected. Hobhouse resorted to, "As soon as the income of the foundation allowed", and writing in 1824 Hoare used the phrase "many years ago."

No reference was made to boys in the surviving Account Books for 1649-1656. When requesting the Opinion of Counsel in 1793 the Visitors stated, "In the year 1659 an Order was made by the then Trustees that Twelve Male Children shod be placed in the said Hospital." (5) The most likely period for the first admission of the boys would seem therefore to be the very early 1660s. By that decade the finances were improving and much more stable, largely as a result of the strict regime imposed by Oliver Cromwell which facilitated the regular collection of rents and although there were isolated examples of the Visitors financing apprentices prior to 1660, such as one in 1638 and two in 1654 referred to as "Gifts Extraordinary", it was in 1663 that their surviving Apprenticeship Indentures commenced. In Edward Cheeke's Accounts for the year ending May 1662 a series of items referred to the boys and indicated that they were already in residence by that month:

"To Robert White for making cleane the Schoolhouse and other work there	10	0
To John Taylor for pr of Bead steeds for ye boyes	14	0
Pd for 4 bedcords	5	4
Spent on the Corporation at the Chosing of ye boyes	1	8
Spent on the Corporation at puting in of the Boyes	2	0

Pd Maurice Bennet for making two formes for the
boyes   3   6

Pd Mr Tryme more for books for the boyes   6   0

Pd Edward Russe for cloth to make ye boyes clothes   2   5   10

Spent on the Sherman that brought home the gowne
Cloth for ye boyes   1   0

Pd James Penney for making the clothes   13   6

Pd William Smart for a paire of shoes for one of the
boyes   1   8

pd Mr Courtney of Salisbury for 12 bibles for the
boyes and for Carridge of them   3   1   0." (6)

The evidence would suggest therefore that some boys were in residence by the time of the financial year 1661-2 and possibly as early as 1660-1, although not necessarily the full number.

Twelve boys were elected in total, based upon the same administrative procedure as that for the old people, namely by the eight Governors. They were the Master of the Free School, the Bailiff of Bruton, the two Constables for the Hundred of Bruton, the two Churchwardens of St Mary's Church, and the two Overseers of the Poor for Bruton: collectively they were referred to as 'The Corporation'. The administrative pattern remained constant: the bellman (or Town Crier) first gave notice throughout the town that an election of boys was imminent and then about three weeks before that occurred at the annual meeting of the Visitors, their Steward would attend the Hospital, assemble the candidates and receive from each one a statement of his claim along with an extract from the Baptism Register to ascertain his age.

In 1794 the Visitors assumed sole control of the election of both the old people and the boys, largely as a result of the complaints they received from the inhabitants of Bruton "in the partial and improper manner in which the elections were carried on by the Corporation." Allegations were made that some of the elderly people were elected to the Hospital far too young and so could live there for decades, and that some members of the Corporation had more than one vote as a result of occupying several posts. The

Visitors' action represented a fundamental amendment to the Deed of Incorporation of 1638, but as far as the election of the elderly people was concerned was a reversion to the method used by the Trustees before that date when they had the exclusive power.

It was not unusual for the ratepayers from the other parts of the Visitors' estates to discuss nominations in their annual Easter Vestry Meeting, although they accepted that their decision was only a recommendation. Such was the interest in Lyncombe and Widcombe in April 1852, for example, that is was reported, "The attendance was so large that the Church was quite crowded." A significant majority supported Charles Goodson, the eleven year old son of a widow.

Occasionally prior to 1794 the Visitors did issue their own Order with which the Corporation had to comply, for example, in their Meeting on 3rd June 1691 they ordered that, "Gerard Grandson to ye Widow Collins be admitted as a poor boy in to the Hospital upon the next void place." The total number remained the same until 1820 when it was decided as the financial situation improved to add one boy a year for three years to increase the number to fifteen, although at the time of the 1841 Census there were just thirteen boys resident. By 1850 there was more flexibility in the system as the total number of boys had again been increased, this time to its maximum of eighteen. The Census of 1851 listed seventeen boys resident but a decade later there were just fifteen. According to Hoare, who had been elected a Visitor in 1786,

"It has been the practice of the Trustees, to elect the Boys from the largest families.........and to give a preference, when the children in a large family have been supported by the parents' earnings, without having received relief; altho' the parent having received relief, does not amount to an utter disqualification of the boy."

Boys granted clothes by the Overseers before entry into the Hospital would seem to substantiate that assertion. In general terms the Visitors preferred not to elect a second child from a family but there were many instances when that did occur, such as

8

William Frederick Deacon aged eleven in 1856 who had had two older brothers in the Hospital, although in most cases the elder brother or brothers had already been apprenticed.

In 1853 there were nineteen applicants, of whom seven had applied before. Between them the families involved had 118 children although not all were still living at the time of the election to the Hospital. Six fathers were classed as Labourers, two each as Masons, Gardeners, Tailors, Ostlers and Carpenters and one as a Blacksmith and another as a "Journeyman in the Silk." (7)

The Visitors preferred to elect boys about eleven years of age so that they could be educated for three years and then apprenticed for seven years at age fourteen, completing their apprenticeship when they were twenty-one years old which was the accepted pattern. Initially as four were apprenticed each year, there were four new admissions to fill these vacancies and of these three came from Bruton and one from other parts of the Visitors' estates and when the number was increased to five apprentices each year, the additional boy elected also came from Bruton. There does seem to have been some flexibility in the numbers as much depended on finance, the suitability of candidates available, both for election to the Hospital and to be apprenticed, and whether any boys had left through illness or had died.

The operation of the whole system was clearly explained by Moses Lumber at his Settlement Examination in September 1747:

"Who on his Oath Saith that he was born in the parish of Brewton in the said county and then & there lived with his mother until he attained the age of twelve years and then by the Corporation of Brewton was placed as a poore destitute Child in the hospitall of Hugh Sexey Esq Situate in Brewton afs where he remained for about the space of two years and then by the Corporation as pursuant to the Charter of the sd Hospitall was some time before the Whitsun Week which was in the year of our Lord 1746 bound an apprentice to one Wm Biggwood of ffrome Selwood Tiler for the term of seven years." (8)

As he had lived with Biggwood for more than forty days the settlement decision was that he should be removed from Bruton to Frome. He had been educated enough to sign his own name.

The support given to the boys was slightly different to that of the old people in the Hospital for while both groups were provided with their clothes, the boys also received all their food but no cash allowance. On admission each boy was given a suit of blue clothes, two shirts, two cravats, one pair of stockings, one pair of shoes and a blue gown and cap, made from three yards and one nail of cloth. In the second year the Visitors provided two more shirts and cravats, a pair of shoes and stockings: the same was the case in the third year. In addition there were often usable clothes left behind by a boy who had just been apprenticed. "Once in two years an allowance is made to each boy of a blue gown and cap, which are delivered at Christmas." If additional shoes and stockings were required the Master furnished them out of the weekly allowance paid to him for each boy. As a result of their costume they were sometimes known as the Blue Boys or the boys from the Blue Coat School. The poor who sought help from the Poor Law and so became paupers had to wear a cloth badge sewn onto their clothes and for many it was a mark of shame. The blue uniform, however, both for the boys and the elderly inmates, was a matter of intense pride.

In 1839 the Visitors resolved,

"That the Master be relieved from the expense of making shirts, converting the boys' cloakes into breeches and trimming them and of mending the boys' shoes." (9)

Although new clothes were provided it is clear that as much as possible was reused and repaired to reduce costs. The expense of clothing the four boys elected in 1793 was £8 8s 4d and a decade later £10 1s 9d. In 1703 an Inventory was made of the clothes available in the Hospital:

"Clothes belonging to ye Boyes

12 blue Gowns, 24 Caps, 24 Shirts, 24 Cravats, 12 Wastcoats, 12 pair Drawers, 20 pair of Breeches, 22 pair of Stockings, 12 pair of Shoes, 21 Coats (12 worn)."

In the nineteenth century the cost of clothing the boys increased as shown in Table 1. (10)

Table 1. Cost of Clothing for boys

Year	No. of boys elected	Cost of clothing the boys elected £ s d	Cost of clothing for boys in Hospital £ s d
1846-7	5	11 0 5	16 17 8
1874-5	6	39 1 4	23 19 5

Election to the Hospital was also viewed as a way of relieving the burden on ratepayers as some of the boys came from the families of paupers. Once boys were admitted the ratepayers were spared any further expense for some ten years. It was not surprising therefore that the Overseers, who were part of the electing Corporation of the Hospital were quite prepared to provide finance for additional clothes on admission.

"1665   Item for apparel for James fflingers boy when he went into ye Hospitall   18   0

1669   Item for Shoes and Stockings for Budds boy   3   6

Item to John Munday for making a suite of clothes for Budds boy for the Hospitall   1   10

Item for a paire of Shoes for Widdow Cowards sonne when he went into the Hospitall   2   0

1670   Item to John Coward when his boy went into the Hospitall   2   0

1688   To Emlyn Lumber to buy her Boy Shoes and Stockings upon his going into ye Almeshouse   4   0."

The Visitors also received regularly petitions from tenants in other parts of their estate, for example, in 1663 they agreed to admit Samuel Gibbs from Lyncombe, the son of John Gibbs "a poore Labourer.... Having six children and no meanes to maynteyne them." They also decided to include one of the sons of Widow Mitchell of Widcombe, "a honest and laborious woman." (11)

The purpose of the education provided in the Hospital was not to raise the boys 'above their station' in life but rather to try and ensure that they became productive, independent members of their community, not reliant upon and a burden to the Poor Laws in the future. The inculcation of what were judged to be the appropriate attitudes was also important as there was no wish to produce young men who might challenge in any way the existing social order.

For these reasons the education provided for the boys under the direction of the Master was initially very elementary, consisting of reading, writing and arithmetic, along with religious instruction. From time to time books were purchased such as in the year ending 1662 Edward Cheek paid Mt Tryme 6s 0d "for books for the boyes" and £3 0s 0d for "12 Bibles for the boyes" from Mr Courtney of Salisbury. He purchased another 12 Bibles from the same source in 1669-1670. Other purchases of unidentified books were made:

"1668-9 payd for Schoole Books for ye Boyes   3 2

14 June 1671 pd for small school Bookes for the Boys   3 6."

Two centuries later small sums were still being expended on books,

"1874 Society for Promoting Christian Knowledge for Books   15 0."

Some of the school work was written on paper:

"10 June 1674 pd for 6 Quire of Paper for the use of the Boyes   3 0", although Hoare noted that as well as writing paper, pens and ink, the Master was also allowed to purchase slates. (12)

In 1840 reservations were expressed concerning the level of attainment of the boys as a result of their lack of education before being admitted to the Hospital. When an Infant School was being proposed for the town it was stated,

"The Almeshouse School is well calculated to produce (what may be termed) confidential Mechanics, but its advantages are not efficiently carried out, neither can they be, in consequence of the untrained description of Boys who abound in the Parish. Much is done for good or evil in Eleven years........ By an improved state of the understanding when the Boy is admitted, it is probable he will be a much improved Character at the end of this time."

The education which was subsequently provided in the National School did ensure for some boys the sought-after access to the Hospital, for example, in August 1867 three boys, Frank Vigar, Henry Gapper and Henry Rawlings, who attended that school were elected to the Hospital to fill three of the five places for local boys, and two years later, four of the five places received National School boys, namely Joseph Day, Richard Cox, William Hobbs and Frank Young. In the years which followed under the headmastership of E.R. Hayter two, three or four boys were elected annually to the Hospital, not always with Hayter's approval. When James Cox, John James, Tabor Flaver and C. White were elected in 1875 he commented, "The first mentioned boy was a very regular & careful boy with his Schoolwork, the others were exceedingly irregular, unpunctual & idle." (13)

Some small developments did occur in the education provided, especially in the nineteenth century. In 1852 the Master was hoping to purchase a copy of the 'Art Union Catalogue of the Great Exhibition' with "more than 300 drawings of great beauty, well adapted to improve the taste of, and qualify the Hospital boys as superior apprentices to the Trades usually chosen." By 1874 the boys possessed a Workshop as £5 was allowed for materials in that year. Very much in keeping with national trends, in the 1860s and 1870s there were references to physical activities with first Sergeant-Major Melhuish and then Sergeant-Major Cross paid £5 a year "for Drilling Boys."

Such an education would ensure that they would be "desirable apprentices", although from the 1850s there was some criticism that the boys lacked general knowledge. It was never anticipated that the boys should seek to improve their position in life beyond that of achieving a skill. A somewhat condescending opinion of the level of their education appeared in 1868, "The education given was suited,

The entrance doorway and the two south-facing windows of the boys' schoolroom in Sexey's Hospital.

perhaps, to the condition in life of the boys who required it, and was quite elementary." (14)

No detailed description of the Schoolroom, which was below the Chapel, has survived, although the presence of two south facing windows meant that it would have been light and in 1703 it contained, "One Table Board, Two Forms," increased to three Forms by 1712. It would have presented a decidedly spartan appearance but one which was very much in keeping with schools of that period. In the mid-nineteenth century it was recorded as nineteen feet long by fifteen feet wide and ten feet high, a generous space especially when there were only twelve boys. (15)

The boys had access to the central courtyard and the garden but there does not seem to have been a dedicated playground until 1801. In 1800-1801 the Visitors re-built the east side of the quadrangle and at the same time purchased for £80 from Sir Richard Colt Hoare a house and garden adjoining the eastern side of the Hospital. Most of this area became the boys' playground but also included a wood store, engine house, pig sty and toilet block. One problem with this playground, which was still being noted half a century later, was that there was no cover and so on wet days the boys had to remain within their schoolroom. The playground was separated from the High Street by a wall approximately ten feet high and which had a doorway in it for access. This extended site on the southern side of the street ended just to the west of the western edge of Cats Lane which was on the opposite side of the road.

The Master received a salary for teaching the boys as well as his accommodation with a large garden. In addition he was given a weekly allowance for the maintenance of each boy, a sum which fluctuated in accordance with the cost of provisions. Initially the Master's salary was fixed at £10 per annum which had increased to £31 in 1798 and £42 by 1824. In the mid-1860s it had reached £75 per year. In the 1790s the allowance for each boy was less than 4s 6d a week but had increased to 7s 0d by 1824, only to decrease by 6d in 1842. The duties of the Master were carefully delineated, for example, an advertisement in April 1798 for a new Master after the death of Robert Surgeon specified, "The master will be required to be properly qualified to educate 12 boys resident in the Hospital House, so as to adapt them for trade and business, and to constantly superintend their morals."

Although the Master was given overall responsibility for the education and welfare of the boys, there was, at least at times, some delegation especially as a Master may have lacked the necessary qualifications, as for example, William Clarke was a tanner. In September 1665 in Answers to the Bishop of Bath and Wells, John Randall, the Minister of Bruton stated, "There is one Edward Drew Cleark of the parish teacheth 12 Hospitall boyes," and added that he was "a man very well affected." In 1666-7 he was paid £10 0s 0d. This was the same Edward Drew, who as Parish Clerk, had been imprisoned for three months with the Minister in the Bishop's Palace at Banwell "for Singing Malignant Psalms" at some stage during the late 1640s or early 1650s. The Parish Register records that a William Clark was buried on 7th September 1663 and it is possible that as well as being Parish Clerk Edward Drew acted as the Master of the Hospital until his death in April 1668. Throughout the 1790s and until October 1811 when his son Stephen took over, John Penny was paid various sums for clothing the boys elected and the apprentices, providing blankets, for the general care of the boys and occasionally for their education, usually during the illness of, or on the death of, the Master:

"1796 May 28 Paid John Penny as Ordered for the
care of the Boys the last year and for educating them   31   0   0
1798 May 31 Paid J. Penny for the care of the
Hospital Boys the last year as Ordered   31   0   0
1807 May 16 Pd John Penny his years Salary   15   5   0."

In 1822 Stephen Penny was paid £6 6s 0d "for superintending the Hospital School previous to the Appointment of the present Master." (16)

In addition to religious instruction in their Schoolroom the boys were required to attend Daily Prayers. These left them in no doubt that they needed to be saved from their sins, that they must work hard and that their life on earth was transient. In the morning there were eighteen short prayers, each one repeated by the boys, commencing with:

"Lord! As thou hast awakened our bodies from sleep, so by thy good grace awaken our souls from sin and make us so to walk before thee this day and all the rest of our lives, that when the last trumpet shall awaken us out of our graves we may all arise to the Life immortal...."

In the evening there were a further eighteen prayers which followed the same themes:

"We most humbly beg forgiveness for every sin we have committed this day....Let it be our firmest belief that nothing can recommend us to thee if we do not lead a holy and useful life....Enable us to improve in virtue and to correct in ourselves every wrong inclination.... Vouchsafe us such refreshing sleep, as may fit us for the duties of the following day. Thou alone knowest how near our death may be, and that every day brings us nearer to it. Grant that we may become every day fitter for it...."

Each Sunday the Chaplain conducted divine service and preached in the morning and evening alternately. He also read prayers on Saints' days. The boys received the Sacrament on four Sundays during the year. (17)

As all the boys were resident in the Hospital their other needs were catered for by the Visitors. This included beds and bedding. In the 1703 Inventory when there were twelve boys it was recorded that there were,

"In the Boys Chamber
Four Beds & Bed Steads, ffour Bolsters, ffour Ruggs, 4 pair of blankets."

This Inventory did indicate that three boys shared a bed but by the late eighteenth century with the same number of boys the Master was permitted six beds and a blanket for each boy, with six new blankets supplied each year. In 1675-6 £1 18s 4d was paid "for 40 yds of canvas to Making sheets for ye boyes." By 1824 the Master was allowed thirty-nine yards of sheeting a year, along with a further six yards for towels and table-cloths. When the number of boys increased to fifteen the Master was granted eight beds. As was quite common in the past there was more than one boy in a bed for the whole of this school's history and comfort for the boys was clearly not a great issue. The bolsters and mattresses on their beds were stuffed with flocks, that is, torn pieces of cloth or wool:

"1665-6   pd for a Bed and bolster   12   6
pd for flock   1   1   8."

Nearly 120 years later in 1794 William Bennett was paid £5 14s 0d "for Flocks for the Boys Beds."

In the 1820s the Charity Inquiry reported that the boys were lodged in three bedrooms but subsequent alterations meant that by the 1850s one boys' dormitory occupied just over half the length of the first floor of the west block of the Hospital at its southern end and was linked to the Master's accommodation by a door up a short flight of stairs.

For all the rigid and rigorous supervision of the boys and the emphasis upon their moral conduct, their close proximity to each other in the dormitory led to disquiet and concern about aspects of their behaviour. The only definite evidence emerged in the 1850s when the Master, James Parfitt, examined the state of the bedlinen and the conduct of one boy in particular. It soon became clear that "indecent practices" occurred amongst a number of the boys, "when I am at supper, then their acts are committed." He believed that the "Boys beds are so close they can lean from one to the other" and then he discovered that far worse a "boy went into another boys bed & polluted him against his wish." While he considered that at least one of the elderly men in the Hospital was setting them a bad example, after questioning the boys he reported that, "one boy told me he learnt it at Nat.[*ional*] School & others told me they practiced it before they came in. I suspect the elders have taught the juniors."

Interestingly Parfitt did not wish to impose a severe punishment but rather to end the practices. "I promised the boys I would forgive them if they helped me to get rid of it and the Trustees should be asked not to disgrace them." The Visitors concurred and felt that he "had acted discretely under the difficult & unpleasant circumstances of the boys." Any scandal was thus avoided but the episode did suggest that attitudes towards sexual abuse were very different. (18)

Each week the Master was given an allowance to feed the boys and to provide any items which were not supplied by the Visitors. Initially the sum involved was small: by 1791 it had reached 4s 4½d per boy per week; by 1823 had increased to 7s and then fluctuated between 6s and 7s for each boy for the remainder of the time that they were resident. When food prices were high the Master was granted an additional allowance as occurred, for example in June 1802 when the then Master, John Parfitt, received £63 12s 0d "for the Boys on acct of the dearness of Provisions." As no provision books have survived until the nineteenth century it is not possible to reach any conclusions about the nature of the food supplied to the boys in the earlier period. The Master had a large garden in the grounds of the Hospital, so it is possible that some fresh vegetables and fruit came from there. A Dietary List for the boys was sent to the Earl of Ilchester by the Master in 1852:

"Breakfast
Bread and Milk porridge – some having bacon with fried
potatoe and bread
Dinner

4 ounces of fresh meat free from bone	)
2 lbs of vegetables	) each
½ a pint of table beer	)

Pulse or rice is substituted for vegetables on Fridays & on Sundays. ¾ lb of fruit pudding with sugar or treacle is given extra.

Supper

3 ozs of Cheese
½ lb of bread
½ pint of table beer."

By 1857 there were monthly purchases of bread, meat, milk, general groceries and occasionally coffee, flour and large quantities of potatoes. In July 1862 a separate cash account was opened for vegetables which averaged just under 7s a month for the following year. Even though the Hospital had its own water supply with a well and later a pump in the main quadrangle, as there was so much concern about polluted water beer was the common drink even for children and that was reflected in the dietary list. The boys would appear to have been receiving a substantial, if not very varied, diet. It was, however, significantly superior to that which many boys of their age and background received outside of the Hospital and meant that their physical condition could also be much better. This in turn, along with their education, would help to explain why there was so much interest amongst employers in obtaining an apprentice from this institution. (19)

Care within an institution did not necessarily protect all the boys from illness and even death, although given the poor background of so many of them with an inadequate diet and dreadful living conditions, the number of recorded cases of serious illness or death is remarkably low. In 1675-6 the Apothecary was paid 3s 5d for medicines prepared for an elderly inmate and for "one of ye poor boyes in the time of their Sickness." Within a short time of the first admission of boys a death occurred:

"1662 pd for burying one of the boyes   12   6

spent on electing of another   2   6."

In 1825 expenses were much greater when an Inquest was required:

"Dec 17 Paid for expences of the Coroners
Inquisht held on the Body of Jno Brown   1   3   0

Dec 31 Pd the Funeral Expences of John Brown   2   3   1."
one of the School Boys

He was buried on 30th November, aged 13 years. Some injuries
were of course self-inflicted. In 1873 a local newspaper reported
that several boys from the Hospital were playing with some
gunpowder "when it accidentally exploded and burnt four of
them."

For most of their three years in the Hospital life for the boys
was rigorous, strictly controlled and in many respects monotonous.
Just occasionally there were variations in routine: the surviving
Account Books for example indicate that from at least the mid-
eighteenth century the boys, along with the elderly inmates, were
treated to an annual feast, usually in December. In addition there
were occasional ad hoc celebrations in the town in which the boys
participated. In 1831 there was a large procession to celebrate the
Coronation of William IV and near the front were the boys of the
Blue Coat School, "carrying a flag, with the initials of the founder,
H.S. on it." On the Abbey Field to the south of the Parish Church
there was then a public dinner with roast beef and plum pudding.
Twenty five years later in 1856 came the opening of the Great
Western Railway through Bruton and another large procession,
this time led by the Blue Boys. A similar feast followed by games
and sports was staged on the Abbey Field. (20)

After three years' education the boys were apprenticed to a
trade for seven years. For the boys from labouring families this was
their objective as the payment required for an apprenticeship meant
that it was generally well beyond their reach. Between c1663 and
1822 four were apprenticed each year then five and eventually six,
which totalled over 900 apprentices in the period of the existence of
the school. Apprenticeship Indentures were drawn up for each one
of these and some 224 have survived: 67 for the period 1663-1714
and 157 for 1741 to 1793. They provide not only an indication of
the occupations followed and of developments in the occupation
pattern, but also of distances covered.

Between 1663 and 1714 some twenty (or 29.8%) were apprenticed to Cordwainers (that is, shoemakers) and fourteen (20.9%) to Tailors. In total thirty-eight (56.7%) became involved in cloth production or products made from it. This industry along with Cordwainers therefore accounted for 86.5% of all apprentices. In the period 1741-1793 Cordwainers remained the largest group with forty apprentices but this represented a decrease to 25.5%. A further twenty-eight (17.8%) were apprenticed to Carpenters and twenty-one (13.4%) to Tailors. In this later period just thirty-two (20.4%) were involved in the cloth industry which meant that this industry along with Cordwainers accounted for 45.9% of apprentices, a marked decrease from the period 1663 to 1714 and an indication of the decline of the cloth industry in the area. Ten (6.4%) were apprenticed to Masons and nine (5.7%) to Tilers and Plasterers. A much greater variety of occupations were represented in the later period including Whitesmiths, Wheelwrights, Plumbers, Saddlers and Collar Makers, an Edgetoolmaker, a Clogmaker and a Tallow Chandler and Soap Boiler.

Tradesmen and employers in Bruton itself were obviously considerable beneficiaries of the apprenticeship system in the period 1663-1714, as may be seen in Table 2. There was a pronounced decrease after 1741 which may be partly explained by the quality of the apprentices compared with parish ones elsewhere but also the development of the transport network, which made travel over larger distances easier, especially as the Visitors were advertising more extensively in local newspapers

Table 2. Apprentice destinations.

Destination	1663-1714		1741-1793	
	Number	%	Number	%
In Bruton	30	44.8	30	19.1
Within 10 miles of Bruton	22	32.8	69	44.0
Over 10 miles from Bruton	15	22.4	58	36.9

Of the fifteen who were apprenticed more than ten miles from Bruton in the earlier period four were sent to London and six, some 40%, to Bath. In the later period just four were sent to London and sixteen (27.5%) to Bath, indicating a much wider range of destinations. In both periods, however, the main focus for the location of apprentices was in Bruton and its immediate area: 77.6% and 63.1% respectively.

More limited evidence is available for occupation or location in the nineteenth century, at a time when Hobhouse expressed the opinion that the boys were apprenticed "to mechanical trades, mostly those of carpenters and blacksmiths." In 1856 the fourteen men who applied for apprentices came from six different trades: of these four men were Boot and Shoemakers and four were Carpenters. Of the remainder there were two each who were Plumbers Glaziers and Painters, Blacksmiths and Cordwainers. None was resident in Bruton and only five came from within ten miles of the town. Of the fourteen tradesmen who applied for apprentices in 1867 four were Carpenters and one a Blacksmith, although in this year nine different trades were represented but once again there were no applicants from Bruton and just two from within ten miles. The Visitors detected a change in the approach to apprenticeships and this was to lead to developments a decade later.

The Apprenticeship Indentures followed a general pattern but were very specific in a number of areas. Most importantly the apprentice was required to serve and obey his Master and undertake no action which could harm his Master or his trade, as well as not absenting himself. Instructions were included for the apprentice's moral welfare as

"fornication he shall not commit during the said Term Taverns Inns or Alehouses he shall not frequent..... at Card Dice or any other unlawful Game he shall not play........"

In return the Master would teach the boy his trade and

"Allow give and provide for the said Apprentice (as well in Sickness and in health) good wholesome and sufficient Meat Drink Washing Lodging Apparel and Mending of all Sorts fitting and necessary for the said Apprentice." (21)

The length of the working day for apprentices had been laid down in the Statute of Artificers 1563 and was meant to be from dawn to dusk during the winter months and until 8p.m. at the latest in the summer, which gave a working day of at least thirteen hours. Specific breaks were defined as an hour at midday for dinner and then three other breaks of half an hour each: one in the morning for breakfast, one mid afternoon and one in the early evening. How far this pattern was rigidly observed is impossible to determine.

From the earliest days of apprenticing the boys, the Visitors were concerned to ensure that they had good Masters and so a system developed which required the Steward to give notice in the town and local villages, often initially using the services of the town crier and then in the eighteenth and nineteenth centuries to place an advertisement in local newspapers a few weeks before the Visitors' Annual Meeting. This notice specified the terms on which the boys were to be apprenticed and informed potential applicants that certificates or testimonials were required, usually from their Vicar, Churchwardens and Overseers. With the spread of Non-Conformity in Bruton and the surrounding area, particularly in the late eighteenth and nineteenth centuries, this requirement became a very contentious issue and was severely criticized by some local inhabitants in an Inquiry in 1880.

The advertisement for 1799 noted, "It being the wish of the trustees to provide good masters for the apprentices, it is requested that none but persons of that description will apply." Such advertisements could elicit a large response, such as the fourteen applicants in 1867, one of whom was T. Thornhill, a Watchmaker, from Middle Street, Yeovil:

"Sirs, I am desirous of obtaining an Apprentice that is of a good character that is honest industrious and quick & not of slight growth as he would have to walk out in the Country often."

He stated that he was a member of the Church of England and a 'Total Abstainer'. In a PS he added:

"The Youth whoever he might be he would have such advantage under my care as few seldom have in regard to knowing the Art of finishing as well as the Rep trade, & jobbing in General."

The earliest testimonials were very individualistic:

"We whose handes are hear under written tenant Too the hospital doo think Simone bush too bee A man fit too take William wiatt one of the hospital boyes too bee his aprentis."

Two hundred years later it had become a set statement signed by the Vicar, Churchwardens and Overseers:

"This is to certify that I believe Mr Saml Bord of Bruton to be a person of good character and to be able and fit to instruct an apprentice in the trade of Carpenter and Wheelwright. Mr Bord is a Churchman."

Even with the care implicit in such a system problems arose as occasionally a Master did not fulfil his obligations:

"1819 Sept. 14 By Cash pd to Thos Gray one of the
apprentices to buy Shoes etc   8   9
Pd Mr Wingrove for his trouble in
endeavouring to compel Gray's
Master to provide for his apprentice   15   0."

In August 1860 Charles Rose who had been an apprentice with John Watts at Somerton for five years, alleged that his Master had returned to his drunken habits and in that state was very violent, having threatened not only Rose but also his own son. Henry Hobhouse recorded, "it is pretty clear that he has neglected to provide proper clothing for the boy who appeared before me in rags that were scarcely decent." He suggested that the Indenture be cancelled, so that the boy could seek his own employment, although he was concerned that the apprentice might be seeking a quarrel for just that purpose. It did however appear that a previous apprentice had also run away from Watts. The outcome was not recorded. (22)

When the boys left the Hospital for their apprenticeship they were provided with clothes so when Thomas Hilbouron "one of the poore boyes of the house" was apprenticed in 1663 to a Bruton tailor,

"pd for a hatt Shoes and Shirt & Clothes for him   1   4   6."

James fflinger proved to be more expensive when he was apprenticed three years later:

"1666-7 payd for Cloth and all things Convenient to make up his Clothes	2	5	1
payd for Stockings and Shoes and a Hatt		7	8
payd for making his Clothes		6	0
payd for making his Indentures		2	0
payd in expences when this Boy was Bound		1	6."

Some entries were much more general,

"1670 Making the Clothes for those 4
Boys Bond apprentices   10   11   10."

By the late eighteenth century each boy received two suits, one of cloth designed for Sundays and a fustian one for working, a hat, one pair of new shoes, two shirts and cravats and two pairs of stockings, as well as the Holy Bible and Book of Common Prayer.

"1796 May 14 By Mr Penny for clothing
for the Boys to be apprenticed out 17
May 1796   20   18   7
4 Bibles for them   1   0   0." (23)

Of considerable interest to the boy's new Master, of course, was the premium which the apprentice brought with him. For the few boys whom the Visitors had helped into apprenticeships before 1660 the figure involved seemed standard:

"1636 Item to Wm Walter 1 Aug last for taking Nich Bakers
sonne apprentice   v li

1654 11 September James Armstrong ffive pound which was given by the Visitors of the Hospitall in Brewton att theire last Meeting unto Roger Burgess for the binding of the sonne of the said Roger Apprentice which is accordingly done unto the said James Armstrong."

With their own boys being apprenticed from 1663 the sum granted was raised to £6:

"1663 Thomas Hilbouron one of the poore boyes
of the house.....7 years apprentice   6   0   0

1666-7 Payd Michaell Atkins when James fflinger
was bound in money   6   0   0

1671 June 14 Willm Walter Bound to John Sandy
a Joyner Bristoll   6   0   0."

In this last case 6s   10d had to be added, "pd in expences at ye Bing [*binding*] this Boy and the Carrng [*carrying*] of him to Bristoll & his diat one ye way."

The premium remained constant for over a century and may well have been insufficient to attract suitable employers but it was not until 1776 that it was increased to £10 and then to £12 in 1783. This figure too proved to be inadequate as one of the Visitors' subsequent resolutions highlighted the result,

"the Trustees finding that from it being so low inferior Mechanics only made Application who seldom had the means of instructing or even maintaining the Apprentice and who in consequence rarely served the full time of his Apprenticeship."

Their resolution suggested that it was quite common for apprentices not to complete their seven years' apprenticeship. In some respects this could be a mutually acceptable position as the Master was absolved from any further expense of maintaining a growing teenager and the apprentice had probably learnt a sufficient amount about a particular trade so that he could set himself up in business or travel around offering it.

They decided therefore to give a further £10 to the Master after four years provided both Apprentice and Master were still living, and that they were satisfied with the Master's treatment of his apprentice. This amended payment was certainly in place by 1797 and according to Hoare,

> "The alteration in the terms has been productive of great benefit.... There has been of late years, seldom any matter of complaint between the masters and apprentices requiring the Trustees' interference."

One implication of Hoare's observation was that such complaints had arisen before that period. The new system also provided the Visitors with an additional means of monitoring the progress and treatment of the apprentice.

Between 1816 and 1822 the Visitors were spending on average £116 7s 10¾d a year on premiums for Apprentices and clothing them. By the 1860s the premium had been increased to £28 when an additional £6 was paid to the apprentice's master at the beginning of the fifth year of the apprenticeship. In return the master was required to pay his apprentice 6d a week from the start of the fifth year, 1s 6d a week in the sixth year and 2s 6d a week in the seventh year. Even with this arrangement there appeared to have been some difficulty in obtaining suitable masters for the boys as after the school had closed it was speculated that if the apprenticeship premium had been increased it might have achieved better places for the boys. (24) In very rare instances no premium was given, for example, in 1825 a note was added in the Accounts after the total for apprenticing four boys, "Rex the other Boy apprenticed to his Father without a Premium."

In the 1660s the Visitors made a payment from time to time to a boy on completion of his apprenticeship, similar to an idea expressed on behalf of the Trustees by Sir Lawrence Hide in 1623 and referred to in the Deed of Incorporation. Such grants which were designed to help them to establish themselves in a trade were rare and appear to have soon ceased.

"1666-7 Roger Burgess 2 li being ordered to be pd when he is out of his apprentis."

There were occasional problems which arose with the apprenticeship system in addition to the inadequate premiums failing to attract suitable masters in the latter part of the eighteenth century. In May 1793 Robert Kiddle was discharged from his apprenticeship for an unspecified reason and in July 1797 the Visitors made a donation of £5 to John Parfit "on account of Thos Biggs his late Apprentice having died before his full premium became due." The Parish Registers show that Thomas Biggs was buried on 23rd April 1797, aged sixteen years. It is not, however, until the nineteenth century that detailed evidence has survived. In 1811 there was a refusal by the parents of the boys and the boys themselves to be apprenticed which may be indicative of the fact that at times some parents attempted to manipulate the system. They supported the election of their sons to the Hospital so that they would receive all the benefits of residence and an education and then tried to prevent an apprenticeship. Instead the boy aged about fourteen would be sent out to earn money for the family, presumably at a higher level as a result of three years in the Hospital. In this instance, however, the Visitors recovered £24 from the parents "on account of their Parents & also the Boys refusing to be placed to good Masters approved of by the Trustees." How many were involved was not specified and only one boy, Isaac White, was named.

Another problem which surfaced in the nineteenth century, and may of course have existed for a much longer period, was "that the boys in many instances were not allowed to choose their own trades, and some of them were put to trades they did not like." The result was that, according to William Bord at the Inquiry in 1880, these boys did not stick to the trade to which they had been apprenticed, "when trades were forced on boys, as was the case in some instance." He went on to claim that he "had frequently heard parents say that their boys were put to other trades and other masters than those they had themselves chosen, and then they were not likely to do well." In evidence which the Inspector was reluctant to accept in such a deferential society, two local men confirmed this allegation. Philip Hill was a very successful plumber and glazier in Bruton and he stated that although "he was eventually allowed to be apprenticed to the trade he had chosen, he had to contend against the wishes of the feoffees, who pressed him to go to other trades, as they had certain masters to whom they had promised boys." He was followed by Charles Atkins, a road contractor, who was apprenticed from the Hospital in 1855. He told the Inquiry that he too wished initially to be a plumber and glazier but the Visitors would not let him as they regarded it as an unhealthy occupation. He was eventually apprenticed to a tailor, did not like it and so ran away. (25)

The allegation by Hill that the Visitors had "promised boys" to certain employers was the only time that such a suggestion surfaced. If correct it does indicate that there could have been an element of corruption in the system, at least in the nineteenth century. Given the class from which the Visitors were drawn and the occupations to which the boys were sent, it is difficult to see what their motivation could have been. It was possibly just another example of paternalism in operation in rural areas.

Three cases illustrated the nature of some of the problems with apprentices themselves, two of which involved running away to join the army during the Napoleonic Wars. In October 1798 an announcement was placed in a local newspaper to alert the public to the fact that John Cox, who had been apprenticed to John Barnes, a cooper in Bruton, three years earlier had run away. "He is supposed to have gone towards Langport to enlist as a soldier." It was stated that, "the most vigorous measures will be taken to bring him to justice", although it was added that if he returned immediately "his past misconduct will be overlooked."

The outcome was not reported. In April 1812 James Whitaker, aged 18, and who had been apprenticed to Thomas Daniel of Westbury, a Plumber and Glazier, for three years ran away and joined the Royal Artillery at Woolwich. His mother, Grace, wrote to Thomas Daniel to apologize for her son's behaviour:

"Sir I am sorry that my child do give you so much trobel. I little thought he would turn out so bad it gives me a great del of troubel and his father Wm I have never a heard from him if I had I would send to you Sir."

Shortly afterwards in June James wrote to his family from Woolwich:

"it is not a bit of use for my master have new indentures and he cannot have me back again but I am verrey sorry to give you such trouble."

He remained in the army until May 1828 when he was discharged due to ill-health with a pension of 9d a day.

Over fifty years later in 1867 James White, who was apprenticed from 1865 to Henry Mabbett, a Carpenter from Tisbury in Wiltshire, alleged that his Master had "not taught him his trade, and done his duty by him." Mabbett denied the accusations but agreed to repay £5 of the apprenticeship money. A letter from his local Vicar, however, gave a very critical view of the apprentice's skills, behaviour and character: he "would not learn: he would not saw a piece of wood straight: could barely plane: and spoiled his materials.

He constantly disobeyed orders, could not be trusted out of sight: could never be believed on his word. Constantly used bad language. When sent to night school would go out in Mischief instead. Was found smoking in Church. Twice escaped imprisonment for punishment for robbing orchards on Sunday, only by the intervention of his Master." (26)

That an apprentice had not been taught a trade was a common complaint against the system. Nationally there is considerable evidence that when a young apprentice joined his master he was given very basic jobs to do such as carrying coal, wood, and other materials, sweeping up and running errands. Some masters realised that if they taught their apprentice just one part of the trade in which he could specialise it could speed up the process and be financially lucrative for him. Such a course of action did not make the boy fit for the trade as a whole.

The Visitors were generally convinced that the increase in the premium paid to masters in the 1790s "has been productive of great benefit" and pointed out in 1842 that although there were some thirty-five boys apprenticed, "there have been of late years comparatively but few matters of complaint between the Masters and Apprentices, requiring the Trustees interfering." Mr Stanton, who compiled a Report for the Taunton Commission in 1868 was less complimentary, "I understand that the apprentice fee had been at various times greatly abused, masters taking and parents binding boys colourably, in order to get it." He did not, however, provide any details but the implication must be that a potential employer and a boy's parents conspired to obtain the apprenticeship fee, split the sum between them and then the boy left his apprenticeship and worked elsewhere for money.

Just occasionally when a boy completed his education he could not become an apprentice as a result of illness:

"1784 June 16 Paid Ann Bond as Order on
account of her son John Bond's afflicted with
the Kings Evil wch render him at present
incapable of being placed out in the usual
course as Apprentice   12   0   0."

It was unlikely that he was apprenticed for long, or even at all, as the Burial Register shows that he was interred on 23rd October 1785, aged seventeen years. (27)

By 1872 the Visitors had become convinced that it was necessary to broaden the educational aspects of the Charity. They were aware that after the Grammar School had reached a low ebb in the mid-1860s, it was recovering but changing in nature. In 1868 it was reported that the Governors had the power to elect five free boys

"but they have had no applications of late, and are indisposed to encourage them, believing that the class of boys who would avail themselves of the privilege would be unsuited to the present constitution of the School."

Most of the boys who attended were the sons of professional men and richer farmers, with just two tradesmen's sons. The only other alternative was the National School to which "many of the poorer farmers send their sons." In addition the Visitors believed that the apprenticeship system as it existed was no longer appropriate in their changing world, "The Trade custom of employing Indoor Apprentices had become obsolete, and special training for that purpose was no longer required." This was a view which was echoed in a local newspaper:

"Whether the change is for the better or the worse, it is a fact, that lads are now seldom sent to live with a master for seven years, to learn a mechanical trade; and it is not often in these days that a premium is paid for instruction in any handicraft."

Some twenty-five years later the Earl of Cork and Orrery, who had been a Visitor since 1856, stated that they had recognised "that the days for apprenticeships were gone", which he attributed to the development of railways and telegraph and better facilities for teaching so that boys no longer had to remain in the district in which they were born. "The days of apprenticeship are past, and we must now look at things as they are at present." These were views which he had already expressed when he formally opened Sexey's Trade School in April 1892. (28)

In 1872, therefore, the Visitors made their first application to the Charity Commissioners to initiate changes and the subsequent negotiations were to continue at various times for some twenty years. A wide range of proposals were discussed and a few led to extensive debate and concern as some Brutonians considered that it was necessary to protect their interests when it was suggested that new schools be built elsewhere. The Visitors most immediate action in 1877 was to close the boys' school without any consultation with the local community. It was a move which was not well received in Bruton and other parts of their estates. When Inspector William Good, at the direction of the Charity Commissioners, was holding an Inquiry at the Wellington Inn in November 1880 on the operation of the Sexey Charity, he was told in no uncertain terms by W.J. Nevill that the removal of the boys' school "was a great grievance both to the people of Bruton and Bath... In past times the school was a most successful one.... He had only to point to men in the town who were educated in that school, and who had become respectable flourishing tradesmen, with a position in the town." There was a strong feeling that if the Visitors had increased expenditure on the school and enlarged it, it would have been even more beneficial to Bruton and the rest of the county. The opinion was also expressed that the quality of the apprentices could have been much improved if the Visitors had extended their period in the Hospital from three to five years, an idea which the Master had championed some twenty years earlier.

In its place they established a school for girls to train them for domestic service, an area which they may have considered inadequately supplied, a view which had been expressed ten years before when it was claimed, "The girls glove; this they prefer to service, and it is often difficult to get servants." (29) It was the first time since the Deed of Incorporation had been signed nearly 240 years earlier that any provision had been made for girls and so ensured that the Visitors still complied with the original requirements in that document and also with their 1623 statements.

b) The Girls.

(i) Sexey's Girls' School

Once the boys had vacated the Hospital the girls moved in. Their school was usually known as Sexey's Girls' School or Bruton Hospital Girls' School but just occasionally as Sexey's Hospital

Industrial School. There were fifteen girls resident who were initially elected from within a two mile radius of Bruton, along with the Visitors' estates in Blackford and Wanstrow, but by 1883 this produced so few suitable applicants that it was decided to extend the area to a four mile radius which would encompass eighteen parishes, with Blackford and Wanstrow as before. It also included the Workhouse of the local Poor Law Union situated in Wincanton.

This alteration produced variable results, for example, in 1890 there were sixteen applicants for five vacancies whereas three years later the Visitors noted that there were few applicants for admission. They resolved that the election of the girls had to be made more generally known. As a result they started to send letters with the appropriate information to prominent men in each parish, such as the Vicar and Schoolmaster and they also placed detailed advertisements in local newspapers. From March 1895 they decided to fill vacancies quarterly rather than at their annual meeting.

The change from boys to girls was not well-received in another part of the Visitors' estates: Lyncombe and Widcombe. Traditionally one boy was elected from this area to the apprentice school but no such provision as made in the new girls' school. At the Inquiry in 1880 representatives from there complained about this omission, especially as they provided significant rental income for the Hospital. R.D. Commans from Lyncombe went so far as to call the new school "this miserable subterfuge", but the Inspector reminded him that the Visitors did have the power to make such changes. There was also significant criticism from representatives from Bruton who claimed that the original intention of the Charity was to educate boys and girls for a specific trade and not to train them as servants. The Visitors on the other hand were delighted with the new school. Inspector Bruce reported in 1887 that, "The Girls' School is considered by the Governors to be the one part of the Charity which they can regard with unalloyed satisfaction." (30)

There were a number of stipulations for entry to the girls' school, such as,

> "Candidates must produce a Certificate from the National School Master of their Parish that they have passed the 3rd Educational Standard, must not be under 14 years of age and are elected subject to a satisfactory report from the Medical Officer of the Hospital."

While the Minute Books record that the overwhelming majority of the girls elected were fourteen years old the Visitors were prepared to be flexible about the age of election for when Alice Trim and Annie Carver were elected in September 1889 they were 13 years 7 months and 13 years 9 months respectively. Flora Hyam was just thirteen when elected in 1884 but "under the special circumstances of her having lost her Father (late letter-carrier at Bruton) being one of six Children and a Bruton girl." Preference was always given to orphans so in 1886 Anise White was elected aged twelve, "both parents being dead." (31)

Once elected each girl was clothed, boarded and trained for three years at the Visitors' expense, as had been the system previously for the boys, with no cost to family or friends. The girls were required to be resident within the Hospital for the whole of this time and it was only in 1909 that the decision was taken to permit them one week's holiday at Christmas and two weeks in the summer. All the girls' parents were contacted in October 1909 and they agreed to have their daughters at home during the holidays but "girls without parents could be temporarily boarded out at the homes of the other girls during the holidays." Each year under the Scheme of Management established in 1881, the Girls' School received a grant from the Visitors, initially £600, later reduced to £450, of which on average £200 a year was expended on the maintenance of the girls and the Mistress.

Just as the boys had done in their time, the girls wore a distinctive outfit: a red cloak and straw hat with a blue serge dress in winter and a printed one in summer, all of which were made by the girls themselves with the aid of a dressmaker. It was very much seen as part of their practical training. They were also provided with shoes and boots which in 1882, for example, cost £11 9s 6d. From 1893 all clothing was regarded as on loan to the girl until she had been in the Hospital for one year. Such a decision may suggest that occasionally a girl had entered the school for a very short time and then departed with the new clothes. Not everyone approved of the new uniform: in November 1880 W.J. Nevill "complained that the manner in which the girls were taught to dress was not fitting for a domestic servant." The Vicar of Bruton, Rev. Ridley, however felt "they dressed in a very simple and unpretending manner." (32)

Few details remain concerning their diet, although in 1889 tenders were accepted from a local baker, A. Budden, to supply four-pound loaves at 4d each, and a butcher, S. Harding, to provide beef at 7d a pound and mutton at 8½d a pound. Once again the conclusion may be drawn that the diet was better in the Hospital than the girls might have expected in their own homes. In 1878 a local Ironmonger repaired their copper Tea Kettle for 6d, put a new ear on their Milk Can for 3d and the following year repaired a Copper Kettle, possibly the same one as before, for 6d and charged 3d to grind their carving knife. He also supplied the School with a Petroleum Lamp for 19s 10d and three dozen Clothes Pegs for 6d, the latter being an indication of one of their major activities. (33)

As they had already received an elementary education to at least Standard III, little time was devoted to school subjects, although there was a limited amount of additional reading, writing and arithmetic which was financed by an annual grant of £5 to the Mistress for books. The emphasis was upon training for Domestic Service: "The girls were taught all branches of domestic work, and received as much instruction in school as time allowed." In fact Inspector Bruce considered that, "Only so much education is attempted as will prevent the girls forgetting what reading and writing they have learnt before their admission." Their moral education, like that of the male predecessors, was not ignored as they were required to attend prayers daily in the Chapel and received some religious instruction from the Vicar of Bruton.

Bruce also discovered that as well as favouring the doubling of numbers, the Matron believed that there could be co-operation with the proposed trade school but that did not appear to have occurred. Just occasionally some of the girls benefited from an external course, such as in December 1893 when the Visitors paid £1 17s 6d for three girls to attend the Butter School which was being held at the Assembly Rooms in Bruton.

Their training was very practical as their Accounts reveal that on average each year they received just over £35 for providing Dinners for the old people. From 1883 they were paid for "Washing done in the School," which started with receipts of £5 0s 4d but by August 1886 had risen to £30 2s 3d. This income remained fairly constant so that in 1908 it was still £29 12s 8d and £24 17s 3d the following year. Such was the scope of the laundry activities in that year that when it was agreed that the girls should have a week's holiday at Christmas, the Master's wife, Mrs Hooper, had to make arrangements for the washing to be undertaken outside of the Hospital.

The amount raised indicated that the girls did not just undertake internal washing but were successful in ensuring that it was brought in from Bruton and its immediate neighbourhood. How far such an enterprise affected the livelihood of those who had previously earned small sums by taking in washing was not recorded. Such activities required a considerable amount of water, pumped by their own manual labour from the Hospital's well, as it was only at the end of the 1890s that Bruton developed a public water supply. On 14th September 1899 the Visitors decided to connect the Hospital to this new system at a cost of £240. While this innovation was undoubtedly welcomed by the girls, this part of their training remained hard, demanding physical labour.

Brief details of the actual operation of the School were recorded in 1909: "The girls act as servants to Mr & Mrs Hooper [*The Master and Mistress*] & are taught all kinds of domestic work. Each girl is assigned an office which is changed every month so that they get practice in all the various household duties, e.g.

as pantry-maid, scullery-maid, cook, etc. They do all their own laundry work & laundry is also taken in." (34)

The girls were initially placed under the control of one Mistress: Miss M. Atkinson until 1884 when she left with a gratuity of £35 0s 0d and then, for nearly fifteen years, Miss Agnes Harvey until she resigned to marry in October 1898. On this occasion the Visitors presented her with a Silver Tea Service, consisting of a Tea Pot, Sugar Basin and Cream Jug as well as with £50. The original salary was £50 a year but by 1882 Miss Atkinson was receiving £70 a year. Miss Harvey was appointed on a lower salary of £50 a year. This rose the following year to £52 10s 0d and by 1889 was £60, where it seems to have remained. There was also domestic help provided in the form of a laundress, although the Visitors amended the description in an advertisement in April 1884 to an Assistant Matron for the Girls' School "not under 25 years of age having a thorough knowledge of Laundry work and able herself to get up fine Linen. Wages £22 and all found." (35)

When Miss Harvey left the Visitors decided not to appoint another separate Mistress, "this arrangement appears not to have been very satisfactory and the Visitors thought that it would be better if everything were under one management." There would seem to have been tensions within the Hospital in relation to the management of the girls but what they were do not appear in the surviving documentary evidence. It may help to explain why Miss Harvey's salary never reached the level of that of her predecessor. The Visitors decided that the wife of the Master of the Hospital should have "special charge of the girls School" - Mrs F.S. Hooper. For this task she received £50 a year. (36)

From 1882 each of the girls was allowed 6d a month pocket-money "subject to the forfeiture of the whole or any part of it for breakages." By the early twentieth century this sum had been amended to 2d per week. Each summer the girls were taken on a trip, usually to Weymouth, but occasionally as in 1883 to Bournemouth, towards the cost of which the School mistress received £5 from the Visitors, for example, in 1889: "A Sum of £5 was granted towards Annual Excursion of Girls to Weymouth." The girls had access to a garden area and their Accounts showed that in the 1880s Samuel Eaton was paid £17   17s   6d a year as the Gardener and that he also received periodic payments for such items as seeds and manure, along with £4   12s   6d in August 1886 for a "Boulton & Co Cucumber Frame." Part of this area was a lawn and in July 1892 Miss Harvey was given £4   4s   0d to purchase a lawn mower. (37)

Although from 1880 "Girls be reported on by Medical Man before admission into Hospital," and from 1882 he was required to "consider their Physical Capacity for domestic service and probable fitness for it," there were problems with illness, but at least the girls were treated by the Hospital's own Medical Officer, for which he received an annual salary of £40. In 1881 when she was forced to leave the school through ill-health, Mary Jane Matthew, was given £3 by the Visitors. In October 1882 Selina Church was unable to go to service as she was suffering from Scrofula and so was sent home to her father, but the following month the Visitors agreed to send her to the Royal Sea Bathing Infirmary in Margate, to which they subscribed £2   2s   0d and paid her expenses of £13   13s   9d. In 1883 they also granted £1   0s   0d "Allowance to Mothers of 3 girls who had contracted an infectious disease compelling them to leave the Hospital for a time." The following year they paid £1   5s   0d to the mother of Emma Parfitt when she too returned home as a result of illness. One unnamed sick girl was treated with "Wine and Stout", which cost the Visitors the not insignificant sum of £5   6s   2d in 1882.

During 1908 the condition of Ada Curtis caused some concern, ranging from the physical to the mental. In February Mrs Hooper informed the Visitors that the girl had a bad knee which required an operation. On the advice of Dr Carsberg she was sent to Bath Hospital and in July he reported that she had "a bony growth removed from her knee", but that unfortunately she might need another operation as "there had since been a recurrence of the growth." In September however Mrs Hooper was able to state "that Dr Edwards of Wincanton Hospital had found nothing bodily wrong with Ada Curtis but that her mind required training... It was decided to give her further time to see what progress she made." Unfortunately there were no further entries. (38)

Initially the girls occupied the accommodation that the boys had just vacated but in 1882 the Visitors decided to build new premises on the playground to the east of the eastern block of the quadrangle, "a suitable house for the Mistress and Girls.........the new School will be quite distinct." The Charity Commissioners approved their plans in August, a tender was accepted from Messrs Clarke and Son of Bruton for £2,786 in September 1882 and the building was ready for occupation in 1883 when it was insured for £1,500 with a further £200 for the contents. The Mistress was expected to insure her property separately so, for example, in 1890 Miss Harvey was paying 3s for £100 worth of cover. The Visitors also took the opportunity to purchase and to demolish five more small old cottages to the east of the playground. Two of these cottages fronted the High Street and the other three were at a right angle to it going south and formed part of the east wall of the playground. Thirty-one perches of land were bought which allowed "the Visitors to effect a great improvement by admitting light & air to the new buildings." (39)

The actual design and contents of the new School building reflected the practical nature of the training available. A brief description was drawn up in May 1909:
"The accommodation consists of

(1) A Laundry. A large & lofty room in the old building
(2) A wash-house with hot & cold water laid on
(3) Kitchen, Scullery & house-maids pantry
(4) Girls dining hall used as a sitting room
(5) Dormitory with 5 Cubicles bathroom & lavatories
(6) Store room for Girls Clothes, linen etc.

The Girls also use the Master's dining room when they sit to do their Needlework." (40)

When their period of training was completed five girls each year were sent out to service, dressed in a new outfit, "That each girl on leaving School for Service be allowed an outfit not exceeding £6 in cost." As an incentive to remain with the same employer and to exhibit good behaviour a Bonus or Gratuity of £2 was given to a girl after one year's service and a further £3 after three years' service "on Employer giving satisfactory Account of Conduct." Conduct was taken very seriously for in 1883 the School mistress reported that,

> "she had received unsatisfactory reports of the conduct of Julia Gulliford and Emily Smith shortly after they had entered Service and would not therefore be strictly entitled to Gratuities."

Bonuses awarded were recorded in the main Minute Book so for example in 1890 Jane White received £2 "for good Conduct during one year's Service," and the following year Sarah Butt and Agnes Wallis received the same. The Visitors monitored the progress of the girls and ensured that care was taken of them if it proved necessary, as occurred in 1880:

> "That Mary Ann Curtis be permitted to enter Mrs Peel's Service and if not strong enough for the work to be allowed to return to Hospital School."

Two years later Elizabeth Ann Gapper "formerly in the School be received at 1/- a day during the absence of her Mistress Mrs Greet."

While some girls entered service in neighbouring towns such as Evercreech, Frome and Bath, others were sent much further afield to places such as Wimborne, Ringwood, Hampton-upon-Thames, Oakhampton, Farrington, Windsor and London. This may be an indication not only of the greater availability of transport but also of the difficulty in acquiring good domestic servants. It was a reflection of the high regard with which the training in this school was viewed. When T. O. Bennett received one request from a potential employer in June 1899 he had to reply that, "I regret to say that all our Girls are engaged for the next year, in fact we could find places for fifty if we had them." More than a decade before Inspector Bruce had made a similar observation: "There were over fifty applications for the services of the five girls who left the school this year."

Girls however were not permitted to take a situation in Bruton itself, a fact which caused some resentment locally especially as no specific reason for that decision was ever recorded. It was possible that as so many of the girls came from outside of the town the Visitors did not wish to prejudice the employment prospects of local girls. In 1894 the Visitors were prepared to make an exception when one of the girls, Ethel Bishop, was appointed the Laundress in the Hospital at an initial salary of £14 a year, rising to £24 a year by yearly additions of £2. (41)

The emphasis upon their conduct while in service was a continuation of the behavioural expectations when the girls were in the School. In 1909 it was commented that, "The conditions appear to be very pleasant, though the discipline is strict." Any breach of discipline was dealt with rapidly and severely, apparently without any appeal. In January 1883 Emily Crossman and Eva Hill were reprimanded for "misconduct" and the next month Annie Gulliver was dismissed from the Hospital for continued misconduct, while Lydia White was allowed to remain on probation for another month and was then permitted to stay. After Sarah Webb ran away in July 1884 the Visitors dismissed her. When Mary Backhouse was involved in petty theft and described as "generally an unsatisfactory Girl", she was severely reprimanded and informed that in the event of another offence she would be "taken before the Magistrates with a view of sending her to an Industrial School or Reformatory." No more was then heard of her case. Not all parents approved of the discipline, for example, in 1894 Mrs Garland complained about the treatment her daughter had received and in consequence removed her from the school. The Visitors investigated and were unanimous that the complaint was without foundation. (42)

By the end of the first decade of the twentieth century education nationally had developed significantly from that of the late 1870s when the Girls' School had been established. The School, however, had not kept pace and this led to an official at the Board of Education noting in May 1909 that while the School was "doing a certain amount of useful work", the locality obtained little benefit from it and the £450 a year received from the Visitors seemed to be far in excess of its needs. He felt, "There is an old world air about the place.... the methods and equipment are hardly up to date." Such comments led to an Inspection by H.M.I.s in July 1909 and they produced a highly critical Report.

After lengthy consideration the Board of Education wrote to the Visitors in April 1910. While accepting that as a charitable institution the School had been a great asset to the neighbourhood, "the educational results shown are poor and in no way commensurate either in quantity or in quality with the relatively large sum expended on the School out of the income of the Foundation." The Board asserted that nothing was done to continue the girls' general education and that there was no "technical training given in classes or with the apparatus of books and note books as would be the case in a modern Domestic Economy school." They felt that the training given was no better than that "a good Mistress would give to her young & inexperienced servants." It also noted that there had been increasing difficulty in obtaining applicants even when the qualifying area of residence had been extended.

The overall conclusion was that,

"while the conditions disclosed by the Report are not such as to make it necessary to raise at the present time the question of closing the school.......an effort should be made without delay to reorganize the school with a view to improving the educational work and carrying out more effectually the intention of the original trusts." (43)

These comments and criticisms prompted a reply from Henry Hobhouse as Chairman of the Finance Committee of the Visitors in May which gave an analysis of the problems as they perceived them. He stated that the majority of the Visitors agreed with the Board that the present school was unsatisfactory and believed that it was necessary to take a broader view of education provision in the Bruton area. They felt that "during the last 33 years there has been a great change in the habits and condition of the poorer classes. It is now comparatively easy for girls from the age of 13 or 14 upwards to get places as domestic servants without such training as is given in the Hospital. It is found that girls prefer the independence of ordinary domestic service to the restrictions necessary in a training institution.... while the training already given is apparently not highly valued by either the parents or the children of the poor, it is also not appreciated to any large extent by the other residents of Bruton, who would, it is believed, prefer to see the benefits of training in domestic subjects extended to the girls of Bruton generally. Some of the Visitors also feel strongly that it is a pity that so much money should be spent on an institution which does not produce valuable results."

The following month there was Conference held in Sexey's Hospital consisting of five Visitors, the Vicar of Bruton, a Churchwarden, the Chairman of the Parish Council and five H.M.I.s. There was agreement that, "as at present conducted, Sexey's Girls' School was of little use" and that there was no likelihood that even if it were made more attractive that more girls would apply to it. It was argued that there was "need for some kind of School for Domestic Subjects." The Conference therefore recommended that such an experiment should be permitted subject to "a complete reorganisation in management, staff and curriculum." (44)

(ii) Sexey' School of Domestic Science.

In August 1910 an official at the Board of Education, W. Galbraith, in a lengthy Minute reviewed the whole case. He was careful to stress on several occasions that the ideas being presented were those of Henry Hobhouse and not necessarily those of the majority of the Visitors, an interesting observation and a reflection of the extensive influence which Hobhouse wielded at this period. Overall he found no reason why the school could not be re-organised as a non-residential Centre for Domestic Instruction for Public Elementary Girls as well as young women and adults in Bruton and its neighbourhood, and possibly even stage Evening Classes and provide more technical education. He commented that, "Since 1877 the cry especially in regard to the poorer classes…. is now for money to be devoted to practical and manual forms of training."

A month later the Board of Education requested a scheme to close Sexey's Girls' School and establish a School of Domestic Subjects. The initial scheme proposed to close the existing school on 1st October 1911 and establish the new School to "provide instruction in all branches of domestic work for

a) Girls of ages between 11-14, attending Elementary Schools in Bruton and the neighbouring parishes
b) Girls and young women resident in Bruton and the neighbouring parishes, who have left school, and who desire to have training in domestic subjects to fit them for domestic service or home life
c) Other girls and women desiring to take course in Domestic work."

Some concern was felt at the loss of the original school. The Chairman of the Wincanton Poor Law Union commented that, "Many of their girls had also had the advantage of a good training at Sexey's Girls' School, Bruton, although he regretted that that source would not be open to them in the future as the school was to be discontinued." (45)

In the year which followed there were lengthy discussions within the Board of Education concerning not only the Girls' School but also the whole of the education arrangements involving Sexey's Hospital in both Bruton and Blackford. Extensive correspondence ensued with the Visitors and other interested parties, most notably Somerset County Council. The final Scheme received the approval of the King in Council on 16th December 1911. The new School of Domestic Science was to receive £150-£200 per year from the Visitors and in a significant development was to have residential places available for pupil teachers and teachers from elementary schools. (46)

These changes required some alterations to the rooms occupied by the former Girls' School to allow for cookery demonstrations, laundry work and housewifery for up to eighteen girls. In January 1912 the Board of Education approved a grant of £400 for the necessary alterations and then in November a further £70 for them and £150 for furniture and equipment. (47)

The idea of some residential students was apparently eagerly embraced by Somerset County Council, of which Hobhouse was an active member. As early as August 1911 their Higher Education Sub-committee had recommended that nine scholarships to the value of £10 each should be offered annually to ex-pupil teachers, or other approved teachers to enable them to attend this school for training. Advertisements appeared in the local press, such as one in June 1913 addressed to Headmistresses or Assistant Mistresses in Public Elementary Schools in the County offering, "Studentships covering six months' training in Domestic Subjects with board and residence, at Sexey's School of Domestic Subjects." (48)

Miss Gertrude Jameson was appointed the Principal Teacher of the new School and commenced Cookery instruction in February 1912, Laundrywork followed in September and Housewifery in November. The School itself was placed under the control of ten Managers of whom at least three had to be female. When a Board of Education official visited late that year he found eight Public Elementary School teachers or would-be teachers in residence, "The PES [*Public Elementary School*] Class in Laundrywork is held on Mondays....When the PES children attend four of the PES teachers assist with the teaching of Children. The other four being engaged in Housewifery. The Principal constitutes the sole staff, so that 4 of the Day Tech students are not under immediate supervision when the Laundry class is being held..... I visited when a Laundry Class was in progress and as far as I could judge (i) the Students assisting the principal were receiving useful indirect tuition in the management of a class & (ii) those students doing housewifery in an adjoining room were going on satisfactorily with their work." He saw no objection to this arrangement as the teachers were about 18-21 years old and "will when they leave the School have to handle classes of children & adults." (49)

In practical terms the resident teachers attended for twenty weeks and then received a Certificate at the end, if satisfactory; twelve other girls attended for cookery for twenty weeks, some of whom also went to ten lessons in Laundrywork and ten in Housewifery. There was clearly some flexibility within the arrangements, for example, a Report on the National School in Bruton by the Board of Education in 1913 noted, "Cookery, Laundrywork and Housecraft are taken at the Centre. The older girls go for a full time course of ten weeks".

The experiment of this School which provided the necessary practical facilities for so many girls was short-lived. In 1920 the Rt. Hon. Henry Hobhouse attended an interview with Board officials and had to report that while the cookery lessons for the PES children still continued, "The training of teachers ceased during the war and for the present at all events could not be resumed owing (1) to the lack of teachers and (2) to the fact that the Course provided was not sufficient to enable students to obtain the Domestic Subjects Diploma." He did however point out that it had only ever been the intention of the Visitors to give teachers sufficient training to enable them to teach practical cookery. (50)

c) The Hospital and educational developments.

Once it became clear in the 1870s that the Visitors intended to undertake changes and developments to the educational provision within Bruton and its neighbourhood, considerable concern became apparent amongst the parishioners. By late 1876 they believed that the Visitors intended, amongst other initiatives, to endow a new school at Shepton Mallet. This news led to a meeting being called on 22nd January 1877 which so many local men attended that it had to be transferred from the Vestry to the National Schoolroom. Its purpose was to consider "the steps which should be taken by the ratepayers of the parish of Bruton aforesaid, to protect their interests in the Estate of the late Hugh Sexey, now placed in jeopardy by the proposed erection and endowment of new schools at Shepton Mallet."

One of the main reasons for all the speculation in the town was that the parishioners did not know for certain what the Visitors were proposing. The latter did not consider that they had any responsibility to communicate with the principal inhabitants and ratepayers and in fact they regarded their discussions as confidential and did not permit the publication of any of their decisions or resolutions. Nevertheless a few days before this meeting took place in an attempt to defuse the situation their Steward, T.O. Bennett, had contacted several of the Visitors, and with the agreement of the Chairman, Mr Dickinson of Kingweston, Theodore Thring of Alford House provided a detailed written account of their thinking to that point and Bennett to read it out at the meeting. It indicated that while they intended to close the boys' apprenticeship school the money was to be used to fund the education of boys from the Elementary School beyond eleven years of age and also to establish in its place a Girls' Domestic School (see section above). There was to be an annual grant for scholarships to King's School and a single contribution towards the cost of building the Headmaster's new house. Finally they planned to set aside £11,000 to purchase a site and build a County Middle School in a town near Bruton.

Bennett then used the Visitors' Financial Statements to calculate that they would spend half of all their income, some £15,000, in Bruton itself. He also went on to point out to the meeting that as they had increased their revenue so substantially, if they did not come up with a suitable Scheme one was likely to be imposed upon them by the Charity Commissioners which might not be so beneficial for the town as they were based in London and perceived as having little understanding of the requirements of individual places in rural areas. With this last point Bennett played upon the decades-old reluctance to allow outsiders to interfere in local affairs. He warned that "it would not be desirable to have three boys' schools of different grades" in such a small town as that would be considered as "a narrow and selfish policy." He concluded by suggesting that the town ask the Visitors to permit the sons of farmers and tradesmen from Bruton and Blackford to be admitted to the proposed new school at preferential rates and that they consider establishing a high school for girls in Bruton, as the latter "would be regarded as a great boon by the neighbourhood." (51)

The attitude of some Brutonians was not well-received in various quarters of the local press. One newspaper felt that as they "had got the lion's share of the good things emanating from the will of Hugh Sexey (*they*) could well afford to allow the remainder to go for the benefit of their neighbours." Another newspaper was very critical of those inhabitants who wanted the money distributed in the town for charitable purposes. It pointed out that it had long been established "that the effects of wholesale systematic alms-giving are mischievous, and that the most useful way to employ charitable bequests is to apply them to educational purposes." (52) From that perspective the intentions of the Visitors were very much within the mainstream of contemporary thinking on charity.

There were, however, those who considered that the Visitors should devote much more money to the support of the inmates of the Hospital itself. One of these was George Mitchell, who signed himself as "One from the Plough", and who alleged "that the people in Bruton Hospital are in a state of semi-starvation - that the place endowed by Hugh Sexey is worse than a workhouse or a gaol." He claimed that, "the whole of the little town, with the exception of a few houses of officials, tradesmen &c. partakes of the squalidity of the Hospital." (53) A range of other different ideas was advanced and discussed: one of the most comprehensive lists was produced for a Vestry Meeting in March 1877. In terms of education this advocated a reformed boys' apprenticeship school, a girls' industrial school, a high school for girls and a county middle school, all in Bruton. In other areas it advocated that married couples should be added to the inmates of the Hospital where all should have increased allowances. There was the suggestion that the Visitors should build cottages for the poor, that the Bell Inn owned by the Hospital could become a public institution and that a Cottage Hospital could be established. (54)

If all or most of these suggestions had been implemented it would have marked a pronounced development in the educational and charitable institutions in the town. It was, however, not to be. As the Visitors were drawn from the landed gentry in other parts of Somerset and neighbouring counties they may have had a broader understanding of what was desirable elsewhere, were desirous of improving conditions in their own areas and may have been more in tune with national thinking. Within Bruton itself the feeling developed amongst many of the inhabitants that as landed gentry the Visitors were actually ignorant of, or dismissive of, the actual conditions of the poor - an idea which was to linger in some quarters in relation to the facilities of the elderly poor in the hospital until well into the twentieth century.

A month after the March 1877 meeting the Visitors published their own Draft Scheme and by 1880 it was clear that they were still pressing ahead with their project for a County Middle School at Shepton Mallet. The discussions, criticisms and proposals for alternatives continued and so in November 1880 the Charity Commissioners sent an Inspector, William Good, to hold an Inquiry at the Wellington Inn on the Charity as a whole. Despite the fact that there were allegations of mismanagement on the part of the Visitors and their paid officials, that the new girls' industrial school was not in accordance with the original wishes of Hugh Sexey and with the proceedings described as "very animated", the Inspector concluded that it was well managed, especially as the total income had reached £4,122 a year and was anticipated to rise to over £5,500 from rents alone as new leases were granted. (55)

The final Scheme received Royal Assent in July 1881 after "Much consideration and of protracted negotiations." It provided for the continuance of Sexey's Girls' School, and of grants to the Grammar School in the form of exhibitions and a capital sum to improve buildings, the establishment of a School for Boys in Bruton, and for a Day and Boarding School in the County of Somerset to be called Sexey's County School. (56)

The inclusion of a boys' school in Bruton satisfied many of the parishioners and it was hoped that rapid progress would ensue: it was, however, not to be so. The advent of Queen Victoria's Golden Jubilee in 1887 gave a new impetus as meetings were held to decide the form a permanent memorial should take. The Committee of ratepayers established to consider the various alternatives ignored all the suggestions and recommended one of their own, namely that as there was the want of a school for the middle classes in the town, they should support the one proposed in the Visitors' Scheme of 1881. Discussions commenced immediately with the Visitors and the parishioners agreed to contribute £500 towards the cost of the building. It was decided that the foundation stone would be laid on the anniversary of Queen Victoria's Coronation Day. At the last moment for some unspecified reason, that proved impossible. Nevertheless confidence in the project remained high, "It should be stated, however, that the building will be commenced shortly." Despite this optimism it was to be four more years before Sexey's Trade School opened its doors. (57)

Bruton was to be more fortunate than Shepton Mallet as the plan for a new County Middle School there did not materialize. The main reason for this and all the delays was the agricultural depression of the late 1880s and 1890s which severely reduced the income of the Visitors. According to T.O. Bennett as reported by Inspector Bruce, the only champion of a school there had been one of the Visitors, Sir R.H. Paget, but when that did not happen he ceased to play any further part. Bennett believed that there was little, if any support, for such a school from Shepton Mallet itself. The decision was made instead to provide £1,500 capital for new buildings at the existing Shepton Mallet Grammar School and to build another school at Blackford in Wedmore where the Visitors had a large estate and this was completed in 1897. When opening the extensions at Shepton Mallet in 1899, Henry Hobhouse explained that to implement all the parts of the Scheme of 1881 would have cost far more than the resources the Visitors had available at that time. In relation to the proposed new school they had only £3,000 and a piece of land at Doulting, the site selected for the county school. (58) The idea of establishing a high school for girls had to be left to others to implement, although T.O. Bennett and Henry Hobhouse remained central to that project as well.

While the educational provision in the Hospital had started in a modest way with just twelve boys, by the end of the nineteenth century it had developed and expanded out of all recognition. Between 1882 and 1897 over £12,000 was spent on capital projects in the area and some £1,100 donated each year to five schools. Hobhouse noted that this represented "nearly a quarter of the gross and half of the net income of the Hospital," and which he estimated assisted the education of some 800 children without affecting the maintenance of the old people.

For most of the period from the mid-seventeenth century, however, the primary function of the education provided by the Hospital was to produce apprentices. For the 900 or so that benefited from the system the opportunity was available to gain skills and then become self-supporting and productive members of their community. It was, on the other hand, a system designed to produce workmen, one that did not threaten the status quo. When the Earl of Cork claimed in 1892 at the opening of Sexey's Trade School that, "apprenticeship has produced most of our excellent and best men," he also recalled the words of the Chairman of the Visitors to a boy when apprenticeship occurred, 'Be a good boy,' and to the Master, 'Take care of your pupil and make him a good workman.' His remarks on the decline of apprenticeship were an implicit criticism of its nature, "the love of freedom, the love of independence on the part of the youth of the present day.....greatly conduces to the abolition to a great extent of apprenticeship in this country."

2

Sunday Schools.

The close connection between religion and education was further developed through the concept of Sunday Schools. Although frequently attributed to the pioneering activities of Robert Raikes, who, horrified at seeing children playing in the streets of Gloucester on a Sunday, established Sunday Schools there, in reality teaching reading of the Bible and occasionally other basic skills on a Sunday may be found amongst some Puritan and evangelical congregations earlier in the eighteenth century and possibly in the seventeenth. In April 1617 in a codicil to his Will Sir Maurice Berkeley of Bruton Abbey instructed that a house with a garden and £40 a year should be given "towards the maine-tenannce of a Reverend preacher" whose function was to be "instructinge and Teachinge the people in the service and feare of god.... that the said Preacher doe preache everie Sabath daye in the forenoone and Catechise in the afternoone throughout the yeare." (1) How far this wish was implemented and for how long is impossible to determine although the Archiepiscopal Visitation in 1634 did record the existence of a lectureship in the town.

The fundamental aim of the Sunday Schools run by Christian groups was to produce the Christians of the next generation. Some Non-Conformist churches increasingly stressed the necessity of their members being able to read for themselves the Word of God as revealed in the Bible. The greatest emphasis therefore was placed on teaching reading to achieve that objective. Such education had to occur on a Sunday as many of the children involved were required to work the other six days of the week. While religious education occupied the most prominent position, these were essentially schools on a Sunday and so virtually all taught reading, a minority also included writing and just occasionally arithmetic. In many of the Sunday Schools the classes were small and taught by dedicated volunteers so the result was that more was achieved in one day than in five days in some of the huge monitorial school classrooms with rote learning.

The creation of Sunday Schools was a significant philanthropic gesture which required local money, time, effort and on-going commitment to ensure success. The overwhelming majority of these schools relied upon local Subscriptions and fundraising rather than receive money from a central fund. At the same time, however, the spread of Sunday Schools across the country may be seen as a response to concerns being expressed about the impact of the Poor Laws upon the poor. Men like Sir Frederick Eden believed that the existing poor laws fostered dependency, increased the demand for aid, undermined the desire to acquire property and discouraged ambition. Adherents of the Sunday Schools were convinced that by teaching virtue, sobriety and industry they could create independent workers who could be supported when necessary by philanthropists. Hannah More, who was instrumental in the formation of Sunday Schools in parts of Somerset, believed that they could be used "to train up the lower classes in habits of industry and piety." (2) To many of the supporters of Sunday Schools the connection between a carefully designed education and a stable political system was obvious.

Although under the influence of the Mores and others Sunday Schools were in operation in areas such as the Mendips in the late 1780s, it is impossible to determine exactly when the first Sunday School was opened in Bruton. On establishing the first Church of England one in January 1835 it was reported that "there had long been one held by the dissenters." (3) Various small groups of Protestant Dissenters had met for worship in a number of houses in Bruton for many decades in the eighteenth century and had registered these Meeting Houses from at least 1780. None however made a specific reference to a Sunday School. (4) In 1800 it was recorded that a group of Independents, later to become the Congregationalists, took over a building in the town which had originally been built by a Wesleyan preacher but was little used; two years later they moved to "a more spacious and convenient chapel" which they registered as the Union Chapel in June 1802 and which became their permanent site in the High Street. This building had space for a Sunday School but it is possible that they had operated one for at least two years before that. By 1818 it was reported to contain ninety boys and girls. (5)

The Wesleyan Methodists, however, do not appear to have been continuously active in Bruton at this period. After Rev. John Wesley preached from the Cross in the Market Place in September 1776 there was some initial interest with a Methodist Society being formed in the town made up of nineteen members in 1777 but it declined to twelve in 1783. It was not until the 1840s that a permanent chapel was built and a Sunday School started.

By the mid-nineteenth century three Sunday Schools were meeting in Bruton but the surviving documentary evidence is very limited, especially for the Non-Conformists. The formation and early years of the Church of England Sunday School may be traced in more detail.

a) The Church of England Sunday School

The careful work of Robert Raikes and the way in which he avoided many of the more radical ideas of some of his contemporaries meant that Sundays Schools spread nationwide in a relatively short time. Yet the Church of England in Bruton seems to have been very slow in embracing the idea which probably indicated some degree of opposition. The decades after 1790 witnessed considerable unrest in England which had a number of causes: the spread of radical ideas associated with the French Revolution; hunger in the mid-1790s with harvest failure; distress post 1815 caused in part by rapid demobilisation and the return of peace after more than twenty years of war; and the agricultural discontent with the Swing Riots in 1830. It was more than enough for opponents to blame the Sunday Schools as Hannah More discovered when a number of her foundations were labelled as subversive. In addition some employers in rural areas saw no need for their workers to have any education whatsoever to perform their manual and routine tasks.

In the 1830s attitudes at a national level towards the education of the poor were beginning to change as in 1833 the first parliamentary grant, albeit very small, was given to aid the two main religious societies which were fostering education: the National Society and the British and Foreign Schools Society. The same change seems to have been the case in Bruton as a Sunday School was established by the Church of England. The unrest in 1830 had come very close to the town as groups of labourers were reported to be on the Redlynch and Stourhead estates, although no damage was done. Some property owners were concerned about the impact of the Poor Law Amendment Act 1834 on the poor and workers. Such concern was not entirely misplaced as in November 1834 there was an arson attack upon Card's Farm at South Brewham, leased by Thomas Hall, the Poor Law Guardian for the village. A reward of £50 was offered for a successful prosecution but none seems to have occurred. (6) A method of instilling the appropriate attitudes became more and more essential from the point of view of the property owning and leasing classes.

In addition for decades there had been rivalry and competition between the Established Church and the Dissenting Congregations. In 1833 a Parliamentary Return indicated that 191 children attended the Sunday School run by the Independents in the town, although how regularly was not specified. This figure represented some 23% of all young people under twenty years of age, as counted by the 1841 Census and would have been an even greater percentage of those under twelve. Such a situation represented a potential long-term threat to the dominance of the Church of England in Bruton and its neighbourhood. (7)

When a steering Committee was established on 18th December 1835 it laid down its own objectives for a Sunday School. It was to be an "excellent and charitable work; which under the Divine Blessing, trains the Young to early habits of order and regular attendance on Divine Service; teaches them the sacredness of the Lord's Day, to the neglect of which is traced the ruin of many unfortunate persons, whose lives and liberty have become forfeited to the violated laws of their Country; makes them worthy and diligent members of society; and brings them to know Themselves, their Neighbour and their God." (8)

This initial meeting was held in the house of John Evett, a Carpenter in Coombe Street, which since January of that year had been the location of the Sunday School. This does raise the question of how far the foundation of a Sunday School was driven by the actions of one man or a small group rather than the church hierarchy in Bruton. No offer seems to have been made to use any part of St Mary's Church or its facilities. In some areas, for example, a side aisle was used, the Vestry or a room above the porch. While the Vicar in the 1830s, Rev. S.H. Cassan, had chaired the initial meeting he appeared to have played no part in subsequent meetings or actions.

In the December Meeting it was resolved to build a new school-house as the existing rooms were "in many respects inconvenient & ill adapted to the purpose." This remark was very much an understatement as in a letter to the National Society some eighteen months later, Captain George Henderson of Berkeley Cottage, who was a major force in the development of the Sunday School explained, "The Children met & still continue to meet in two places - they cannot be called rooms (for during the week they are used as Carpenters' shops) - & are both by position & state ill calculated for such purpose, especially in winter being neither wind nor water tight." He added, however, "still the Children have not been deterred by very inclement weather from attending." (9)

In the December Meeting £75 0s 0d was subscribed immediately towards the project and another £5 0s 0d promised.

In the following months the philanthropic nature of the town raised £214 10s 6d as cash was received from eighty-four sub-scribers, of whom at least fourteen were female and twenty-nine were non-resident. These non-residents subscribed some £84 2s 0d and indicated the importance of the support of influential patrons and of the social network of the area. This list was headed by the Earl of Ilchester of Redlynch, the Bishop of Bath and Wells, the Right Honourable Henry Hobhouse of Hadspen and Sir Richard Colt Hoare of Stourhead, who provided timber. An analysis of the list indicates that many others were former residents of Bruton or related to them such as Rev. Richard Michell, Rev. T. Henderson, W.B. Henderson, Lieutenant Henderson and Rev. John Dyne. Thirteen pounds was received from "Friends" of Bruton residents.

Some thirteen of the subscribers were clergymen, headed by the Bishop, confirming the importance of the role played by the Church of England, although the Vicar of Bruton did decline to subscribe. The largest sum was £20 from Rev. John Goldesbrough and then £10 each from the Earl of Ilchester, Rev. J.C.J.H. Abrahall, Mr Dyne, Captain Henderson, Mr C. Michell of Whaddon, Mr J.S. Ward and 'A Friend'. The smallest donation of 1s 6d was received from Mr Frame and eleven more Bruton subscribers gave 2s 6d each. In addition, once alterations to the building were under way Sir Richard Colt Hoare who wished to "have nothing to do with brick and Mortar" provided timber for the new floor, Jonas Lucas carriage of the timber, Mr Peplar of Coombe Farm carriage of Keinton stone and Mr Ross a stone Door Case. (10)

The original intention was to purchase a site and erect a new building but by May 1836 Henderson was forced to admit that "the low state of the Funds" made that impossible and so it was decided to convert an existing building "at once into a temporary School House." A Vestry Meeting convened in July 1836 for the purpose of disposing of the old Poor House, after the new Union Workhouse had been opened in Wincanton, agreed to sell to the newly created Trustees of the Sunday School "the Western part of the Building (commencing with the party wall now standing between the Hall & the Long Room) to Bow Bridge." The result was that after the resolution of various legal issues, including dealing with the Board of the local Poor Law Guardians and the Poor Law Commissioners in London, the property was transferred to the Trustees in March 1837 for £50, "for the purpose of erecting a School Room for the Instruction of Children in the Religion of the United Kingdom of England and Ireland." (11) This part of the old Poor House was rectangular in shape with the long southern edge bordering Silver Street and the shorter western edge bordering the alleyway which led to Bow Bridge. The former garden between the building and the River Brue became a yard.

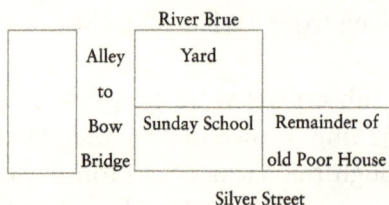

	River Brue		
	Alley	Yard	
	to		
	Bow	Sunday School	Remainder of
	Bridge		old Poor House

Silver Street   [Not to scale]

The conversion work entailed the creation of two large rooms, one on each floor, by the removal of any partitions: the ground floor room with a new Keinton stone floor was thirty-three feet two inches long by fifteen feet one inch wide and the upper one with a new wooden floor was thirty-seven feet eleven inches long by fifteen feet one inch wide, slightly longer as it extended over the alley which linked Silver Street with Bow Bridge. A staircase was inserted, along with two privies and two Arnott stoves for heating which cost £12 from an ironmonger in Bath who charged a further 3s 0d for a scraper and poker.

The total cost of the conversion work was £150 which was paid to local builder Mr Ross. A further £8 19s 10d was paid to John Evett for two armchairs, eight small chairs, fourteen joint stools, ten long forms and four short forms. Comfort for the children was not a primary concern. The final cost of the project was £238 6s 3s which created a deficit of £23 15s 9d, which was eventually met with additional subscriptions over a period of several years.

The conversion work was undertaken during the winter and spring of 1837 to 1838 and Ross was paid the balance due to him in August 1838 when he "reported the building complete was far as his Verbal Contract went." In fact such was the demand for a large internal open space that even before the children had occupied their new rooms one of them was used for celebrations for Queen Victoria's Coronation in July 1838: "One hundred and twenty of the oldest inhabitants were regaled with the best of Old English fare in the Sunday School-room"

The Accounts for the first seven years indicated that the steady flow of philanthropy continued. Table 3 does however show that there were deficits in 1839 and 1840 which may be largely explained by a rapid increase in numbers attending, by the fact that economic times were hard, and that additional subscriptions were being raised for another building project. (12)

Table 3. Sunday School Accounts 1835 to 1841.

Year	Subscriptions/ Receipts			Expenditure			Balance		
	£	s	d	£	s	d	£	s	d
1835	34	13	0	28	10	8	6	2	4
1836	37	14	0	29	4	3½	8	8	9½
1837	34	0	6	31	7	6¾	2	12	11¼
1838	34	10	1	29	0	5	5	9	8
1839	29	16	0	36	18	5½	-7	2	5½
1840	29	4	6	35	12	0	-6	8	6
1841	33	7	4	31	2	0	2	5	4

These early Accounts also indicated that once the conversion was completed there was on-going maintenance expenditure, such as between £1 0s 0d and £1 13s 0d a year for cleaning the rooms and lighting the fires, 9s to D. White for whitewashing the rooms in 1839 and in the same year 5s for levelling the yard, while John Evett was paid £3 9s 10d for additional chairs, stools and repairs and the following year 3s "for Repairs." In 1840 an iron pipe for an unspecified purpose cost £1 14s 6d. Repairs to the Stoves in 1841 cost 9s and John Evett submitted a bill for £1 1s 10d.

Unfortunately no curriculum details have survived from this Sunday School but it would undoubtedly have followed a pattern similar to that clearly expressed by Hannah More for her schools, "the Catechism, broken into short questions, Spelling Books, Psalter, Common Prayer, Testament, Bible." (13) The initial meeting in Bruton on 18th December 1835 resolved, "That the Books used by the School be only those published by the Society for promoting Christian Knowledge", an organisation which had been publishing religious books and material since 1699. The Accounts indicated that between 1835 and 1841 £37 19s 0½ was spent on such books, much of which would have been devoted to Bibles and Prayer Books for the pupils. For the care of such books which were kept on the premises Sir Richard Colt Hoare presented the Sunday School with a Box for their storage in 1836.

A major issue that the Sunday School had to deal with was that the overwhelming majority, if not all, of the children who attended were illiterate. One method which was widely used to teach reading was gradually to recognise and build up letters and then words from Cards. Capital letters with straight sides such as HTLNZ were taught first, followed by those with curves, such as BRSO. Then came small letters usually taught in alphabetical order, abcde and so on. Gradually letters were placed together to spell short words and allow recognition. The letters were all on Cards which could be moved around on a board. The Accounts for Bruton Sunday School show that in 1835 and 1836 some 17s 0d was spent on Card Boards, Trays and Slides for Cards.

There is no evidence to suggest that writing was ever undertaken in this Sunday School, although it was possible that it did so once the Infant School was established as more resources would have been available. There was a requirement that the day should start and end with a short prayer. In addition the children were expected to attend some services in St. Mary's Church and to that end in May 1835 a local carpenter, Henry Feltham, was paid £2 19s 1d "for new Stools for the Sunday School Chn[*children*] in the Church." (14)

The new Sunday School targeted "the Children of the Poor" and the numbers included in the initial statements of Accounts indicated that there was a good and increasing demand. See Table 4.

Table 4. Number of Children attending Bruton Sunday School 1835-1841.

Year	Boys	Girls	Total
1835	65	73	138
1836	61	83	144
1837	59	105	164
1838	77	121	198
1839	89	148	237
1840	84	146	230
1841	82	140	222

These numbers seem to have remained fairly constant for the rest of the century as in 1842 when the Sunday School was "admirably conducted" there were 214 pupils, about 200 in 1859 and 179 in 1888. (15) Unfortunately none of the returns of pupil numbers specified the ages of those attending. In some parts of the country it was not unusual to find adults present in the hope of learning to read. There is no evidence for this practice in Bruton, especially as the pupils were referred to as 'Boys' and 'Girls'.

Once the Sunday School scholars had moved into their newly converted rooms in 1838 there was certainly enough space for their activities. The rooms, however, seem to have remained spartan, each heated by just one stove, with wooden benches for the children to sit on and there was little indication that there was much in the way of stimulating material adorning the walls, although in 1836 5s 6d was spent on mounting a map of the Holy Land. Exactly which books were available was not specified although donations of money for them were received on an annual basis for at least six years from the Castle Cary District Fund. The Bible and the Book of Common Prayer remained the dominant resource and in 1836 Sir Richard Colt Hoare donated thirteen Bibles and eleven Prayer Books "part of the proceeds of the pious bequest of Henry Hoare, Esq. made in 1724."

While the Church Sunday School was successful in attracting children, their attendance could be irregular so methods were required to retain them. Reward schemes were widely adopted, with in some places items of clothing for good attendance being given. The Bruton Sunday School Committee decided upon a system of rewards for good conduct and so in 1835 at a cost of 11s 7d some 2,160 Tin Tickets were purchased and a further 200 the following year for 1s 6d. These were issued to the children as appropriate and had a nominal financial value. In their Report accompanying the Accounts for 1836 the Committee were delighted to state that, "Many of the Scholars, greatly to their credit, have requested that the amount of the Rewards may be appropriated to the purchase of Bibles and Prayer Books - fifteen of the former and four of the latter have been obtained, and there are no less than fifty Scholars whose Rewards (at present amounting to £3 3s 9d) are thus accumulating." In 1841 the Committee was able to report that "the Children have obtained 96 Bibles and 198 Prayer Books through the medium of their Reward Tickets" and there was still available £12 17 5d for further purchases.

A second method used to retain support was the Annual Treat. In 1835 the Accounts recorded a payment of £1 15s 4d "For cakes, &c by Henry Ball at Whitsuntide." Subsequent Accounts referred to this event as the "Annual Feast at Whitsuntide", with expenditure increasing from £2 4s 7d in 1836 to £5 1s 0d in 1841. Whitsuntide was a traditional holiday in Bruton and many other areas when local Friendly Societies held their Club Day with a Church Service, parades and considerable celebration with huge quantities of alcohol. A major reason for the Sunday Schools selecting this date was that the children could be removed from witnessing the worst excesses of drunkenness. (16)

An annual treat continued throughout the nineteenth century and usually took the form of a substantial tea and games, often on the Abbey Field. There could be some variation as in June 1875 when all the Sunday School children were taken to Burnham-on-Sea by train from Cole Station. On arrival they were fed with bread and meat, played games on the beach during the afternoon and were then provided with tea. For many of the poorer children this will have been the only time that they either travelled by train or saw the sea. Such events were widely reported in local newspapers and provided excellent coverage for the Sunday School.

By the 1860s another treat was becoming common and that was usually given to the children in the winter months. In December 1864, for example, "Instead of the usual cake and bread and butter, there was a plentiful supply of beef and bread, to which the children did ample justice." The rest of the evening consisted of games. In February 1867 after the traditional tea of bread and butter and cake some 130 children experienced "various amusements.... The chief attraction being two 'German Trees'." By the 1890s the treat had become even more elaborate: "The teachers and scholars met in the infant school-room at three o'clock. A procession was formed and marched to the Abbey field, headed by the Bruton Excelsior brass band.... Various games were indulged in till half past four o'clock, at which time a capital tea was provided in the schoolroom." Heavy rain meant that they could not return to the Abbey Field so the Band played music for dancing in the Schoolroom. The following Thursday the postponed "sports and other amusements did take place." The finance for all these treats came once again from local philanthropy, including an annual subscription of five guineas from the Visitors of Sexey's Hospital, and the changing nature of some of these events is perhaps a reflection of how children were perceived as the nineteenth century advanced. The Trustees themselves also maintained a small account in the local Savings Bank so that sums could be paid in and any bills settled. In September 1899, for example, it reached £5 1s 8d, when it was transferred to a Post Office Account. (17)

There were also ad hoc treats for the children to celebrate various events. In May 1837 on the birthday of Princess Victoria "the children of the Church Sunday School were treated with cake and tea on Mr Ward's lawn." In 1872 on the re-opening of the Parish Church after restoration the children of all the Sunday Schools in the town marched around the streets and were then provided with tea on the Abbey Field, followed as usual by games. (18)

As well as instructing the children in religion another function of the Sunday School was to teach good habits which it was felt certain would benefit them in future life. Saving money was perceived as one of these and so in 1838 a Penny Club was established although it was stressed that it was not restricted to that sum. It was claimed in the 1839 Accounts that "the children learn the value of Money as well as the benefit of regularity and honesty." The system was simple: when the depositor's savings amounted to 10s, the sum was placed in a Savings Bank in the depositor's name. It was pointed out that if a person saved 1s a week for twenty-one years, with Interest the total would be £79 4s and, perhaps rather optimistically, if the saving continued for forty-two years the sum would be £238. It would seem, however, that most deposits were withdrawn annually, for example, on 13th December 1888 there was £30 5s 10d in the account but on 27th of that month some £30 5s 0d was withdrawn.

The key appointments in the Sunday School were those of the Master and Mistress as they set the tone and direction. The first Master was John Sparks, described as a 'schoolmaster' as he and his wife kept a boarding school in Patwell Street, on a salary of £5 a year. He left Bruton at some stage in 1840-1841 after the death of his wife Jane aged forty in childbirth in January 1840 and then the death of his daughter aged three months in April of the same year. He was succeeded on a salary of £4 by Thomas Rawlings. The first Mistress was Mrs Lydia Fish who was appointed on a salary of £3 a year. It has not proved possible to determine what, if any, qualifications or experience they possessed. (19)

They were supported by a number of assistants, the overwhelming majority of whom were "selected from the School." Between 1835 and 1841 a total of twenty-six young people fulfilled this role, of whom nineteen were female. The names of some thirteen of these assistants appeared for only one year but Eliza Eastment held the position for six of these years and Charlotte Taylor for five. The largest number of them appeared in 1839 when there were twelve and each one received a payment of 8s per year. The use of these assistants indicated that the children were split into groups for at least some of the time, if not all of it. To encourage these assistants to continue to study the Bible themselves each year Mr Daniel Ward provided an incentive: "A Valuable Bible is, after examination, presented every half-year to the Teacher (not having previously received one) who exhibits the greatest knowledge of its contents."

Once a Church Day School was in operation the role of the Sunday School in teaching reading decreased and much more emphasis was placed upon religious instruction. In their Report for 1841 the Committee commented, "the main object of the School.... is, 'to bring up the children in the nurture and admonition of the Lord,' and teach them their need of a Saviour, and the hope of salvation through his merits alone, to make them under God's blessing, faithful members of Christ's Church on earth, that they may be partakers of His Kingdom hereafter." In many places which started a day school the paid assistants were then replaced with volunteers from the parish and the overall control of the Sunday School passed to the Master of the day school so in Bruton by 1851 George Perrott was in charge of both. The Sunday School was normally in session from 9 a.m. to 11 a.m. and from 2.15 p.m. to 3.30 p.m. (20)

The success of the Church Sunday School in Bruton may be seen in various ways. Certainly in its early years before the establishment of a day school the activities each Sunday were very important in teaching a large number of local children to read. The Sunday School was successful in maintaining a regular attendance throughout the nineteenth century and in so doing maintained the religious knowledge expected at that time. The instigators of the Sunday School were delighted "by a willingness, on the part of some who have been nurtured in the School, to attend, in the days of their youth, the Sacrament of the Lord's Supper." They felt that this was an ideal example not only for others of their age but also "to others of riper years." In 1841 the Committee was also pleased to report that local employers "who have thus an opportunity of observing their daily behaviour" were clear "that there is a marked improvement in them, visible in a decency and quietness of deportment, which, whilst it shews the good effects of this early training, affords at the same time the best hope of a right conduct in after years." Some degree of social control was clearly in operation.

For centuries death was an ever-present occurrence for all people, with infant and child mortality very high. (21) For the Victorians therefore preparation for death was still an important part of life. It was an area which the Committee commented upon in 1840 in order to judge one aspect of the success of their Sunday School: "Since its establishment, several of the children have been removed to an eternal world: in their sickness, the instructions they received, soothed their dying hours; and instances are not wanting, that they departed in full assurance of the Redeemer's Merits and all-sufficient atonement, whereby alone remission of sin can be obtained."

b) The Sunday School of the Independents.

Documentary evidence for other Sunday Schools in the town is much more limited. The Independents had started their Sunday School very early in the nineteenth century and it was supported, at least indirectly, by Silk Mill owner, John Sharrer Ward, for when asked by a member of a Parliamentary Select Committee what instruction the young children whom he employed in his Mill from the age of seven received, he replied, "I recommend them all to go to a Sunday school, which there is established in the town for any one." (22) The Independents continued to flourish throughout the nineteenth century and when their re-built Chapel was opened in October 1836 it was noted, "the old chapel adjoining is appropriated to convenient school-rooms and vestries." Competition from the Church of England's Sunday School may have affected their numbers as in 1840 there were about 120 children in attendance, compared with 191 in 1833, and the same number in 1859 when it was reported to contain about seventy girls and fifty boys, along with ten teachers. At that stage they clearly felt that action was required: "It was agreed at a Previous Meeting to canvass the town for additional Scholars," although it proved to be a slow process as there was some lack of enthusiasm from the congregation and other problems. (23)

In May 1864 at the Sunday School anniversary tea the hope was expressed that "members of the Congregation will take more interest in our Sunday School than they have manifested for a few years past." Occasionally there were serious disagreements as an entry in the Church Record Book for 1869 revealed. "Mary Evett has been kept back from uniting with the Church by the ill-advise of her Teacher (in the Sabbath School) who is amongst the enemies of the Lord's people and his cause here." A number of disputes within the Church seem to have come to a head in the late 1860s and were only resolved when several members left the Chapel. (24)

In April 1871 the Pastor was able to comment that, "The Sunday School has not been in a more prosperous state for several years." He added, "There is peace & unanimity between the Superintendent and the Teachers", but gave no indication of what the problems had been. The Sunday School succeeded in maintaining and increasing their numbers and so in 1880 it was decided to renovate the old Schoolroom and add more classrooms. When this work was completed in 1881 they had created "five

The former Congregational Chapel in the High Street. The rooms on the first floor and in the basement served as schoolrooms.

excellent classrooms on the top floor, which had hitherto been used as a lumber room; also a classroom for infants in the ground floor." (25)

Most of the teachers seem to have been volunteers, for example, one was Miss Skinner, the daughter of the pastor, who taught in the Sunday School for over fifty years from 1850 and in 1901 received a certificate from the Sunday School Union "in recognition of long and valued services." She was to continue for several years after that and during much of this time she also ran a small private school in Quaperlake Street. (26)

The existence of a large indoor space in the centre of the town meant that it was often in demand for other meetings. As the Non-Conformist churches were generally opposed to alcohol it was not unusual for appropriate organisations to hold public meetings there. In August 1876, for example, a meeting of the Bruton Band of Hope and Abstainers' Union was held in the Schoolroom and in June 1882 a meeting of the Blue Ribbon Army. In May 1891 the Temperance Society staged a musical evening there. Other lectures were delivered such as one in November 1882 by Professor Berlyn on the social, moral and religious position of the Jews. (27)

As with the Church of England Sunday School, to encourage continued attendance the children of the Independent one also received an Annual Treat. In 1858 B. Mullins lent them his grounds and the children were treated to tea followed by games. In May 1863 the festivities were held in a field at Discove lent by Thomas Green with the Castle Cary and Bruton fife and drum bands in attendance. Staging this event at this time of the year was once again no coincidence as it was specifically stated in one local newspaper, "Whit Tuesday is selected for this treat in order to draw away from the scenes of drunkenness which accompany club feasts at this period." On this point the various churches could find common ground. The pattern of the day was still much the same thirty years later: "Tea was provided for the Scholars at 4.30, and a public tea at 5.30, after which various games were indulged in, and a very enjoyable evening was spent. (28)

Occasionally there was a more ambitious treat such as on Whit Tuesday in June 1862 when one hundred and fifty children from the Sunday School with their teachers joined an excursion train at Cole Station, which already contained children from the Baptist and Independent Sunday Schools in Wincanton, "so that about 700 were in the carriages" and which then went to Burnham-on-Sea. (29)

To finance the Sunday School and any developments philanthropy and self-help once again played a prominent part. Very early the Independents adopted the idea of a Tea Meeting, which became an annual event and which took place for the rest of the century, so that, for example, in January 1889 some fifty-one persons sat down to tea. Any money raised was devoted to the Sunday School but in addition such meetings had important social implications, "they felt still more happiness in the social chat and friendly intercourse which the occasion furnished." They were undoubtedly a significant boost for the volunteer teachers, as on this occasion when more than 150 people attended, "The teachers of the Sunday School felt greatly cheered by the presence and sanction of so many of their friends as well as by the encouragement which had been held out to them by the Ministers and others who had addressed them."

By 1880 it had become necessary to increase the school accommodation and so fundraising commenced: in November a large bazaar was staged on the premises of Mr Read in Quaperlake Street. The stalls which were open for two days were under the control of ladies from the church and more than £100 was raised. The children themselves were encouraged not only to help to raise money for their own Sunday School but also to be involved in that required for Missionary activities. In 1831, for example, they collected some £1 11s 1d for that purpose and continued to do so for decades, such as 13s 1d in 1855. (30)

c) The Sunday School of the Methodists.

Although Wesleyan Methodism had faded away in Bruton after the 1780s it had revived by the 1830s as in September 1836 it was placed on the Service Plan of the Frome Wesley Circuit with a service to commence each Sunday at 2.30 pm. Along with open-air Meetings on the site of the old Market Cross, many of these early services were held first in a cottage on Tolbury and then in one behind the Castle Inn. In 1842 the present Chapel then seating 165 persons was opened at the West End on the road to Wyke Champflower; it was formally registered as a place of Religious Worship in May 1844 and a Sunday School started there on 4th October 1848, so it was recorded as celebrating its fortieth anniversary in October 1888. (31) It was well-established by 1852 and in 1854 a specific Sunday Schoolroom was added at a total cost of £53 5s 10, with the stone and timber being donated by Charles Michell, esq., and transported to the site at no charge by others.

Money was raised through twenty-eight subscribers, the largest of whom was James Harding of Whaddon Farm with £10 and at the other extreme 1s was received from each of 3 people, Miss White, C. Corps and J. Budden. Along with general collections and proceeds from the Opening Service £55 5s 10d was raised. Local tradition claims that there was so much opposition to the schoolroom that the walls had to be built from the inside.

The Schoolroom provided a useful space for other activities associated with the Methodist Church, most notably meetings of the Wesleyan Mutual Improvement Class. A Bible Class which contained over forty members also met there. (32)

Unfortunately, no details have survived about the teaching within this Sunday School or the materials used. Some indication of what was expected of the children may be gathered from a late nineteenth century poster displayed in their new Schoolroom built in 1897.

> "It is expected of the
> SCHOLARS
> in this school that they be
> Regular in Attendance
> Punctual Morning and Afternoon
> Obedient to Teachers
> Attentive to Lessons
> Careful in the Use of Books &
> Kind One to Another."

As with the other two Sunday Schools the Wesleyans were concerned to ensure continued and regular attendance. One of their methods was prizes which were awarded for lessons, attendance and good conduct. Such prizes were invariably in the form of books which in 1889, for example, cost nearly £3. In that year Mrs Cruse presented the prizes and then gave every child an orange. (33)

Similarly the concept of a Treat for the children was in place by 1852 when a reference appeared to the "Children's Tea."

It seems to have followed the same pattern in subsequent years. Unlike the other Sunday Schools, however, the date of the event seems to have varied as it occurred in either June, July or August. By the 1890s it too had become rather more elaborate: "22 June. The Scholars, attended by their teachers, assembled at the School at two o'clock, and after forming a procession marched to the Jubilee Park where various games were much enjoyed. At 4.30 tea was provided. There was also a public tea at 5.30, which a large number of townsfolk attended. The children passed the evening with sports, swings &c." On this occasion the Bruton Excelsior Band provided the music. In this decade and in the first years of the twentieth century it was common for the event to be staged in a field loaned by one of their principal supporters, Josiah Jackson of Durslade Farm. (34)

Their Sunday School Treat in July 1896 included swings, cocoa nuts, bowling "and an amusing washing competition, for which there was keen competition. Prizes were offered by Messrs Lever Bros, the winners being Mr J. Miles, 1st prize, one dozen plated spoons and tongs in a leather case; 2nd prize Mrs George White, 32lbs [pounds] Sunlight Soap." (35) Perhaps here reinforcing the Victorian idea that cleanliness was next to godliness. There was some variation in the Treats, for example, in July 1892 "the Wesleyan scholars" were to be found "journeying to Stourton in brakes." In August 1904 Josiah Jackson lent the Sunday School a wagon with two horses and a driver to help transport the children to Stourton Tower.

There were other more ad hoc Treats for the children, for example, in September 1858 all the Sunday School children and their teachers were treated to a Harvest Home tea with cakes by James Harding of Whaddon Farm. In January 1887, after a Service of Praise during which the Sunday School Scholars gave recitations and sang, "Through the kindness of Mrs Jonathan Cruse, those who took part in the service, and also the scholars of the Sunday School, were entertained to a sumptuous tea, which was much enjoyed by all." (36)

As well as maintaining the attendance of the children the Wesleyans were concerned to retain the active support of their parents. On 1st March 1860 they were invited by the teachers to a Tea Meeting and a large number attended. "The object of the meeting was to set before the parents the necessity of attending religious worship on the Sabbath, and the injurious effects produced by the neglect of this duty on themselves, their children, and the teachers of the school." It appeared to have had the desired effects as the following Sunday there was "the attendance of many of them at several places of worship." (37)

Attendance figures are not available for this Sunday School for most of its existence but by the mid-1890s the existing Schoolroom had become too small as there were 117 scholars in August 1895 and over 130 were on the Register in 1897. Conversations on future developments were clearly taking place in March 1895 as may be seen from a series of entries in Josiah Jackson's Diary and in May of that year a piece of waste land opposite present day 89 High Street and Silk Mill House and almost opposite Town Mill at the West End was purchased for £45 from Mr George. Starting at the end of October and on many days in November Jackson sent one or two of his men with a horse and wagon to clear all the rubbish from the site.

On 10th February 1896 a meeting took place to consider purchasing an Iron Church which already existed in London and on 15th Jackson and Mr Jones travelled by train to Chiswick to view the building and "make enquiries about taking down, hauling to station, supposed cost of carriage, erection at Bruton." Within a week they had decided not proceed with the purchase but rather to erect a new building of brick or stone. There followed a period of about a year during which the Building Committee had to ensure sufficient money was raised. Then in April 1897 an advertisement was placed in local newspapers requesting tenders to construct the new building and in May the one for £530 0s 0d from Messrs Clarke and Son of Bruton was accepted. Once again Jackson sent men and a wagon to help transport soil from the site to Yonder Park, then stone for building to it and later tiles. (38)

On 17th June 1897 foundation and memorials stone were laid: "Mrs Amor laid the first stone in memory of her late dear husband George Amor who filled the office of Superintendent of the school for 48 years having founded it on October 4th 1848." Two of the 132 scholars, Hubert King and Ida King, laid another stone and

Foundation Stones in the new Wesleyan Schoolroom 1897.

presented £7 2s 11d which had been collected by the children. Mrs C. Lockyer laid a third stone and donated £5 and Mrs Jackson a fourth along with a gift of £2. (39) These stones, carved with various initials, may still be seen to the right and left of the main entrance facing the road. Originally the words 'Wesleyan School Room' were carved around the upper window but were erased as a condition of the sale of the building to the Red Cross in the late twentieth century. The date was allowed to remain.

The new Schoolroom which was opened by Mrs Cruse on 28th October 1897, was lit by gas and was some forty feet long by sixteen feet wide and twenty feet high with several attached small rooms and could accommodate about 280 persons. Although Jackson attended the opening he gave no details, unlike a report in dialect which appeared in the 'Castle Cary Visitor'. A local working woman was asked if she had seen the building: "Lor' ees but I cooden' get inside 'un cos I was feared the babby'd meak a noise. But I thought I'd bide outside an' lis'n. Lor' did'n thic man taak. I comed whome and zed to our Char's, 'Ther' thic man's words comed out of his head just like stoones out of a wuld wall'." (40)

Once again such a large indoor space proved to be a valuable resource as not only was the Schoolroom used for its intended purpose but was available for others to hire. A wide range of activities occurred within its walls as well as religious ones, for example, in November 1911 Miss Beatrice Heginbothom with her Orchestra gave a concert and in December of the following year Miss Paynter's Collegiate School staged their annual concert there. When eighteen boys formed a Boy's Brigade in October 1912 they used the school-room for their drill practice. As war drew closer in 1914 a large public meeting was held in the school-room in August with a view to forming a civilian volunteer force and 110 young men signed their names. The following month an army recruiting meeting took place there "at the call of Lord Kitchener" and eighteen men volunteered. (41)

As with the other two Sunday Schools it was local philanthropy which funded it and financed the buildings. In January 1888, for example, a bazaar was held which George Amor stated "was in aid of the Sunday School and that most of the work had been done by the Scholars." It was reported that the attendance was very large and as well as stalls and refreshments there was

The new Wesleyan Schoolroom 1897.

musical entertainment. A year earlier during a Service of Praise, "A Collection was made to defray the children's books, which they had received at Christmas last." The building of the original Sunday Schoolroom had been financed mainly by subscription and the same occurred in 1896-1897 but on a larger scale and with some variations. In October 1895 it was suggested that shares could be sold a £1 each; in August 1897 a bazaar was held in the Assembly Rooms in Coombe Street; sometimes there were straightforward donations such as £50 from Mr Lockyer of Gant's Mill in March 1897 and a much smaller one of £1 from G. Francis on 27th August 1897. The provision of men, horses and wagons by Josiah Jackson saved a significant amount of money. (42)

Nationally Sunday Schools thrived during the nineteenth and early twentieth centuries. In Somerset alone in 1861 the Church of England ran 726 such schools with 31,974 children, the Methodists 125 with 8,806 children and the Congregationalists 56 which 8,692 attended. A number of Sunday Schools existed near Bruton, at an early stage, for example in 1818 there was one in Shepton Montague with thirty children and a combined one for North and South Brewham with 146. Pitcombe had a Sunday School for forty-six apprentice girls from a silk factory in 1818 and then in 1833 another commenced for local children with sixty-seven attendees. For children in the Shepton Montague areas it was also noted that, "The poorer classes have the opportunity of attending a Sunday School at the neighbouring hamlet of Redlynch." This Sunday School was in fact older as in 1814 Rev. John Goldesbrough subscribed £1 1s 0d to it and in 1817 Lady Ilchester was subscribing £2 a year. In 1833 it was attended by thirty-three children. (43)

The existence of these Church of England Sunday Schools in some of the surrounding villages before 1820 does in fact make it even more surprising that the foundation of one in Bruton itself was much later.

The Sunday Schools played an important role in the local community on several different levels. In terms of education they produced a religious education for a large number of children and thereby probably ensured a constant supply of new members for the congregations of the various churches. For many children there was also some basic elementary education with reading and possibly some writing. The role of philanthropy was of key importance in the foundation and survival of these schools, as well as the provision of Annual Treats, but with that went an element of the creation of status as the publication of Subscription Lists, particularly by the Church of England ensured the identification of those with sufficient resources to make donations. On-going support through a range of activities from visiting the schools, to attending prize-giving, to supporting treats for the children were widely reported in the local newspapers and again ensured such recognition. Some element of social control cannot be overlooked as the very young children could be exposed to the various aspects of belief which suited those in the higher social ranks and which found expression even in the hymns which the children were taught, such as 'All Things Bright and Beautiful' and 'Jesus Bids me Shine."

There was obviously a role for female members of the churches in the Sunday Schools as teachers, and reports of the Sunday School Treats often concluded with thanks being expressed to the ladies who provided the tea. In addition they supervised the stalls at public events such as bazaars and were responsible for many of the accompanying decorations. It is also possible that there was some working class involvement in the Sunday Schools, especially in the Non-Conformist chapels with their more inclusive organisational structure, but as the names of the vast majority of individual teachers for Bruton have not survived it is not possible to trace their origins. On the death in 1909 of William Thomas who carried on the business of shoemaker and draper, it was noted that he had been a Sunday School teacher in the Congregational Chapel "for fully fifty years." In the same Chapel Thomas Hannam Jones, an outfitter, was for thirty years until his death in August 1908 the Sunday School Superintendent. Within the Wesleyan

Chapel the Superintendent for some fifty years was George Amor. Reflecting the society of their day men retained the higher roles. Countless volunteers gave freely of their time and experience to teach the children and demonstrate another aspect of the on-going philanthropic approach. (44)

3

The National Schools.

In the nineteenth and twentieth centuries formal schooling became progressively more important. Before that time most working people had functioned perfectly well being illiterate or partially literate and generally learned their trade or skill through experience with no need to be able to read or write. With industrialization and increasing competition from abroad attitudes began to change. It was felt that an educated workforce would lead to the economic development of the nation with greater productivity and innovation. For those who wished to extend the vote to working people, such as the Chartists in the 1830s and 1840s, education was seen as essential so that these newly enfranchised people would be able to understand the issues involved and so use their vote wisely.

Concerns however continued to be expressed that once the working classes could read and write they might become more critical of the social order. In 1842 one local newspaper believed that the solution to prevent unrest was more moral and religious instruction. "It is to a judicious system of education based on, and regulated by religious instruction - by the extension of the salutary influence of the Church into the hovels and humble dwellings of the poor, that we can hope to make them submissive under privation, and contented with their allotted station." There was certainly a great deal of work to be done in Somerset as five years earlier Robert Weale, an Assistant Poor Law Commissioner had found, "the education of the peasantry and the lower order of artisan.... in a degraded state." (1)

Two religious organizations were established to deal with education: the first was founded by Quaker Joseph Lancaster in 1808 and became the British and Foreign Schools Society in 1814; the second was the National Society for promoting the Education of the Poor in the Principles of the Established Church, usually known as the National Society, and founded by Andrew Bell in 1811. It was the latter to which the school in Bruton turned.

a) The Infant Day School.

When members of the Church of England in the town had considered their new Sunday School building they had also contemplated that in the future it might serve as a day school as well. In 1837 Captain Henderson stated, "it would be desirable to carry out the plan & use the rooms as an Infant day school during the week." The financial situation, however, meant that their efforts had to be concentrated on establishing the Sunday School. By the autumn of 1839, with that successfully in operation, an Infant School was again under consideration along with the addition of two small rooms to serve a practical purpose:

> "The late exceedingly wet weather has shown the great want there is for a place of deposit for clokes Umbrellas & pattens..... considering the great possibility of a day school being established the great want of a place of deposit for Pattens &c and also a retiring room for various purposes, We directed Mr Ross, Carpenter, to furnish us with an estimate for the cost of building two rooms, one over the other."

Ross provided an initial estimate of £20 for the rooms, each of which was to be eight feet by thirteen feet.

During the winter months further discussions were held and the idea of an Infant day school became firmer so that on 16th March 1840 "the First Meeting to Consider the Propriety of Establishing an Infant School" was held. It was agreed that a self-supporting infant school should be created to be called, "The Infant & National School of Bruton." Their discussions became so detailed that a complex system of class-based fees was proposed to ensure adequate on-going finance and "to better to classify the population.": the first child of a Labourer would pay 2d per week and then all others 1d; small Tradesmen and Mechanics 3d for the first child and 2d for others; 'Housekeepers and Tradesmen' 4d and then 3d. The proposed scheme obviously provoked some criticism for at the second meeting a week later on 23rd March it was abandoned in favour of a flat rate of 2d per week for all children between the ages of two and seven.

Modification was then required to their building plans for on 30th March it was decided that the proposed new rooms should be increased in size to nine feet by thirteen feet at a cost of £30 and the wall next to the river raised, presumably for safety reasons as well as to reduce the risk of flooding, which took the total cost to £46 16s 0d. Once again it became necessary to solicit subscriptions and leaflets were duly printed which stated that it had

> "become more absolutely necessary to put the Building in a fit & safe state that it may be used during the week as an Infant Day School. When it is considered also how useful the School building has been found on several occasions, there is every confidence that the inhabitants of Bruton will give their cheerful ready aid towards the creation of funds to complete the School building." (2)

Twenty-four subscriptions were received, totalling £36 18s 0d, including £5 each from Sir Hugh Hoare of Stourhead, Mr Stockwell and the Bishop of Bath and Wells. When replying to the latter in June 1840 Henderson, as the Honorary Secretary, stated that the works were "so far advanced as to leave scarcely a doubt but they will be completed within a short period." He added optimistically, "I lk [look] forward to ye gt [great] period when e'en a cup of cold water shall have its full acknowledgements. When such hum[ble] exertions as we are making receive Countenance & approval, our reward is cheer'd & we lk [look] forward to a glorious harvest not that we can fix the period but that we may continue to sow in hope." (3)

There was certainly some support for the scheme from some wealthier members of the community, for example, Colonel Coles wrote to Henderson, "I believe it to be the happiest idea as regards the education of the Poor that was ever hit up as it insures priority of possession, before evil is fixed, in the Infant mind & early impressions are always lasting."

To maximize support an Address was drawn up which listed the benefits for parents, children and the Parish. Parents were informed that, "It is easier and safer to instil good principles in the Mind before evil is learnt, than afterwards." Children would receive education from the earliest possible age when parents themselves were too occupied to do this. On a practical note it was claimed that as the children would be at school for five hours a day there would be "less wear & tear to their Clothes" and while their children were being supervised, parents would be able to work and so pay the small fees. Two advantages were specified for the children:

"1st They are taught 'the Holy Scriptures which are able to make them wise unto Salvation.'
2nd Health, Cleanliness, Order, Instruction, & Happiness."

For the Parish it opened the prospect that, "The rising generation are improved by being early taught good principles" and so better prepared for Sunday Schools and "therefore better recommended for admission to various employments; the more likely to prove useful Members of Society hereafter."

On subsequent occasions to encourage attendance further reasons were advanced. One centred on the boys who might apply for admission to Sexey's Hospital Blue School and who would have "the great advantage of going there well advanced" so that,

"they would make great advances & be more fitted to take hereafter places of trust & greater profit than others who go into that school knowing not a letter of the Alphabet (which I have heard from Mr Parfitt is not an infrequent case)."

There was also the slightly bizarre suggestion, "that those inhabitants who kindly give soap to large families should make it a stipulation the Children of that family of fit age shd. be sent to the School."

The possibility of sending very young children to the School while mothers as well as fathers went out to work seemed to have proved popular in the early days of the new school. In addition as another child was added to the family it was a method of relieving the burden on the mother at home. The 1851 Census, for example, indicated that some eighteen children - 20% of the total - classed as 'scholars' were under five with one being just two years old. By 1861 the number of three and four year olds attending had fallen to thirteen, or some 10.8%, with none specified as being two.

By the end of October 1840 the additional attached rooms were built, with a window on the first floor of the existing building converted into a door to give access to the new small upper room from the upstairs Schoolroom. They had also included in the new ground floor room pins and racks for outdoor clothes and umbrellas. Ross was given a list of small items which required attention, along with a request for his final bill by the end of December. The Infant and National School was ready for its official opening at the beginning of 1841, with boys taught in the ground floor Schoolroom and girls on the upper floor, the same arrangement as with the Sunday School.

A list of eight Rules was prepared and published: children between two and seven years old were eligible to attend the new school which operated from 9am "when it will be opened with prayer" until 12 noon and then from 2pm until 4pm from Monday to Friday; lack of punctuality or irregular attendance could lead to removal; every Monday morning each child had to bring 2d; parents could only be in the Schoolroom at the time of public examination. Great care was taken in relation to health and hygiene as children were required to attend "<u>clean</u> and <u>neat,</u> with their hands and faces washed, their hair short and combed." If a parent allowed a child to attend school "knowing or suspecting that it has any symptoms of infectious disorders, such as measles, hooping cough, scarlet fever, or the like" then it could lead to expulsion. Finally it was stated that if a parent found a "cause of complaint against the Teacher, they are requested to inform the Managers of the same." (4)

The first Managers of the School were all prominent members of the Church of England, most of whom had served on the Committee which had established the Sunday School and then this one. In an interesting note to an item which he proposed for discussion Henderson wrote, "Managers - Ladies as Managers." The outcome of any discussion on this topic, if it took place at all, however, was not recorded nor were the names of subsequent Managers and so the extent of female involvement at this level cannot be determined for certain. In October 1874 the Committee was all male as were the new members elected to fill the vacancies and in 1878 it was noted that the National Schools were managed by "a committee of 13 gentlemen, Mr. T.O. Bennett, jun., being the hon. Secretary", which may suggest that this was the pattern for most, if not all, of the nineteenth century. Even when the Education Act 1902 required a new structure for the Managers, those elected were all male.

For a large part of the nineteenth century the Managers were drawn from the most prominent inhabitants of the town who were members of the Church of England. It was only in the closing decade that leading Non-Conformists, such as Josiah Jackson were elected to the body. These men were also amongst the largest ratepayers in the area, a not insignificant matter when so much of the finance for the School had to be raised locally. Most of the men were drawn from the ranks of the clergy, retired military men, solicitors, doctors, principal traders and shopkeepers, land agents, mill owners and larger farmers.

In general reports from H.M.I.s in rural areas found that the Managers were devoted to their schools and showed great personal interest. The frequency of visiting, involvement and the concern for this school shown by the Bruton Managers would seem to substantiate this observation. There was genuine sorrow when one of the Managers died, such as Daniel Ward in February 1859 when all the children of the National Schools walked at the head of the funeral procession and he was described as "one of their truest and warmest friends" At his funeral in September 1893 William Muller was said to have been "especially beloved by the children of the National Schools.... in whose welfare he took such great interest." Even the death of the daughter of Manager T.O. Bennett in November 1900 led to the attendance of some sixty of the older children and their teachers: "They wore mourning, and each child carried a bunch of white flowers, which were thrown on the coffin at the close of the service."

Some of the support received was over a long period of time, for example, Captain Dyne was a Manager for some fifty years and T.O. Bennett was the Honorary Secretary and Treasurer for nearly forty years. The Log Books after 1870 indicated that some of the Managers were regular visitors to the School, along with the Vicar and a number of prominent ladies of the town, such as the wife of the Headmaster of King's School, Mrs D.E. Norton.

Their concern for their school was best demonstrated on the occasions when they perceived that it was threatened by external events, such as Foster's Education Act 1870 and the potential for a Board School being imposed upon them. They were absolutely determined to maintain a fundamentally Christian education in Bruton, based of course upon the beliefs and teachings of the Church of England. As late as 1906, for example, they called a meeting to protest at an Education Bill which they felt threatened that belief. Rev. Hayward, the Vicar of St. Mary's Church, as Chairman spoke against it "as a Christian, a Churchman and a parent." The meeting passed a number of resolutions of protest, which were seconded by Headmaster Hayter. "It does not give any national recognition of religious teaching of any kind. Because it disregards the right of Church parents to have for their Children Church teaching in Church schools during school hours by the school staff."

Evidence from elsewhere in Somerset such as Skilgate and Writhlington, indicated that occasionally the Headteacher and the Managers did not agree on a range of issues, from the state of the buildings to the competence of the teachers but neither of the Log Books for Bruton National School made any reference to such disputes. As the Minute Book of the Managers does not appear to have survived their perceptions of the actions taken by the Headmaster are no longer available. (5)

b) The new National School.

Nationally the number of schools increased significantly after 1830. This development was in part aided by the fact that in 1833 the Government gave its first grant to the two religious groups. It was initially £20,000 but increased to £30,000 in 1839 and was £837,000 in 1851. In Bruton in the 1840s members of the Church of England decided to revive their original plan to build a completely new school with a Master's house attached. They had been encouraged by the success of their Sunday School and the Infant School as numbers steadily increased. In addition their finances seem to have become more secure.

A more immediate cause was that the existing Schoolroom narrowly missed a disaster in November 1848. According to newspaper reports some 400 local people were attending a lecture on emigration being delivered in the upper schoolroom There was a loud crashing noise which was at first thought to be a fire "but the real cause of the alarm was the giving way of the floor, which sunk considerably, leaving a deep cavity, the beams which supported it being severed in two." Fortunately most people ran towards the ends of the room so a tragedy was avoided but, "It need scarcely be added, that the audience made their exit with all possible expedition." (6) There is no direct evidence for the immediate aftermath: whether the damage was repaired or the girls moved downstairs to share the room on the ground floor with the boys as the year before there had been sixty-six boys and sixty-three girls on the register so there was adequate space. The wording of the application for a new school building did imply only the use of the ground floor.

The site for the new school was soon found as a plot of ground was available immediately to the west of the existing schoolrooms, between the alleyway to Bow Bridge and the lane leading to the ford through the river which ran along the eastern side of Plox House. In the eighteenth century it had been the location of the Coach and Horses Inn which by 1798 had been converted into a house. Exactly what was the nature of the building which was there in 1851 was not specified but the site cost £90 0s 0d when purchased from Benjamin Ellis of Shepton Mallet, druggist, and William Ellis of Bruton, Maltster.

In March 1851 Rev. White and four other inhabitants completed a building application for a National School to be submitted to the Lords of the Committee of the Council on Education who had the power to grant up to 50% of the cost of building a new school, provided that it was for the children of the 'poorer classes'. (7) They proposed to erect a school for 100 boys and 100 girls along with a house for a Master and Mistress, the latter being a recommendation of the Council from 1835. They stated that there were only a few dame schools in the district and claimed, "that the present School is incommodious - insecure - too low - too narrow - imperfectly ventilated & lighted - has a stone floor - not large enough - no class rooms - and ground floor not sufficiently elevated. No Master's residence attached & was merely converted into a Sunday School from a Poor House." They estimated that the total cost was likely to be £944 0s 0d, of which they expected to have £440, including obtaining £90 for existing stone and timber and a grant of £50 from the National Society. They had in fact overestimated the cost as on completion the total was to be £787 5s 10d.

At the same time Rev. White applied for the new school to join the National Society, which included inserting an appropriate clause to that effect within the existing Trust Deed before it was enrolled in Chancery. On 29th July 1851 the Committee of the Council on Education approved the plan and gave a grant of £171 15 0d towards it. Clearly confident of success, by that stage an advertisement for tenders to build the new school and Master's house had already appeared in local newspapers. Once again the contract was awarded to Ross of Bruton. (8)

The formal opening of the School was marked by a church service on Wednesday 19th May 1852 when nearly 200 National and Sunday School children attended. "After the morning service, a highly respectable company of ladies and gentlemen of the town and neighbourhood, upwards of 100 in number, sat down to an elegant and substantial collation in the new Schoolrooms." (9)

The new National School was a single storey building, con-structed of local stone with walls one foot nine inches thick and a slate roof and with two large schoolrooms, one for the boys and one for the girls: mixed classes would not be countenanced. As was customary at that period there were two separate entrances: the one for the boys was from Silver Street which led to a small hallway, on the left of which were "offices", that is toilet facilities. To the right of the hallway was a schoolroom, thirty feet long by twenty feet wide and fifteen feet six inches high. It had a wooden floor raised two feet above ground level, which allowed for two cold air 'drains' from the outside to lead to two cold air ventila-tions in the centre of the floor in each room and one in the class-room. There was one large window facing south and two smaller ones facing east.

The girls' entrance was through a door from the alleyway leading to Bow Bridge and it opened directly into their schoolroom

The girls' entrance to the National School from the alleyway to Bow Bridge and the east-facing window of their school-room, now overlooking a car park.

which was thirty-three feet long by eighteen feet wide and fifteen feet six inches high. This room was located at the northern end of the boys' schoolroom and at a right angle to it, so forming an L shape and separated from it by a moveable partition wall. At the western end of the girls' schoolroom a door led to a cloakroom nine feet by eight feet and a small yard with toilet facilities. The Schoolroom had a large window facing east and a smaller one west onto their yard. The sills of all the windows were some six feet above the floor to ensure that pupils when sitting would not be distracted by looking through them at passing carts and carriages, animals or people. (10)

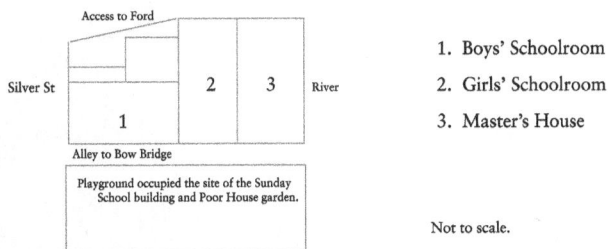

Access to Ford

Silver St

2 3 River

1

Alley to Bow Bridge

Playground occupied the site of the Sunday School building and Poor House garden.

1. Boys' Schoolroom

2. Girls' Schoolroom

3. Master's House

Not to scale.

The original intention was that the new schoolrooms would be sufficient for 100 boys and 100 girls. The National Society regulations however stipulated that each pupil should have six square feet of space. Because of the restricted nature of the site the number of girls therefore had to be reduced by one to ninety-nine to conform with this requirement. There was also a third much smaller classroom to which both boys and girls had access: the girls directly through a door in the south-west corner of their schoolroom and the boys through a doorway at the northern end of the entrance hallway. This room was originally fourteen feet by thirteen feet and nine feet six inches high, but by 1902 after some internal alterations was extended to eighteen feet by sixteen feet.

As both sets of toilet facilities and the WC from the Master's house adjoined the lane to the river, the contents initially emptied into a drain which went straight into the river. The system may have originally relied upon a manual input of water as in 1859 a Report recommended that, "The offices ought to be provided with a tank for collecting the water from the roof and flushing the pans." The same Report also indicated that there were problems with ventilation, a problem which was to bedevil the School for much of the rest of the century. "Though the room is lofty, the ventilation is bad, owing to the want of apertures in the windows. (11) The total cost of the actual school building itself, excluding any fittings, was £268 13s 0d.

The boys' entrance to the National School from Silver Street, with the bell turret above, and the large south-facing window of their schoolroom.

Although there was no specific building plan for schools at this period most tended to follow the pattern of one or two large rooms and in Somerset as a whole were built of local stone and tiles. This was a style with which the builders were most familiar and so tended to be cheaper. The ceilings in the rooms were also high as this allowed the noise to be dispersed. When it came to windows some schools favoured the 'Tudor' style with square-top windows and others the Gothic style with pointed windows as in churches. The former was simpler and cheaper to build but many schools including Bruton National School did decide on the latter, possibly as they were much more dominant and impressive (and these windows still look out over Silver Street and the car park today.) In practical terms the restricted nature of the space available meant that in Bruton no other plan would have been feasible.

Once the new National School had been built the old Sunday School and Infant School building was demolished, immediately improving the natural light available in the new schoolrooms. The area which it had occupied, including the old Poor House garden, which together stretched from Silver Street to the bank of the River Brue, became the new School's playground, with apparently no tangible boundary with the street.

Attached to the northern side of the School, but with no direct access to it, and overlooking the river was a cottage for the Master and Mistress. There were three rooms on the ground floor - parlour, kitchen and scullery, with three bedrooms above. The parlour, kitchen and one bedroom measured thirteen feet by twelve feet and the other rooms were smaller. Outside to the north-west was a very small yard and along the northern side a paved area for access. The yard and pavement were constructed to be twelve feet above the bed of river as it existed at that time and so was designed to place the cottage and school above any flood level. The total cost of building this house was £124 13 8d. It was certainly not spacious as the Census Returns for 1861 showed that Daniel Byles, the Schoolmaster lived there with his wife who was the Schoolmistress, two daughters aged two years and four months,

The Master's house attached to the northern side of the National School and overlooking the River Brue.

his brother-in-law aged sixteen, two female Pupil Teachers, both aged fifteen, and a female General Servant aged thirteen. (12)

(i) Attendance.

Attendance at a school was always problematical in rural areas. A Return for the Wincanton Poor Law Union on 1st July 1853 found that of 360 children who were chargeable to the poor rates throughout the Union, 169 attended a school at a cost to their parents or relatives, thirty-four had their fees paid by "other Parties", but 157 or 44% did not attend any day school. This figure was slightly above the Somerset average of 37%. The Return also revealed that in the Wincanton area 85% of those who attended a day school were under ten years of age. In some families it was essential for children to work to supplement family income, for example, in 1862 Elizabeth Hill, a 41-year-old deserted wife, was unable to find any employment in South Brewham and relied upon the 2s a week earned by her nine year old son. Although she was able bodied the Board of Guardians directed their Relieving Officer to give her 1s 6d and one loaf of bread a week until such time was she could find work. (13)

In 1861 Rev. James Fraser reported that in agricultural areas "there are such successive demands on juvenile, almost infantine labour, that anything like regularity of attendance or continuity of instruction is impossible.... on the average, you must not expect in an agricultural district to be able to keep the boys under instruction after 10 nor girls, at the outside, after 12." He considered that many Guardians of the Poor Law Unions did little to encourage parents on outdoor relief to send their children to school, "They do not feel very strongly on the subject as employers, and still less so as guardians." Change, however, was beginning as he perceived "that the farmers, as a class, are beginning to see the superiority of the educated labourer... the scientific methods of cultivation require more knowledge and intelligence in the cultivator."

Nevertheless there continued to be those who questioned the value of education and retained a desire for the old ways. As late as 1910 W.H. Hudson declared that he wished, "we had a more rational system of education for the agricultural districts, one which would not keep the children shut up in a room during all the best hours of the day, when to be out of doors, seeing, hearing, and doing, would fit them so much better for the life-work before them."

In 1869 the Guardians in the Wincanton Union felt that while there were appropriate arrangements for education in their area it was "not always taken advantage of; parents are apathetic about it, and many will not send their children even if the pence are paid for them." They also noted that, "boys themselves would rather do work than go to school." One of the Bruton Guardians, Amor, stated that boys went out to work as young as six or seven when they led the horses, scared off birds and picked apples. He was in no doubt that, "They must work because wages are so low." More than half a century before J.S. Ward had admitted that while he employed a small number of children under eight years old in his Bruton Silk Mills, "Principally to oblige their parents," he had no idea how many others worked at home "for their mothers." He claimed that he did nevertheless "recommend them all to go to Sunday School." Another factor which may have influenced some poor families was the expense and availability of suitable clothes. To attend the Infant and National Schools in Bruton children were required to be "clean and neat" but as one manufacturer in Somerset claimed, "It is difficult to persuade the work people to send their children, even to a Sunday School, on account of the expense of decent clothing." (14)

In the late 1830s and 1840s many head teachers and H.M.I.s considered that about two years of education, spread over three to five years up to about ten years of age, was adequate for working class children, although interestingly a pre-1851 Return for Bruton which included ages listed twenty-five scholars aged ten and under fifteen and one aged fifteen and under twenty. The remaining thirty-eight were aged five and under ten. (15) By 1870 very little had changed but the introduction of compulsion extended the period in schools significantly until it reached some seven years. In 1893-4, for example, some three-quarters of working class children aged twelve and thirteen were still attending a school. The first hesitant step towards compulsion had come in Lord Sandon's Act 1876 and was completed in Mundella's Act 1880.

Early statistics suggest that there were some ninety pupils on the Register of Bruton National School in 1853 and that this had risen to 120 by 1859 when the average attendance was 101. When the Diocesan Inspector visited the School in March 1868 there were 108 children present and the number of children on the books above three years of age in October 1874 was 191. As expected average attendance rose significantly after the introduction of compulsory education, as may be seen in Tables 5 and 6. (16)

Table 5. Average Attendance at the National School 1882-1898.

Year	Average Attendance
1882-3	163
1883-4	165
1884-5	170
1885-6	191
1886-7	222
1887-8	210
1888-9	203
1889-90	205
1890-1	197
1891-2	215
1892-3	210
1893-4	237
1894-5	248
1895-6	237
1896-7	251
1897-8	257

Table 6. Number on Roll and Average Attendance 1900-1914

Year	Number on Roll			Average Attendance			
	National School	Infant School	Total	National School	Infant School	Total	% of Attendance
1900	191	108	299	170	77	247	82.6
1901	183	103	286	168	79	247	86.3
1902	201	97	298	173	69	242	81.2
1903	186	99	285	175	71	246	86.3
1904	174	102	276	172	83	255	92.4
1905	184	95	279	177	84	261	93.5
1906	174	87	261	159	72	231	88.5
1907	180	83	263	171	78	249	94.6
1908	158	86	244	149	78	227	93.0

(continued)

Table 6. Number on Roll and Average Attendance 1900-1914 *(continued)*

Year	Number on Roll			Average Attendance			
	National School	Infant School	Total	National School	Infant School	Total	% of Attendance
1909	162	86	248	147	76	223	89.9
1910	153	88	241	145	79	224	92.9
1911	146	88	234	138	79	217	92.7
1912	139	92	231	131	77	208	90.0
1913	152	103	255	144	87	231	90.5
1914	145	107	252	137	87	224	88.8

The number on the Register was of course always higher than the average attendance, for example, in 1887-8 when average attendance was 210 the National School Register contained 190 names and the Infant School 92 which gave an average attendance rate of 74.5%. Similarly in 1890-1 with an average attendance of 197 there were 202 and 78 pupils respectively on the Registers which gave an attendance rate of 70.3%. In the years before 1914 it was in fact claimed that the average percentage attendance was almost the highest in the eastern part of Somerset. (17)

From 1880 the legal position was absolutely clear: each parish was required to have an elementary school attended by children between the ages of five and ten. National attendance rates rose only slowly from 68% in 1870 to 76% in 1885 and 82% a decade later. Bruton National School did not appear to have been able to keep pace with these national figures which may indicate not only the reluctance of parents to send their children to school regularly but also the continued unofficial use of child labour in the area. As Table 6 shows, however, in the early twentieth century attendance rates improved markedly, reaching a peak of 94.6% in 1907. The population of Bruton declined after 1871 but at the same time, as Table 7 indicates, the average attendance percentages showed that a great percentage of that population was attending the National School.

Table 7. Percentage of Population attending the National School 1881-1911.

Year	Population	Average attendance	% of population
1881	1849	163	8.8
1891	1788	215	12.0
1901	1776	247	13.9
1911	1755	217	12.4

Needless to say in every year after 1900 attendance at the Infant School was lower, largely explained by the tendency of younger children to be susceptible to illnesses, of which there were many in circulation.

When E.R. Hayter was appointed Headmaster of Bruton National School in 1870 he started a new Log Book and so information is available after that date on the reasons for absences or low attendance until 1914. (18)

– Illness and Disease.

References to illness and disease appeared very frequently in the Log Book. Sometimes it was undefined and just included in general terms:

"29 September 1871   Much sickness in the town.

1 March 1872   A large number of children absent through sickness.

15 January 1892   Attendance during week very bad. Many cases of illness."

Some of the illnesses were those associated with the winter months:

"5 March 1874   A number of children absent from colds & Chillblains.

9 March 1877   Some children absent from broken chillblains.

| 30 November 1877 | Several children absent from severe colds & low fever. This has been the case for the past few weeks. |
| 28 January 1878 | The influenza epidemic is spreading & the attendance of this week has been very bad in consequence. Where the children are not suffering from it, they are kept home through the parents being ill." |

With medical treatments often being very limited a number of diseases had the potential to be very serious. Chicken pox was reported on a number of occasions amongst families in the town such as in March 1884 and March 1907, but although no comments were made on attendance as a result a number of pupils suffering from these diseases, some children were brought to school by their parents and then had to be sent home. Significant outbreaks of measles were recorded on at least ten occasions between 1878 and 1908, often lasting several months and having a profound impact on attendance.

| "2 April 1884 | Attendance bad. Measles spreading. |
| 11 December 1893 | The measles have spread very rapidly. Only 111 children present this morning." |

There were times when the Medical Officer of Health had no hesitation in ordering the closure of the school, such as for five weeks during an outbreak of measles in January 1902 when "Almost every child in the School had had measles."

Whooping Cough was another disease which kept re-appearing, especially in the 1880s and 1890s and this led to infected children being sent home. The longest outbreak seems to have occurred between July and October 1905. Mumps made an occasional appearance such as in February 1893: "attendance very bad. A number of Children absent through 'Mumps'." In January 1909, "Many cases of Mumps", when some children had to be sent home already suffering from the disease.

Undoubtedly the disease which caused most concern was scarlet fever. There was a serious outbreak in the town in September 1874 and local doctors ordered the School not to allow children from families where there was the disease to attend the School. It continued through October and November when once again pupils were sent to school already suffering from the disease. On 3 November it claimed the life of George Atkins of Standard II. "Disinfectants have also been placed in the School & Yards." The opening of the School after Christmas was delayed until 11th January and Hayter noted, "During the holidays the school premises have been thoroughly cleansed. The fever has sensibly abated." Two more pupils had however died by this time, Nellie and Bessie Billett.

Scarlet fever reappeared in January 1877 when "Children living in Providence ordered not to attend School at request of Dr Heginbothom." Attendance dropped significantly as the result of another outbreak in October 1905, from 169 to 142. It lingered until at least Christmas and then there was a fresh outbreak at the end of January which lasted throughout February. In January and September 1907 children from different parts of the town such as Tolbury were ordered by the Medical Officer of Health not to attend School because of the disease. In fact school closures as a result of scarlet fever were not limited to Bruton National School as it affected other local villages and hamlets, such as Hadspen, Pitcombe and Wyke in 1893 when on this occasion the Medical Officer of Health ordered the closure of Pitcombe National School.

– The Weather

At times the weather had a major impact on attendance. Heavy rain could be a problem:

"5 September 1870 Very wet morning, attendance small.

16 February 1880 Weather very bad. Raining in torrents. Small School."

After heavy rain and some flooding in the morning on 13th November 1888, "School opened in afternoon but only 66 Children present." On 15th January 1900 as a result of heavy rain, "There was no School in the afternoon, as all the approaches to the room were flooded." Just occasionally the reverse happened as on 25th April 1890: "Heavy rain last night caused a flood, and the children who attended School could not go home till nearly one pm, the roads being impassable." Four years later on 12th November 1894 Hayter recorded, "Owing to the heavy rain the town was flooded. The river rose very rapidly & the Children were dismissed at 11.45 to enable them to get home. The roads were impassable in the afternoon, and the School was not opened."

Snow and intense cold also had an impact on attendance as the following entries indicate:

"30 January 1873	Heavy Snow. The number present was consequently very low.
3 February 1873	Weather intensely cold. Snow. Attendance very small.
24 February 1873	Weather very tempestuous. Deep snow on the ground. Attendance very small.
10 January 1879	Attendance very small, on account of intense cold.
13 January 1880	A very heavy fall of snow considerably reduced the attendance.
13 March 1891	Deep snow this week has made the attendance very low.
22 February 1898	Heavy snow during the night & this morning. Streets and roads were almost impassable. Only nine Children put in an appearance, & these had their feet & legs so wet with coming through the snow that they were at once sent home. The snow in places was knee deep."

On just one occasion the reverse was noted: "16 July 1897 A falling off in the attendance this morning. Several Children suffering from the effects of the great heat of yesterday."

– Rural Activities.

As agriculture was such an important activity in the Bruton area it was also inevitable that its requirements would have an impact on school attendance. In 1868 the Taunton Commission pointed out that "many of the poorer farmers send their sons" to the National School and this was a group which could not afford to employ other labourers.

"2 September 1870 Low attendance caused by children being kept home for potato digging."

In September or October of virtually every year for the rest of the nineteenth century a comment to that effect appeared in the Log Book. Earlier each year of course the potatoes had had to be planted and children played a part in that as well:

"24 April 1874 Attendance rather irregular, many Children being at work planting potatoes.

2 April 1883 Attendance bad: potato planting occupying a number of the Children."

In the same autumn months and sometimes into November children were absent as a result of apple picking, even though this infringed the terms of the Employment of Children (Agriculture) Act. The Headmaster did make some enquiries about the reason for an absence "but in nearly every case answers were sent to the effect that they were apple picking for farmers." (22nd November 1875) These activities had occurred for generations as had gleaning:

"26 August 1871 Several Children absent gleaning."

One month earlier haymaking occurred and children were expected to play their part in that:

"9 July 1872 Several children absent Hay making.
13 July 1891 A number of Children absent haymaking."

– Miscellaneous.

A number of other reasons for a fall in attendance appeared in the Log Books:

"30 August 1870 Attendance smaller than usual Wesleyan Sunday School treat & Election day at the Hospital.
7 June 1883 Very small attendance in the afternoon; 'Independent' Sunday School treat."

On 15th July 1886 attendance was once again noted to be very small, this time as a result of the Girls' Friendly Society Festival and Wesleyan Sunday School Treat. Gradually, but very slowly, it became accepted that these annual events would have an impact and after 1900 the School generally closed on the afternoon of the Wesleyan and Independent Sunday School Treats. The Headmaster was less keen to close the School for Club Days but was forced to do so on the afternoon of 1st June 1883 when "so many applications were made for 'leave' and so many children were absent for the Shepton Montague Club Day." The School did remain open during the Brewham Club Day on 6th June 1887 but it was noted that, "Several children gone with parents to Brewham Club." The abundance of alcohol on these Club days was one of the main reasons why they were so much opposed by schools.

One reason for absence which clearly annoyed Headmaster Hayter was Maypole Dancing for on 20th July 1896 he noted, "The work has been interfered with today by a number of girls being absent. They belong to a troop of Maypole dancers. Originally formed as a means of recreation for the girls, they have now got into the hands of a woman who has started touring with them. They were absent from School some three weeks ago." Five years later the problem remained for on 29th May 1901 he recorded, "A number of girls were taken away from their work today to a fete near Warminster, Maypole dancing."

It becomes very apparent from the Log Books that some reasons for absence analysed so far remain constant in the period under consideration, most notably illnesses and the weather. Others however become less of an issue through the decades, possibly aided by the changes to the regulations relating to school leaving ages and the availability of some part-time schooling. After 1900 there does not appear to have been the same opposition to compulsory attendance as occurred twenty years earlier.

One problem with attendance remained and occupied an increasing amount of time:

– Truancy.

Truancy was a recurring theme throughout the Log Books. On 17th July 1875 the Headmaster noted, "John James Standard III who has been repeatedly punished for playing truant has been again absenting himself without leave." On 1st April 1887, "John Annett, St III (an inveterate truant) has been playing truant since March 7th", and on 19th June 1905, "Rose Garland playing truant."

After 1876 the Board of Guardians of the Wincanton Poor Law Union were required by law to nominate twelve of their members to become the Attendance Committee for their Union and in May 1877 appointed their Relieving Officers as the School Attendance Officers for their respective Districts. (19) The reception which the Officer covering the Bruton area received from Headmaster Hayter was initially favourable. He commented, for example, on 30th November 1883 that when "active measures" were adopted average attendance increased rapidly and when in November of the following year the Officer visited weekly the effects were very noticeable. In the years which followed, however, his degree of success was clearly limited so his attention had to be drawn to a whole series of truants such as Edith Hiscox, William Read and Amelia Harding on 16th December 1888 and then on 5th May 1893 to Ada Eddington, absent 181 times, Ada Reed, absent 189 times and Linda Harding, absent 191 times.

Over the twenty years from 1881 the Bye-laws issued by the Wincanton School Attendance Committee became more and more complex. On 2nd March 1881, following Mundella's Act 1880, they required all children between the ages of five and thirteen to attend school unless they had reached the Fourth Standard or if they were to be "beneficially and necessarily employed" and had reached the Second Standard, raised to the Third Standard in August 1893. No exemptions were permitted after the 1880 Act until a child was ten years old, raised to eleven years old in 1893 and twelve in 1899. In an ideal world all children were to achieve Standard VII before they left school but the education provided to the required Standards II and III was very basic indeed. Such a low level of attainment was a very good indication of the prevailing attitudes towards the employment of children in rural areas: the lower the level the higher the demand for child labour.

In 16th July 1901 the school leaving age was raised to fourteen but a pupil did not have to attend after the age of twelve if he or she had reached the Fifth Standard, but they had to make five attendances a week (that is half-time) if they had only reached the Fourth Standard or had made 300 attendances in the previous five years. Those aged thirteen and fourteen who were "to be beneficially employed" did not need to attend school if they had achieved 350 attendances in the previous five years. To make the system even more complex, children over eleven who had reached the Fourth Standard and were to be employed in agriculture need only attend 250 times in a year. If any of these requirements were breached a fine of £1 was imposed.

These laws on compulsory attendance were the first ones in British history which required children to attend school for a minimum period of time. As such they had a profound effect upon the lives of working class families as they were no longer able to rely upon the wages of their children to add to the family's income. There had of course been earlier legislation relating to the employment of children in factories and mines but it was much more limited whereas these measures affected every family with children in the country. It was viewed by some people as the first time that the state had interfered in the relationship between parent and child by not only reducing their income but also by imposing new patterns of behaviour on both: parents were obliged to send their children to a school and they had to attend.

If a pupil was going to take advantage of any of the provisions relating to their attendances and employment a Labour Certificate was required and it particularly irritated Hayter that the Attendance Committee allowed children under the appropriate age to leave school without such a certificate. The lack of urgency with which the Attendance Officer operated he found hard to understand, for example, on 26th November 1897 the Officer requested information on Eliza Parsons, Stanley Hayward and Henry Balch. "The first left in 1896 her mother stating that she was 13 years of age. Actually she was under 11. The Attendance Officer was informed of the case at the time, but nothing has been done till now. The two boys are both at Work without certificates, both being under 13." (20)

The lack of promptness in taking action did raise the question of how far some of the Guardians with close connections with local agriculture were committed to enforcing the various measures. In fact in the rural parish of Brewham there were never any prosecutions for non-attendance. In addition it was an administrative nightmare not only in terms of the interpretation of the clauses but also of establishing the exact number of attendances and the precise age of a particular pupil and paved the way for innumerable disputes. On the whole Headmaster Hayter became less and less impressed with the work of the Attendance Committee.

"4 November 1892	The Wincanton Attendance Committee does not seem to be of the slightest use.
27 November 1896	As far as I can see the great object of the Wincanton Attendance Committee with their officer is to assist the parents in framing excuses for their children's absence from School.
14 December 1900	There is little hope for improvement while the Wincanton Attendance Committee & their Officer have charge of the business.
26 April 1901	....the summoning before the Magistrates so spasmodic as to be useless."

Part of the problem as Hayter perceived it was that far too much emphasis was placed upon sending out letters and notices rather than undertaking visits to homes. He did however admit that some of his pupils were adept at manipulating the system as on 21st November 1890 he noted, "Some of the Children reported to the new Attendance Officer, Mr Dyke, are old offenders and appear to be taking advantage of the change of Officers."

The Attendance Committee did have many successes, however, such as for example on 7th November 1879 Thomas Wood's name was removed from the School's Register "he having been sent on board 'Formidable' training ship: his father having disregarded three successive Magistrates Orders to send his child to School." From time to time the Committee did prosecute parents for failing to send their children to school, for example, George Meaden, Alfred Clothier, William Glover and Annie White on 23rd December 1878. In each case an Order was made for attendance. Ann Hopkins and Eliza Rideford received similar Orders on 28th March 1881 and Thomas Lumber on 30th May 1881, Ada Reid 4th December 1891, John Parsons 10th October 1909, George Brown 11th March 1910, John Andrews, Frederick Pilley and John Davis 3rd June 1910.

As well as believing that there were not enough of these prosecutions another major problem as Hayter perceived it was that few of the Orders were actually followed up. There were exceptions such as George Hayter who was fined 9s 4½d or seven days in prison for non-compliance with an Order on 26th June 1889, as well as Francis Lintern 2s 6d in December 1891, William Harding 3s in November 1892. George Corps 5s in January 1902, William Mills of Dropping Lane and William Windmill 5s each in March 1914. (21)

The Headmaster in fact was not alone in his criticism as the Castle Cary Education Committee expressed great dissatisfaction in April 1912 at the leniency of the Magistrates when dealing with non-attendance. They considered that too many nominal penalties were given or just Attendance Orders. The Committee was suspicious of the behaviour of some parents in Bruton. "Several parents appear to have taken advantage of the recent outbreak of mumps to keep away from school children who were perfectly able to attend." The following month they acknowledged that while attendance was generally down in their district for genuine reasons "at Bruton also by some 'shamming'." They resolved to initiate proceedings in three cases and were still doing the same in October. In March 1914 they were still suspicious of some Bruton parents as they requested the Medical Officer of Health to produce a report on children excluded from school there for ringworm "some of whom have been kept from school for long periods." (22)

ii) Curriculum.

The curriculum was very elementary, consisting of Reading, Writing, Arithmetic, English Grammar, Geography, Music (according to the Hullah System), along with Religious Instruction. The materials which were available in the first Infants' School would have been continued:

"Books &c to be used in School
The Lords Prayer
Childs 1st Prayer

Graces before and after Meals
The Creed
Commandments
Catechism
    Catechism Church plain
          do   broken in 2 & A[*nswers*]
Reading
    National School Books 1 & 2
Trimmers Spelling Book with Short Stories
Summary of Bible.
Prints from Old Testament
    "   " New "
A Box of Objects." (23)

The emphasis upon the religious nature of the National School was plain to see. The teaching of Reading through the recognition of letters and then words continued in the same way as in the Sunday School. From that stage the children moved onto Sarah Trimmer's carefully graded books which contained short stories all of which had a moral but also were graded by syllables: a Step One book had stories with words with just one syllable, Step Two books had two syllables and so on.

Step One: The Wolf and the Lamb

"One hot day a Wolf and a Lamb came at the same time....." (all one syllable).

Step Two: A Foolish Stag

"A Stag, who chanced to come to a clear fountain to quench his thirst... He saw a pair of branching horns...." (maximum two syllables)

One former pupil of Wincanton National School recalled that in the 1840s to help them remember the alphabet they sang it to the tune of a well-known hymn. (24) For many children who came from homes where there were no books or other reading material and whose parents were often illiterate or at best semi-literate, especially until at least the middle of the nineteenth century, learning to read was a real struggle.

Writing initially consisted of long periods of time copying letters from a blackboard or printed sheet, ensuring the correct shape and size. The children would start with small letters and then progress to capitals. In many schools for the youngest children this work started with a sand tray: a monitor would point to a letter on an alphabet sheet which was hung on the wall, would say its name which was repeated by the children, and then they would form it in the sand. Once they had mastered the letters the children would progress to write on slates with chalk and which could be rubbed clean. It was not until 10th March 1905 that the Headmaster noted in his Log Book that, "All the work is now done on paper." Arithmetic remained at a simple level with addition, subtraction and then some multiplication and division. Being able to do simple calculations involving money was important for their future lives.

It is not possible to trace how far the work of the National School improved literacy in Bruton in the first twenty years of its existence. Nationally male literacy rose from 67.3% in 1841 to 75.4% in 1861 and for females from 51.1% to 65.3%. An Inspector's Report for Bruton National School in August 1859 would suggest that progress was being made but that more needed to be done. "The School is in very fair order and the Children are lively and ready in answering. The writing from memory and from dictation might be improved and extended lower in the School. Reading and Writing are carefully taught. Knowledge of number is not satisfactory in the lower division of the School. (25)

Nationally a very significant change occurred in education in 1862, largely as a result of increased costs with the introduction of the Revised Code, or Payment by Results. This Code ended grants which had been introduced in 1846 to augment teachers' salaries, grants to pupil teachers and for school maintenance. Under the new system each child could earn the school a grant of 4s through regular attendance and 8s depending on the outcome of an examination. An Inspector would deduct 2s 8d if not satisfied with the child's performance in Reading or Writing or Arithmetic. All children over six years of age had to be presented for examination in one of six newly defined 'Standards'. Within the school each child was examined at the end of the year and if he or she passed then was advanced to the next standard.

The Committee of Council on Education issued very detailed instructions to its Inspectors on the conduct of the examination. "All children will remain in their places throughout the examination. You will begin with writing and arithmetic, and you will direct the teachers to see that all who are to be examined under standard I have before them a slate and pencil." The children in Standard I then had to stand up in their places so that the teacher could confirm their identity, after which they were told to sit down. "You will then dictate the letters and figures which they are to write down." The same procedure was followed for each standard and then after the children had done this, "You will then call them name by name from the examination schedule to read, which you will hear each do...." The passage to be read was usually taken from one of the School's Reading books, which some pupils had read so many times that they knew it by heart. For Standard V there were a few lines from a poetry book used in the school and for Standard VI a short paragraph from a newspaper

The same was true for writing as to assess the child's hand-writing a very short passage from the Reading book was copied out and then there was some dictation - such as a sentence for Standard III and no more than a short paragraph from a news-paper for Standard V. There was an approved list from which Spellings could be taken and once again the children were very familiar with them having spent countless hours in practice. The arithmetic could be slightly more of an unknown but having chanted their Multiplication Tables for hours the children at least had a good grasp of them. Standard I had to be able to write fig-ures up to 20 and add or subtract figures up to 10 orally, Standard III had to work out a sum involving money and Standard IV one with weights or measures.

In practical terms therefore each year ended with every pupil in the school being examined: passing meant that he or she moved up a Standard but failing led to the year being repeated. The result was that it was not uncommon to find children of different ages in the same classroom group. In 1894 in one school in Bath, for example, Standard I still contained two ten-year-olds and one twelve-year-old, whereas in Standard IV there was an age range from eight to fifteen.

The general outcome of this new system, which was widely unpopular in schools, was that teachers concentrated on the subjects to be examined and so the curriculum narrowed in many schools. It also meant a significant increase in rote-learning. Before 1862 there had been a tendency in some schools for the teachers to concentrate more on the children who attended regularly, were keen to learn and who were bright. Those who were poor attenders, did not adapt to the rigid conditions within the classroom or who were 'dull' were sometimes given less attention as long as they were not disruptive. After 1862 it was essential for the finances of the school that the teachers raised as many pupils as possible to the basic level required in the examinations through rote-learning and in the process less attention was paid to the brighter pupils. In many cases the children, having listened to the teachers were expected to memorise material and then be able to repeat or reproduce it for the teacher, visitors and later an H.M.I. Mental arithmetic was a prime example of this method and in Object Lessons huge numbers of facts could be given and then repeated.

There were modifications, such as in 1867 when a grant could be earned for other subjects such as History and Geography and after 1875 'class subjects' were permitted when a grant was given based upon the performance of classes not just individuals. A Code of 1882 established classifications of 'fair', 'good' and 'excellent' for merit grants. By the 1890s the original intention of the Revised Code had been largely undermined.

The introduction of the Revised Code was not popular locally as one newspaper commented in 1865, "The New Code is not likely to become very popular in this district, nor, we fancy, in any other. One point in this Code seems to strike us as particularly unfair, viz. whoever is absent on that day, never mind from what cause, the money which he would bring to the school is lost." It does, however, seem to have led to some improvement as in July 1867 H.M.I. Rev. Barry commented that for Bruton National School, "there is great improvement in every respect," and two years later, having individually examined 127 pupils he "expressed himself as being much pleased with the considerable progress made in the attainment during the past year." (26)

The Inspectorate began in 1839 with just four men to cover the whole of the country but gradually their numbers increased, but nevertheless in 1851 there was just one Inspector to cover some 156 schools in Somerset, Dorset, Devon and Cornwall. The Reports which they issued after a visit to each school indicated that they played a crucial role in the development of schools as they were able to advise Headteachers and teachers about the latest expectations and changes - an important matter when so many small schools operated in virtual isolation. They were able to offer advice on what improvements needed to be made and if necessary make quite detailed criticisms of the management of a school. From the point of view of a Headmaster they could be crucial in attempting to persuade Managers that it was necessary to make some changes or improvements to buildings and facilities.

Once E.R. Hayter became the Headmaster in July 1870 he recorded the main comments of the HMIs in the School Log Book. (27) There was also some extension of the curriculum, especially in the 1880s and 1890s, as compulsory attendance for longer meant that more time was available. Reading and Writing attracted many comments: initially not always too complimentary. In 1875 the H.M.I. remarked, "The spelling is indifferent throughout the School.... The Reading is wanting in accuracy and intelligence." The following year he commented, "Reading requires especial attention there being an absence of fluency and expression and specifically of distinct articulation."

The School clearly took the comments very seriously as by 1880 Reading was regarded as "the best point" of a fair examination and in 1884, "English has been taught with considerable success." The following year, "The Reading was good and fairly intelligent; the Spelling was good and the Writing neat." It was a pattern which was to continue as in 1910 it was noted that, "Reading is well taught on the whole" but a proviso was added, "The importance of the Blackboard in teaching Reading has yet to be recognised."

Arithmetic never seemed to have been the School's strongest point. In 1875, for example, "in the higher Standards there is room for improvement in Arithmetic", although the following year the H.M.I. acknowledged some progress. In 1878 the Arithmetic of the Fifth Standard "was indifferent." By 1883 "much further improvement is needed, especially in Arithmetic" and the 1885 Report believed, "More practice is required in Mental Arithmetic." By 1910 little had changed for it was reported in Arithmetic that the upper standards required attention although then the comment was added, "but considering the history of the school this is not to be wondered at." This may well refer to the frequent changes in staff noted elsewhere in the Report. Just before the outbreak of the First World War it was the lower part of the School which was causing concern in Arithmetic, "the work of Standards I & II is weak and should have the Head Master's attention."

In general terms arithmetic, which included both oral mental arithmetic and written work, concentrated on addition, subtraction, multiplication and division, with measurement and weights introduced in Standard III and fractions in Standard V. As far as possible the examples which were used were of a practical nature, perceived to be important for the future of the children. Questions such as the following were common:
"A farmer at a fair sold 3 oxen at £15 12s 6d each; A horse for 30 guineas; and a score and a half of sheep at 32s 9d per head. His expenses were 9s 10½d. How much money did he carry home to his wife?"

"A tradesman bought a chest of tea containing 24½ lbs at 3s 8½d per lb. He sold it on at 4s 4d per lb. How much did he gain on the whole?"

One question set in some schools was to tell the pupils the exact time, day and year when their school was opened and then ask them to calculate how long it had been open to the day on which they were working. Many children found the concept of time very difficult to understand and manipulate. A problem which sometimes arose in measurement was that while there was standard measurement there were local variations and this was particularly true of Somerset where there were usually 24 poles to a rod compared with the standard of 22 used elsewhere - pupils had to be able to cope with both.

The Class Subjects of Geography and History received occasional mention in the Reports, again not always complimentary. In 1878, for example, "The Class subjects especially the Geography require improvement" and in 1884, "The fifth standard failed almost entirely to answer some simple questions on History." A decade later however the Inspector was able to report, "Class subjects have been intelligently known." Geography tended to start with the locality around the School and then move on to give significant coverage to the United Kingdom. Finally the British Empire was studied - possibly given the extent of the Empire in the Victorian and Edwardian periods it is perhaps surprising that it did not figure more prominently. History tended to be taught only to the upper classes as it used Readers and a good degree of reading ability was required. These Readers tended either to take a chronological approach or to concentrate on teaching history through the lives and exploits of heroes or famous people, usually men, associated with this country. Singing had been an element within the curriculum since the beginning of the School and was particularly important to E.R. Hayter so that in 1874 it was regarded a good and in 1880 was seen as "creditable."

Physical exercises did not appear until later in the nineteenth century and became much more important in the early twentieth century when so many men who volunteered to join the army to fight the Boers in South Africa were rejected as physically unfit. By 1874 Drill was well established in Bruton National School and in that year the Inspector regarded it as good and in 1878 and 1881 the School was said to be "well drilled." The usual practice was for the children to march around the playground, often under the direction of a former army officer or non-commissioned officer. The use of such a person may not have always been the case in Bruton as the Headmaster served for many years in the Somerset Volunteers and drilled them himself. On 6th February 1903 it was reported that, "A Class for drill instruction was started with the teachers this week. Teacher E.R. Hayter, qualification - War Office certificate." Drill could be interrupted for a number of reasons such as in July 1906 "on account of the intense heat", so Reading and History were substituted instead! In June 1904 and again in February 1907 Drill did not happen for more than a week as a result of drains being laid through the playground. In January 1899 and December 1903 it was too wet.

In 1909 Drill was still important as Headmaster Chancellor commented on 20th September, "School piano arrived. Great improvement in march in from playground on account of piano." It must have required absolute silence from the pupils for the piano to be heard. By this time, however, the School had acquired other "Gymnastic Apparatus" in the form of "Dumb Bells and Bars" for the main school and "Bar bells for the Infants." (28)

When the National School started in Bruton the curriculum was the same for the girls as for the boys but as the century advanced several variations appeared with an emphasis upon domestic subjects after 1870. In the middle of that decade Mrs Ridley, the wife of the Vicar, was instructing girls in knitting on Monday afternoons. Needlework however soon came to be regarded as of greater importance, not only for its practical applications but also because it became a compulsory subject and contributed towards the grant. It was considered to be out of the question for a girl not to be able to sew: it was essential as a way to save money within the family by undertaking all the necessary tasks, particularly making clothes and repairing older ones; for some it provided the skills to be able to earn a living; and for some it provided a recreational activity such as embroidery or making soft toys. Sewing often led to considerable manual dexterity which was much sought after by employers in other industries that required intricate work. It was not unusual that by the age of five a girl would be able to tack up a hem for her mother to sew it.

When E.R. Hayter became the Headmaster in 1870 his wife was listed as the Teacher of Needlework. This time corresponded with the period when more and more handbooks for teachers were being published which frequently outlined a definitive method for performing basic actions, such as putting on a thimble, threading a needle, holding the needle and the position of the fabric: during all of these procedures the correct posture would be maintained. It did become very regimented but it also meant that following the same methods, often aided with illustrations, even very young children could make good progress. Once the basics had been mastered then the girls learned a variety of stitches, followed by buttonholes, how to fit a sleeve into a garment as well as cutting out a range of garments.

Reports by HMIs on the effectiveness of the teaching of Needlework varied through the decades: in 1876 it was stated that, "More specimens of needlework should be shown another year." By 1882 it was considered that, "The needlework wants more attention." Initially however little was done as five years later the H.M.I. was critical: "Needlework specimens done for the day for the Examination were scarcely satisfactory.... More attention must be paid to Button-holing and patching." By 1894 it was regarded as good and in 1896, "The Needlework deserves especial mention." A decade later it had deteriorated again, probably due to the person employed to teach it. Two years later it was still poor with many of the wrong methods being employed, but the new Headteacher, W.T. Chancellor, added a note, "Should be better as now in charge of qualified teacher - Miss Gulliford." His optimism proved correct for in 1910 Needlework was found to be "most successful. Great attention is paid to repairs." More detail was given in the Report of 1913, "The Needlework scheme of instruction is good. The girls draft their own patterns and learn to use a machine." It was, however, felt that they should be able to make more than one garment in a year. The Inspector did accept that, "The work is done under very trying conditions. The teacher has a class of 52 girls and the seating accommodation is quite inadequate."

The extent of the development of the curriculum for girls may be glimpsed in the requirement in 1899 that girls in Standards IV to VII should cover, "Domestic Economy. Food, its composition. Clothing & Washing. The skin and personal cleanliness." Further curriculum developments for girls had to wait until the twentieth century. Many girls learned very little in the way of cooking at home as their mothers often had few skills - an emphasis upon bread, potatoes, soup, stew and possibly three or four other basic recipes was the maximum. On 19th February 1908 it was noted that, "the first division of the Cooking class was sent to the Wesleyan Schoolroom where the class is held. Work from 9.30 am to 12. The second division works from 2 to 4.30." After 1912 the girls were able to take advantage of the changes which had occurred within Sexey's Hospital. "Cookery, Laundrywork and Housecraft are taken at the Centre. The older girls go for a full time Course of ten weeks."

Comments such as the latter make it absolutely clear that for most girls, especially those from working class families, even with full-time education which could last eight or more years, the perceived expectations were low. For many marriage, a home and bringing up a family still constituted their horizon.

For the boys as well there were some curriculum developments. On 20th October 1890 the Managers decided to introduce Drawing, in connection with the Science and Art Department. It was scheduled to take place from 3 to 4 o'clock on Monday and Wednesday afternoons. While much of the early work centred on freehand drawing, it was often linked as well to arithmetic and mensuration, especially geometry and surveying. Clay-modelling was also introduced for the upper standards in 1901 with a view to extending it later to the lower ones but no details were given. It may have been used to help teach 3-D shapes.

On 29th March 1912 Chancellor received permission to introduce Gardening as a subject and started immediately on a plot of land on the other side of the River Brue from the School. In November he and a group of boys went to Pitcombe to dig up twelve fruit trees which were given to them by Rev. J.R. Dummelow. The Report of 1913 regarded gardening as "very successful. The practical work is well done and excellent use is made of the garden for lessons in Nature Study, Arithmetic, Mensuration & Drawing. The notes are original and record many interesting observations made by the children." The Report also noted that as there was more outdoor space available, "A Bee Keeping Company has been formed by the boys on a profit sharing basis. They have now two stocks of bees and teacher and boys are learning beekeeping together." It was not unusual, when the need arose, for new bee hives to be designed in drawing lessons and the various dimensions worked out in arithmetic and mensuration lessons. The actual construction then followed in woodwork lessons. As with the girls the boys were clearly being given instruction in various practical activities which could have some bearing on the future working life of some of them.

An overall syllabus list was prepared for a Schools' Enquiry Form in 1902 and indicated the differences in the curriculum for boys and girls.

Boys	Girls	Infants
English	English	Reading
Arithmetic including	Arithmetic	Writing
Mensuration	Needlework	Arithmetic
Drawing	Geography	Kindergarten
Geography	History	Needlework
History	Object Lessons	Drawing
Object Lessons including	including	Object Lessons
Elementary	Domestic	Singing by note
Science and Nature Study	Economic &	Physical
Singing by note	Hygiene	Exercises
Military Drill with	Nature Knowledge	
Physical Exercises	Singing by note	
	Physical Exercises	

Detailed breakdowns of the Course of Instruction were rare but Hayter did include one in the Log Book for 1901.

"English.

Class 1. [*the top class*] Reading from three books - History, Geography and Literary, also from Newspapers and Magazines.

Recitation 100 to 200 lines.

Reproduction of passages read to children, or of stories told by the teacher.

Essays, letter writing. Grammar rules bearing on Composition.

Class 2. Reading from three books - History, Geography and Literary.

Recitation 80 to 100 lines.

Formation of Sentences orally and in writing.

Writing substance of a lesson.

Letter writing.

Class 3. Reading from 3 books, History, Geography and Literary.

Recitation 60 lines.

Formation of easy sentences, orally and in writing.

Dictation of similar sentences.

Class 4. Reading from two books, Geography and Literary.

Recitation 40 lines.

Formation of easy sentences - oral.

Similar Sentences dictated.

Transcription

Class 5. Reading from two books.

Recitation not less than 20 lines.

Formation of very easy sentences, oral.

In Reading lessons, the children to be encouraged to give answers to questions in sentences.

Arithmetic.

Class 1.

Group (a). Averages, percentages.

Boys - Mensuration of plane figures, with work from own measurements.

Girls - Household accounts.

Group (b). Fractions, vulgar and decimal, Simple interest, Simple proportion.

Group (c). Practice, simple and compound, Vulgar fractions to division (proper fractions only), Simple proportion, Bills.

Class 2. Compound rules, Money.

Reduction of money, and Common Weights and measures.

Class 3. First four rules, and addition and subtraction of money.

Class 4. First four rules, simple division only.

Class 5. Simple addition and subtraction.

Geography.

Class 1. The British Empire.

Class 2. Scotland, Ireland, Canada.

Class 3. England.

Class 4. Geographical terms, outlines of England: physical.

Class 5. Geography of the neighbourhood.

History.

Class 1. Period covered by History reader.

Class 2.   "   "   "   "   "

Class 3.   "   "   "   "   "

Elementary Science.

Classes 1 & 2.

Boys - The Dairy Farm. Work for different seasons.

Soil - formation and constituents.

Orchards, Management, Pruning, Grafting.

The Cow, Butter and Cheese making.

Girls. Domestic Economy, lessons on the choice of food and drinks.

Methods of dealing with common ailments.

Simple lessons in first aid.

Class 3. Lessons on Minerals and Manufactures of England, and on imports from our colonies.

Class 4 & 5. Lessons on Garden work. A plant and its growth, illustrated by plants grown in school and by the children.

Bees and bee keeping.

Farm animals and their produce.

The children are to be encouraged to procure specimens illustrating the lessons, and the Boys in Class one will attend any lectures or practical work given in the neighbourhood by the County Council's lecturers.

Drill

Boys. Military drill.

Girls. Physical Exercises.

Singing, Drawing and Needlework were to conform to external Codes.

The lessons in Elementary Science, Class 1 will be illustrated by simple experiments."

Two years earlier the 'Poetry for Recitation' had been listed in the Log book:
"St. I   'Up, Up'!
St. II   'Birds Nests' & 'Spring'.
St. III   'The May Queen'."
The remaining Standards used selections from Cowper taken from vol. XXXIII of 'The Penny Poets.' As a number of these were very patriotic they formed a good basis for teaching the history of Britain through the story of its heroes. Recitation and songs were an important part in school life as Visitors to the school were often entertained in this way and the impression created would be transmitted throughout the local community. It was then just one step further for the children to give a public performance in

concerts for parents and visitors. In his Report in 1910 Inspector Tillard noted that, "Recitation is generally well said especially by the girls and the meaning of the poems learnt by heart is well understood." He was less complimentary about the Composition: "The Composition of the First Class was disappointing. It was common place and in many cases ungrammatical."

When Grammar was taught it tended to be in the same way as for Latin, namely the identification of parts of speech, such as a verb, noun, adjective and adverb and then the construction of a sentence. As Somerset speech patterns and dialect could be very pronounced in rural areas, this could not have been an easy task. Both handwriting and spelling had a high priority in the nineteenth century and countless hours were spent copying words and passages from the blackboard and as a result of dictation to develop both of these. The word 'Composition' only appeared in the 1901 list for Class 1; for the others it was writing a summary of a lesson or dictation - imaginative or creative writing was not of significant concern.

There were two other parts to the Curriculum: when the original Infant School was established in 1840 one of the first purchases was a Box of Objects. Object Lessons in varying forms remained constant throughout the whole period under consideration, even though in many schools they were not introduced until 1860 and made compulsory in 1890, then requiring the approval of the H.M.I. The original aim was to select items which were familiar to the children and in which they would be interested, although gradually rather more exotic items were included, sometimes reflecting the expansion of the British Empire. A central list was drawn up and the Headmaster allowed to make a selection from it. Hayter included in his Log Book a list of what had been approved for 1898-1899:

"Standard I.
Object Lessons.
    Animals (familiar):-

126

Cow, Horse, Pig, Sheep, Dog, Rabbit, Hen, Duck, Goose.
Animal products:-
Milk, Butter, Cheese, an Egg.
Clothing
Leather, Woollen, Cotton.
Plants:-
Roots, Stems, Leaves, Flowers, Fruit.
Metals:-
Iron, Copper, Tin.
Standard II.
1. Animals:- Domestic & pets.
    Dog, Cat, Rabbit.
2. Animals: Wild, compared.
    Lion, Tiger, Wolf.
3. Insects, Varieties & Structures.
    Bee Keeping.
4. Food.
    Bread, Butter, Tea, Coffee, Sugar, Cocoa.
5. Clothing:-
    Linen, Woollen, Cotton, Leather.
    Standard III.
1. Plant Life:-
    Parts of a Plant, How seeds and plants grow. (Plants
    to be grown in class). Roots - forms of, Leaves.
2. Animal Life:-
    Vertebrate, Invertebrate, Mammalia,
    Cat and Dog - compare.
    Cow, sheep, goat, horse.
3. Wild Animals
    Rabbit, Hare, Fox.
4. Common things:-
    Paper, Coal, Iron, Glass, India-rubber, Silk, lead
    pencil, Candle, Slate, Tea cup, Glue."

While dealing with the familiar was a sound educational idea
and undoubtedly led in some schools to imaginative ideas and
approaches, object lessons generally were often not held in high

regard particularly because of the way that they relied heavily upon the teaching of facts. Such an approach proved a fertile source of criticism as may be found in the writing of novelists such as Charles Dickens in 'Nicholas Nickleby' and 'Hard Times'.

The other part of the Curriculum, and in a Church of England school one of major importance, was Religious Instruction. As well as an inspection from the government's H.M.I. the School received an annual inspection from Diocesan Inspectors, the Reports of whom are generally available from 1869. The vast majority for Bruton National School were favourable, an indication that these Inspectors tended to be more generous in their appraisals than H.M.I.s: in 1877 for example Rev. W. Mitchell found the School, "most satisfactory in discipline and in knowledge and intelligence of the work prepared." In 1888 Rev. F.W. Weaver felt, "It was a real pleasure to examine such a thoroughly efficient school." In 1892, "The children passed very creditably in the subjects presented for examination showing careful teaching", a view reiterated five years later, "The children shew by their answers and repetition that they have been systematically and intelligently taught over a full syllabus of Scripture, Catechism and Prayer Book services."

There were of course sometimes areas for improvement as in 1903 when the Inspector found, "The Scripture repetition was lacking in accurate knowledge"; in 1907 when the repetition was felt to be "a trifle too fast"; in 1910, "The top division was somewhat disappointing. I could not get answers requiring thought from the Children." This last remark was not only an indication that rote-leaning was still prevalent but also that there was a movement away from just knowledge to its application in their lives.

There was clearly somewhat of a mistake in April 1878 as Hayter noted in the Log Book, "The majority of the questions given to group II and III were based on portions of the Bible which the children had not been working at, although a syllabus of the past year's work was sent to the Inspector a week ago!" The result was that the School was inspected again in June and this time the Inspector found that the children "answered intelligently, showing signs of careful and painstaking teaching", although he did add, "Very few children knew private prayers from home use; this should be attended to." (29) This last remark provided an interesting glimpse into the religious expectation of the time: that all working families who sent their children to a Church school should be practising religious observance at home as well.

Perhaps the most complimentary observation appeared in the Report in July 1913, "This School is excellent in every way."

c) Headteachers.

All headteachers in National Schools had to be members of the Church of England but as the nineteenth century advanced that became a source of considerable resentment for Non-Conformists as those in the teaching profession were barred from some 14,000 headships. The original intention in Bruton was that the new Infant School should be under the control of a married couple but that did not appear to have happened, possibly as initially no accommodation was available.

George Perrott may have been the first master but no documents bearing his name have survived until the late 1840s and he was listed as the schoolmaster in a Directory for 1850. His departure probably coincided with the opening of the new school buildings in 1852 which contained accommodation for a married couple. A contributory factor may have been his failure to be elected as the Master of Sexey's Hospital. In November 1851 the existing Master, George Parfitt, died and one of the Visitors, F.H. Dickinson, suggested to Perrott that he might apply for that position. He did so even though in reply to Dickinson he claimed, "I had no intention of giving up my present Situation" and that Rev. White, the Vicar, did not "wish me to be a Candidate." The Committee of the Management of the Bruton and National Schools, as they called themselves, provided him with a suitable Testimonial: he has "since his appointment to the situation discharged his duties in a Manner most Satisfactory to the Committee and that they would deeply regret the loss of his Services." (30) He was not appointed however as the post was awarded to Parfitt's son and then he seems to have left Bruton during 1852.

The post of Schoolmistress in this early period was filled by spinsters. The 1850 Directory lists Miss Ward as Mistress and in the 1851 Census Mary Warren aged 20, who lodged with the Postmaster and his wife in the High Street, was listed as 'National Schoolmistress.'

The first married couple to occupy the post of Master and Mistress and also the new accommodation were Mr and Mrs Rand. Unfortunately no other information seems to have survived about them and their period in office except that in 1852 the salary for the Master was £35 0s 0d and £32 10s 0d for the Mistress. They remained in post for two years.

When they were succeeded by Mr and Mrs Daniel Byles in March 1854 their duties were carefully specified: Daniel Byles was to teach and superintend the teaching of the boys in the day school and his wife Elizabeth Jane the girls, to whom she would also teach sewing and needlework. In addition they were responsible for the Sunday School to be held between 9 o'clock and 11 o'clock and again at a quarter past two until three-thirty pm each Sunday. They also had to superintend the Evening School held on Monday, Wednesday and Friday evenings between seven o'clock and eight-thirty. Any Pupil Teachers were also their responsibility and they were required to provide at least one and a half hours tuition for them each day. Outside of the School the Master was to be the Choir Master for the parish church, a very common requirement for such an appointment.

While fulfilling all these duties and responsibilities they were to receive a joint salary of £70 0s 0d, considered to be £60 for the Sunday and Day Schools and £10 for the Evening School. In addition they were entitled to their newly built house rent free. (31)

One problem which existed nationally in the first half of the nineteenth century, and in some cases far beyond, was that many of the early teachers in these elementary schools had few if any qualifications and some had little experience. No documentary evidence remains for Bruton's teachers until the appointment of Daniel Byles who did not appear to possess a Certificate as when he was appointed it was stated that he was to "undertake to apply for a Government Certificate as soon as conveniently may." Amongst other Testimonials, however, there was a Government Certificate signed by the Poor Law Commissioners that Mrs Byles was competent to undertake the supervision of Pupil Teachers. This evidence may suggest that they had started their teaching careers in a Workhouse school. An appointment in a National School was viewed as a definite promotion, and certainly better paid.

On 22nd October 1859 when some prizes were being awarded "the able and zealous Master and Mistress" arranged some entertainment for the crowd of parents and other children who packed the schoolroom. "The entertainment consisted for the most part of songs and chants, intermixed with recitations of poetry, dialogues, &c., by the pupil-teachers and the children of the school." It was clearly well-received and indicative of an aspect of the School which was to continue for the rest of the century.

Mr and Mrs Byles were held in high regard in the town for to mark seven years of "faithful and efficient services in this town" they were presented with "a silver cruet stand, with cut glass cruets, together with a purse of money and pair of trays." They were also involved in the wider area, for example, in March 1856 Daniel Byles delivered a lecture, "On Corporal Punishment in School" to the Schoolmasters' Association for Somerset. In December 1859 Mrs Byles read "a valuable and well written paper to the East Somerset Schoolmasters' and Schoolmistresses' Association, entitled, 'The Teachers' Studies and Recreations after School'." (32)

By May 1864 Mr and Mrs Byles had resigned from the National School and established their own school for boys in the town; "has kept and still keeps a School of his own of the same class of Boys." This observation was made when the suggestion appeared that he should temporarily teach in the Grammar School in the absence of the Headmaster there. Opposition centred on the fact that he had not received a Classical education and so could not teach Latin, Greek or French. For two years advertisements appeared in local newspapers for their 'Middle Class Boarding and Day School' and then Daniel Byles was appointed Master of the Shepton Mallet Workhouse and Elizabeth Byles the Schoolmistress. He was to hold this post for some twenty years until his death in May 1887 at the age of fifty-six. The timing of their departure from the National School so soon after the introduction of the Revised Code may indicate either their disapproval of it or that they were unable to implement its stringent new requirements. (33)

They were succeeded in 1864 by Mr and Mrs James who remained in office until 1870. As the existing Church organist, P. Williams, had left Bruton in 1862, when Charles James was appointed he took over that role as well. By November 1867 he had established a Singing Class which was reported to be "quite a success," and in May 1868 gave a 'Grand Vocal and Instrumental Concert' in the National Schoolroom which "was most fashionably attended." Unfortunately little documentary evidence has survived about them personally and their time in Bruton. The comments from the various Inspectors, however, tended to be favourable: in 1867 the Diocesan Inspector was satisfied overall and the following year he was particularly pleased with the pupils "order, neatness and general progress." In July 1867 H.M.I. Rev. H.B. Barry reported, "The School is in good order, and there is great improvement in every respect." In July 1868 he noted, "There has been a considerable increase in the attendance since the inspection last year, and the general result of the examination was very satisfactory."

When Charles and Mary James resigned they were presented with "a beautifully embossed electro-plated sugar basin" by the children and a purse of ten guineas by the local inhabitants. (34)

They were replaced by Mr and Mrs E.R. Hayter from the school in North Cadbury.

Edward Hayter commenced his Log Book on 12ᵗʰ July 1870 at the age of twenty-seven and was to remain at the School for the next thirty-eight years. He had been trained in 1861-1862 at St. Mark's College, Chelsea. The salary, as that of his predecessor, was fixed at £70 but the following year it was agreed that in addition "in consideration of Mr Hayter's attention to the Night School and his general efficiency in the Day School, he be paid in future one third of the Annual Government Grant." In 1871 he was listed as a Certified Teacher of the Second Class which by June 1879 had been raised to the First Class. His wife was one year younger and the 1871 Census indicated that they had one son and two daughters.

Hayter clearly made a good start in the School as less than two months after he was appointed an H.M.I. visited and reported, "The numbers have considerably increased, and the classes are under good control. Considering all circumstances, very fair progress has been made in elementary subjects, and the School seems to be improving under the new master." One year later another H.M.I. commented, "The schools are in a satisfactory condition." It was also the case that by then the Government Grant was between 50-60% higher than ever before. (35)

As well as being a meticulous teacher himself, Hayter carefully monitored the work of the other teachers and recorded comments in his Log Book, such as 21ˢᵗ April 1871, "During the week the work has been carefully done," and on 12ᵗʰ August 1872, "The School work during the week has been very well done, the teachers appearing to take a thorough interest in their work." On the last day of each school year he inspected all the Standards and tended to report a good year's work. In June 1900 he found that some children had made such good progress that they had moved up two Standards in a year, rather than the usual one. He could be somewhat critical and less than sympathetic if children did not move up a Standard. On 30ᵗʰ June 1905, for example, he remarked that the small number who had not made sufficient progress were, "in all cases children who have been admitted from other schools, with a small part of the year's work done, or children of somewhat defective intellect."

Hayter always expressed concern about the need to catch up with work if the School had had to be closed as a result of illness, such as the severe outbreak of measles in January 1902. "The ground lost through the School being closed for measles has not been made up," was his comment on 2nd May 1902. After the School was closed in late 1905 as a result of Scarlet Fever, cases of which were still occurring in February 1906, he was able to report on April 6th of that year, "Both teachers & children had worked hard to make up for the time lost by the closing of the School."

Hayter had a deep love of music and as Headmaster of the National School he became not only the choirmaster but also the organist of St Mary's Church. Every year from his appointment in 1870 he organised a benefit concert in the National Schoolroom which was usually crowded. "There was a full attendance, the reserved seats being filled by the elite of the town and neighbourhood. The programme was a very good one, and of the eighteen items, nine were encored." In these concerts "he was assisted by several ladies and gentlemen, amateurs of the town and neighbourhood." The concept of a benefit concert was not new, having been the practice under a previous organist, Williams, who was also a harpist, in the 1850s. (36)

Hayter seems to have had considerable success as the choirmaster as on his retirement in 1908 it was commented, "It was due to his never failing energy that Bruton choir has reached its present high standard." He was also deeply involved with the Bruton, Castle Cary and Wincanton Choir Festival Association and served on its Musical Committee. He invariably took part in all Choir activities and went with them on their annual excursion, usually to Weymouth. (37)

He could often be found providing entertainment when he attended meetings in the town, for example, in April 1890 he performed a recitation of 'The Jackdaw of Rheims" when he was present at one of the meetings of the Mutual Improvement Society. Before moving to Bruton he was a frequent helper with the entertainments at the Castle Cary Young Men's Society.

"And Mr Hayter, too, is press'd
To sing a song as well's the rest." (38)

Hayter clearly took his musical expertise elsewhere for as early as 1875 he was listed as the music master at the Grammar School and was referred to as the singing master at Prize Day in July 1888. Earlier that year he was the Leader of the Bruton Philharmonic Orchestra and between 1880 and 1889 he was the Bandmaster of the Castle Cary Volunteers. (39)

After 1870 professional organisations for teachers developed, such as the National Union of Elementary Teachers which became the National Union of Teachers. The general aims were to raise the status of teaching and to campaign for better pay and conditions. By 1885 it had some 11,000 members, a figure which was to double by the early years of the twentieth century. There was a branch of this organisation based in Castle Cary and Hayter was elected its vice-president in November 1896. (40)

As well as the School and music, Hayter became involved in a range of activities within the town. Between 1880 and 1889 he was a Sergeant in the 3rd Battalion of the Somerset Light Infantry Volunteers. He was an extremely good shot so that in 1883 he came second in the annual shooting match, winning £2 10s 0d. It was no surprise therefore that when a Church Lads' Brigade was formed in the town in 1898 he became their drill instructor. When a Jumble Sale was arranged for their benefit in the Schoolroom in 1899, "the lads of the brigade gave exhibitions of drill and physical exercises (musical) under Sergt-Major Hayter." He was a member of the Royal Clarence Lodge of Freemasons in Bruton from at least 1873, served as its Worshipful Master, was Secretary of the Somerset branch and wrote a history of the Bruton Lodge which was published in 1898. (41)

Hayter was probably known and involved with a greater number of local people through his membership of a Friendly Society, the Ancient Order of the Foresters, with the Bruton branch being the Court, 'Sons of Briton'. On no less than fifteen occasions he was elected their Chief Ranger. When a large procession and fete was staged by the Foresters in July 1887 for the first time in seventeen years Hayter was the Chairman of the Organising Committee. He organised the annual procession in 1893 when there were reported to be over 300 people and forty horses in it. At the same time a Flower Show was initiated by Hayter and he was careful to ensure that the categories included the gardens and produce of labourers. He acted as its Secretary for many years. He was listed as attending the annual Whitsuntide dinner of the Blue Ball Friendly Society but there is no evidence of any deeper involvement in it. (42)

As a prominent educationalist Hayter was a member of the Bruton Mutual Improvement Society which met weekly during the winter months for lectures and discussions. After January 1891 he was its Secretary and delivered lectures himself, such as one on 'Humane Beekeeping' in February 1888. There was usually a concert staged for the last meeting of each season in which he played a large part but also it was not unusual for musical items to occur during the course of other meetings. After a lecture on 10th February 1888, for example, Hayter conducted amongst other items, 'The Marvellous Work' and 'The Heavens Are Telling' by Haydn and 'Gloria in Excelsia' by Mozart. (43)

He also appeared to have had some interest in sport as he was instrumental in the formation of the Bruton Cricket Club in 1871, and was still its Treasurer in 1895. He himself may not have been a great cricketer as on one occasion in September 1882 when playing against Frome and District he was out for a duck. In political outlook he was a Conservative/Unionist: attending Unionist lectures as in May 1890 but also delivering lectures himself to the local Conservative Association, such as one in April

1889 entitled, "Ireland, the Spoilt Child.", at a time when Irish Home Rule was very topical, when he traced the history of Ireland and pointed out its many advantages. (44)

As a prominent middle class member of society in Bruton he was called upon to perform other roles. It was not unusual for him to be summoned to be part of the local Coroner's Jury and on many occasions he was the foreman, as in February 1888 on the death of a six year old girl, Emma Jane Hopkins, when a verdict of natural causes was returned and as a gesture the jury gave their fees to her mother. He was appointed one of the Overseers of the Poor for the year 1899-1900. Even with all his other responsibilities he took time to be involved in the long drawn out campaign to obtain a clean water supply for the town. In March 1896 he wrote to a local newspaper to draw attention to the fact that for years the Local Government Board had condemned the well water as, "more or less unfit for drinking, and that many of the cottages have to carry water long distances uphill." He included an emotional appeal: "Can anyone see (as we do scores of cases daily, hot or cold, wet or dry) children, many of them of tender years, toiling uphill with buckets and cans of water, that in some cases they seem scarcely able to lift, and not feel pity for these little ones, and an anxiety to see them relieved of this daily and toilsome burden?" (45)

On 25th March 1908 Hayter retired after thirty-eight years in the School, a length of time equalled by about a quarter of headteachers in Somerset in the later Victorian era. His entry in the Log Book was simple and factual: "I this day finish my work as Head Teacher of this School. At the conclusion of this morning's work the Vicar attended and presented me with a pair of Silver Candlesticks from the Teachers and children as a parting gift." From various groups within the town with which he had been associated he received a purse containing £75, several illuminated addresses, and from the Choir a large framed photograph of themselves. He retired to Sidford in Devon and became the church organist there. He died in April 1912 aged sixty-nine.

The influence which he had had over generations of Bruton children and the wider community was immense. Through his range of activities he was known to every person in the town.

On 26th March 1908 the new Headmaster took office: "I William Thomas Chancellor began duties as Head Teacher of the School today." He had in fact been a teacher in the School since 10th July 1905, when he was aged twenty-two. He was often known as 'Buck'. He was a qualified teacher having studied at Exeter Training College. Despite some early accusations of excessive punishments, the Managers had little hesitation in appointing him to the post, which some of them may have had in mind when he was first appointed. In one change in policy the Head Teacher was no longer required to be the church organist and choirmaster; that position was filled by Arthur Clements.

Chancellor initiated some modest changes immediately such as a new timetable and the re-arrangement of desks in Standards I-IV and of cupboards to avoid entering various classrooms to get books and apparatus. In October he managed to purchase fifteen new dual desks which an H.M.I. thought was a good improvement and suggested even more of them. For all his undoubted talents, hard work and dedication as a Headmaster, Hayter may have become too set in his ways, too tolerant of the standards being achieved and so some change was required. An H.M.I. Report on 12th May 1909 as a result of three visits commented, "The condition of the School is steadily improving under the present Head Master.... The tone and order of the School are distinctly better than they were twelve months ago." The following month the Diocesan Inspector reported, "I found the School generally greatly improved in their knowledge of the Bible and Prayer Book subjects."

In May 1910 H.M.I. Tillard felt, "The School gives very good promise of becoming thoroughly efficient in the course of two or three years. Already the painstaking and intelligent work of the Master and his assistants has produced a marked improvement in many directions." Chancellor went on to introduce Gardening and Beekeeping so that in 1913 Tillard's assessment was that, "This is one of the most promising of the Schools engaged in the practical work scheme. The Headmaster has devoted much time and thought to the organisation of the instruction."

Not everyone in the town was enamoured with Chancellor and in November 1913 Harry Atkins, who had three children in the School, assaulted him and threatened to shoot him. The exact cause of his action was never explained or detailed. Initially Atkins had shouted obscenities at Chancellor as he was cycling from Pitcombe to Bruton and later as the latter was in his garden feeding his chickens Atkins approached him and according to Chancellor said, "I am going to do for you. If I had a knife I would stick it in you. If I had a gun I would shoot you." He then approached Chancellor with his fist up and clenched but as he was so drunk the latter struck him first and pushed him away. Atkins next attempted to purchase a revolver from the shop of William Buckley, an ironmonger who was also a gunsmith, but he refused and Atkins was eventually arrested. Wincanton Police Court decided that as drink was such a major factor that he should be bound over in his own recognizance to keep the peace for six months. (46)

d) Monitors, Pupil Teachers and Assistant Teachers.

The National Society advocated the 'monitorial system' of teaching. Under this system a small number of older pupils, usually those aged ten and eleven, would be allocated a group of younger pupils, often ten but it could be as many as twenty. Before all the children arrived in the morning the Master would go through the lessons of the day and explain to the monitors what they had to teach to their group of children. He would then deliver the main lesson to all the children while the monitors ensured that discipline was maintained. The monitors would then take their group to its allotted space and would undertake the designated task such as to hear each pupil read from text on a sheet on the wall, either individually or as part of a group. The Master would be available to walk between groups to ensure that this was being undertaken and achieved and that discipline was being maintained. If the system was implemented correctly then at the end of the day the Monitors would be rewarded by being taught their own lessons by the Master. For some it was the first step to becoming teachers in their own right.

Two advantages of the system were that it could cope with large numbers of pupils and it was very cheap to implement and operate. The main criticism, however, was that untrained and unqualified young children were attempting to instruct even younger pupils. The system remained in use throughout the 1830s and into the 1840s but was increasingly being criticised, particularly by Dr James Kay-Shuttleworth who became Secretary of the Committee of the Privy Council on Education when it was created in 1839. The following year Her Majesty's Inspectorate was established and it too was soon not in favour of the system.

In 1846 Kay-Shuttleworth initiated a new era in teacher training with the Pupil-Teacher Scheme, which eventually replaced the monitors with apprentices. At the same time financial incentives were introduced to encourage schools to appoint pupils teachers and to improve their training Queen's Scholarships became available for them, tenable at the newly introduced training colleges. Pupil-Teachers had to be at least thirteen years of age, apprenticed for five years during which time they had to improve their own knowledge, and had to pass an annual examination conducted by an H.M.I.: failure to do so had implications for the grant the School received. There were also other grants for trained and efficient teachers. The system seems to have worked as in 1849 there were 681 certified teachers and 6,878 by 1859, along with thirty-four training colleges.

Bruton National School conformed to the general pattern, although it may have been slow to adopt the system of Pupil-Teachers. It would seem that under George Perrott in the late 1840s and early 1850s there were still four unpaid monitors. Once the new School was in operation the Managers applied for

Pupil- Teachers for the girls. Their initial wish was to have two but the number of pupils did not justify them. "The numbers in average attendance [90] do not admit of the maintenance of more than one Pupil Teacher at the Public expense." A month later another letter stated, "I am to add that should the numbers in your School increase sufficiently during the current year you will be in a position to apply for the engagement of another Pupil Teacher." This appears to have happened quite quickly as in December 1856 the Inspector reported on two Pupil-Teachers. The School also found an interesting way of adding to its number of Pupil-Teachers, namely by appointing an Honorary Pupil Teacher, to which the Committee agreed in December 1856:

"Sarah Fanny Mills (Honry PT) is accepted as Honary apprentice.

Whenever the School becomes entitled to the maintenance of another Pupil Teacher in it at the public expense, My Lords will be happy to sanction Mills as a regular Apprentice, provided that her conduct and progress up to that date have been satisfactory." So that there could be no misunderstanding they emphasized that neither she nor the Mistress would receive any payment till then from the Parliamentary Grant. (47)

When a Pupil-Teacher was appointed, usually after an advertise-ment in newspapers, an Indenture was drawn up, as in December 1857 for Sarah Freeman from Stockcross in Berkshire. She agreed to "faithfully and diligently serve the Mistress.... shall not, except from illness, absent herself from the said School during school hours and shall conduct herself with honesty, sobriety, and tem-perance, and not be guilty of any profane or lewd conversation or conduct, or of gambling or any other immorality." She was required to follow all the instructions of the Mistress and "regu-larly attend divine service on Sunday." The Master was to ensure that he provided, "The Pupil Teacher with all proper lodging, food, apparel, washing, medicine, and medical attendance."

Attached to the Indenture was an Appendix which covered the areas for examination of the Pupil- Teacher each year and so by implication what she had to be taught. Table 8 gives an indication

Table 8. Extracts from 'Subjects for Examination for Pupil Teachers'.

	Grammar	Writing and Composition	Arithmetic and Mathematics Male Pupil Teachers	Arithmetic and Mathematics Female Pupil Teachers
End of 1st year	The Noun, Verb, and Adjective; with their relations in a Simple Sentence.	To write from memory the substance of a more difficult narrative	Practice and Proportion.	Practice and Bills of Parcels.
End of 2nd year	The Pronoun, Adverb, and Preposition; with their relations in a Sentence.	Composition of a Class Report or the Abstract of a Lesson.	Vulgar Fractions.	Simple Proportion.
End of 3rd year	The Conjunction; with the Analysis of Sentences.	Composition of the Notes of a Lesson on a subject selected by the Inspector.	Decimal Fractions; and Euclid Book I, to end of XVth Proposition.	Vulgar Fractions.
End of 4th year	More advanced exercises in preceding subjects; with a knowledge of Prefixes and Affixes.	Composition of an account of the Organisation of the School, and of the Methods of Instruction used.	Simple Interest; Euclid Book I; and Algebra, First Four Rules.	Compound Proportion, ad recapitulation of preceding exercises.
End of 5th year	The same subjects.	Composition of an Essay on some subject connected with the Art of Teaching.	Problems in Arithmetic; Euclid Book II; and Algebra, to the end of Simple Equations.	Decimal Fractionsand Simple Interest.

of what was required in Grammar, Writing and Composition, Arithmetic and Mathematics.

In addition Reading, Religious Knowledge, Geography, Drawing and Music were included along with History from Year 3. From the Appendix it was very clear that the expectation in Arithmetic between Male and Female Pupil-Teachers, and hence of their pupils, was very different. (48)

As a result of examining the progress of pupil-teachers in Bruton National School one H.M.I. was not completely satisfied as he commented in December 1856, "Hall should attend to Geography. Wheaton should be cautioned to work hard to pass a good examination next year in Geography, Arithmetic, and Grammar." Some Pupil-Teachers were more successful. One local newspaper reported in February 1865, "We are happy to state that Miss M.A. Thomas, the late pupil-teacher of these schools, obtained a first-class scholarship at the Christmas examination of HM Inspectors", and so obtained a Queen's Scholarship. It went on to add that, "It is most gratifying to say that every pupil-teacher who has served her time in these schools has been successful in obtaining a Queen's Scholarship." It was a pattern which seemed to have continued, for example, in December 1881 Miss Milborne was presented with a silver locket by the teachers and children when she was successful in the Scholarship examination. (49)

The Revised Code 1862 was a pronounced setback for the Pupil-Teacher system. In the first place the syllabus of work became much narrower as schools began to concentrate just on those subjects to be examined but, more importantly, the apprenticeship idea with the headteacher no longer existed as the grant for pupil-teachers ceased and any money in future was paid directly to the Managers. Although there were attempts to modify the arrangements, by 1866 the number of pupil-teachers had decreased by a third.

These developments may explain why when E.R.Hayter became Headmaster in July 1870 he listed just one Pupil-Teacher,

Annie Ross who was at the end of her second year, and a paid Monitor, Mary Ross. For a year he referred to her as a Monitor but the H.M.I. in 1871 listed her as a Pupil-Teacher of the Second Year. This may be explained by the fact that Annie Williams was taken on as a probationary Monitor on 10th July 1871. Thereafter the term 'monitor' was rarely used, although occasionally it did appear, such as on 22nd June 1883, "Agatha Hayter & Bessie Milborne have been employed as monitors", and on 14th October 1887, "Annie Randall appointed monitor in the place of Mary Thompson, left." As the names of several other girls who were not Pupil-Teachers were mentioned from time to time, it would seem that a version of the old system did remain in Bruton, even though some of them were promoted to be Pupil-Teachers.

From entries in his Log Book it did appear that Hayter faced a whole series of problems with his Monitors and Pupil-Teachers. Potentially one of the most serious was that their lessons were poor. Throughout September 1870 he complained that the lessons of Mary Ross were "imperfect" or "very badly done", although when she died of consumption on 19th August 1872 he recorded that she "was a good & painstaking teacher." The lessons of Annie Williams were likewise criticized in 1875 and 1876 as very bad and in 1876 she failed the examination and did so again the following year and so on 29th June 1877 Hayter recorded, "Annie Williams engagement as Pupil Teacher terminated."

Part of the problem was that these young people, being not far removed in age from the children they were meant to teach, had little idea of how to maintain discipline. On 13th October 1870 an entry read, "3rd Class kept in at 12, for extra reading lesson, inattentive during regular reading lesson and the teacher M. Ross not sufficient to be diligent." On 30th January 1873 Hayter recorded, "J. Tanner and Clara Bord cautioned as to maintaining discipline in the Senior boys, a point on which they have been rather lax."

In order to try and maintain discipline there was a tendency to resort too readily to physical punishments. No documentary evidence has survived for the early period of the School before 1870 but on 1st September of that year, just two months after Hayter became Headteacher, Julia Bell's mother came into the School "and complained that Mary Ross had been beating her child. From the appearance of the child's ears, they had evidently been severely boxed." At the end of the same month on 30th September Hayter recorded, "Pupil-teacher again cautioned about striking the children." Exactly three years later on 30th September 1873, "A. Trotter cautioned not to strike the Children." On 14th July 1880 the father of Alice Coward complained, "that his Child had been struck by the pupil teacher & was ill in consequence." In this instance the unnamed pupil teacher denied all knowledge of the girl being struck.

Another problem was that the routine of the School was adversely affected by pupil-teacher and monitor absence which was usually the result of illness. "14 June 1872 Pupil Teachers absent the whole week both suffering from disease of the lungs." Late in November 1874 Jane Tanner was "suffering from a severe attack of Scarlatina" and two were absent in January 1888 suffering from bronchitis. On 8th September 1873 Annie Williams was late in the morning, "When sent for her excuse was that her mother was going away for a few days and she was wanted. Cautioned."

Hayter of course had to deal with these young girls when they fell out with each other:

"27 June 1871. Monitors cautioned against quarrelling after School hours, an offence of which they had been guilty the previous evening. M. Ross very impertinent."

"2 May 1874. Pupil teachers cautioned against quarrelling in the School-room, after School hours."

In the 1890s the School was receiving male Pupil Teachers, one of whose behaviour led to an intriguing entry in the Log Book:

"18 October 1898. In consequence of a complaint made by Mrs Morgan of Brick Kiln that Francis Plenty, PT 4th Year had been behaving in an improper Manner in Wincanton, I suspended him." Four days later his father requested that he be released from his position as it would be difficult for him to return. No other explanation was given.

There were of course successes within the system. On 23rd April 1884 Pupil-Teacher E. Randall was appointed to take charge of the Infant School as there was an outbreak of measles in the lodgings of the Infant Mistress. Her performance was so good that when the Mistress left Miss Randall was appointed in her place on 26th September. In April 1899 Miss C.M. Kelley was presented with a Teachers' Reference Bible when she left to become assistant mistress at St. Michael's Mixed School in Bath. On 29th September 1905 Hubert Bending was appointed a Pupil-Teacher and following the practice adopted in the twentieth century to improve the knowledge and quality of his education, he was sent to a local centre to continue his studies, in his case from 20th February 1906 to Sexey's Trade School in Bruton on Monday, Tuesday and Thursday mornings. His progress was so good that on 2nd August 1906 he left to attend St Mark's Training College, Chelsea. Day Centres had in fact been established in 1880 and were linked to local Universities, in this case Bristol. Their intention was to relieve headteachers of the burden of instructing pupil-teachers and to raise standards.

A career path was now in place. With the introduction of the Pupil-Teacher system there was a real opportunity for a bright child from a working class background to become upwardly socially mobile. A successful pupil-teacher could expect to join the teaching profession and become part of the middle classes. This was a massive advancement in just one generation.

Before these local centres were in operation the education and training of the Pupil-Teachers continued to be the responsibility of the Headteacher of a school, some of whom were better equipped than others and some more conscientious. Hayter seemed to have taken his responsibility very seriously as he started their lessons at 7am, some two hours before the school day began for the children.

Before the arrival of Hayter in 1870 the School had relied largely upon the Master, the Mistress, Pupil-Teachers and Monitors, along with some part-time assistance. On 12th July 1870 the Log Book recorded that as well as one pupil teacher and one monitor there was also a Teacher of Needlework. When a Return was completed in 1902 Hayter had five other teachers on the main site and three more in the Infant School. (50)

The training experience of the assistant teachers appointed varied: some had attended a recognised training college such as Miss S. Dilke from Fishponds Training College who was appointed Mistress of the new Infant School on 8th February 1877 and William Chancellor who had attended Exeter Training College before his appointment on 10th July 1905. Other assistant teachers seem to have gained their experience as pupil-teachers, such as Miss E Randall who was a pupil-teacher in Stoboro Dorset before her appointment on 1st July 1883, Miss M.E. Tabor who was a pupil teacher in Milborne Port before she came to Bruton on 7th November 1902 and Miss Eliza Hancock, the Mistress of the Infant School in 1903, who had been a pupil Teacher in St Matthew's Infant School, Bristol between 1891 and 1895. It was, of course, the practice at that time to appoint only single women.

There was often movement between schools by assistant teachers which at times reduced continuity for the children and occasionally made replacement difficult. When Miss Tabor resigned in February 1907 Hayter reported to the Managers that he was unable to obtain a replacement until April and that that had made life difficult within the School. Assistant teachers did of course move within the National School system, such as Miss E. Garrett who was appointed from the one in West Coker in February 1903 but part of the reason for all this movement was that the salary paid in the new Board Schools after their introduction in 1870 was often higher than in Church Schools. In addition the new schools did not impose religious restrictions such as regular church attendance on a Sunday.

In rural areas life must have been very lonely for single female teachers in particular as they often did not have family or friends nearby. They were expected to be examples of moral rectitude so that some guidelines for their behaviour in towns in 1902 stipulated that they should be in their home between 8pm and 6am unless attending a school function. The same guidelines laid down that they should not travel beyond the town limits without the permission of the Managers and never travel in a carriage with any man except a father or brother. Even what they wore was controlled as the colours had to be plain grey or black and their dresses must not be more than one inch above their ankles. While a headmaster such as Hayter could be involved in a wide range of activities within a community the same did not seem to have been the case for female assistant teachers.

The Log Book contains many entries which mentioned the departure of teachers, for example, of the five teachers listed in 1902 two had left by February 1905 and in addition Miss Long who was appointed after 1902 resigned in July 1905. When Miss Tabor left in 1907 it was after four years. Only on rare occasions was a reason recorded: on 10th September 1906, for example, following the usual expectation at that time, Miss Beatrice Warren resigned as she was getting married; on 30th April 1910 Miss Owen left as she had been appointed to a headship in Leigh.

From time to time there were problems with an assistant teacher, for example, on 24th June 1885 Miss Shean's employment was terminated, "conduct & attention to duties for some weeks past very unsatisfactory." No specific details were included but Hayter did record that as it was so immediate one of his daughters had to be transferred from the Infant School to the main site and two monitors from Standards VI and VII sent to assist in her place in the Infant School. On several occasions in March and May 1886 Miss Jackson was cautioned for beating and "unkind treatment" of children. She clearly did not heed these warnings as her engagement was terminated on 2nd July. On 9th May 1911 an entry was made in the Log Book in the Vicar's handwriting,

"In consequence of certain statements regarding Miss Perry's conduct the Managers decided to suspend her pending inquiries." No other details were given but on 25th May Miss Perry resigned.

Details of the salary of individual assistant teachers were never given. The Headteacher was paid £95 in 1902 and the Infant School Mistress £75 in 1903. As a percentage of the total expenditure of the School, however, the overall salaries bill was high, for example, in 1893 out of a total expenditure of £392 7s 1d salaries accounted for £270 17s 8d, some 69%. (51).

e) Pupils.

For pupils in the nineteenth and early twentieth centuries school life was very regimented in barn-like schoolrooms, often with poor ventilation, heating and lighting. Every moment that they were there was accounted for by one instruction after another and any breach of the strict discipline would result in a sharp reprimand or something more physical.

From the very beginning of the weekday school in Bruton the school hours were fixed at 9 o'clock to 12 o'clock and 2 o'clock to 4 o'clock, Monday to Friday. It was made clear that, "Children cannot be allowed to stay in the School, who do not come punctually at the hour of School." Such times could be long sessions for children who were between the ages of two and seven. By the time that Mr and Mrs Byles were appointed in 1854 there had been some amendment: the morning session remained the same but the afternoon became 2 o'clock to 5 o'clock during the summer months, defined as May to September, and 2 o'clock to 4.30 o'clock in the winter months. (52) When Hayter became Headmaster in 1870 he reverted to the 4pm closure in winter, although by 1881 it was again at 4.30pm. The final change came in June 1908 when Chancellor commenced afternoon school at 1.30pm.

The original two hour break at lunchtime did allow all the children to leave the premises and walk home to have their meal and then return, summoned as always by the ringing of the school bell. It also meant that if there had been a problem during the morning session a child or group could be kept behind. On 13th October 1870, for example, Hayter kept the whole of the 3rd Class in a 12 o'clock, "for extra reading lesson, inattentive during regular reading lesson." Unfortunate instances could arise such as on 23rd July 1898 when Miss Burt kept H. Plowman in at 12 o'clock "for inattention. She told him to keep his seat till she told him to go." She then went home for lunch and forgot about him and it was only when another teacher returned at 1.45pm that he was found and sent home. Hayter added that, "teachers have been told on several occasions that pupils not to be kept in more than 30 mins without telling me & work given to them." He did send Miss Burt to explain to the parents.

There was one break in the morning and one in the afternoon although the decision was taken that these should be staggered because of the number of pupils and the limited space in the playground. It was only in July 1907 that Hayter amended the time-table so that all the children could "have play together 10.40 to 10.55 in the morning 3.10 to 3.30 in afternoon." It is not hard to imagine the noise that will have emanated from the playground alongside Silver Street when the children were released from their rooms on fine days. In the nineteenth century games involving a chase and leap frog were very popular. Playing with hoops and marbles was possible if any parts of the playground were smooth enough. Skipping accompanied by rhymes always found ready participants. As the River Brue flowed on one side of the playground if any boys managed to obtain a ball, often made from the bladder of a recently slaughtered pig, for kicking great care had to be exercised.

The Rules drawn up in 1840 remained in force through much of the rest of the century: parents were not permitted in the classroom except during an examination and this did prevent any disagreements with the teachers being seen by the children or cause them any distress at being left at the beginning of the session. With the ever present threat of illness and disease spreading rapidly in an institution which had so many children close together, the requirements for the children to be clean and free from any disease were rigorously enforced as may be seen from entries in the Log Book when such children were sent home. Punctuality and regular attendance were the requirement not only to ensure that there were no breaks in their education but also to instil these concepts for their future employment. As the century advanced there were minor alterations to the rule that any child who was more than half an hour late could be sent home. In February 1884, after attendance had become compulsory it was ordered that the Register should be marked in black ink at 9.05 and then again at 9.50 with any latecomers marked in red ink. This latter time was brought forward to 9.45am in 1902.

Education for much of the nineteenth century was not free, it sometimes being argued that if the working classes paid a small contribution they would take it more seriously. There were those who were somewhat cynical about these payments:

" Infants of humble, busy wives who pay
Some trifling price for freedom through the day."
(George Crabbe)

One or two pence a week was the usual amount and in relation to that Bruton was typical. In 1840 the Infant School started with a flat rate of 2d, paid every Monday morning but this was soon modified to become 2d for the first child and 1d for any others in the family. This contribution was known as the School Pence and for the year ending Christmas 1852 it raised £28 11s 5d. The level of payment did seem to have remained constant for more than thirty years for it was only raised from 29th October 1877 when it became 3d if there was only one child in the family in the School and 2d if two or three and then 1d for each additional child.

It is easy to understand how some families would have struggled with these amounts if they had several children in the

School. For the very poor, those on Outdoor Poor Relief, there was some help from 1875 when the Poor Law Guardians were given the authority to pay the fees from the poor rates. There was no enthusiasm for such a move within the Wincanton Poor Law Union as on 28th June 1880 Hayter noted that they were paying the school fees of just one family. A year later the Guardians paid 5s 6d in School fees for Bruton but by February 1887 it had risen to £17 0s 0d. (53) The introduction of compulsory education in 1880 clearly had a profound financial impact on the Poor Law System and indicated how many children from pauper families were added to the school roll, having previously been denied such an opportunity.

There was little doubt that the introduction of compulsory education made it much more difficult to force parents to pay the fees but they nevertheless lingered for another decade for it was not until 1891 that education became free when a special fee-grant of 10s a head was introduced. On 31st August 1891 Hayter noted that, "the Managers having decided to accept the fee grant, no fees were colled [*collected*] this morning." For the first time elementary education for all children of school age became free in Bruton and as a result average attendance figures in the 1890s rose.

In the days when children had had to bring their School Pence on a Monday morning, that could create its own problems. On 11th July 1887 Henry Lintern was sent home, not for the first time, to get his School Pence and a "message sent for the parent to come with him." When his father duly arrived it emerged that he had been given his money but had spent it on the way to school!

The original rooms in which the children received their lessons were those converted within the old Poor House, boys on the ground floor and girls upstairs. They were plain and simple, a little smaller than the barn-like schoolrooms in the new School. There is little evidence that the walls were covered with much in the way of stimulating material. The Sunday School had purchased prints of the Old and New Testament and these were presumably left on the wall for the day school. Although at least one map was subsequently purchased in 1876, the H.M.I. commented that, "Maps appeared to be wanted."

The walls themselves were whitewashed, partly to reflect as much light as possible. From time to time Hayter noted that a fresh coat of whitewash was added, always during a holiday to prevent disruption. "12 August 1872. The premises have been thoroughly cleaned and whitewashed during the holidays.
24 May 1874. The School premises have been thoroughly cleansed & whitewashed."
Similar entries appeared for the rest of the century, for example, on 29th August 1892, "The School premises have been thoroughly cleaned, whitewashed and painted." It is interesting to note that for some unspecified reason it was only in the summer of 1897 that wainscoting was introduced, "The walls have all been thoroughly wainscoated all round inside to the height of four feet."

The National Society recommended that in a schoolroom there should be desks generally about eight feet long to allow the children to rest on to write and that these should be around the outside of the room facing the wall so that the children could not be distracted. The remaining central area could then be used by children standing in groups or squares for instruction by their monitors. The original 1851 Plan for Bruton National School proposed a slightly different arrangement with three rows of desks in three blocks along the west wall of the boys' schoolroom and three rows also in three blocks along the north wall of the girls' schoolroom. The comfort of the pupils was not a consideration: hard wooden benches with no backs were the order of the day.

When the Sunday School was established there had been some expenditure on benches and forms and these would have been used initially in the new day school. There were however no desks and so in 1840 some were purchased for £11 10s 0d but unfortunately no funds were available and so a special Subscription was raised with ten different donations ranging from £5 to 2s 6d. In the new building the desks, which had a slight slope towards the pupils, had wooden benches attached for seats which did not have any back rests. In the front row the desks were two feet two inches high, in the second row two feet three inches and in the third row two feet five inches. In each row the desks were one foot wide. The seats which were one foot two inches high for the front row rose in the same number of inches as the desks in the next two rows. In the first two rows the distance from front of desk to front of desk was two feet five inches and three feet for the third row.

In the 1850s Rev. White attempted to obtain an additional grant from the Committee of the Council for more desks and benches to cope with the greater numbers of pupils but that was finally refused on 8th June 1855. For most of their lessons, therefore, the children stood in their groups around a monitor or pupil teacher. In some schools the exact location of the groups was marked on the floor in chalk and was frequently a circle, although for higher Standards it would be a semi-circle so that these pupils could all face a blackboard or sheet of paper fixed to the wall. In some parts of the country these small areas were referred to as 'drafts'.

The Committee did, however, offer to pay half the cost of a gallery. Under this arrangement some seats were constructed in tiers so that the children, especially the youngest, could all see the monitor or teacher. The Managers would appear to have accepted the offer and a gallery was duly put in place. It remained there until 1909 when in his Report on 29th January Inspector Millard recommended its removal and so it was taken down later in the same year. Such galleries were removed in most elementary schools in the first decade of the twentieth century as ideas on education developed and changed. An increase in numbers, especially after the introduction of compulsory attendance meant that the supply of desks and benches was inadequate. On 18th November 1881 Hayter noted, "The want of proper desk accommodation has been much felt this week. All the desks & forms in the School will seat only 120 Children, while more than once this week there have been 150 children present." (54)

Exactly how well the desks survived the attention of the children is impossible to determine but being wooden they could be repaired such as on 23rd October 1899, "The desks have been repaired. Carpenters at work all day." The damage was not necessarily always the fault of the children, as on 4th December 1903 Hayter complained that, "The surfaces of some of the desks were damaged yesterday while they were in the playground." They had been moved outside to make room for a Jumble Sale in the Schoolroom the day before.

There were occasional purchases of new desks such as on 14th July 1899, "The new desks supplied through aid grant were fitted and placed today." On 30th October 1908 Chancellor noted, "The 15 new dual desks arrived today", and these the H.M.I. in his 1909 Inspection thought were a good improvement and added that more were needed. These dual desks tended to be more comfortable for the pupils as they had separate chairs which allowed for some flexibility in relation to size and growth. On 19th November 1912 six more dual desks arrived. Nothing seems to have been done for the teachers in relation to their desks even though in 1911 an H.M.I. had commented that, "The Teacher's Desk is past service."

In the early days of the existence of the School very few books were used. Those that were purchased tended to be from the list of books approved by the National Society. There were often not enough and the condition of those that existed deteriorated so that in August 1871 an H.M.I. commented that, "New books are wanted." Unfortunately the Log Books did not list the titles of any books purchased but ones such as 'Royal Readers' published by Nelson and 'New Code Readers' published by Collins were very popular in schools. Collins also published titles such as 'Arithmetic'. Much more emphasis was placed upon children copying from a blackboard once they had mastered basic reading and writing. Such a process had the significant advantage that it allowed them to practise these two skills at the same time. There was an emphasis upon learning material by heart and so recitation became an important aspect of activities, even for the youngest children who were expected to be able to recite not less than twenty lines of poetry.

Two important developments occurred in the late nineteenth and early twentieth centuries: the first was the introduction of reading from newspapers and magazines which had the added advantage of giving even young pupils some indication of what was happening in the world around them. The second development was the creation of a small library. This was formed in 1901 as on 15th October Hayter noted that, "The School library has been catalogued, the Vicar kindly undertaking the work. The books number at present 161." He added that while a few had been bought with the aid of the grant most had been presented by friends of the School. On 18th November he recorded that, "The first issue of books took place this morning. The children seem very eager to avail themselves of the privilege of using the books." It was to be more than another decade before a similar free library was in operation for adults in the town itself. The system in the School was not without its problems for when Chancellor became the Headmaster in March 1908 he found that thirty books were missing from the Library. Nevertheless it continued to expand as in January 1911 £67 6s 9d was spent on new Library Books, the money being raised through an "Entertainment".

It cannot have helped the children to concentrate that the new National Schoolroom suffered from poor ventilation which led to overheating in the summer and cold conditions in the winter, a very common problem in nineteenth century schoolrooms. As early as 1859 an Inspector had commented that, "Though the room is lofty the ventilation is bad, owing to the want of apertures in the windows." Yet nothing was done. On 16th June 1871 Hayter complained, "Room very close and uncomfortable. Defective ventilation very apparent." A month later on 17th July he noted that the weather was very hot and the children "noisy and inattentive," suffering from the effects of bad ventilation. On 17th July 1874, "The Schoolroom has been very hot and Close,

& the Children have been consequently fidgety & troublesome."
After many more of his complaints on 20th April 1885 he was able
to report, "Workmen being employed putting ventilators in the
roof." That attempt at a solution, however, was not a complete
solution. Such was "the great heat of yesterday" that attendance
was much lower on 16th July 1897.

Almost exactly two years later on 19th July 1899 he recorded
that a serious situation arose as the weather was "intensely hot"
that week. "Yesterday with all the doors and windows open the
thermometer reached 86 degrees." [*fahrenheit*] The Vicar was
summoned and he advised the School to close in the afternoon,
"It being a real case of Emergency." By 1914 virtually nothing
had been undertaken to improve the ventilation as an internal
memorandum at the Board of Education was scathing, "The
alterations are not satisfactory." In the boys' schoolroom, "None
of the top lights have been made to open. In each of the two
East windows one of the bottom lights has been made to swing
(horizontally) but they have not been hoppered [*hinged at the
bottom*] and there is a bad down-draught from them. The large
south window is untouched." In the Girls' Schoolroom nothing at
all had been done." (55)

Far worse for the children was the fact that the one stove in
each room was totally inadequate in cold weather. Hayter's most
outspoken criticism was made on 2nd December 1879, "The want
of some efficient warming apparatus for the Schoolroom was much
felt today. Several of the smaller children were crying with cold. The
work was much interfered with to allow the Children occasionally
to go to the fire place and get a little of the heat that did not go
up the Chimney." It was a very cold winter for he noted on 26th
January 1880, "Weather intensely cold. The thermometer this
evening registered 12 degrees Faht." A year later on 24th January
1881 he recorded, "The thermometer at present marks 18 degrees
of frost." Such readings were not uncommon: 17 degrees Faht on
11th January 1895 and 25 degrees of frost on 8th February 1895
when "I found it necessary to light all the gas jets in the School

on Wednesday, Thursday and Friday mornings." On 5th February 1912 Chancellor found the temperature in Standard I and II's room to be 32 degrees. Inspectors such as Millard also commented, for example on 26th January 1909, "All three rooms are inadequately warmed. On the date of the visit of inspection the thermometer never rose above 45 degrees all day in any one of the rooms."

The officials of the Board of Education were of the opinion that the Tortoise stoves used to heat the rooms were totally inadequate. The response of the Managers was to introduce a portable stove which led one official to comment that it was "by no means satisfactory", and that it was "a deadly thing that ought not to be allowed in any School" as there was no outlet for any of the fumes produced. (56) Such a situation was in fact nothing new as inadequate ventilation and poor stoves meant that on more than one occasion the schoolroom began to fill with smoke. The most serious of these was on 24th October 1880 when Hayter recorded, "This morning the room was so full of smoke, that after an hour's work, the children did nothing but cough & wipe their eyes." The Vicar was sent for and he ordered the children be dismissed for the day.

This event was not the first time that the room had filled with smoke but on the previous occasion it was due to the weather rather than the heating system. On 29th March 1878 the children were sent home as Hayter explained that, "This morning owing to the tempestuous wind the room was so full of smoke, & covered with soot, that it could not be used."

Given the regulations introduced later in the twentieth century in relation to the level of warmth to be observed in classrooms, it is hard to imagine the misery from cold which the children in this School must have experienced and had to endure on some days during the winter months. The reluctance of the Managers to undertake corrective work must be seen in conjunction with their failure to deal with other problems relating to the buildings and playground and which will be considered in the section on 'Buildings'.

As well as heat and cold for the children there were also problems with lighting in one classroom. No adverse observations seem to have been made about lighting in the two main Schoolrooms which had large windows and gas lighting. After alterations to the small classroom in 1896 there was some criticism of lighting but it was not until the Inspection of 1909 that it was branded as inadequate. This in fact led the School being placed on the "School Premises - Black List" which listed defects. "Small classroom is inadequately lighted, owing to the proximity of some neighbouring houses [Plox House] which block the light. Position of boy's offices prevents additional windows being made." Inspector Tillard visited the School on 19th June 1909 and met with the Vicar and one of the Managers, R.T.H. Hughes, and as a result of that he suggested, "An immediate improvement could be effected by painting the walls white & substituting prismatic reflecting glass for that in the lower panes." These and other suggestions in a letter of 2nd July provoked a critical response from the Managers. They pointed out that no complaint had ever been made about the lighting until they coloured the walls green, believing it "to be restful to the eyes of the children." They also reminded the Board that they had approved the plans.

The Managers did, however, repaint the wall in white but then when another Inspector felt that the lighting was still inadequate in 1911 they sent a furious response. They pointed out, "It is lighted on the West side by a large mullioned window, with large clear panes of glass. The window is 9 feet high by 7 feet wide. There is also a smaller 3 light window high in the South wall, close under the Roof." They claimed that since they had painted it white the light had been much improved and no one else had complained. Their view was that as the house across the lane was just twelve feet away, there was nothing else to be done." (57) Time and again the Managers displayed a reluctance to spend money but above all they resented interference from outside.

As National Schools were supported by the Church of England there was naturally great emphasis upon religious instruction and

159

careful inspection by Diocesan Inspectors who produced annual reports. In addition the religious aspect of the School was apparent in other ways. From the very beginning the day for the children started with Prayers and until 3rd April 1871 morning school ended with Grace being sung before they went home to a meal. Throughout the Log Books the visits of the Vicar were recorded - he did after all live just across the road. Rev. H.T. Ridley visited the School at least once a week and frequently more so he was a well-known figure for the children. His support was clearly much appreciated as on 12th November 1884 he was presented with a Barometer as a birthday present "and as a proof of their appreciation of the interest he takes in the welfare of this School & Scholars." On 30th November 1893 he was presented with another gift, this time an inkstand of polished oak with a silver mounting to mark his twenty-five year connection with the School. Such visits were continued by his successor, Rev. Llewelyn Hayward who was to be seen on the premises two or three times a week.

On some important religious festivals all the children crossed the road to St. Mary's Church to attend a Service. In early to mid-February they were present at a morning service on Ash Wednesday and continued to be so until 1906 when the Vicar arranged a special service for them at the end of afternoon school and Hayter recorded "nearly all attended." For many years the children were also taken to the Church for a service on Ascension Day.

There were occasional less formal connections with the Church, such as the rural tradition of strewing flowers in the path of a newly married couple as they left the Church, as happened, for example, in July 1864 on the wedding day of Emily Stockwell, the daughter of the local doctor. (58)

Close proximity to the parish church meant that it was a straightforward matter to march the children from the playground, across the road and along the path to the North Tower entrance. There was, however, one significant disadvantage - the bells. On 5th June 1878, for example, Hayter complained, "The school-work was interrupted very much this afternoon by the Church Bells, which were ringing nearly all the afternoon." He did not specify the reason for the bells being rung but it was most likely the annual Club Day of one of the town's Friendly Societies.

Before the commencement of the surviving Log Books in 1870 there is no documentary evidence for the holidays which the children were permitted. It is, however, reasonable to assume that those mentioned in 1870 and immediately afterwards conformed to the existing pattern. The longest holiday of four weeks was from late July or very early August to late August and was usually referred to as the 'Harvest Holiday', indicative of the importance of child labour at that time of year. A shorter holiday of some two weeks occurred over the Christmas period. The third holiday of about ten days centred on Whitsuntide, coinciding with the Friendly Society festivities.

Easter was not a time for a lengthy holiday, just Good Friday and Easter Monday but that changed in the 1880s when ten days then became standard in place of the Whitsuntide holiday. This change may be a reflection of the growing importance of the Temperance Movement and the concern that young children were being exposed to the excesses of alcohol and the drunkenness so common on Club Days. An exception was made in the case of the much more highly disciplined and organised Ancient Order of Foresters, of which Hayter himself was a prominent member, when they staged their parade, fete and flower show in July. The Foresters did have a Juvenile branch and in 1887 Hayter commented, "A large number of the boys in the School belong to this Order." In the early twentieth century the Co-operative Society established a significant presence in Bruton, particularly in Patwell Street, and it soon started its own Gala Day in July. This became another regular half-day holiday.

Throughout the year there were also a number of full-day or half-day holidays, which reflected either national holidays or local events. Traditionally Shrove Tuesday had been regarded by working people as a holiday and time of festivities, often involving alcohol and so not always the most peaceful. For the children it was a half-day holiday, a custom which survived into the twentieth century. Another half-day holiday was granted to coincide roughly with Bruton Feast in late September each year. This celebration at the end of the harvest season was traditionally a time of rural games, feasting and an abundance of alcohol. (59) By the late 1870s this old tradition was beginning to decrease in importance and change its nature, once again under the influence of temperance and the attitude of the Victorian middle classes.

Every year the children were given a half-day holiday so that they could attend the Athletic Sports Day at the Grammar School and another to coincide with their Commemoration Day Celebrations of Corpus Christi. Since the early nineteenth century Bruton had an Agricultural Society and each year they staged a major Agricultural Show, initially this was in December but by the 1880s had moved to October. As this was such a significant event in an agricultural area with important attractions, such as a performance by the tight-rope walker Blondin, the School was closed for the whole day. By 1880 the national attitude to holidays was changing and a Bank Holiday was introduced at the beginning of August. In 1880 the School attempted to remain open on that day but Hayter found that the attendance was very small in the morning so the children were dismissed at 10am for the rest of the day. The next year the School closed for the whole day.

When added together all these regular holidays amounted to over eight weeks. In addition there were a number of ad hoc holidays most years. There was usually a half day holiday associated with the School's own "Treat" but in addition as the Church Sunday School Treat was always on a weekday and as so many of the day pupils attended on Sunday, it led to closure for half a day as well. The time of year varied so it was for example in February in 1873 and September in 1878. Other activities associated with the parish church led to closure such as the general holiday in the town on 20th June 1872 to celebrate the re-opening of the parish church after restoration. As the latter had proved very expensive money was still being sought five years later and so on 19th April 1877 the children were dismissed at noon so that the room could be prepared for an Entertainment in aid of the Restoration Fund.

At 11.50am on 22nd January 1877 the School closed so that a Vestry Meeting could be transferred there and on several occasions such as 24th March 1879 and 27th February 1882 the School shut for the afternoon as the room was required for Confirmation candidates. As might be expected the School did not open at the time of the funerals of Managers or friends such as 28th March 1898 for Rev. H.T. Ridley and 18th January 1906 for Mrs Dyne. Possibly because of Hayter's musical activities the school closed on 12th July 1883 for the Diocesan Choral Festival at Wells and most years in July on the day of St. Mary's Choir's Excursion, usually to Weymouth.

National events were yet another reason for closure, especially if associated with royalty. Half-day holidays resulted from the marriages of Queen Victoria's children: Princess Louise on 21st March 1871, the Duke of Edinburgh on 24th January 1874 and the Duke of York on 6th July 1893. The School closed at lunchtime on Monday 2nd July 1887, "so many children being absent assisting in decorating the town" ready for Queen Victoria's Golden Jubilee. It remained closed for the rest of the week as on Tuesday and Wednesday it was used for public dinners, principally for the old, sick and infirm, although the children were treated to a Tea and given a Jubilee Mug. Then the School had to remain closed on Thursday and Friday as it was necessary "to wash the floors which were in a very greasy & dirty state." The Queen's Diamond Jubilee a decade later led to closure again but this time for just two days. The School was also closed for half a day to celebrate the birthday of King Edward VII on 20th November 1901 and for a whole day on 20th May 1910 on account of his funeral.

Holidays for other national events included half a day on 1st March 1900 to celebrate the relief of Lady Smith in South

Africa and after receiving news of the end of the Boer War on 2nd June 1902 "the children after singing the National Anthem were dismissed by the Managers for the rest of the day." Empire Day also led to a holiday on 24th May 1906.

One sign of the times was that the School was closed on a number of occasions to act as a Polling Station at the time of a General Election. As a result of the Reform Acts of 1867 and 1884 the franchise had been extended to include many working class men and from 1872 votes had to be cast in secret and not by a show of hands so a suitable space had to be found. The School closed on various days, such as 27th November 1885, 13th, 14th and 15th July 1892 and 25th and 26th January 1906.

There were of course from time to time closures for reasons which to the modern perception appear unusual. On 22nd May 1873 the School closed for the afternoon so that the Sunday School children could attend a tea given by Rev. Peel and again on 29th July all the children having been invited to a tea given by Mrs Dyne. On 2nd February 1876 there was a half-day "to enable the Master to attend a drill Certificate Examination" and on 25th September 1906 so that the teachers could attend the Prize Distribution at Sunny Hill Girls' School. It seems to have been a common practice to grant a half day holiday after an inspection such as one in July 1867 "as usual" after the examination by an H.M.I. and September 1882 the Headmaster was so pleased with the way the children approached the Diocesan Inspector's examination that they were given a half-day holiday "as a reward for their good work and attention." A half-day was given on 14th July 1905 when a visiting circus staged a children's performance in the afternoon.

As the Schoolrooms were such a large, important space and resource for the community, the children receive many half-day holidays when preparations were being made. These events included evening entertainments, such as dramatic productions and concerts, some of which were for the benefit of the School itself, such as one on 17th January 1896 to raise money for alterations to the classroom. Preparations needed to be made for a range of events and meetings such as jumble sales and teas.

Some of the School closures and consequent holidays were beyond the control of the Headmaster and the Managers. The weather played its part with access prevented as a result of floods such as in October 1882, November 1888 and November 1894. Snow forced the School to close in January 1891. Occasionally work on the School buildings which could not be undertaken during a normal holiday period forced closure. On 31st October 1877 there was no School as carpenters were undertaking some unspecified work; on 20th April 1885 workmen were installing ventilators in the roof; on 5th September 1899 problems with the drains in the girls' offices necessitated closure; and on 18th March 1905 alterations in the boys' yard. The longest forced closure for this sort of work was from 12th October 1900 when the School remained closed for a week to allow alterations to the toilets and water to be laid on. This last work was very successful, "The alterations are a great improvement."

The most prolonged forced closures and additional holidays were the result of illnesses when the local Medical Officer of Health ordered the School to close in an attempt to prevent the spread of a particular disease. Measles was a much more serious illness throughout the nineteenth and early twentieth centuries. On 12th April 1884 the Medical Officer of Health ordered the School to close for two weeks; on 12th December 1893 for a month; for three weeks from 10th January 1902 and then for another two weeks as the disease continued to spread; on 2nd June 1908 for three weeks and the same from 12th March 1913. In November 1904 diphtheria was present in the town and on 5th December the Medical Officer ordered closure for three weeks.

The most serious outbreak of disease appeared to have been in 1905 when the School was closed for two weeks from 8th September because of the prevalence of scarlatina and whooping cough. Within a week of it being re-opened scarlet fever broke out and spread throughout October. The result was that the Medical Officer of Health ordered the School's closure on 23rd October and this time it did not re-open until 8th January 1906, some two and a half months later. It was a major disruption to the education of the children but when Hayter examined them in April he noted, "Both teachers and children had worked hard to make up for the time lost by the closing of the School." An H.M.I. commented that the work was generally satisfactory although he considered that spelling had suffered most as a result of the closure.

As well as the subjects specified in the curriculum there were other activities for the children. The most prominent of these was the provision of an entertainment by the pupils for their parents, families and friends. The first recorded concert was on 21st December 1854 when the School broke up for Christmas and it was arranged by Mr and Mrs Byles. About eighty children "ranged in a gallery, formed the choral body, who sang Christmas Carols, songs with choruses, and four-part rounds with a precision and animation, which reflected much credit on the skilful training of their Master and Mistress." After the presentation of some prizes in October 1859 there was an entertainment which "consisted for the most part of Songs and Chants, intermixed with recitations of poetry, dialogues &c... and all of them performed their parts most creditably."

As Edward Hayter was so interested and involved in music it was natural that he continued this activity. On 5th November 1879, for example, there was an entertainment for parents and friends and "As a reward for their exertions they had a half holiday this afternoon." As well as the children Hayter himself performed, for example, he opened an entertainment in May 1881 by playing a duet with his daughter and later performed a monologue which he had written and which touched upon various local topics, including the Whitsuntide Club Walking. (60) He continued to deliver such monologues to various groups and societies for more than another twenty years and press reports indicated that they were very popular and well-received.

Throughout the nineteenth century schools were concerned with the basic education of children rather than their physical well-being. They were not, however, insulated from problems associated with childhood. As national statistics and Bruton's Burial Register indicated, death was an ever-present reality for children, fortunately decreasing as the century progressed. In fact in the period 1870-1914 there were remarkably few recorded in the Log Books for Bruton National School. In 1874 the School lost three pupils during an outbreak of Scarlet Fever: George Atkins of Standard II aged seven in November and sisters Nellie and Bessie Billett aged seven and six in December. On 26th April 1907 Stanley Clark of Standard I aged eight was "accidently drowned" but no details given.

There were at least three other tragic deaths: the first occurred on 4th November 1873 when two brothers, William and George Day, went into the cottage of Mrs Cox near the School during the mid-day break. William, the elder brother aged twelve, found a gun which had been left here, pointed it at his nine year old brother and it went off, hitting George in the neck and chest so that he died instantly. Hayter recorded that the Vicar went into the School in the afternoon and "spoke to the Children very feelingly on the sudden & dreadful death of their schoolfellow." A Coroner's Inquest ruled that it was an accident but severely criticised the owner of the gun for leaving it loaded.

The second death occurred on Saturday 26th March 1887 when Julia Hann of Standard I aged six was knocked down and killed on the corner of Silver Street and Church Bridge by a horse and cart laden with coal, the wheel of which ran over her head and fractured her skull. Although the coal merchant George Moon was not with his horse but on the bridge talking to another man, the Inquest merely censured him but did not recommend a charge of manslaughter. "The girls of the National Schools attended the funeral, most of them carrying nice bouquets and wreaths of flowers. A splendid wreath of choice hothouse flowers was sent by the teachers of the schools."

The third death occurred in 1905 when William Viney aged eight who lived near Cogley Wood was sent to School as usual on the morning of Wednesday 21st June but never arrived. He was found unconscious in a field near the railway station the following morning. He had a fractured skull with a wound some seven inches long. A local doctor operated to relieve pressure but the boy died on Friday morning. The doctor speculated that the wound could have been caused by the kick of a horse. A Coroner's Jury returned an open verdict: "The deceased died from fracture of the skull with compression of the brain, the result of extreme violence, but how and under what circumstances the fatal injuries were caused there is no evidence to show." (61)

There were also very few accidents in the School which were serious enough to be recorded in the Log Books. On 11th May 1908 Harold Ovens of Standard III, the son of Mr Ovens the baker, was playing in the playground when he tripped over the kerbstone of the pavement and broke his thigh bone. A local newspaper added that, "Mr Chancellor, headmaster, carried him to the doctor and his leg was set. The little fellow is progressing favourably." (62) On 8th February 1911 John Benjafield cut Albert White's hand with a modelling knife, "The cut bled rather freely so I sent him to the doctor who dressed it." No mention was made about whether it was an accident or deliberate. Five days later Maggie Curtis "fell down in a fit during prayers this morning." After first aid by Chancellor the doctor was called and advised that the girl should go home.

All the other serious accidents occurred outside of the School. In March 1874 Samuel Elderkin of 2nd Class was severely injured when a railway truck ran over his leg. On 24th March 1882 John Cockerell of Standard IV was run over in the High Street after School had finished and his leg broken in two places. The same fate befell Meaden of Standard IV when her leg was run over by a timber wagon also in the High Street in January 1895. Five days later Francis also of Standard IV had his ankle broken when it was run over close to the School. The following day yet another

Standard IV pupil, Stone, fell down going to School, probably as the result of ice, and injured her collar bone.

In the nineteenth century children's health and physical condition was generally not a great priority in the majority of schools, although preventing the spread of potentially killer diseases was always a major concern in institutions which brought large numbers of people together in close proximity to each other. From the very beginning of the Infant School in 1840 parents were instructed not to send their children to school if they were ill or even if they suspected that they were. Some parents ignored this requirement as the Log Books after 1870 contained a number of examples of pupils being sent home. On 2nd November 1874 "A boy named White, living on Walk" was found to be suffering from Scarlet Fever so he and his two sisters were sent home. In October 1878 Henry Trim was sent home suffering from Measles and Spratling the next day. In December 1880 a number of children were removed suffering from Mumps, a situation which repeated itself in March 1909. In September 1887 two brothers were sent home as there was Quincey in the house and the next month Joseph Goverd with an unspecified skin disease.

The beginning of the twentieth century witnessed a change in attitude with much more concern being expressed about the physical state of children in schools. Compulsory education after 1880 had brought some childhood problems into much sharper focus: bad health, neglect, lack of proper nourishment, problems with eyes, teeth and physique generally. As early as 1890 the London School Board had introduced medical inspections for its schoolchildren and other places such as Bradford followed in 1893. It was, however, the Boer War between 1899 and 1902 which really caused alarm as about half of all men who volunteered for the army were found to be physically unfit for service. In 1901 a pioneering study by Seebohm Rowntree found that a quarter of the population of York were living in poverty and as a result suffering physically. The whole question of future manpower both in war and peace was discussed as a matter of urgency. In 1904 a Board of

Education committee drew attention to the need for a systematic medical inspection for all school children. In an Education Act in 1907 the duty to provide such a medical inspection was placed on the Local Education Authority.

Some sort of system in Bruton was well under way by November 1909 as on the 6th of that month all girls over twelve were inspected. Increasingly children were sent home if they were found to be dirty or verminous. What is perhaps striking by its omission is that there was not one entry to that effect while Hayter was headmaster. On 2nd April 1909 Chancellor recorded that he sent Annie Warr home "again this morning to clean her head. She was in a very bad state, literally crawling." On 18th November 1909 a complaint was made about the dirty and untidy appearance of Edith Apsey and Gertrude Eddington and the result was that both stayed away the next day. Oatley Barber was excluded on 24th March 1911 when he was found to be verminous as were six girls on 22nd July 1912. Two months later two sisters May and Kate Carver were excluded on account of ringworm. An interesting entry was made in the Log Book by Chancellor on 30th October 1908, "I was obliged to send Sidney Carott home, as his Clothes were in such a filthy condition and smelt so strongly." Personal hygiene was something for the distant future for many poor families in the early twentieth century.

Just before the outbreak of the First World War a much more vigorous and punitive approach was being taken towards the condition of children. In March 1914 four parents were summoned in front of the Magistrates in Wincanton "for sending their children to the elementary school at Bruton with their heads in a dirty and verminous condition prejudicial to the health of the other School children." The County Council nurse in evidence stated that she had visited the School and advised the parents what to do but they had ignored her instructions. Two parents were fined 5s each for one child, one 2s 6d for each of two children and one 2s 6d for each of three children. Four months later George Sibly was fined 5s for a similar offence. (63)

From 1906 it had been possible to provide meals for children but there is no evidence that this occurred in Bruton before 1914, probably because of the limited nature of the site for introducing the required cooking facilities. The children did, however, benefit from a School Dentist as on 5th November 1914, "School Dentist attended at Church Room.... Children treated." There was no doubt that such a person was urgently required as in 1913 the Chief Medical Officer of the Board of Education estimated that of the six million children in public elementary schools in England and Wales some 50% suffered from injurious decay of their teeth. He also estimated that 10% had a serious defect in vision, 5% defective hearing and 10% unclean bodies. There was clearly still a great deal to be done. (64)

It was only in the last quarter of the nineteenth century, particularly after the introduction of compulsory education, that any significant attention was paid to children who had physical or mental problems: those who were blind, deaf or suffered from a physical or mental handicap of any kind were largely ignored and little if any special provision was made for them. While teachers could easily see that a particular child had a problem they did not have the knowledge or training on how to deal with it. In general such a child was left alone provided that he or she did not disrupt other children. Most rural schools had one or two pupils who were very, very slow in their understanding and actions and so labels such as the "village idiot" were all too common.

After 1870 some Board Schools, generally the larger ones, did try to develop appropriate help and teaching methods but Church Schools were under no obligation whatsoever to do so or even to admit such children as pupils. The requirements of the Revised Code of 1862 in relation to all children being examined certainly did not encourage their presence. It was often the case that many of them made little progress and it was felt that they hindered normal teaching. If such a child was present in the School the usual procedure was to inform the Managers that they were there and that they had a problem. On 31st May 1886, for example, Hayter

171

noted that, "Attention of Managers called to Ethel Thick (loss of eye) Car Jones & Maud Thick, Dulness."

Occasionally a local doctor would make a recommendation on the treatment of a particular individual. On 19th May 1885 Dr Smith confirmed that Emma Farthing was suffering from heart disease and "must not have any pressure with school work." On 7th June of the following year Dr Stockwell reported that Laura White of Standard I was "not sufficiently strong to attend School regularly, or to be worked hard in School." On 24th October 1887 he ordered that William Farthing "is to do little or no School work, as he is too weak." Just over a year later on 26th November there was another entry for the same boy, "Wm Farthing, suffering from an affliction inside the head, has been ordered by the doctor, to leave School; in his present state of health, School work would be likely to cause inflammation of the brain."

By the mid-1880s it was possible to place a child on an 'Exception List' so that they did not have to be examined. The following examples are representative of the Log Book entries:

"1886 October 19	Edith Westcott, Exception, Suffers from deafness.
December 10	Geo Chamberlain & Joseph Farwell St I have been added to the exception list. Both dull & Chamberlain frequently unwell. Farwell now laid up with Bronchial attack.
1887 May 12	Edith Hiscox, exception. A weakly Child & constantly absent through illness. Ada Frances, exception. Suffers from pains in the head."

On 21st November 1887 eleven children were added to the Exception List as being weakly, having pains in head, sleeplessness, bad eyes, deafness and "Somewhat defective intellect." On 23rd November 1888 Hayter listed seven children "unable to do work of their Standard":

"Ada Eddington,	a weak child, no previous instruction	)
Matilda Harris,	bad eyes	)
Charles Jones,	a weakly child	) St I
Fred Hill,	mental incapacity	)
Joseph Biss,	a weakly child	)
Edith Westcott,	St II Deafness	
Joseph Attwood,	St II Dullness. This boy had to be retained in Infant School one year extra, owing to same reason." As he was baptised on 1st February 1880 he was nearly nine years old.	

Such entries continued in subsequent years with little indication of what was to be done with these children or any indication of much sympathy for their situation. The costs involved precluded any significant action.

f) Punishments.

Punishment in all its forms was felt to be essential in the Victorian and Edwardian classroom where it was obligatory to keep control of large numbers of children, especially as they were undertaking the most boring and mind-numbing activities. Absolute obedience was judged to be necessary not only there but also as a preparation for their future working lives. The level of punishment in Bruton National School is difficult to assess as no separate punishment book has survived and there are only a small number of references in the Log Books.

In many instances a simple caution was sufficient, such as to William Lucas of Standard III on 4th February 1878 "about using bad language." Being kept in at the end of a school session was certainly used, as witness the whole 3rd class being kept behind at lunchtime on 13th October 1870 for inattention during a reading lesson. Before January 1885 Thomas Hole was kept in regularly as he was regarded as idle. On 23rd July 1893 H. Plowman was kept in at noon for inattention.

The reverse process also happened in that pupils could be sent out of a lesson, sent home or even suspended. On 25th November 1873 Mrs James complained, "that her boy is often sent out by the teachers for punishment without cause." That allegation prompted a reply from Hayter that, "She was, however, informed that children in School are rarely punished except for such breaches of discipline as come immediately under the Master's notice." While it was not uncommon for children to be sent home if they were ill or in contact with illness, or later were judged to be dirty or verminous, they could also be sent home for a breach of School Rules as Emily Hyam discovered on 22nd September 1879. She went to school in the morning "with her hair in curling papers. As this has always been forbidden by the School rules, she was cautioned. As she came in the same way in the afternoon with an impertinent note she was sent home again." On 16th February 1872 Charles Weeks of Standard II was suspended for theft but interestingly it had occurred at home and not in School, an indication of the power and influence a determined Headmaster could have in a small community. The boy had taken nearly £4 from his sister's pocket, apparently not for the first time. It was left to the Managers to decide if and when he should be re-admitted. Unfortunately their decision was not recorded.

Expulsion from the School was yet another punishment available, as Leonard Day of Standard V discovered on 29th July 1878 when he was found "guilty of embezzling several sums of money belonging to his father, his name was struck off the Register this day." Another example of an activity outside of the classroom having repercussions for the offender in the School. On 8th January 1885 Thomas Hole of Pitcombe was dismissed by the Managers as he was, "Idle and insubordinate." He was also a pronounced truant as he "is allowed by his parents to remain from School as long as he feels disposed." Charles Tucker was also a truant as well as "very idle and unpunctual", for which he had been cautioned and punished on 8th May 1890. Hayter commented that, "His example is having a bad effect on some of the younger boys." Matters came to head on 4th November of the same year when he was "guilty of impudence to his teacher & of making indecent remarks before a mixed class of girls and boys." As he was over the school leaving age he was immediately expelled.

A more unusual punishment was given by Chancellor on 18th March 1910 when R. Mainstone was accused of stealing a ball from King's School. His father refused to produce the ball and sent "an impudent message." Chancellor recorded, "I punished him (the son) by declining to give extra lessons out of school hours until the ball was produced." The boy was withdrawn and transferred to Castle Cary School. Unfortunately no information has survived on the nature of these extra lessons.

Other examples of punishment were recorded throughout the Log Books but the exact nature was not specified, for example, on 6th December 1870 T. Burston was "guilty of insubordination" as was George Farwell on 21st September 1886. Truancy attracted an unspecified punishment, although in this case probably corporal as on at least one occasion the parents were informed before the punishment was administered. Willie Hurden and John Annett were punished on 18th April 1883 but it did not stop their activities as the same happened on 14th October 1884. On 1st April 1887 John Annett was referred to as "an inveterate truant" who had been absent since 7th March. His case was drawn to the attention of the Attendance Officer, an action which seemed to have happened increasingly, and his parents were held responsible and were eventually charged in the Magistrates' Court in Wincanton.

Corporal punishment was used extensively in all educational establishments in the nineteenth century, from public schools to Dame and Workhouse Schools. Most adults believed that to teach children some kind of physical discipline was essential. The large number of pupils in one room, along with the inexperience of monitors, pupil teachers and some teachers encouraged corporal punishment as many felt it was the only way that they could cope with the numbers and demands of the job. Corporal punishment was also considered necessary in order to ensure that a child concentrated and remained focussed. It followed that errors in a pupil's work, such as a spelling mistake or incorrect sums and even poor handwriting with ill-formed letters, was the result of the inattention of a child who therefore needed to be punished. Discipline, punctuality and obedience were essential not only in schools but also in later employment so there had to be strict rules and regulations. The canings themselves were generally carried out with a variety of sticks, leather straps and wooden rulers, often in public.

The attitude of parents towards punishment was somewhat ambivalent as some, particularly those of girls, did not approve of what the School did and were quick to complain whereas others accepted that it was necessary and in a few cases insisted that it was administered. There is evidence that some of the monitors and pupil teachers did use corporal punishment in Bruton National School after 1870 but it was thoroughly disapproved of by Hayter. On 1st September 1870, just three days after the School had re-opened following the Harvest Holiday, the mother of Julia Bell came into the School at the end of the afternoon to complain that Mary Ross "had been beating her child." Hayter examined the girls and noted, "From the appearance of the child's ears, they had evidently been severely boxed." Mary Ross was cautioned but it had little effect as she was cautioned again for "striking the children" on 30th September. On 23rd June 1871 the Log Book included the following entry: "Monitor Mary Ross guilty of insubordination by boxing children's ears after having been repeatedly cautioned not to do so." On 30th January 1873 A. Trotter was cautioned "not to strike the Children."

More than a decade later in 1886 Hayter experienced trouble with Miss Jackson. By March of that year she had been cautioned more than once for "beating the children in her class." On 4th May Mrs Steeds came into School to complain of Miss Jackson's "unkind treatment of her daughter." Hayter added, "Complaints from parents have become very numerous as to Miss Jackson's using corporal punishment and 'bullying' the children." On 2nd July she was dismissed. On 25th April 1898 Hayter received a complaint from the mother of Christine Hussey that "her child had been beaten with a pointer by Miss Birt." He took the opportunity to remind the teachers that, "they are under no circumstances to administer corporal punishment."

With the appointment of William Chancellor in 1905 complaints about the treatment of boys came the following year. On 7th May Hayter received a complaint from Mr Mainstone about the "excessive punishment" of his son in Standard II. It was referred straight to the Chairman of the Managers but no outcome was recorded. Matters came to a head in October of the same year when the mother of G. Fowler complained on the 4th that Chancellor had punished her son "Excessively - for making a noise and annoying the pupils in the Evening Continuation Class." Hayter investigated and stated, "the boy's hands were found much Swollen." He referred the matter to the Vicar as Chairman of the Managers only to be told that he too had received a similar complaint from another parent. On 17th October Mrs Butler complained again that her son Stanley "had been severely punished by Mr Chancellor." Hayter reported, "Livid Stripes were visible on the child's buttocks, & the punishment certainly appears to have been excessive." Once again the incident was reported to the Vicar and on 26th October Hayter was informed, "that Corporal punishment is to be inflicted only by Head teachers." Chancellor must have protested for a note was added in the Vicar's handwriting, "This order rescinded in reply to application by WTC."

No other explanation was given and two years later Chancellor was the Headmaster with a reputation for very strict discipline which was to remain with him until he retired. He was reputed to have been very free in his use of the cane, or any other implement which was close at hand. The result was that an element of fear could be engendered. On 12th October 1910 he found George

Clarke "writing indecent words on a piece of paper." He referred the matter to the Managers who decided that he should receive corporal punishment which was duly administered the next day. It is very noticeable that in the early twentieth century far more cases were recorded as being referred to the Managers for their opinion or decision. It may reflect the way in which membership of that body had been extended with the spread of democracy as the result of extensions of the franchise.

Some of the allegations may have been vexatious as they met with strong denials. On 14th July 1880 Hayter recorded that, "A complaint was made by the father of Alice Coward that his child had been struck by the pupil teacher & was ill in consequence. On enquiry the pupil teacher denied all knowledge of the striking of the child." No more was heard of this allegation.

As Headmaster Hayter himself did administer corporal punishment but the references in his Log Book were very rare, presumably as he had a separate Punishment Book which has not survived. On 24th January 1883, for example, "punished (corporally) four boys for playing truant the day before." On 23rd May 1894 G. Vigar of Standard VI was "exceedingly insubordinate & impertinent" at the end of morning school. He returned in the afternoon but was sent home and a request made that his father should see the Headmaster. When he heard what had happened he insisted that his son "might be severely punished." Hayter recorded some difficulty, "Corporal punishment was administered, it was a somewhat awkward task, as the boy's Manner was defiant throughout." There is a small amount of documentary evidence that the headmaster was prepared to cane girls as well, albeit on the hand. On 18th November 1895 he included the following entry, "Martha White St V punished for insubordination & impudence. Her father called this evening and complained that she had been unduly punished. As a matter of fact she received one stripe on the hand with the cane, and was placed apart from the rest of the children the remainder of the afternoon."

Even with all the punishments which were available and inflicted there were occasional hints that the discipline in the School was not as good as it might have been. In 1856, for example, the H.M.I. was said to have spoken "in qualified terms of the discipline." In 1874 the Inspector recorded that, "The discipline wants attention." In 1884 in his Report the H.M.I. felt that Standards I and II "did not seem to be under very good control" which led to several cases of copying during the examination. An H.M.I. in 1904 also had reservations as he noted, "There is a tendency to talk during School time among the boys, which should not be allowed and is destructive to good work."

The expectation was that the discipline, behaviour and values taught in a School would be transferred to the conduct of the children outside of school. Judging by some of the letters which were printed in the local press that was not always the case. While it is not possible to state categorically that those involved in the following incidents attended Bruton National School most did occur after education became compulsory. In January 1882 a letter appeared which complained of the way in which boys were shooting catapults at passers-by, little children, birds and animals. It was alleged that this sort of behaviour tended "to make boys who use them cruel and heard-hearted."

In May 1888 another correspondent reported the activities of "ill-behaved boys" who gathered in groups and insulted young ladies entering shops. When one of the recipients of the abuse threatened to report them, "They then used language not fit for men, let alone boys." A week later the writer of another letter was convinced that if the local policeman and magistrates did not act decisively the town would descend into "lawlessness and disorder." Another correspondent joined the debate but claimed that it was not just boys, "The 'young ladies' are, if anything, rather worse than the boys." Two years later the boys were still congregating in groups around shop windows and "howling" but if criticized and told to move away, "you get nothing but abuse." For good measure he added that something ought to be done to stop them letting off fireworks in the streets every evening as this was frightening horses and causing them to bolt. (65)

In rural parishes it was expected that the local police constable would deal with some of the behaviour of the children in his area. This took many forms: from a reprimand to a threat to tell their parents to a 'clip around the ear.' Sometimes the constable would go into a school to talk to groups of children but there was no entry in the Bruton National School Log Books to indicate that that ever happened there. The view was prevalent in many areas that the whole of the community had some responsibility for the way children behaved. On 18th July 1874, for example, one of the Managers went into the School to deal with a local incident. "Captain Dyne & Messrs Palmer & Mills attended at the School this morning for the purpose of identifying some boys who had set fire to a cow stall belonging to Mr Mills, and some trees belonging to Mr Dyne. The culprits turned out to be John James, Albert Shepherd & Henry Meaden. Captain Dyne cautioned them, and on their promise of better behaviour in future Mr Mills undertook not to prosecute them."

g) Rewards.

In the days before attendance became compulsory it was necessary to devise ways of ensuring that children not only attended school but also did so regularly. Once in school they had to be encouraged to achieve as much as possible. One method was to offer prizes. In the 1850s in Bruton National School it was customary to give some prizes "to the most deserving scholars." Such actions were well-received by pupils and parents as "the award of prizes was accompanied with cheers and congratulations which must have been as encouraging to the children as it was gratifying to the master and mistress." Once the Revised Code was in operation that could have a bearing, such as in August 1878 when the Vicar presented six children "with handsomely illuminated Certificates for their good Conduct and Success in the recent Examination."

By the 1880s the reasons for awarding prizes had become more extensive. By that time the "ladies of the town" were awarding prizes "for the best specimens of needle work and knitting prepared for the Government examination", and also for good conduct and attendance. In 1888 prizes were awarded to over sixty different children, including fifteen for needlework, seventeen for knitting, sixteen for good conduct and attendance and Walter Thomas was given a prize "for best behaviour in school." Infants received eleven prizes and eleven certificates of proficiency were awarded. At the end of the proceedings each child was given an orange. For many years in the late nineteenth and early twentieth centuries at their annual flower show the Foresters awarded three prizes for pieces of needlework "worked in school by children on the books of Bruton National School."

As attendance was so important it merited special attention and therefore in 1883 some fifty children were rewarded for their attendance. By that stage there was a financial incentive as each child who made 400 or more attendances received back a quarter of the School Pence that he or she had paid. Those who made over 350 and under 400 attendances were given one fifth of their contributions. In October 1904 seventeen boys and twenty-eight girls were rewarded for over 400 attendances each. In 1906 Hayter noted that 103 pupils qualified for an attendance prize and that thirty-four received one, of whom twenty had not missed an attendance. The following year seven boys and eleven girls recorded full attendance and so received a prize. There were occasionally new prizes, for example, in October 1908 Mr Ernest Jardine, who in 1910 was elected the Unionist MP for East Somerset, offered two prizes of 10s 6d each, one for a boy and one for a girl, "for general good work, good fellowship, and influence for good." By 1910 at the Foresters' Flower Show the Headmaster was offering an extra prize to boys for the "best drawing of plant or flower in water colour or crayon." (66)

The second method of rewarding the children was generally referred to under the broad heading of "Treats". The main one of these was the Annual Treat which in some years in the nineteenth century was staged together with the Church of England Sunday School. In August 1855 some 300 children assembled in the Schoolroom and then marched through the town to the Abbey Field "where they were plentifully regaled with cake and tea." There was usually a band in attendance, such as the Shepton Mallet Union Brass Band in 1863, the Frome Band in 1865 and Bruton's Drum and Fife Band in 1869. After the tea there were games and activities until about 9pm: in 1865 cricket, football and jumping were included with prizes awarded for running and jumping in sacks. The various bands could be relied upon to provide music for dancing. In July 1886 Hayter felt that, "a most enjoyable afternoon & Evening was spent by all," and in July 1885, "the treat was a perfect success." There was an added attraction in August 1860 when after the tea and cakes which "were despatched with marvellous swiftness", and various games, "two large balloons were let off from the lawn of the Vicarage, the children cheering vociferously." (67)

The Annual Treat did create a problem for Hayter if the weather proved unreliable and consequently the children had their tea in the Schoolroom. On 16th September 1870 he recorded that that had happened the day before and as a result he was unable to start the school until 9.30. "It took over an hour to replace desks, forms etc. Holiday given in the afternoon that Room might be washed," - a good week for the children: their Annual Treat and the School closed for two half days!

There was also a range of ad hoc treats for the children. Some of these were organised under the general auspices of the School or those associated with it. On 14th October 1880, for example, the Managers of the School arranged for about 190 children to visit after school Wombell's Menagerie. On the afternoon of Friday 16th April 1886 several "gentlemen and ladies of the Town" made arrangements for the children to attend a performance of a visiting Circus. In the evening when the School broke up for Christmas in 1888 the children were treated to a series of Dissolving Views and as they left each child received an orange. A more unusual treat came on 3rd August 1911 when an aeroplane landed nearby, "Allowed children a few minutes to go to a field to see an aeroplane."

The children were also beneficiaries of celebrations within the community as a whole. National events, especially those associated with the royal family, were always celebrated. When the Prince of Wales married in March 1863 there was a day of festivities which included "rural sports" on the Abbey Field in the afternoon along with football and a jingling match which caused much amusement: "some of our friends say they laughed until they were ill." One of the two men who played with "untiring energy" was Headmaster Byles. After the games the school children assembled in the National Schoolroom "where they had a plentiful supply of tea and cake, but the room was so densely crowded, that it was almost a wonder they could find a way to their mouths." After the tea there was a Magic Lantern Show.

There were also significant celebrations in the town at the time of Queen Victoria's Golden Jubilee in 1887. In preparation for the day Hayter and the Vicar, Rev. Ridley, had constructed an arch from the National School over the road to the Vicarage, complete with the words, "God save Victoria, for 50 years our Queen." During the afternoon there were various entertainments such as steam roundabouts, shooting galleries and a Punch and Judy Show. At 4.30 some 600 children marched onto the Abbey Field headed by the Drum and fife Band with all the boys waving flags. They were then provided with a tea in a large marquee and each child was given a Jubilee Mug.

Local events were likewise celebrated by the whole community and the children treated. One such celebration was the opening of the railway in September 1856 when there was a huge procession through the town to the Abbey Field which included the children from the National and all the Sunday Schools. Some 450 children consumed that number of large buns and tea before which they had sung Grace:

> "Be present at our table, Lord,
> Be here and everywhere adored,
> These mercies bless, and grant that we
> May feast in Paradise with Thee."

The food was followed by "Old English Sports" which included hurdle jumping, racing, climbing the pole for a hat and ribbons, along with dancing.

Some events were even more local and specific. In May 1870, for example, T.O. Bennett, junior, Secretary to the Managers of the School, married a daughter of J.R. White of Coombe Hill, himself one of the Managers. Together they provided a tea for local inhabitants, and especially the children of the various schools in the town, and it was estimated that in the end nearly 1,600 people enjoyed that tea in a marquee in a field alongside Coombe Hill. In January 1910, for the second year as a result of a public subscription, a Children's Tea and Entertainment was arranged for about 250 children attending the National and Infant School. Because of the numbers involved it was held in the Wesleyan Schoolroom. One again there were games and a Punch and Judy Show. Before they left each child was given toys, mince pies and oranges by Santa Claus. (68)

A third type of reward was available to a very small number of young people and that was the prospect of social advancement. The first step was to be selected as a monitor as it gave some responsibility, experience of limited teaching and controlling children and usually extra lessons for themselves. Those who were successful as monitors had the possibility from 1846 of becoming a pupil-teacher. This position marked real advancement as it usually included formal extra tuition, study in their own time, yet more teaching experience and for the successful access to a Training College. It was a route for social advancement for a bright working-class boy or girl. An added benefit was that there were no training fees to be paid which was a great benefit to children from a poor background. A number of examples may be found in Bruton National School: J. Tanner started in the School as a monitor late in 1872 and within two years was a pupil-teacher. In his Report in 1876 the H.M.I. recorded that, "JM Tanner has passed fairly & is now qualified." Miss A. Randall was already a pupil teacher in Dorset when she moved to Bruton in June 1883 as an Assistant Teacher and within a year became a fully qualified teacher in the Infant School. Former pupil Hubert Bending was appointed a Pupil Teacher in September 1905, attended a local pupil teacher centre at Sexey's Trade School and was then accepted at St Mark's Training College.

Another reward for a very small number of boys for all their effort and progress at elementary school was election at approximately eleven years of age to Sexey's Hospital Blue School. Once there they continued their education for another three years before being apprenticed to a trade. Those who completed the process became skilled craftsmen in their own right. In the late 1860s at least three boys a year came from the National School, such as Frank Vigar, Henry Gapper and Henry Rawlings in 1867 and Joseph Day, Richard Cox, William Hobbs and Frank Young in 1869. (69) This trend continued under the Headmastership of Hayter, although in 1873 there were just two, Walter White and George White. Hayter was not always impressed with the Visitors' selection as in 1875 while he felt that James Cox of Standard V was "a very regular & careful boy with his Schoolwork", the other three John James and T. Flower both of Standard III and C. White of Standard II, "were exceedingly irregular, unpunctual & idle."

When the Visitors changed the nature of their operation in 1877, Hayter was able to record on 31st October, "9 girls in Standard III & upwards who were elected by the Trustees of Hugh Sexey's Hospital to enter the New Industrial School for girls, went into Residence today." Although such elections continued for over thirty years, Hayter gave few details, although he did note on 11th October 1907 that Olive Longman was elected.

The opening of Sexey's Trade School in 1891 was yet another opportunity for a very small number of boys. On 18th September 1891 Edmund Green of Standard V gained an open scholarship for three years there and four days later John Steeds also of Standard V was awarded a scholarship valued at £10 a year for three years. This particular scholarship, funded by the East Somerset Agricultural Society, was open to the sons of farmers and tradesmen of Bruton and the surrounding parishes - his father was the landlord of the Old Bull Inn in Patwell Street. On 18th November 1895 Steeds returned to the National School as a probationer and later in his career became the Headmaster of Cranleigh Elementary School and then Newdigate Elementary School. (70) On 10th February 1896 Francis Plenty returned to the School having been a pupil there and then a County Scholar at Sexey's School for three years between 1892 and 1895. He remained until October 1898. The pattern continued into the twentieth century, as, for example, in 1910 both Fred Martin and Stanley White gained free scholarships there. The former became an H.M. Inspector of Taxes and the latter made a career for himself in the Royal Navy.

h) The New Infant School.

Up until the 1860s far less attention was paid to infants in schools but as they were in the same rooms a principal objective seemed to have been to try and ensure that they did not unduly disturb the work and concentration of the older children. In the 1860s their education was taken more seriously and with Forster's Education Act in 1870 infant departments became a permanent part of elementary schools, especially as the Code of Regulation of 1871 created an infant stage below Standard I for the five to seven age range. This measure, probably more than any other, led to the final disappearance of Dame Schools. An additional Code in 1885 required infants to be suitably instructed for their age and this was amended four years later "to their age and capacity." Such changes were reflected in the comments which the H.M.I.s made as result of their inspections so that in 1874, for example, the

Report on Bruton National School noted, "The progress made by the Infants is not satisfactory", and the following year, "The infants are too crowded and interfere with the instruction of the elder Children."

By the end of 1871, however, the Managers had been made aware that more accommodation was required. A Report on 22nd December 1871 by an Inspector based upon the Census Returns of that year indicated that school accommodation was needed for 272 children, a figure which was soon increased to 300. The existing School was judged to be able to accommodate 170 pupils so 130 more places were required. The Managers decided that a separate Infants' School was the way forward and by early 1873 had agreed upon a site in the High Street. At this point there appeared to have been a breakdown in communications with the central body, possibly as a result of finance not being available or more likely the usual resentment at what was perceived to be external interference, an attitude found so many times in Bruton when dealing with other national agencies such as relating to the Poor Law, Public Health and Water Supply.

On 10th March 1873 the Managers had placed an advertisement in local newspapers requesting tenders "for converting the old Town-hall and premises situate in the High Street, into an Infant schoolroom and Teachers' Residence." Less than a month later on 1st April the Secretary of the Education Department wrote to the Managers with details of the increased numbers. Unfortunately there was an error in the letter with the shortage of places being given as just 30 and not 130. The letter was clearly not well received as it was to be six months before T.O. Bennett replied to the Department on 10th October, pointing out their error and stating, "It will be evident to you that we must be clearly informed before we can take any measures to provide for the deficiency." The Education Department considered that the Managers were procrastinating but it was to be another ten months later on 12th August 1874 that they demanded that the matter be resolved within six months or they would impose a School Board on the town under the terms of Foster's Act 1870 and order the construction of a new Board School. (71)

That threat had the desired effect as in October a committee was formed to resolve the issue of the accommodation and a sub-committee established in February 1875 to consider the most appropriate means of raising the necessary money. As most of the large ratepayers were opposed to a Board School they agreed to pay a voluntary contribution of 1s in the £ and continue to finance an Infants' School and the salary of a Mistress through subscriptions. After the necessary conversion work the new Infants' School was formally opened by an H.M.I. on 24th July 1876. When the term began on 18th September Hayter recorded, "The infants were this morning drafted off to the new School Room." There had apparently been further delay caused by the weather as T.O. Bennett stated, "The wet Spring made earlier occupation dangerous." Unfortunately he did not elaborate but as later there were to be drainage problems those may have had a bearing. He did however express the disappointment of the Managers that as the Inspector had made such favourable comments, "we rather expected a letter of Congratulation on the way in which the additional Accommodation had been applied. We have had trouble enough about it." (72)

The converted premises were formally handed over to the Managers by the Visitors of Sexey's Hospital who owned the site by an Indenture dated 12th September 1876.

"All that site of the old Town Hall situate on the North side of the High St in Bruton aforsd with the Playground adjoining containing by admeasurement 0 ac[res] 20 p[erches] ....
to be applied as a site for a School for the instruction and Education of the poor Children of the said Parish & for the residence of the Schoolmaster or Schoolmistress of the said School."

The building had a frontage on the High Street which measured fifty feet and the site stretched back north one hundred feet towards Backway, then called Lower Backway. (73) The Infants now had one large room alongside the road 39 feet 7 inches long by 27 feet wide and 15 feet 8 inches high, with the residential accommodation on the western side of it. These measurements meant that each child, based upon average attendance, had fourteen square feet of space, and eleven square feet based on maximum attendance. The playground of some 214 square yards with the Offices was to the north behind the buildings. It was during these alterations that the alleyway (now called Warren's Close) linking the High Street and Backway was created.

The Infant Schoolroom on the north side of the High Street, converted from the old Market Hall which had been built in 1684. The photograph shows the south-facing window and the original entrance which is now blocked up. The Masonic symbol was inserted in the twentieth century after its use changed when the children were transferred to the new elementary school in Higher Backway.

Once the Infants were in a separate building the teaching at their level became much more focused with appropriate teachers so that the various annual reports over the next forty years were generally favourable. The Diocesan Inspector in 1888, for example, felt that there was "an efficiency observable throughout." Two years later an H.M.I. found, "The order is very good and the instruction has been successful." In 1899 the Report stated that, "The various classes have been taught with care and skill, and the order is excellent." The following year the Diocesan Inspector was likewise satisfied, "The little ones did well, and many of them said their repetition very nicely. They seemed to be in very good order."

There were of course occasional concerns depending on exactly what the Inspectors saw and their own inclinations. In September 1891, for example, an H.M.I. noted, "The attainments of the infants' classes do not soar to an ambitious height, but they are sound as far as they go." Two years later came the comment, "The upper classes are well taught, but the lower ones need more attention. The staff seem hardly strong enough." (74) Much of the improvement thereafter may be attributed to the quality of the Mistress appointed: such as from 1894 widow Mrs Georgina Stonelake who was still in post in 1902. When Chancellor became the Head teacher his wife assumed the role of Mistress of the Infant School.

A draft of Inspector Millard's Report in July 1913 gave a detailed assessment of the Infants' curriculum and a very favourable impression of their School just before the First World War.

"The Schemes of instruction are admirably planned, the teachers' methods sound, and the progress of the children highly satisfactory.

A high standard is maintained in Reading, always a strong feature of this school since the present Head Teacher took charge.

Recitation is well said.

Speech training receives careful attention and the children are encouraged to converse freely with their teachers. A little written composition is successfully attempted.

Numerous songs of a good class are sung tunefully and with spirit

Handwriting is good.

The means adopted in the teaching of Number are varied, ingenious and very successful.

The Drawing gives evidence of close observation and is very fairly executed. Much of the work is spoiled by the coarse ribbed texture of the brown paper upon which it is done.

The very large Baby Class is managed with conspicuous success." (75)

The teaching of infants in Bruton National School had certainly made large advances once their new schoolroom was open. From time to time as might be expected Headmaster Hayter had his own views on the standard of what was sent to him from the Infants' School when the children were generally six or seven years old. On 7th September 1894 he commented, "A draft of children rather a large one and most uneven in their work, received from the Infants' School. Some of these children do not know their letters, and are over 8 years of age." On 3rd July 1899 he received a draft of forty-three children of whom two were over eight and eighteen under seven. "The children with about 2 exceptions are fairly intelligent." The number who transferred each year did vary significantly as, for example, in July 1910 Chancellor noted that he admitted twenty-five from the Infant School.

i) Bricks and Mortar.

During the whole of the time under consideration no provision was made for accommodation for any of the teachers except the Headmaster: the expectation was that they would find either a house or lodgings for themselves. On the main site there was no specific space dedicated for the use of these teachers so that they would have to remain either in the main schoolrooms or the smaller classroom. The same was the case in the new Infants' School. At lunchtime it was expected that they would leave the premises and return to their own accommodation for a meal.

Even with the new Infant School in operation the main National School building still suffered from overcrowding. On 7th September 1879 Hayter noted, "School very full. There is not sufficient seating accommodation for the number present." Once education had become compulsory average attendance rose rapidly from 163 in 1882-3 to 222 in 1886-7. In November 1881 he had already bemoaned the fact that with all the desks and forms in use they could only seat 120 children.

As the youngest children had been successfully transferred to another site, consideration started to be given to the removal of some of the older pupils from the Silver Street site by the creation of an "Upper Department" elsewhere in the town. The driving force behind this idea was the Managers' Secretary, T.O. Bennett, who was also the Seward and Land Agent of the Visitors of Sexey's Hospital. On their behalf on 28th January 1882 he reported to the Charity Commissioners that he had inspected sites which "would be suitable for the erection of a Building for an Upper Department of the National Schools." This action may be seen as part of the Visitors' reappraisal of their educational role in Bruton after the closure of their own Boys' School.

Various sites were considered such as Plox House garden between the house and the Grammar School in Silver Street, the gardens on the opposite bank of the river to the Headmaster's house and between the lane to the ford and the northern entrance to Bow Bridge, and the site of the cottages and gardens in Lower Backway immediately to the north of the Infant School. The favoured one, however, was the area immediately to the west of the Infant School. "It consists of Houses, Cottages and gardens and is most advantageously situated in the centre of the High Street.... forming an area of 968 square yards." By this time Bennett had already purchased the whole area on the Visitors' behalf for £450 and pointed out that if it was not used as a school it would be an investment for them. (76) The Managers, however, decided not to proceed, possibly concerned about the cost but also because the Visitors were discussing the possibility of a trade school for boys in the town.

It was to be more than a decade later before any alterations were made to the existing buildings and that was only as the result of pressure from the Education Department. The Managers established a Committee on which local farmer Josiah Jackson served and a series of meetings were held. The result was that late in June 1895 T.O. Bennett sent to the Department Plans and Specifications for an extension of the classroom, new boys' and girls' cloakrooms and a new W.C. for the girls. He added a note that, "the Managers have had considerable difficulty in consequence of the very restricted site which is bounded on three sides by public thoroughfares and on the fourth by the river wall." The Plans were approved and work started almost immediately. When the school resumed on 3rd September, however, the builder was still on site, "The builder met with many difficulties owing to the confined space in which the men had to work." It was not until the end of January 1896 that the final touches were made. The most noticeable change was the extension of the classroom to 18 feet 9 inches by 16 feet 1 inch. It proved to be an expensive operation and to help raise money in January 1896 one of the Managers, R.T.H. Hughes produced a farce, "The Magistrate", by W. Pinero. It attracted a large audience in the Schoolroom where there was standing room only. (77)

Although the National School suffered major problems with ventilation and heating, it was extremely well-built in stone and slate so that there were no references to structural repairs being required prior to 1914. There were odd mishaps such as on 3rd December 1884, "while the school-bell was being rung for afternoon Assembly, it fell from the turret & was smashed." Fortunately no one was underneath at the time.

A much more fertile source of contention centred on the toilets and drains. When the new National School was built the Committee of the Council on Education acknowledged that while the location of the privies beside the classroom wall was not ideal they "cannot be conveniently placed elsewhere." They did feel however that, "They need not be at all unsightly or inconvenient where they are." By 1859 an H.M.I. was recommending that a tank should collect rain water from the roof and flush the pans. It is now perhaps difficult to imagine what it was like for the children in this school to have had to go outside in all weathers, pouring rain and freezing conditions to use these facilities, ones which would have given off a terrible stench especially in times of hot weather. After the new elementary, later primary, school was built in Higher Backway, even in the late 1950s the toilets were at the far end of the playground with the boys' urinal trough open to all weathers. At least by then the cubicles were enclosed.

It was not until 1886 that a defect was found in the brick drains, the common construction method in the earlier part of the century, so they were all dug up in the girls' yard and replaced with a glazed pipe. Beyond that there was practically no mention of the toilets in the Log Book before the twentieth century when the Board of Education became much more involved. Elsewhere in Somerset in village schools ditches were used, cesspits and occasionally a septic tank. In many of these schools H.M.I.s frequently drew attention to the state of the offices: the need to be cleansed, emptied more often, the contents mixed with ash, leaking roofs repaired, worm-eaten seats replaced and cubicle doors added. It is unlikely that this school escaped some of these problems. (78)

The second half of the nineteenth century witnessed significant progress in the understanding of the causes of a range of illnesses and diseases as well as developments in attitudes towards public health. It has to be said, however, that Bruton was not in the vanguard of improvements in either public health or a clean water supply. (79) The result of these changes in attitude at national level towards many of these issues meant that the Managers of the School came under considerable pressure to undertake improvements in the years before the First World War.

In his Report in 1909 Inspector Millard, while approving of the instillation of a new lavatory basin, noticed that, "there appear to be leakages in the joints between the pans and soil pipes." Why no-one else was aware of this problem was not explained. The main criticism was the cramped space in the offices and the proximity to a classroom window. An internal memo in the Department in June 1909 declared, "This arrangement is not one that can be allowed to continue indefinitely", and recommended that the Managers purchase the land immediately across the river from the Headmaster's house and re-locate the offices there, the pupils having to go over Bow Bridge to reach them. This suggestion, when it was communicated to them, produced a furious response from the Managers in October as they considered, "that the importance of this question of the offices is much exaggerated" and that anyway the land in question was not for sale. Once again it was clear that the Managers were not going to accept what they considered to be interference in the way in which they ran their School. Two years later they were re-iterating the same points, this time supported by Henry Hobhouse, "The offices are well-ventilated and flushed, and kept in good order." After a further inspection on 3rd July 1911 the Board decided that no immediate action was required. (80)

Another area of the School which attracted significant criticism in the early twentieth century was the size of the Playground. With the increasing concern about the lack of fitness in the population as a whole much more emphasis was placed upon Drill and other physical activities. The playground of the National School was formed from the site of half of the old Poor House which had been demolished and its garden, stretching from Silver Street to the River Brue. No barrier was ever erected alongside Silver Street so there was always the danger to the children from passing horses, carriages, farm wagons and later motor vehicles. During their breaks the children must have spilled onto the road as on 16th December 1912 Chancellor gave an order to them "not to play on the road during playtime." There was also the public thoroughfare passing alongside the western side of the playground to give access to Bow Bridge.

In 1902 the playground was claimed to consist of 420 square yards, but that measurement may have included any pavement beside the road and the path to Bow Bridge as in 1911 it was measured at sixty-one feet by fifty-two feet, which equated to 352 square yards. The Board came to the conclusion that it was insufficient for the number of pupils and so suggested the site across the river. (81)

This perceived interference provoked a detailed critical response from the Managers. First they pointed out that they had been advised, "that there is no obligation thrown upon them to provide playgrounds." Secondly they stated that the owners of the gardens in question were not prepared to sell them. Two years later they were still arguing their case but this time stressing that their existing playground was perfectly adequate for purposes such as Drill. They claimed that play areas were not essential in rural parishes as there were other open spaces available for the children, most notably some 4,000 acres of land around Bruton which was mainly pasture. Once again the Board decided not to press the matter further. (82)

From 1876 of course the Managers had to maintain the new Infants' School as well as their original school buildings. Before long it became clear that there was a significant problem with the drains of this School, possibly as a result of the fact that they had not been altered or extended to any great degree when the building was converted from the old Town Hall. "The drainage at the Infant School has for some time been in a very defective condition, and several times during the heavy rains, the drains have been choked causing the water to run into the school-room. This, of course, is dangerous to the children's health." The Managers decided therefore to "renovate the drains." To help finance this project a Grand Fete was held on the Abbey Field on 1st August 1889, Hayter serving as the Secretary. Unfortunately the extent of the alterations and their success was not recorded.

As the issue of the drains was decided by the Managers there was no problem but when it came to dealing with the central authority the same pattern emerged in relation to the Infant School as for the main site, that is until the twentieth century there were few if any complaints from their inspectors about the building but from 1909 the criticism started and it elicited the same, often hostile, response from the Managers.

In his Report in January 1909 Inspector Millard considered that the gallery should be removed and "the substitution of some modern desks in its place." That suggestion did not seem to have been a particular issue as it was not mentioned again. A second recommendation was that as all the children were in one large room, "A classroom for 'Babies' is desirable" and he suggested a moveable glass partition which could be placed against the chimney breast on the south side of the room. In 1911 the Managers were "prepared to admit that a Partition would be desirable" but it would be expensive and they already had debts which would not be paid off until 1913. They were therefore considering moveable partitions and "have already applied to the County Council to allow them to experiment with these Partitions." This action seemed to have been successful as in his Report in July 1913 Inspector Millard commented, "The partition is a great boon: it allows the youngest children to indulge in activities appropriate to their age without disturbing the lessons of the older children."

In 1909 Inspector Millard drew attention to the fact that the heating of the large room was inadequate. The Managers in 1911 did not agree as they stated that the room was heated by two large open fire grates, which they claimed the teachers preferred and that there had been no complaint until 1909. To ensure that their case was sound they did decide to monitor the room temperature during the following winter. It must have been satisfactory as there was no further action before 1914.

The issue which appeared to have irritated the Managers the most centred around the ventilation in the Infants' Schoolroom. From 1909 the Board was informing them that it needed to be improved and that hopper windows should be installed. The Managers were not impressed and in 1911 pointed out that the room had two large windows, one in the north wall and the other in the south wall, which provided natural light for the room and that each window was ten feet square, and that each contained an opening area and that a hopper window had already been installed in the north window. It gave they believed, "a thoroughly good cross ventilation from Window to Window, high above the Children's heads." They also reminded the Board that there were two doors, one in the north wall and the other in the south one, as well as two ventilators in the ceiling. "The Managers consider therefore that this complaint is absolutely ill-founded." Once again by 1914 nothing else was done. (83)

The lack of action by the Managers was prompted by a number of motives. In the first place they often believed that the criticisms which were being made were unwarranted. From their perspective their school buildings were fit for purpose, although it should be borne in mind that few of the Managers actually had their own children educated there. In 1911 they had no hesitation in claiming that it appeared to them, "that the Board wish to condemn every Building, unless it is built and constantly reconstructed in accordance with ever changing modern notions." Secondly, while the Managers had a deep commitment to Bruton National School, it was on their terms and viewed from their perspectives. While some of them gave their services freely for many years they had their own understanding of what education was suitable for the children of the poor in a rural area and how they should be cared for. They tended therefore to judge that the facilities which they provided were perfectly adequate for that purpose and took extreme exception when the central board suggested otherwise: "The complaints made by the Board seem to imply that the Managers are indifferent to the health of their children, and they very much resent such an imputation." (84)

Thirdly, money was always a significant concern. So much of what was spent had to be raised by public subscription or various fund-raising activities, especially in the early days of the School. As Board Schools after 1870 were financed from the local rates they tended to have a higher per capita figure than the schools of the religious groups. That situation had profound implications for what was available to be spent.

Finally, as a local market town Bruton had a long tradition of managing its own affairs. Time and again as centralization increased in the Victorian era the principal inhabitants of the town, who were also the largest ratepayers, expressed their opposition and continued as far as possible to run their own affairs as they had always done. It was almost a war of attrition as the Managers seemed to wish to wear down the central Board. In this desire they had some success as Inspector Tillard added a note to one Report on heating and ventilation, "I am heartily sick of this Case."

Such a policy, however, had its dangers. As early as 1909 the Managers were worried that the Board was unlikely to continue recognition of their School "for any considerable length of time" if they did not undertake the improvements which were being indicated. The Managers were clearly no fools and they did just enough as in July 1911 an internal memo to Inspector Tillard recommended that as some developments had occurred and as the cramped site of the main School, along with the cost, meant that any other improvements would be extremely difficult to implement, the threat of closure should be removed. "After reviewing carefully all the circumstances of the School and the representations of the Managers the Board do not feel that they need require the immediate erection of a new School upon another site, but they feel that this is the solution which the Managers should keep in mind." (85). It was to be a solution which the latter would keep very much at the back of their minds for another twenty years.

j) It All Costs Money.

The establishment and financing of a Church of England day school in 1840 and its maintenance thereafter for the whole of the period under consideration, was a remarkable achievement. As the decades passed central government in various guises, and then the new local government, started and increased their contributions

199

but a significant burden fell on the local ratepayers and inhabitants of Bruton. It was a clear example that the philanthropy which had operated in the town for centuries was still an active and flourishing feature of the community's life.

The conversion of part of the old Poor House into rooms for the Church of England Sunday School which then was also used as the first Infant Day School in 1840 was financed almost exclusively by voluntary subscriptions. Such subscriptions continued through the 1840s reaching £53 6s 8d in 1850. The following year the Vicar, Rev. James White, anticipated that they would remain at around £50 a year and he was reasonably accurate as in 1852 for example they amounted to £48 13s 0d. At that stage another important source of income was the School Pence paid by the pupils, £29 0d 9d in 1850 and £28 11s 5d in 1852. Rev. White expected that these payments would remain around £30 per annum. (86)

By the time that the new National School was built in 1851 the Committee of the Council on Education was prepared to make a contribution of £171 15s 0d but as Table 9 shows most of the money was still derived from private sources, a pattern which was repeated in many schools across Somerset. (87)

From 1833 the Government provided grants for the schools of the two religious societies which by 1851 had reached some £837,000. Bruton National School benefitted from a small share of this grant, in 1854, for example, it amounted to £13 6s 8d but by 1856 had risen to £34 3s 0d. By the 1880s it was substantially larger, reaching a peak of £244 4s 0d in 1890-1. It became a significant item in the annual Accounts as in many years it represented about half of the total income of the School, for example, in 1891-2 the Grant was £206 19s 0d out of a total income of £410 4s 10d. It assumed an even greater importance in the twentieth century, for example, in 1902 the total amount received from grants amounted to £453 16s 6d when the expenditure on all aspects of the School reached £603 8s 8d. (88)

Table 9. Building Account 1851.

Source of finance	£	s	d
To private Subscriptions of £5, or upwards	289	0	0
of £1, and under £5	14	17	0
under £1	1	12	6
To Grants from Charitable Societies vizt -			
National Society	50	0	0
The Trustees of Bruton Hospital	25	0	0
Grant from the Chumley Society	30	0	0
To Collections from Sermons	36	16	2
To Money received from any other Sources	168	5	2
Total Amount already received	615	10	10
To Amount of Grant to be received from Committee of Council on Education	171	15	0
Total	787	5	10

The introduction of the Revised Code in 1862 and its subsequent many amendments did introduce an element of uncertainty into the finances of schools because so much depended not only on the performance of the children when examined but also their very attendance. It is interesting, however, that this was not an issue which Hayter commented upon in his Log Books.

Even with the various grants the philanthropic element remained strong in Bruton. Voluntary contributions continued to be made and reached £88 16s 0d in 1892-3, which in fact equated to 7s 6d for each child based upon average attendance. Through the decades a huge effort was made to raise money through a range of activities. One method was special collections in the parish church such as during the two services which were held when the School was opened in 1852, with a total of £36 16s 2d collected. In September 1863 "An eloquent and impressive Sermon was preached" on behalf of School funds which raised some £6. In March 1856 Rev. George Davies of Ditcheat, a noted local lecturer at the time, gave a lecture entitled, "Allegory and Faith" which concentrated on John Bunyan's 'Pilgrim's Progress'. The lecture was announced to be for the benefit of the National School, "and at the appointed hour a numerous company were assembled to testify as well their sympathy for that excellent Institution, as their respect for the talented lecturer." (89)

Other perhaps rather more enjoyable events for a wide cross-section of the town's inhabitants also took place to raise money. Shortly after the new Schoolroom was opened a two-day bazaar was held in it for that purpose; in May 1860 there was a concert of amateurs occurred there which filled the whole schoolroom and included a number of songs which were "well-received and rapturously encored", including those by the then Headmaster Daniel Byles. Another amateur concert was staged in January 1865 as, "The school funds are considerably in arrears", and when an "unusually large attendance of the clergymen and gentry of Bruton and the adjoining parishes showed how willing they were to co-operate in such a good cause." During this concert the former organist of the church, W.P. Williams, gave a series of solos on his harp. On a larger scale "a grand fete" was staged on the Abbey Field in August 1889 which included a band, open-air concert, a public tea and a variety of other entertainments, all under the management of the Fete Secretary, Headmaster E.R. Hayter. (90)

From time to time there were donations, for example, in 1846 a grant of £15 was received from the Factory Office and then another one from the same source in March 1852 of £10 "to the general Funds of the Bruton National School and request that in the distribution thereof due regard may be had to the particular want of the scholars who are employed in the Bruton Silk Factories." Regular subscriptions could also be started such as one from the Visitors of Sexey's Hospital for £15 15s 0d to the National School and £10 10s 0d to the new Infant School, both of which were paid for the first time in 1874-5. Thereafter the subscription was steadily increased until by 1892 the joint subscription had risen to £52 10s 0d but on 10th September of that year the Visitors had to inform the Managers that as a result of the agricultural depression and the fact that they had been forced to reduce their rents, the subscription was to be halved. (91)

After the introduction of the Board Schools in 1870, even though the National Schools received a larger grant, an increasing disparity developed between the two systems: the religious schools were often hard pressed for cash whereas the former had the vast resources of the rates upon which they could call. By 1880 the average cost nationally for each child attending a National School was £1 14s 10¼d whereas the Board Schools were spending £2 1s 11¾d on each child, that is a difference of 7s 1½d per pupil. By 1890 as rural areas felt the effects of the agricultural depression the gap widened to 9s and by 1900 to some 11s 6d. Such a situation had the effect that the better resourced Board Schools were able to offer superior facilities and often higher salaries which attracted the best teachers.

In the late nineteenth and early twentieth centuries there were clearly significant financial problems in maintaining Bruton

National School. On 18th July 1901 Josiah Jackson recorded that he and others agreed, "that some more money should be taken up on the Infants School & House to help carry on the National school", and he himself subscribed £1 10s 0d. By 20th September the situation was judged to be so serious that he attended a Managers' Meeting to consider "the advisability of having a school Board." That idea was once again rejected and on 23rd December Jackson agreed with eleven others to offer "a guarantee up to £300 to carry on the School for another year." This decision seems to have been sufficient and the crisis passed, just before the new local education authorities came into force. (92)

1901 was not the first time that the concept of School Board had been discussed and dismissed in Bruton. The Board Schools which were created in 1870 were generally in areas where there were no schools or an inadequate number or where the H.M.I.s found existing schools to be unsatisfactory. This may well have been the case in Wincanton, for example, as a new Board School was established there and the existing National and British Schools closed. Bruton National School had no difficulty satisfying an H.M.I. and there was a pronounced determination to maintain the existing school for when a Vestry Meeting was called on 24th November 1870 to consider the future of elementary education in the town, "The meeting was unanimous in rejecting all thought of a school board which they considered would do no more for education although it would entail more expense. A subscription for maintaining the school under the present system was then opened, and liberally responded to." This Meeting was reported to be "one of the largest that had been held for years."

Just over four years later when the Managers were being threatened with a School Board if they did not stop delaying the construction of a new Infant School another meeting "found that the feeling of the inhabitants generally was against a School Board." The principal ratepayers agreed to a voluntary rate of 1s in the £1 in the pound for the necessary work. Certainly such a decision was far from unanimous and after ratepayer William Bord of Wyke Champflower had written an open letter detailing the immediate and on-going costs likely to be involved, several other ratepayers, such as George Amor also of Wyke, withdrew their support for the proposed building.

The discussion at that time elicited a more emotional response from G. Mitchell who signed himself as 'One from the Plough'. He argued that not only should Bruton have a Board School but that it should take over all the educational charities in the town. "There was a time when voluntaryism was *the* thing for Dissenters; but time changes. True Liberalism can only be identified with Government education - free, secular, and compulsory, as far as possible. Depend upon it, Sir, the Dissenters and working men will no longer be bamboozled and tom-fooled by the sham-voluntary Church-Catechism party, but will cry out with me 'Hurrah for the School-Board!'"

Undoubtedly one of the principal opponents of School Boards and a driving force behind the retention of the National Schools was T.O. Bennett, a man who was involved with and influential in virtually every organisation in the town. During the course of one of his speeches in May 1895 he declared, "he would say he always should endeavour to have a National School in Bruton and he hoped they would have one as long as he lived. He should do his utmost to prevent a school board in the town being of opinion that the existing schools were quite as efficient and certainly more economical than a school board would be. (Applause)" (93)

How far the absence of a Board School created resentment or discontent within the Bruton community is difficult to determine as virtually no documentary evidence has survived. Non-Conformity in the form of both Congregationalism and Methodism was strong in the town. There would seem to have been considerable concord and cooperation between the groups and in the 1890s and early twentieth centuries at least one staunch Non-Conformist, Josiah Jackson, served as a Manager.

The Managers of the National School had no control over the last change to the financial arrangements before 1914 and that was as the result of Balfour's Education Act 1902. By the end of the nineteenth century at national level attitudes to elementary education and state involvement were changing. Such a situation led to the formation of a Board of Education in 1899 and then by this Act in 1902 County Councils, which themselves were just over a decade old, were designated the local education authorities. These new local authorities were required to maintain existing voluntary schools which included the payment of teachers. In return the Managers of these schools had to provide the school premises free of charge. It gave real security to denominational schools in return for some degree of public control. Somerset County Council designated 1st July 1903 as the day when they assumed their responsibilities with the County Treasurer paying teachers' salaries. A significant burden had been lifted from the Managers.

k) The School as a Community resource.

In the mid-nineteenth century the number and range of large indoor spaces in which to stage gatherings in Bruton was limited: the Assembly Rooms in Coombe Street were well-used as were some large rooms in local inns. The new National School became an important centre for a variety of activities, frequently unconnected with education. When John Skinner was composing his history of Bruton in poetic form in 1861, while taking some liberties with the size of the building he did give an indication of its use:

> "The National School is a building complete,
> In length forty-eight, and height twenty-seven feet;
> And serves - when the shadows of evening fall -
> For Lectures, or Concerts, or Soirees, a Hall."

One of the most significant uses was as a venue for local concerts, both vocal and instrumental. Most of these concerts were organised and performed by local men and women such as one in April 1858 to celebrate the opening of a new organ, attended by "about 180 of the elite of Bruton and its neighbourhood." One newspaper report was not entirely flattering: "Of the vocal music we have little to say - it probably was as good as amateur performances are in general - but the instrumental music no one could fail to be delighted." Many of the concerts were designed to raise money, such as one in May 1860 by the Bruton Glee and Madrigal Union in aid of the funds of the National School itself. In May 1881 a concert was staged on behalf of the funds of the Working-Men's Club, "The programme was an unusually good one (Haydn's trio in G). It is to be hoped that we shall hear more of such music as this, as well as the so-called popular pieces." In November 1887 the Bruton Philharmonic Society organised a concert which included children from the National School and in which Hayter played the violin-cello in a trio. The Bruton Choral Society held their annual concerts there and in March 1899 were ambitious enough to perform Handel's 'Messiah', "in an admirable manner."

There were occasional concerts by visiting performers such as the Cremona Musical Union in November 1864 which attracted considerable comment as it consisted of eight brothers and sisters. Two of the female members between them played the violin, flute, piccolo and side-drums which led to the observation about "the novelty of seeing lady performers on such instruments." In January 1886 Madame R. Rose RAM, assisted by Misses Mabel and Belle Harcourt, "gave one of her drawing room concerts." They were supported by "some local amateurs." (94)

The Schoolroom was also used for a range of other entertainments, as examples from the mid-1860s indicated. In September 1865 Mr Trevori gave a "Ventriloquial Entertainment" which included a well-received rendition of pieces on the concertina. Other parts of his performance met with some criticism: "We cannot help thinking his entertainment would be greatly improved by introducing something new in the ventriloquial department." The following year local gentlemen, "who take the most active part in all schemes for benevolent purposes", staged some amateur dramatics to crowded rooms to help pay off a debt on the Reading Room. It included the trial scene from the 'Merchant of Venice' by William Shakespeare and the farce of 'Box and Cox'. In January 1867 "an entertainment of electrical and optical illusions" was presented by J.A. Rudge of Bath on two successive evenings. The entertainments were regarded as "the best we have witnessed for a long time." (95) Similar reports may be found in local newspapers for the following decades.

The Schoolrooms were even regarded as sufficiently large to stage Balls. Throughout the 1860s, for example, the annual Ball of the 23rd Somerset Rifle Corps was held there, attended by up to ninety local inhabitants. Dancing usually started at 9pm and finished about 5am. (96).

On a more educational theme it was common for the Schoolroom to be used for lectures. In 1856, for example, J.R. White of Coombe Hill delivered a lecture there on "Atmospheric Air." In February and March of the same year Rev. George Davis of Ditcheat gave at least three lectures on topics such as "Allegory and Faith", and one entitled "Antiquity of the Earth", which suggested that the Earth with its various geological strata was "probably more than one hundred thousand years old." There was also a lecture by William Finch of Bruton, "On projectiles illustrative of the firearms used in the present war." [Crimean War] Finch had a considerable interest in gunpowder and was usually deeply involved in any firework displays in the town: his preparations for one of these some three months later led to an explosion which damaged his left hand. In May 1867 Mr Hall delivered a lecture with illustrations on the "Travels of Captains Speke and Grant in Central, South and Eastern Africa." In October 1870 Mr Baker gave a lecture with dissolving views, "some of them were very good." (97)

For educational purposes a series of Penny Readings was started in the Schoolroom in December 1865 on a fortnightly basis and included, 'Notes of an army Chaplain in the Crimea' and 'The Cornish Grants', which was "specially read for the Amusement of Juveniles." Each reading was interspersed with songs and music so that in any evening there could be six separate readings and at least four musical items. "We sincerely hope that the young men and labouring classes of Bruton will show their appreciation of these efforts for combining amusement with instruction, by attending in still larger numbers at the next meeting." The Penny Readings were clearly successful as they were still being staged in the same format in the 1870s and continued into the 1880s when at times "the room was completely Crammed." The Readings were initially delivered by local middle class men, such as members of the clergy, factory owner J.R. White, land agent T.O. Bennett, solicitor William Muller and shopkeeper William Finch. These evenings represented not only an easy way to provide entertainment and to gain knowledge but also to ensure that the required values were transmitted. (98)

The Schoolroom was also used as a venue for teas on various occasions. In March 1863 to celebrate the marriage of the Prince of Wales the school children from all denominations "were supplied with an abundance of cake and tea." In October 1886 there was a public tea there in connection with the harvest festival celebrations when "Tea was laid for about 150, but so large was the company that the tables had to be laid the second time." In 1888 after a service in the Parish Church the Bruton Branch of the Girls' Friendly Society adjourned to the schoolroom for tea. (99)

The Schoolroom became an important location for meetings of all kinds. In August 1857 it was the venue for the nineteenth Annual Meeting of the Somerset Archaeological and Natural History Society. In the 1860s and 1870s the Bruton branch of the British and Foreign Bible Society held their annual meeting there. Occasionally so many men attended a Vestry Meeting that it had to be transferred from the Church to the schoolroom, as happened for example in April 1873 when the whole question of the admittance of the press to such meetings was being considered. Needless to say the decision went against the press. Further Vestry Meetings had to be held in the Schoolroom when a large number of ratepayers attended to review the drainage of the town. As such a scheme was likely to entail considerable expense there was the usual procrastination and various other meetings had to be called.

Gatherings with the potential of large numbers attending were also scheduled there such as a public meeting in February 1863 to discuss how to celebrate the wedding of the Prince of Wales. In 1870 a meeting was held in order to collect subscriptions for the sick and wounded of the armies of France and Prussia at the time of the Franco-Prussian War. Some £6 was donated immediately and arrangements made for a house to house collection. A controversial topic led to a large assembly in March 1882 when there was a motion to close public houses on Sundays. "The room was crammed... but the greater part were on mischief bent" and so in consequence of the singing and whistling most of the speeches could not be heard. The local paper commented that, "Such a noisy meeting has not been held in Bruton for sometime" but a supportive petition was forwarded to the county MPs.

Late in the nineteenth century with the spread of democracy it was the location for political meetings, such as one in January 1889 to support the candidature of Henry Hobhouse MP, as a County Councillor for the Bruton and Castle Cary Division of Somerset. He was duly elected. Involvement in political matters was not always beneficial for the School as on one occasion in November 1885 on Polling Day at least eleven men were involved in breaking the windows of the building. They were subsequently charged with that offence and rioting. Ten of them were fined and all bound over to keep the peace for twelve months. (100)

The opening of the new Infant Schoolroom in the High Street created another large indoor location for community use. Almost immediately it became the meeting place for the Mutual

Improvement Society. Week after week through the winter months the members met there to hear lectures on a wide range of topics such as, for example, in January 1888 on 'Astronomy' by Dr. Coombs of Castle Cary, and 'Ants' by Dr. Still of Bruton. There were debates on various issues, including Capital Punishment. They also invited entertainers, such as Professor Dupres in April 1889 with his conjuring and magic, at the end of which there was a private séance where "The 'Dark Half Hour' was much enjoyed." Members were certainly kept abreast of contemporary developments as in November 1896 when William Knight, Headmaster of Sexey's School, gave a lecture on 'The New Photography of X-Rays' during which he took an X-ray of a hand. In October 1899 Arthur Picton brought along and demonstrated a gramophone, "The instrument was entirely new to the greater portion of the company." After the establishment of parish councils in 1893 the Infant Schoolroom became the location for their regular monthly meetings. The room was also used for concerts, such as one in February 1893 given by a choir of boys and girls from the Princess Alice Orphanage in Birmingham and it raised over £6 for them. (101)

Just occasionally the use of the room caused some controversy as was revealed in a letter to a local newspaper in February 1894. "A short time since the Infant School-room at Bruton was granted for holding a public tea when Blondin was visiting the town. Within the last few days the same room has been refused to the Congregationalists for holding a concert, on the ground that the building was to be used for educational purposes only. A 'Lover of Truth' wishes to ask the vicar and his friends whether they consider a tea in honour of an acrobat's visit to the town greatly conduced to the education of the young people. The only remedy for this kind of unfairness is a School Board for Bruton." No reply is recorded. (102)

l) Bruton Evening Continuation School.

One further use of the National School premises was for teaching in the evenings. In Bruton such classes were originally called an

"Evening School" or "Night School" but by the latter part of the nineteenth century was referred to as "Bruton Evening Continuation School", although Frederick Wood who superintended the School at that stage, did acknowledge in 1899 that some locals still referred to it as the "Night School."

This form of education played an important role in rural areas where the demands of employment, especially in agriculture, and the need of a family for any income, meant that for many children their time in a school was often very short, intermittent or non-existent. Even with compulsory education and then an increase in the school leaving age their time there could be limited. [For details of Evening Classes see Section on 'Other Schools'.]

4

Sexey's Trade School.

a) Introduction.

The establishment of Sexey's Trade School, later Sexey's Boys' School, was the result of a combination of national and local factors. At national level there was an increased demand for the provision of education for the middle and working classes which was greatly stimulated by elementary education becoming compulsory and free. There was an awareness that many existing elementary schools did not have the resources to cope with this change and to offer the appropriate courses. The views of these groups in society were increasingly important as a result of the extension of the franchise in the Reform Acts of 1867 and 1884.

Much more fundamental, however, was the on-going dramatic change in Britain's international industrial and economic position. More and more Britain's dominance was being threatened as between 1870 and 1913 while her industrial output doubled that of the world in the same period quadrupled. In 1913 Britain still managed one seventh of the world's output of manufactured goods but in 1870 it had been one third. Germany and the United States of America were emerging as Britain's main industrial competitors and both of these countries had invested heavily in education. One civil servant, Sadler, who studied the education systems of these two countries expressed the view that the survival of the British Empire would depend on "sea power and school power."

Traditionally the skills required for employment in a particular trade or occupation were obtained largely through the apprenticeship system but that was changing as the nature of the labour force changed. There was a greater demand in the late nineteenth century for more technicians, engineers and accountants as well as clerks in government, industry and commerce. The recognition was developing that knowledge did not necessarily have to come from experience but could be obtained from books and teaching.

While unprepared to invest large sums of money in technical education various British governments did establish Commissions to investigate and report. The Samuelson Commission on Technical Instruction in 1884 came to the conclusion that some kind of technical education would have to be funded from local rates as the Science and Art Department, which had been founded in 1853, was no longer adequate. "Our industrial empire is vigorously attacked all over the world. We find that our most formidable assailants are the best educated people." The beginning of change was achieved in the Technical Instruction Act 1889 which transferred responsibility for this form of education to the newly created County Councils.

Developments thus moved to the local level so local factors became important. Surprisingly Somerset became a leading example for promoting technical education because there was "a small group of progressive gentry making fairly creditable contributions in a conservative agricultural setting." (1) Prominent among these men was Henry Hobhouse who embraced the drive towards technical education with considerable enthusiasm. He was later to write a pamphlet on Technical Education which used Sexey's Trade School as its example. It was through his vision, determination, commitment and pressure that this school was finally built. Reflecting nearly twenty years later on the role of Somerset Education Committee, Professor Sadler commented, "The Somerset Education Committee, at a critical time in English Education, set an admirable example.... It was one of the first, if not the first, to bring out a carefully considered system, which had done much for technical education, and it had encouraged practical education of all kinds." (2)

The most immediate local factor was the recognition by the Visitors of Sexey's Hospital that the days of the apprenticeship system were over and that their revenue should be used for other educational purposes. In this desire they were greatly aided by an Act of 1869 which reshaped the Charity Commission and required it to re-organize existing educational endowments to make more resources available for secondary education. The closure of the boys' school in the Hospital led to an intense debate in Bruton with inhabitants being absolutely determined to ensure that the town benefitted from a new school and that money from the Hospital's revenue was not diverted to elsewhere in the County.

Almost immediately the Visitors published a draft scheme on 23rd April 1877 which was "the subject of much consideration and of protracted negotiations with the Visitors and others interested." The outcome of these deliberations was that a new Scheme was finally sanctioned by the Queen in Council on 15th July 1881. As well as continuing to support their new Girls' School in the Hospital itself and giving financial aid to the Grammar School, it sanctioned £1,000 to be made available to provide buildings for Sexey's Trade School and a further £250 a year to cover salaries, maintenance and scholarships. The controversial part of this Scheme was the proposal to establish Sexey's County School elsewhere in Somerset.

A range of protests followed: a letter was sent from the parish-ioners of Lyncombe and Widcombe pointing out that for two cen-turies boys from there had been educated in the Hospital and then apprenticed. They stressed that the Visitors received some £300 a year in rent from their estate there and that the sale of recently enclosed waste lands had realised an additional £3,000 for the Visitors. They pleaded that they had "no special educational advan-tages of any kind" for a large labouring population. They received a blunt reply from the Secretary of the Charity Commissioners, W. Richmond, on 15th February 1881 to the effect that as it was a new scheme the parishioners had no rights whatsoever and reminded them that they were a parish within the wealthy City of Bath.

A long letter was also written by the curate of Milton Clevedon, Rev. F.W. Weaver, who had been the curate of Bruton and an assistant master at the Grammar School. He stressed the opposition in Bruton and its neighbourhood to the proposed County School, "that such a school is not wanted at all... I assure you that the general feeling in Bruton is a very sore one." His letter received an even blunter reply: "The Overseers and Visitors of the Hospital, who are noblemen and gentlemen of leading position in the County of Somerset and have actively promoted this Scheme are probably in as good a position as he is to judge whether its object is a good one." (3)

b) Establishing the new school.

i) The Scheme of 1889.

Although enthusiasm amongst the inhabitants of Bruton for a Trade or Technical School in the town remained strong, for six years nothing happened. The main reason for this delay as far as the Visitors were concerned was that, despite the fact that £15,000 was set aside for educational developments by the Sexey's School Foundation under the Scheme of 1881, their financial position was deteriorating. Initially the cause was a technical issue with the Charity Commissioners over obligations under the 1881 Scheme and the latter's refusal to release various dividends. A "Paper Debt" was thus created and the Visitors were not prepared to proceed until that issue was resolved: this was largely achieved as a result of meetings and lengthy correspondence between the Visitors' Steward, T.O. Bennett, and the Charity Commissioners. In addition by the mid-1880s the apparent agricultural depression was beginning to lead to a decline in their rental income.

In order to help break the deadlock the principal inhabitants of Bruton offered to donate £500 towards the new school in the town as a permanent monument of Queen Victoria's Golden Jubilee in 1887, an offer which the Visitors accepted at a Special General Meeting on 5th April. (1) Delay followed and so, increasingly frustrated, the parishioners at a Committee Meeting on 22nd October stipulated that the foundation stone should be laid by the end of the year. It was at this point that the Charity Commissioners despatched an Assistant Commissioner, W.N. Bruce, to hold meetings with both groups. This he did on 25th October. After his meeting with the Visitors he recorded that while they did not wish to proceed at that point with a County School, they were prepared to build a Trade School in Bruton once the financial position was resolved. Surprisingly considering all the discussions during the previous six years he found that, "The Governors said they did not feel competent to express an opinion as to the demand in Bruton and the neighbourhood for the proposed trade school." It was an indication again, given their backgrounds, of how out of touch some of them were with local feelings - even so they stated categorically that they did not want a representative element on the proposed school's governing body.

When Bruce then met a deputation of parishioners he experienced a much more positive atmosphere. Their spokesman, W. Muller, explained "that the people of Bruton were surprised and disappointed that the scheme passed in 1881 should be still almost a dead letter.... and were much irritated at the cold and tardy response made to their efforts." The parishioners were clear about who was responsible, "The committee did not wish to lay the blame of the deadlock which had occurred since 1881 upon any particular shoulders (though it was hinted that they were more disposed to think ill of the Visitors than of the Commissioners), but they thought it fair to state that they had had great difficulty in suppressing a very violent explosion of feeling on the subject." They had by this stage already drawn up a potential building plan for a school to accommodate fifty pupils at an estimated cost of £1,200. They considered that some provision should be made for boarders, probably because they realised the commercial advantages for the town that boarders such as those at King's School brought.

Bruce reported that he felt that Bruton was a suitable location for a technical school as there were good transport links, there was no other such school in the county and the town was close to a wide range of rural industries, which could benefit, such as cloth works, paper mills, rope manufactures, lace works and mining. He concluded, "I found the townspeople hopeful, energetic, determined to do all in their power to make the school a success, and only asking to be allowed to begin at once." (2)

Once again however nothing happened immediately. In September 1888 Bennett wrote to the Charity Commissioners to inform them that, "The effects of the Agricultural depression have so entirely disturbed all reasonable Estimates which were made ten years ago, and the outlook is still so uncertain that the Visitors feel that, at this juncture, no reliable financial plan can be formed for the future." He added a much more positive comment which probably reflected his own views, "The 'Trade School' is earnestly desired in Bruton, and has enlisted the unanimous support of its inhabitants." In fact the necessary propaganda continued to be disseminated in the town, for example, in December 1888 under the auspices of the Mutual Improvement Society a lecture was delivered by an H.M.I., A.P. Graves, on "Technical Education and Trade Schools". Unsurprisingly the Chairman that evening was Henry Hobhouse. (3)

The Charity Commissioners however were undaunted by the Visitors' attitude and proceeded to produce a draft scheme which after due consultation and amendment was approved by the Queen in Council on 28th November 1889. "The Technical or Trade School for boys by the scheme of 1881 directed to be established and maintained shall be established and maintained under this Scheme in the parish of Bruton as a School for boys under the name of Sexey's Trade School." For this purpose a capital sum of £2,750 was made available, "As soon as conveniently may be the Governors, appointed by Somerset County Council, shall provide for such School proper buildings, suitable for not less than fifty day scholars." The nine Governors could award scholarships for free places to boys who had attended a public elementary school for at least three years. For all other boys fees were fixed at between £3 and £5 a year. Exhibitions were to be available, tenable at places of higher education for boys who had been in the school for at least three years. Details were also included on the subjects to be taught. (4) This was the point at which a school which had been discussed for over a decade became a reality, although not as yet a physical one.

After all the delays progress became much more rapid: in April 1890 Bennett was able to report to the Charity Commissioners that the nine Governors had been appointed by the County Council, holding their first meeting on 3rd May. In July they elected William Pearce, an accountant, as their Clerk. (5)

ii) Building the new school.

The original intention, as the Visitors informed Bruce at their meeting in 1887, was to build the new school on a site in the High Street, immediately opposite the Hospital and then occupied by the former Bell Inn (now Sexey Villas). The advantage as they perceived it was that they already owned the site and the land on both sides and behind it so that future expansion was feasible. At that stage the local inhabitants also accepted this idea as their plan envisaged the main school building being constructed alongside the High Street and detached workshops on the raised ground behind it, thus avoiding excavating into the hillside itself.

By 1890 however another potential site had emerged: the Cliffe House Estate at the top of Lusty Hill on the northern side of the road leading to Pitcombe and Cole. No reason was specified for the rejection of the original choice but it may have proved to be too limited and difficult a location for such a project. Both Henry Hobhouse and T.O. Bennett wrote to the Charity Commissioners in 1890 extolling the advantages of the new site. In this instance it is impossible to determine with absolute certainty who was the driving force behind the decision but it was most likely Hobhouse who as a landowner would have realised the limitations of the original site and the potential for expansion on the new one. On the other hand, Bennett's main occupation was as a local Land

Agent and so he had excellent knowledge of the nature of the land and as early as July 1890 he was consulting local farmers such as Josiah Jackson about a site for the new school. (6) The owner of the Estate, John Stroud, had died in 1884 and fortuitously the Trustees of his Will decided to sell it in 1890. In total it consisted of the small mansion known as Cliffe House along with nine acres and five perches of land. Although the new school required about three acres of land, the Trustees were only prepared to sell the Estate in its entirety.

At their monthly meeting in August 1890 a Committee of the Visitors considered, "the desirability of purchasing the 'Cliffe House' property, with a view to sparing a portion of the land for the Trade School site." A Report was then ordered to be presented at the Annual General Meeting in September where it was agreed to purchase the Estate for £2,000, having received an assurance from Henry Hobhouse, as Chairman of the Sexey's School Foundation, that the Governors would purchase about three acres at the rate of £200 an acre as a site for the Trade School. Early in December the Visitors paid a deposit of £200 for the Estate. (7)

The final step was to convince the Charity Commissioners that this was a beneficial purchase for the Hospital so that they would sanction the sale of Consols, in which the Visitors' surplus cash was invested, to allow the transaction to be completed. Two long letters were therefore despatched: the first from T.O. Bennett as the Visitors' Steward. He gave a description of Cliffe House and its outbuildings, the amount of land involved and the current rental value which was £91 a year, of which £65 was for the house itself. He drew their attention to the fact that at that time the Consols to be sold yielded just £55 a year so the Visitors would receive an additional income of £36 a year. He stressed that the Governors were anxious to purchase part of the site as they "are strongly of opinion that the site is the best in or around Bruton." In particular he noted it was within easy reach of two railway stations which would allow potential pupils to travel from surrounding areas. To strengthen the case even further he informed the Commissioners that, "the Public throughout Bruton and the neighbourhood are strongly impressed with the peculiar advantages this site affords." He concluded that, "the Property is a very good investment at the price of £2,000."

To his letter Bennett attached a copy of the letter which Henry Hobhouse had sent to the Visitors in September 1890 requesting them to purchase the estate as, "After prolonged consideration of the subject and numerous enquiries we have come to the conclusion that there is only one satisfactory site available for the School." He confirmed that the Sexey's School Foundation had passed a resolution to "bind ourselves" to purchase about three acres of the site from the Visitors at £200 an acre. The Commissioners clearly still had some reservations and so on 8th November Bennett wrote a second letter to them to reassure them that, "the Land proposed to be purchased will not be sufficiently near 'Cliffe House' to detract from its letting value nor to prejudice its Residential character." He felt that a "Farmer, or Tradesman, might be only too glad to avail himself of such a Residence for the education of his sons."

The Charity Commissioners were convinced, agreed to the purchase and on 31st December 1890 the whole property was conveyed to the Visitors who paid the balance of £1,800 to solicitors Dyne and Muller on 7th February 1891. The small portion of land required for the new school was then sold to the Governors of the Sexey's School Foundation for £635: "The said Hospital grant and convey…. to the said Governors all of that patch or parcel of pasture land containing by admeasurement three acres and twenty-eight perches or thereabouts being part of a certain close called 'Solomon's Cliff'."

Almost immediately advertisements were inserted in local newspapers requesting tenders by 15th May 1891 to build the new school, with the plans, which had been drawn up by Architects G.J. Skipper and F.W. Skipper of Norwich, being available to view in the offices of T.O. Bennett. The speed with which these events occurred suggest that designs and plans were produced before the

Sexey's Trade School as proposed in a sketch and plan of 1891.

purchase process had been completed and were an indication of the confidence of the Visitors that their proposals would be accepted by the Charity Commissioners. No reason was ever stated for the selection of Architects from the other side of the country. (8)

By the specified date eight tenders had been received which ranged from £2,327 16s 0d to £2,890 0s 0d and the contract was awarded to Messrs Francis of Castle Cary for £2,340 0s 0d, "after very careful consideration of the quality of the work of the two Builders in other circumstances." The Governors then attempted to keep the actual cost of the building itself to £2,100 by deferring the erection of the proposed larger workshop and the inclusion "of a hotwater apparatus and Gas fittings to the Schoolrooms.... It is also believed that a considerable sum may be saved by using the good local Stone which has been found on the site." The discovery that the site contained appropriate stone was not only very fortuitous but also an indication of the lack of a detailed survey beforehand. In fact the final Accounts showed that £57 10s 0d was saved, along with a further £15 by using bricks made locally.

Once construction had commenced a whole range of extra work was found to be necessary, such as boarding the roof and laying hair felt under the slates which cost £52 15s 0d, and another £18 for building the chimneys in Doulting Freestone rather than local stone. Making and fixing picture rails in the Schoolroom cost £2 11s 2d. When the building was completed in March 1892 the Architect specified that the work completed totalled £2,450 0s 0d.

Further expenditure was still required on furniture and fittings, such as blinds which cost £7 11s 6d; "Making platform under Master's desk" £1 0s 0d; Classroom desks £20 16s 0d; "Lecture Table with all fittings complete & with teak top" £10; "Chemical Laboratory Fittings" £166 2s 7d; Table and three chairs in Masters' Room £2 7s 6d; "Fitting up Carpenter's Shop with tool racks" £2 5s 0d; "Cuting for & fixing oak sills & beams in well arching.... Fixing pump & rods, also pump trough, making & fixing boarded & slated shed over pump £22 17s 0d." Finally £68 7s 10d was paid to Longbottom and Co. for Heating Apparatus.

By the time that the Building Account was finally sealed in May 1893 the total cost, excluding the purchase price of the land, was some £3,220. To meet this cost £2,850 was provided by the Visitors of Sexey's Hospital, £250 came from a grant by Somerset County Council and £120 was contributed by the Governors themselves when they discovered "that the Funds at their disposal were insufficient." (9)

iii) Opening the School.

Even before the purchase of a site had been completed and building commenced an advertisement was drawn up for a Head Master to take up responsibilities by Easter 1891 "for an Endowed Trade or Technical School for 50 day scholars.... A young, able energetic man, well trained in practical science preferred." The salary was to be £120 a year with capitation fees of £2 per boy and rent and rates paid. There was also an allowance for coal and gas. Six candidates were called to an interview in January 1891 at a cost to the Governors of £16 7s 6d and William Albert Knight aged twenty-four was appointed. In the nineteenth century it was not uncommon for young men to be given such responsibility in their twenties, as may be seen, for example, with the appointment of Rev. J.C.H. Abrahall at the Grammar School in Bruton aged twenty-five and Edward Hayter at the National School there aged twenty-seven.

The appointment of Knight was in one respect a very daring gamble as he had to establish and lead a new school which was in many ways to offer a significantly different approach to education when he himself had received a classical education for three years at the King's School in the town under Rev. D.E. Norton. The explanation for the appointment undoubtedly rests with Henry Hobhouse: he had a vision for the direction of technical and scientific education for the future and what he required was a man of similar ideas, capable of translating this vision into an effective reality. In Knight he saw that man and together they constituted a formidable partnership. [For details on the role of Knight see section d).]

It was also essential to publicize the existence of the new school and an advertisement duly appeared late in 1890. It anticipated that the new buildings would be available in the spring or summer of 1892 and informed prospective parents that as an interim measure the temporary Technical or Trade School would open after Easter 1891 in 'The Glen'. "The School is intended for the sons of tradesmen and small farmers between the ages of 10 and 17." Tuition fees were to be £4 a year and there "will be a few free places reserved as scholarships for promising boys." An initial Prospectus, based largely upon the Scheme of 1889, specified the curriculum which, as well as the general subjects, stressed that for older boys there would be instruction in book-keeping, mensuration and land-surveying which would be accompanied by practical science with many examples being cited. "The scholars should thus on leaving the School be fitted to take their place at once as useful and intelligent assistants in the farm, work-shop, or manufactory." Shortly after Knight's appointment a revised Prospectus was issued which named him as the Headmaster and gave the opening day of the new school as Monday 6th April 1891. A similar announcement appeared in local newspapers. (10)

On the appointed day the new school duly opened, as the Headmaster recorded in his Log-book: "April 6th, 1891. Opened school in temporary premises at The Glen, Bruton, with 15 boys." This house in Quaperlake Street was also to serve as his home for the first year. There was no formal opening ceremony, although William Muller "spoke a few words of encouragement to master and boys." He had been instrumental in leading the local inhabitants' campaign to establish this school and had been appointed one of its nine Governors.

The first boys to attend regarded their schoolroom, which was some twenty feet by fifteen feet, as an idyllic location. There was a large French window which looked out onto a lawn which itself stretched down to the River Brue. Around the edge of it were various trees: hornbeam, tulip-tree, alders, acacias "and a magnificent beech, whose height many of the first pupils remember measuring with more or less accuracy." Practical work from the very beginning. Closer to the house and French window "clustering or climbing were rose trees in profusion, wisteria, sweet-smelling clematis and jessamine." The major downside as far as the boys were concerned was that Knight insisted upon an examination, "the result of which showed that a great deal of comparatively humble study in the merest elements was necessary before higher branches of knowledge were attacked."

The first two scholarships were awarded in August 1891 to Edgar Pound of Castle Cary and Edmund Green of Bruton. Three more scholarships were then added by the East Somerset Agricultural Society, of which Bennett was a leading member, and in January 1892 the first seven County Scholars arrived. By this stage as numbers had increased to nearly forty the Governors appointed an assistant master, W.G. Watson, who was to teach the junior boys. This appointment was an important step as it allowed for the better division of the School into junior and senior sections. Watson also taught Woodwork which had to take place in an adjoining cottage.

The first year ended with the examination required by the Scheme and was conducted by H.J. Walker, a member of the Bristol School Board and an ex-president of the National Union of Teachers, who was suitably impressed. "I beg to say that from the results of my examination and from a careful inspection of the work performed by many of the boys when first admitted to the school, I am convinced that real progress has been made. Mr Knight has carefully organized his school, has adopted intelligent methods of teaching and is, in my opinion certain of future success." Walker was to examine the School on future occasions and after he retired remained in contact with Knight, providing advice and valuable experience.

Renting 'The Glen' cost the Governors £45 for the year but they were aware from the very beginning because of the anticipated number of boys and what Pearce described as the "inadequate character of the present Premises," that it had to be temporary. (11)

iv) To Lusty Hill.

While the new school premises were being built it became fashionable to walk out from the town to see the progress being made. At this stage there was some confusion about the name which was going to be adopted. On the site a large board which faced the road called it a "Trade or Technical School." The word 'Technical' was not understood by many local people and it required constant explanation and definition: a source of considerable irritation to T.O. Bennett to whom many of the queries were directed. In a letter to a local newspaper announcing the establishment of the East

Somerset Agricultural Society Scholarships he gave his opinion and additional information.

"Having been frequently asked to explain what I consider the meaning of the word 'Technical' I would venture to say that, perhaps, if 'Practical' had been substituted, it would have expressed more intelligently the kind of instruction proposed to be given. For instance, the sons of farmers will be taught how to measure an acre of land, a piece of timber, or rick of hay - small matters it may be said but certainly useful in the everyday occupation of a farmer; the sons of tradesmen will be taught those subjects likely to be of the greatest practical usefulness in afterlife - all the boys instructed not simply from *books* but from *objects* immediately surrounding them."

Before long the word 'Technical' disappeared.

This School was not alone in adopting the word 'Trade' as there was, for example, a Trade School in Keighley in Yorkshire and 'Taunton's Trade School' in Southampton. By including the word 'Trade' in Bruton it clearly distinguished the new school from King's School. For some tradesmen however it still appeared to have been misleading as it was not unusual for small tradesmen to apply to the Headmaster for an apprentice, just as their predecessors had done in the days of the boys' school in the Hospital. The expectation may have been better educated boys bringing a good premium with them.

In the mid-1890s as the School gained so many County Scholarships and a large number of County scholars from elsewhere in Somerset chose to be educated there, it was suggested that an alternative name might be the "East Somerset County School." The idea however was not pursued. In 1908 the Governors decided "to ask that the official name of the School may be in future 'Sexey's School, Bruton' instead of as at present 'Sexey's Trade School'." In his letter the Clerk, F.W. Hooper, did not specify a reason for the request but it may well relate to the emphasis which was being placed upon academic success as well as an excellent practical education. The Board of Education declined to sanction the change but in the Scheme of June 1910 directed that it should become 'Sexey's Boys' School'. Their decision was to draw a clear distinction between this School and the nearby expanding girls' school, referred to as 'Sunny Hill Girls' School.' (12)

One year after starting in 'The Glen' masters and pupils moved to the new school buildings on Lusty Hill. The formal opening ceremony occurred on the first Prize Day on 19th April 1892 when the day started with a short service in the parish church conducted by the Vicar, Rev. H.T. Ridley. The Governors and principal guests were then provided with lunch by Henry Hobhouse, as Chairman of the Governors of the School. At 3p.m. the opening ceremony was held in the Schoolroom "before a large company assembled to witness the distribution of prizes and to hear the Earl of Cork declare the School open." The Earl of Cork and Orrery, as well as being the Lord Lieutenant of Somerset, was a Visitor of Sexey's Hospital and a Governor of the School. One of the guests was Josiah Jackson who noted in his Diary in his usual succinct way, "There was a good number present & the thing passed off very well indeed."

In his speech the Earl traced the origin of the School, especially the decline of the apprenticeship system and stressed the importance of education but added that, "It was not so much what a man knew as *what he was* that would determine his conduct and success in life." After other speeches and the distribution of prizes some of the boys sang various pieces. Specimens of the boys' work were on display: some from when they had entered the School the year before and some from the week before this opening ceremony to illustrate their progress. The Governors then invited the guests to tea in the Infants' Schoolroom in the High Street after which they were entertained with a short concert. In addition the bells of St. Mary's Church were rung at intervals during the day and 'The Star of the East' Band from Baltonsborough was engaged to play periodically selections of music. (13)

v) Room to expand.

The new School, which was built on what was regarded as "an attractive and healthy site", was designed for fifty boys. It originally consisted of a spacious entrance porch and a large schoolroom thirty-six feet by twenty-four feet which was able to seat fifty boys, with a double-gabled projection on the front and an open bell turret with copula and vane on the roof. The four windows gave plenty of natural light and ventilation. There was a lecture room twenty-two feet by eighteen feet which could accommodate thirty boys, a chemistry laboratory equipped for twenty boys as well as a workshop, cloakrooms and lavatory. To the west of the schoolroom was the Headmaster's house with three reception rooms, five bedrooms and offices but by 1904 this was the subject of some criticism. "The Headmaster's house, in accordance with the traditions too prevalent at the date of its erection, has hardly a single room of decent size."

There were about two and a half acres of garden and playground attached to the buildings. Within this area there was the water supply in the form of a well. As early as April 1890 when this site was being considered T.O. Bennett had informed the Charity Commissioners, "The most competent authority in the neighbourhood has inspected the Land and says there is no doubt there are two different points on the site selected which will yield ample supplies." The Building Account recorded that £57 4s 9d was spent on "Sinking Well."

There was some thought given to a range of details: "Comfort and health were considered as well as educational efficiency" claimed the School Chronicles. The buildings were heated with hot water on a high pressure system rather than with grates and stoves; the laboratory was fitted up with gas, water and electricity as well as "all the latest improvements." Wood block flooring reduced the noise level compared with wooden floor boards. The rooms had large windows which gave good light and ventilation, although as was common in the Victorian period the sills were placed so high that seated pupils could not look out of them and be distracted from their studies. In the Workshop were benches along with an assortment of tools and a lathe donated by Henry Hobhouse. "The same care and liberality were bestowed on the selection of furniture; a special pattern of desk was chosen which has served as a model to more than one other new school since." (14)

The success of the School and the consequent increase in numbers meant that the accommodation was soon insufficient. Fortunately the site purchased allowed for some expansion and by Easter 1894 two new classrooms and a gymnasium had been built and were ready for use. The gymnasium itself was largely furnished as a result of subscriptions from Governors, parents and friends of the School. The building work cost £450 0s 0d and at the same time £5 10s 0d was spent on "Two pairs of Sliding Blackboards hung & balanced in oak frames & with Iron Runners." Improvements in ventilation cost £10 and new Closets £25. The total came to £490 10s 0d and so not for the last time Henry Hobhouse stepped in with a loan at 3% interest. The Charity Commissioners were annoyed that they had not been consulted about the proposed expenditure but eventually agreed, although the affair dragged on until February 1895. (15)

The new gymnasium had a very short lifespan as within three years the accommodation in the School once again proved to be too limited and did not meet the requirements of the curriculum. In January 1897 William Pearce informed the Charity Commissioners that in conjunction with the Science and Art Department they wished to provide "the Trade School with a properly equipped Physical Laboratory. They are for this purpose converting and altering their present Gymnasium into a Laboratory and are erecting a new Gymnasium, store &c. in the rear of their present School Building." They anticipated that the cost would be £387 or £430 if equipped with apparatus.

This decision created two problems: the first was that the size of their proposed Gymnasium meant that there was insufficient space on their existing site and so they required an additional piece of land. Negotiations commenced with the Visitors to purchase an additional five perches of their land at the rear of the existing buildings. At their Monthly Meeting in March the Visitors agreed to sell the required land for just £4   0s   0d as they considered the Governors had paid such a good price for the original site. The second problem was financial but in the end Somerset County Council gave a grant of £125, the District Education Committee £25 and £103   10s   0d came from the School's own resources. This left a deficit of £150 and once again Henry Hobhouse provided a loan at 3% interest. In fact the Governors were able to repay Hobhouse in January 1898 without any interest charges as they received a larger than expected grant from the Science and Art Department The new buildings were a considerable asset although in 1904 the Inspectors did point out, "The usefulness of the Gymnasium is at present restricted by the fact that no facilities exist for heating or artificial lighting." (16)

In the 1904 Inspection it was reported that "the classroom accommodation is insufficient and the addition of at least two classrooms is urgently needed.... Some extension is imperatively demanded if the School is to maintain its present position." The Governors were well aware of the situation and a scheme for extensions had been drawn up but not costed by that stage. During the Prize Day the following year Hobhouse had to report that their plans would involve considerable expenditure and as a result tuition fees had had to be raised to £5 a year. By the time of the visit of H.M.I. Battiscombe in August 1906 the work was well underway. He noted, "These alterations represent a very real improvement in the equipment of the School, upon which the Governors are to be heartily congratulated." The Report the following year enthused about the changes: "an enormous improvement in the accommodation of the School." The Science Rooms were together in one block and the new Physics Laboratory was longer and wider than the previous one. There was a new Dark room and four new benches in the Chemistry Laboratory. A new Woodwork Room with accommodation for twenty-six boys was built and the old one converted into a Lecture room. "The old Physics Laboratory, which is now available for class teaching, is excellently arranged and is now the best room in the School." A new lavatory with cement floor had been built, the lighting in several classrooms improved and the gymnasium fitted with gas lights.

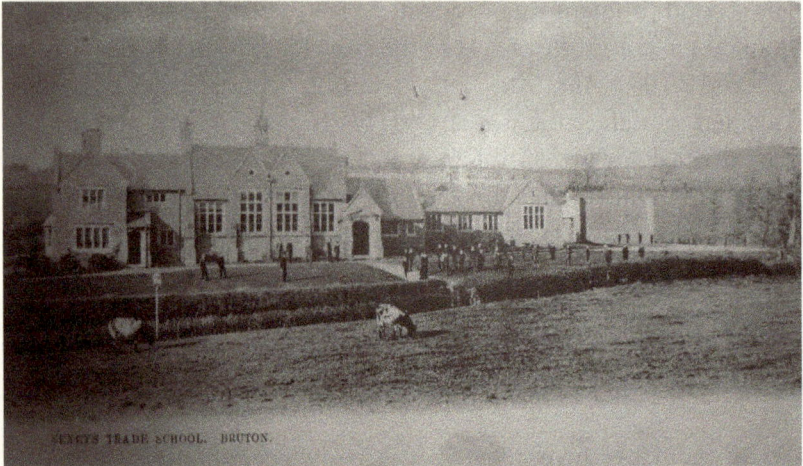

Sexey's Trade School, c. 1908. A Fives Wall may be seen to the right of the buildings.

The only other major development before 1914 was that in 1910 a new small block was built at the rear of the School alongside the Gymnasium which consisted of Headmaster's Room, Assistant Masters' Room, Library and Waiting room. Once again it was built by Messrs Francis of Castle Cary and cost £504 3s 10d.

At the outbreak of the First World War the School could accommodate 120 boys in the main large Schoolroom and four other classrooms. It boasted a Lecture Room which could seat forty, a Chemistry and a Physics Laboratory together holding forty-six boys, a Dark room, a Balance room, Gymnasium, Carpentry Shop for eighteen boys and Metal Working Shop for twelve.

The buildings did not always appear to have been as secure as they might have been as in May 1895, "It was found that some person had effected an entrance to this school during the night and had ransacked all the boys' desks and stolen about 30s contained in one of them." The intruder used a ladder to gain access through a window. No one appears to have been caught. (17)

c) The Governors.

The Visitors of Sexey's Hospital were drawn predominantly from the ranks of male landowning gentry in Somerset and the neighbouring counties. It was not surprising therefore that as the Hospital's money was to finance this new enterprise they wished to retain this arrangement and hence control. During a meeting in 1887 with Assistant Commissioner Bruce from the Charity Commission they did however acknowledge that they did not know how much demand there was a for a trade school in Bruton. This admission led him to suggest that in order to "secure the confidence of the public in its management" it might be advisable "to include a certain element representative of the inhabitants of Bruton," so that they could "obtain an authoritative expression of local opinion on matters connected with its management." The Visitors were not impressed and informed Bruce that, while they would pay attention to local opinion, they "considered themselves the most impartial, unselfish, and capable set of men that could possibly be obtained for the work." They further explained that they objected to a representative element chiefly "on the ground of the excitement, party feeling, and jobbery which are in their experience the offspring of public elections." In light of these views it is possible to speculate that had it not been for the dominance and persuasive powers of Henry Hobhouse, the direction which the School was to take might have been very different.

Two years later when the Scheme of Management was published it was clear that the Visitors had not entirely achieved their objective for while there were no elected representatives, amongst the nine Governors of the Trade School, as well as two involved in manufacture and trade, were two from Bruton: T.O. Bennett who had been so instrumental in the establishment of the

School, but at least from their perspective he was their Steward, and solicitor William Muller who had spearheaded the local inhabitants' campaign for a school to be built in the town. He was also a Manager of the National School but unfortunately died in September 1893 and was replaced by local doctor, Frederick Stockwell. Of the other seven Governors three were already Visitors of the Hospital and two more became so in a short time: Henry Hobhouse in 1890 and Arthur Goodford in 1893. The latter was also Chairman of Somerset Technical Instruction Committee from 1890 and Chairman of the County Council before Hobhouse from 1900 to 1905. (1)

The Scheme required the Governors to build the new school for fifty boys and to maintain it. They were given the power to appoint and "at their pleasure dismiss" all teachers, as well as fix and pay their salaries. They had overall control of the finances and were able to determine the level of the fees. Each year they were required to appoint an Examiner who was to report in writing on "the proficiency of the scholars and on the condition of the School, as regards instruction and discipline." The Headmaster also had to present in writing a statement on "the general condition and progress of the School." They could grant scholarships as free places in the School and award Exhibitions tenable at places of higher education.

When Inspector Lefroy presented his Report of his visit to the School in 1894 he included statistics showing the attendance of the Governors at meetings, of which there had been eighteen. See Table 10.

It would appear that a small group of about five Governors formed a core for attendance in the early years but none of them was present on more than eleven occasions or some 61%. Proximity to Bruton was clearly an important factor in attendance and men such as the Earl of Cork had a significant number of other commitments to fulfil. He did however retain a strong interest in the School and presented the prizes on a least three occasions before 1914. Sir R.H. Paget had campaigned hard for the foundation of a

Table 10. Attendance of Governors at Meetings.

Name	Residence and Occupation		Date appointed	Meetings attended. Max.18
The Earl of Cork and Orrery	Marston,	Lord Lieutenant	1890	1
Sir R.H. Paget	Cranmore Hall,	M.P.	1890	3
J.F.F. Horner	Mells Park,	J.P.	1890	8
Henry Hobhouse	Hadspen House,	M.P.	1890	11
Arthur Goodford	Chilton Cantelo,	J.P.	1890	10
John Donne	Castle Cary,	Twine Manufacturer	1890	11
Edmund Hill	Evercreech,	Cheese Merchant	1890	10
T.O. Bennett	Bruton,	Land Agent	1890	11
Frederick Stockwell	Bruton,	Physician	1894	—

County School in Shepton Mallet and when that did not happen it was claimed that he lost interest in attending meetings in Bruton, including those of the Visitors. On the more positive side it may be that the Governors had so much confidence in the ability of Knight that they considered regular, stringent scrutiny unnecessary. (2)

As a result of amendments and alterations in the new Schemes of 1897, 1901, 1906 and particularly June 1910 a number of changes occurred relating to the Governors. There were still nine Representative Governors appointed by Somerset County Council of which three had to be Visitors of the Hospital and a further two resident in Bruton. If the total was increased it had to be with the approval of the Board of Education and appointed by a Local Education Authority. Religious opinion or attendance was not to be a barrier to becoming a Governor and they had to publish annual accounts. "The Governors may at pleasure dismiss the Head Master without assigning cause", although a resolution to do so had to be passed at two special meetings at which at least two thirds of the Governors were present. (3)

As a result of the success and outstanding organization of the School under Knight's leadership the Governors found that they had no reason to interfere in the way in which it was managed. Their attitude was best summed up by Henry Hobhouse in his speech at Prize Day 1916: "The principle which they as Governors of the School observed was that so long as the School was flourishing and things were going smoothly, they should not interfere more than they could help. That was a rule which they had strictly observed during the long period of Mr Knight's headmastership." Some fifteen years previously at an earlier Prize Day Hobhouse had gone so far as to state that, "He did not know that he could report much progress, because the School had attained such a high state of efficiency that further progress was almost impossible." Future reports were to show that in fact even more could be achieved. (4)

The Governors of course were not detached from the School and at times their role was crucial. Year after year Hobhouse in particular provided vital support: at Prize Day after Prize Day he kept reiterating the function and value of the School to a wider audience. "It was to be a technical school where a thoroughly practical training was given, and they wished to give the boys a sound foundation for agricultural and industrial work, and other branches of life.... They wished to give the lads habits of thought." Time and again he urged farmers and those associated with the land to encourage boys to remain longer at school so that they would be better equipped to face the foreign competition of the late nineteenth and early twentieth centuries. Such support from a leading local and national politician was crucial for the success of the School. (5)

The Governors had overall responsibility for the finances of the School and although the Budget could be very tight, for the overwhelming majority of the period under consideration they kept the School in credit. [See section k).] They were responsible for the maintenance of the buildings and once again with their limited resources they spent money as necessary on repairs, such as £73   19s   1d for the year ending 31st December 1897. Above all the Governors had to respond to the success of the School which led to demands for additional buildings and in this area they were generally successful. [See section b)v.] The one aspect which was to haunt them for years and which was not resolved before 1914 was the provision of boarding accommodation. [See section g).]

d) The Headmaster.

William Albert Knight, or 'Wacker' as he was invariably called by the boys in the School, usually behind his back although occasionally by mistake within his hearing, was twenty-four years old when appointed Headmaster. He came from the locality as his father was the manager of the string and twine factory in Castle Cary and was one of nine children. (1) When he was very young Knight had the task of marking the ends of balls of string with blobs of red paint so that customers could find them. He was educated at Castle Cary Elementary School between 1870 and 1877 and then at the age of eleven he was sent to the Grammar

School (King's School) in Bruton and remained there for three years. By the end of that time it appears that he had decided on a career in teaching as he worked as a Pupil Techer in Castle Cary between 1880 and 1884 and then for six months at St. Thomas's School in Islington in London.

The following year he was admitted to St. John's Training College in Battersea in London which was one of the first Teacher Training Colleges founded in England and which, most significantly for his subsequent career, stressed the importance of applied education, that is, of linking academic studies with broader practical experience. In 1886 he was awarded the Board of Education's Certificate and for the next two years was teaching at Nightingale Street Board School in Marylebone but at the same time working towards the University of London, Inter B.A., First Class, which he was awarded in 1887. While in London he became the Queen's Medallist in Science, South Kensington.

He obtained his first headship in 1888 at the Higher Grade British School in Maryport, Cumberland and remained there until 1891. In the mid-1880s a group of local men had attempted to establish a Higher Grade School in Maryport but by 1887 had failed to do so. At that point the Managers of the existing British School stepped in and offered to establish such an institution, together with evening classes overseen by the Department of Science and Art. This institution was to be carried on as a separate department of their school. It was this department which Knight was to head. It was also in 1888 that he married Annie Florence West.

Many years later in 1920 he was awarded an honorary M.A. by Bristol University and became an Honorary Associate of Reading University but at the time of his appointment to Sexey's Trade School Knight may not have had the level of academic qualifications of some candidates although he was able to offer varied practical experience. One of his subsequent pupils, Hubert Phillips, was later to write that, "his paper qualifications were slight." That was certainly the case as his Inter B.A. was awarded after just one year's study but Phillip's added that, "he happened to be one of those visionaries with a genius for organization." (2)

Knight had his own views on the reason for his appointment which he confided to his granddaughter many years later. "There were half a dozen of us interviewed. One of the questions asked was: 'How many assistant masters will you need?' As the candidates came out they told us what they had answered. Most said about six. I was last in and when they asked me that question I replied, 'None. My wife and I will be able to teach all the lessons at first and then, as the School grows, we will take on extra Staff to suit the circumstances.' That's how I got the job." (3) The reality was of course different for while such an answer may have swayed an undecided member of the interviewing panel, the dominant force was Henry Hobhouse who undoubtedly saw other qualities in Knight. His cause may well have been helped by the fact that one of the Governors was John Donne, his father's employer and who would have known him for many years.

The first headmaster has been described as, "A tall, spare figure with penetrating dark eyes" along with dark hair and moustache. Another former pupil recalled that when "he strode into a classroom, or sauntered past a group of boys in the playground, you were automatically on your best behaviour." He "was a man of unbounded energy and the most catholic tastes. In many things he was far in advance of his time." Prominent amongst these was the emphasis upon the sciences: chemistry, physics and botany. "Above all, he taught us how to learn," a concept which would not be out of place in the twenty-first century.

Like many Victorians, however, he believed that there must be a general education before vocational training. In the process a boy's overall intelligence would be improved and there would be academic competence. The 1904 H.M.I. Report noted that, "Premature specialisation is discouraged." In 1911 Knight was

W. A. Knight.

reported as stating that he "steadfastly opposed attempts to convert the School into a so-called Agricultural School" because he believed "that specialized and utilitarian teaching can only be given to older boys, after they have had their general intelligence trained, and the general principles of knowledge instilled in due proportions." In his evidence to the Acland Committee in the same year he commented that while there should be "regular instruction in Handicraft as part of the ordinary course for boys in secondary school" it was only "at about the age of 15 or 16 (that) it should be possible for a boy to specialize in the direction of his probable future career."

Knight experienced no problems with the prevailing ideas relating to instilling the appropriate attitudes such as loyalty, obedience, initiative and leadership. His success in this area was seen in a thriving Old Boys' Association and the careers which so many of his former pupils pursued. In 1919 Henry Hobhouse commented, "The abilities of the boys had been thoroughly developed, and what was still more important, their character had also been developed on a high plane, and a wonderful amount of *esprit de corps* had been evolved." Old Sexeians attributed their success to Knight's methods of teaching: "his power of throwing into strong relief the essentials of his subject, and of simultaneously imparting life to those essentials. The ability to discern essentials, and the habits of reasoning and constructing from first principles, are among the leading characteristics of the Sexeian. We Old Sexeians know further that it was at School we learnt to work, and to work not under protest but with an enthusiasm and zest caught from our Headmaster." (5)

From the very beginning the School was a success in terms of attracting boys and in achieving good examination results. In practical terms it had to be in order to survive as there were so many other established and well-regarded schools catering for boys, although not necessarily from the same background, within a twenty mile radius of Bruton. The nearest was King's School in the town and then others in Shepton Mallet, Wells, Yeovil and Sherborne. The 1904 Inspection Report considered that the success of the School was due not only to Knight himself being "a stimulating and successful teacher" who had such a knowledge of other subjects in the curriculum that he could exercise control over all the teaching, but also that he had superb powers of organization. The Report of the H.M.I.s on their 1910 Inspection continued to analyse the reasons for the success of the School. They noted "a very definite bias in the direction of Science" and in so doing it had "achieved extraordinary success and has gained a number of Scholarships out of all proportion to its size." Their conclusion was that, "The remarkable success of the School is a tribute to the exceptional organising power of the Head Master.....He keeps a firm hand on every branch of the School curriculum and supervises every department of School activity.... He has succeeded in establishing certain ideals and traditions of work which are felt in every classroom." Such a system could be maintained while numbers were relatively limited and the headmaster retained a firm grip. One danger inherent in such an approach was that it could lead to a rapid turnover of teachers if they felt unable to experiment with other methods or introduce different material. (6)

In March 1923 Knight was invited to distribute the prizes at Huish Grammar School in Taunton where he took as the theme of his speech, "What a Good School should be." During this speech he identified so many of the factors which had made his School such a success under his leadership. He dismissed a school being good because it had high fees, large numbers, beautiful buildings, success on the games field or even the number of scholarships. "There must be a steady, persistent effort for efficiency in the staff and boys carried on day after day, month after month, year after year." Time must not be wasted in any way and there must be careful classification so that the boys in each form were of the same intellectual standard and that their work was carefully planned. He believed that it was necessary to resist the temptation of over-crowding the timetable, a point which he considered particularly important. A good school in his opinion required firm discipline in which each boy was treated according to his temperament. Staff must have the highest ideals and "above all, that one quality, enthusiasm. The keynote of a good school, the vital thing of all which counted more than anything else was the personal influence of the staff upon the mind and soul of the individual boy." (7)

Knight seemed to have had a favourite quotation which in many ways summed up his philosophy. It has been attributed to Charles Reade but its origin has never been determined for certain:
"Sow an act, and reap a habit; sow a habit, and reap a character; sow a character, and reap a destiny."

In the early years of the School's existence Knight taught a wide range of subjects, especially science, but when he was in a position to employ more assistant masters he began to concentrate on Mathematics and French. It was in fact his French lessons that a number of former pupils remembered most clearly: "Wacker taught French, and taught it well enough to ensure, at least, excellent results in examinations." He did, of course, sometimes use an incentive (or bribery) by promising that if a boy managed to translate correctly the ten sentences he had dictated to them, he would give them half a crown (2s 6d). "I well remember Wakker's French lessons and his vivid attempts to describe the sound of the vowels: the 'u' was produced by pushing his lips out and mixing the sounds of 'e' and 'u'. I watched fascinated as this procedure caused the hairs on his moustache to splay out in all directions." (8)

Although looking for excellence in the boys and certainly achieving it as witness the number of scholarships and university/ college places obtained, Knight was not a supporter of too many external examinations. In 1913, for example, he commented, "The present system of external examinations exerts an unhealthy and undue influence on the curricular of Schools, and requires simplification and control." He remained firmly of the view that it was necessary for each school to determine its curriculum depending on the nature of their locality and their school population. It was very much an opinion shared by many schools at that period. (9)

For all his labours the salary of the Headmaster was fixed at £120 a year with a share of the capitation fees. As the number of boys in the School increased it did mean that he received a rising sum: £234 in 1893, £269 in 1897 and £361 in 1904. The first H.M.I. Inspection in 1904 commented, "it is to be regretted that the circumstances of the School have not hitherto admitted of such increase in his net profits as under more favourable conditions, the length and value of his services would probably have secured." Hobhouse and the Governors took exception to this comment and pointed out that the Headmaster's overall salary had risen and that he received his house rent free along with coal and gas. They added that he only paid a rent to the Governors of £32 for Cliff House.

In a Note attached to Hobhouse's letter an official at the Board of Education, Ellis, drew attention to the fact that any increase in income came not from salary but from capitation fees. "The boarding house practically brings him in nothing: the increase in the boarding fees just saves him from an actual loss.... He has personally had to do several improvements at his own cost." Ellis was led to believe that Knight had been offered the headship of Crewkerne School which had a large boarding house and a good private house. He did however add that he did not wish to imply that the Governors had been "niggardly in their actions towards Knight: but I do think that, if they want to keep him, they must somehow or other make it more worth his while to stay." Finally he pointed out that Knight himself was not complaining but merely stating a fact. In the years which followed the salary did rise so that by 1914 it was £140 but the capitation figure remained at £2 per boy. In the end Knight chose to remain: it may have been that his freedom of action, support from Hobhouse and the control which he exercised helped to influence his decision.

The other financial provision which the Governors made for Knight was the establishment of a Pension Fund. On 7th October 1893 they passed a Resolution to pay £15 a year into a Sinking Fund provided that Knight paid the same amount, which represented some 12.5% of his salary. It was clearly well invested as by 1903-4 the Dividend was £7   10s   0d and by 1908 the capital sum had reached £596   16s   3d. It was of course to be nearly another twenty years before Knight benefitted from it. (10)

Although the School was the main focus of his attention Knight was involved in a range of other areas. In fact by 1920 there were so many that H.M.I. Battiscombe in a confidential section of an Inspection Report stated, "that HM was conducting the School in the same efficient manner as he had always done and added that although he had many public duties in connection with various committees the School did not appear to suffer in any way." Hobhouse was satisfied: he had reported that, "the GB [Governing Body] had had doubts as to the School suffering by the occasional absence of the HM", especially as he had recently been nominated to serve on the Burnham Committee.

A number of Knight's other commitments related to education, for example, he was originally a member of the National Union of Teachers and served as the President of the Castle Cary branch in 1893. He gave lectures to groups of teachers, such as one in February 1892 on, "The Teaching of Drawing" to the Teachers' Association at Sparkford. Shortly afterwards he joined the Incorporated Association of Headmasters, became Chairman of the Examination Committee and in 1924 was elected its President. From 1903 he was a member of Somerset Education Committee, being described in 1912 by another member, J.E. Wakefield, "as a very helpful, courteous, kind, tactful comrade.... who had given them much valuable advice, especially with regard to their secondary school work." He also served as an Examiner to Wiltshire County Council for Junior Agricultural Scholarships and was a Governor of Sunny Hill Girls' School, Bruton, from its foundation. (11) He also found time to write articles relating to teaching in various publications, such as one on Drawing in the 'School World' in 1903 and one entitled, 'The Measurement of a Field', in the Ludgate Nature Study Readers in 1904.

Knight was always involved with the local community and was a regular attender and speaker at the winter monthly meetings of the Bruton Mutual Improvement Society. By the mid-1890s he was on the Committee of the local Cricket Club. He campaigned hard for a footpath to be added beside the road from the Queen's Head Inn at West End to Lusty Bridge, making it safer for boys walking to the School. The narrowness of the existing Legg's Bridge and the possibility of the County replacing it led to the postponement of this idea until after he had retired.

His passion for science was always evident. In the 1890s it was common for Knight to conduct Science classes on the School premises on Tuesday evenings, sponsored by the County Council. These tended to be practical Chemistry classes, "The attendance is fair. No opportunity should be lost of attending these classes, which are very instructive," was the view of one local monthly publication. He possessed a telescope and the boys were always keen to be permitted to use it under his guidance as happened in February 1917, for example, when they were allowed to view the great sunspot group which was said to be the largest ever observed, being some 125,000 miles in length.

He was a local pioneer of the use of X-rays or Rontgen rays as they were called, having been discovered by a German Wilhelm Rontgen on 8th November 1895. One year later in November 1896 Knight delivered a lecture in the Infants' Schoolroom on "The New Photography or the X-Rays." He explained the apparatus he possessed and traced the general advance of Science, expressing "the opinion that it would be better for future generations of Englishmen if more interest were shown in scientific matters." With the aid of the Magic Lantern he showed negatives of a selection of objects he had taken, including a lady's hand and a box of drawing instruments that he had taken at the beginning of the meeting. It was not hard to understand the wonder that such a demonstration caused, although Josiah Jackson was very matter-of-fact, "I came back [from Bruham Lodge] & heard Mr Knight Lecture on the X rays."

In fact it was in the large Lecture Room in the School that Knight gave the boys one of the first public demonstrations of X-rays. Amazement was created when they were able to see their arm-bone structure displayed on a nearby fluorescent screen. He was to give similar demonstrations in meetings in many local towns and villages. That in itself was a considerable feat "because he needed so many heavy electrical cells to produce the necessary power, he had to transport them everywhere in a large horse-drawn cart." (12)

Such was the quality of the results which Knight achieved with his X-rays that on 14th May 1895 he registered five of his resulting photographs with the Copyright Office and Stationers' Company:

an adult lady's hand "showing rings and sesamold bones of thumb", a box of brass weights; various objects including "an aluminium match box, ebonite triple lens, mica and Dutch Metal"; another group of objects - "coin, wooden match, lead pencil"; a child's hand "showing epiphyses, aged 7." Two days later he added one more photograph: this time a leather purse containing a key, coin and a pearl link." This collection would seem to suggest that he wished to demonstrate that X-rays would work with a range of different materials. (13)

Considering that at this very early stage in the development of X-rays their dangers and the damage which they could do to human beings as a result of prolonged exposure was not understood or appreciated, and the fact that there was no protective clothing or equipment, Knight was extremely fortunate that he did not appear to have suffered any ill-effects.

Knight's public service continued after the outbreak of the Great War as in November 1917 he took the necessary oaths to become a Justice of the Peace for Somerset.

As well as his deep interest in Science Knight was a great enthusiast for matters relating to his native county. "He has an extensive knowledge of Somerset topography, history, and antiquities: he is well versed in the dialect and folklore of the eastern part of the county; and it has been whispered along the historic road which leads from Cary to Camel that 'he can tell a tidy drop o' zider, looky-zee, zo well as one here an' there, when he do clap eyes upon a quart o't!'" He encouraged the boys to take an interest in such areas at a time when it was far from fashionable. The first performances of several plays in the Somerset dialect took place in the School, such as "Dumbledore's Droa" in December 1910 and for which Knight acted as the Stage Manager. This play was subsequently published as a supplement to the School Magazine at Easter 1911. Many other items of local interest appeared in these magazines, such as, "A Bruton Worthy: Stephen Bateman", and rainfall statistics on a regular basis. (14)

The Old Sexeian Amateur Dramatic Society.

DECEMBER 26TH. 1910.

A VERSATILE AND TALENTED COMPANY WILL PRESENT

"DUMBLEDORE'S DROA,"

A DIALECT PLAY IN TWO ACTS.
By PODYPLUS

DRAMATIS PERSONÆ.

Programme for first performance of a dialect play at Sexey's Boys' School 1910.

In keeping with so many Victorian Schools, under Knight a school hymn as adopted. It was recorded in the first School magazine in February 1897, but it may well have been written earlier:

"Hear Mighty Lord,
Thy Sexeians' humble cry;
Hear, mighty Lord,
Inspire with motives high;
For work and School,
For students here and past,
Grant thankfulness,
And endless rest at last."

In the version recalled by Phillips the penultimate line was "Grant Victory". The School also adopted the song "Forty Years On" which was borrowed from Harrow School. While the first verse was appropriate, subsequent verses contained references to a game played at Harrow: "Bases attempted and rescued and won." According to Phillips the boys also persistently sang 'arguing' instead of 'auguring' which was the word in the original

248

"How we discoursed of them one of another,
Auguring triumph or balancing fate."

Not only was this song sung in the School but for decades
afterwards at meetings of the Association of Old Sexeians, the AOS.

"Forty years on, when afar and asunder
Parted are those who are singing today,
When you look back and forgetfully wonder
What you were like in your work and your play -
Then it may be there will often come o'er you
Glimpses of notes, like the catch of a song;
Visions of boyhood shall float there before you,
Echoes of dreamland shall bear them along."

As well as inspiring generations of boys with Science that was
also the case with one of his three daughters, Edith. As a schoolgirl
she was regarded as a tomboy, nicknamed "Boy Knight" as she
often wore trousers or riding breeches and smoked cigarettes. In
1914 aged eighteen she started to work on a farm in Buckinghamshire
and remained there throughout the First World War but then in
1918 Knight persuaded her to study Agriculture at Reading
University. In 1920 she entered Liverpool University Veterinary
School and in 1923 became the first woman to be awarded a
veterinary degree, MRCVS, and then BVSc in 1926. (15)

When Knight finally retired in 1927 after some thirty-six years
as Headmaster he received a large cheque and a bird-bath that
his wife had always wanted! The AOS produced an Album which
contained two pages of hand-written text in various colours and
gold-leaf. There followed hundreds of signatures which clearly
overwhelmed Knight who in a reply commented that, "It is rare
that a Headmaster's services are so fully appreciated." (16)

When a Sexey's School Register 1891-1952 was published a
poem was inserted by a former pupil, R.W. Gregory (1894-1899),
who had become an electrical engineer:

"You made us men, we boys of your own breed;
And like the glowing steel, our mother wit

With cunning hand you hammered into shape,
And tempered for keen service to our kind.
You made our School: a thousand boys and more
You showed the way of life; and thorough men,
Through all the continents of mother earth,
Hold you in honour." (17)

e) Assistant Masters.

During his years as Headmaster Knight appointed some forty-four assistant masters of whom thirty-three had been in place before the end of 1914. Many of these were very young men just starting out on a career and the result was, as may be seen in Table 11 a large percentage remained in the School for only a short time. Knight was very much in the tradition of some Victorian headmasters who welcomed such young men so that they could train them in their philosophy of education and methods of teaching.

Table 11. Length of Service of Assistant Masters.

No. of Years	1 year or less	2 years and under 5	5 years and under 10	10 years and under 20	Over 20 years
No. of Masters	12	15	4	0	2

In 1905 Hobhouse commented that, "They could not expect in a school of that kind to keep their assistant Masters for a great many years, and they were glad to think some of them had gained the promotion they deserved." In fact twenty-seven or nearly 82% remained in the School for under five years. Of those who left at least five became headmasters of other schools and a number entered higher education so that two became professors: Hubert Britton, Professor of Chemistry at University College, Exeter, and Charles Moss, Professor of Botany at Witwatersrand University, Johannesburg, South Africa. Three more, Sydney Bowler, Rhys Harris Jones and Oliver Tunnell were killed during the First World War. Another master, Sydney Brown, was severely wounded but he did resume teaching at the School in 1917. Of the two longest serving Masters, Hubert Crowther taught Chemistry and Physics for thirty-three years from 1904 to 1937 and Stanley Lane Woodwork and Metalwork for thirty-seven years from 1914 to 1951, although he served in the Royal Engineers for four years during the First World War.

The first assistant Master appointed late in 1891 was Walter G. Watson who was to teach the junior boys and woodwork at a salary of just over £6 a month. He was soon involved in the community as well with woodwork classes held at the School as part of the Continuation School. He also gave lectures to other teachers, such as one on the "Teaching of woodwork" in April 1893 in which he used a range of examples from his own pupils. Watson left the School in 1895 and two years later died from typhoid fever while in Leipzig. In January 1898 a memorial to him was unveiled by Lady Verney in Newport, Monmouthshire. (1)

In the first decade of the life of the School some ten different masters were appointed of whom seven remained for four years or less. One of these young men was Joseph Bell who was at the School between January and September 1893 and had taught with Knight in his previous School in Maryport. He left to attend University College, London. At any one time therefore the Headmaster had just one or two Assistant Masters as Inspector Lefroy remarked in his 1894 Report: "For a School of 80 boys three masters are hardly enough" A decade later, even though by then there were five full-time Assistant Masters the H.M.I. Report noted that, "If the subdivision of the School is to be effective, the number of Assistant Staff must be increased." They added that, "It is greatly to the credit of the Head Master and his Staff that the efficiency of the School has been maintained at its present high level when some of the classes are of unwieldy size and contain boys of such unequal attainment." Within a year one more Master was employed.

By the time of the 1910 H.M.I. Inspection there were still six assistants which elicited the comment "that the present Staff is numerically insufficient. There are really eight Forms for only

P. W. RANDELL

six Assistant Masters." A decade later eight full-time and one part-time assistant teachers were in place. (2) As the number of Assistant Masters increased so did their salary bill: in 1897 it stood at £392 18s 2d but by 1914 had risen to £955. One potential problem which became evident at times was the calibre of some of the Assistant Masters. The main reason for this was that the salaries were low: in 1894, for example, the two assistant masters received £90 and £100 respectively. Phillips speculated that during the six years that he attended the School they were about that level or slightly higher. He commented: "You couldn't get double firsts at that figure." He added that, "Teaching at Sexey's was no cake-walk either. There were too many clever boys, their wits sharpened by constant competition." From time to time there was some concern such as in 1898 at the instigation of the Science and Art Department. In September William Pearce, the Governors' Clerk, wrote to the Department to inform them that "the Governors have decided to dispense with the services of Mr Crew and to appoint a well-qualified assistant Master for English subjects." Albert Crew was in fact not a trained teacher but a lawyer and later became a barrister at the Old Bailey. The Department also raised concerns about Frederick Wood who was unqualified and taught elementary practical Geometry and was responsible for Manual Instruction. The School decided to retain him and he remained there until 1902.

In their 1904 Report the H.M.I.s expressed the view that one Master who was "careful and conscientious.... under a weaker Head Master he might have trouble in preserving discipline." The 1910 Report was much more forthright: it recorded that of the six Assistants five were trained certified teachers and one held the Cambridge Teachers' Diploma. Four of them were graduates of English Universities. "While they are all doing useful steady work there is nothing remarkable in their teaching.... It seems very desirable in a School of this importance that there should be on the Staff one or two Masters of higher academic status and teaching experience." (3)

All the Assistant teachers appointed before 1914 had one thing in common: they were all male. Like so many of his contemporary

252

headmasters Knight clearly did not believe that female teachers had a place in a boys' school. The First World War forced a change upon him and by 1920 some nine female teachers had been appointed, of whom seven were wartime appointments, a number being in post for short periods. The first female teacher to teach in the School was a probationer, Miss Annie Paradise from 1st January 1916 and she remained until 23rd May 1918. Some indication of his attitude of scepticism but tempered with limited praise was expressed in his speech at Prize Day in December 1916. He reported that there had been "numerous changes in the Staff during the year, the war compelling them to engage several lady teachers, and although they had not quite maintained their standard, it was better than he expected. He hoped they would be able to maintain discipline at its former level. When he knew that they would have to engage ladies upon the staff, he was very doubtful about the result, but he thought they were to be highly congratulated upon their efficiency."

Knight returned to this theme two years later: "The educational work had been as difficult as could be imagined, owing to Staff troubles. Every eligible man, without exception, had left the school, and lady teachers had been substituted, but there had been no serious lowering of the standard of work, except perhaps in manual instruction. They had been obliged to close their workshops." No record exists that Knight ever publically praised his female teachers or gave an indication of any positive features that they brought to the School or the lives of the boys.

Once the War was over the men returned and the ladies gradually departed: the last to go was Miss Ada Dent who taught Mathematics between 1916 and 1921 and was the only female member of staff at the time of the H.M.I. Inspection in May 1920. "Her lessons are characterized by great clearness and directness, and she created a very favourable impression", although the inspectors added, "it is felt that in the highest Form it ought to be possible to aim at a higher standard."

For the remainder of his headmastership Knight was to appoint just one other female to teach the boys and that was at the very end of his time to fill the gap that his departure created, when Mrs Muriel Herridge taught French from 1927 to 1928. As Miss Simmons she had been his Secretary between 1920 and 1927. In total ten females compared with forty-four males. (4)

f) Pupils.

The Scheme of 1889 declared that the School was to be open to all boys "of good character and sufficient health" and the result was that between 1891 and 1914-5 it witnessed a dramatic increase in the number of boys attending, at one stage it was nearly ten times the original fifteen. As the sample of years in Table 12 shows, however, there was some variation from year to year, which in many instances may be explained by the different months in which

Table 12. Number of boys in the School.

Year	Number of Boys
1891	15 rising to 40
April 1892	57
July 1893	66
1894	80
October 1894	81
July 1895	99
July 1896	100
December 1903	120
October 1904	124
June 1905	119
June 1906	114
June 1907	127
October 1907	146
January 1909	134
February 1910	137
1911	140
1914-5	125

the figures were compiled: the end of the school year could often be lower than at the beginning as boys left for employment purposes.

Although the Scheme of 1889 did not specify the ages for attendance, the first Prospectus stated that the School was intended for boys between the ages of ten and seventeen. The detailed statistics produced for three inspections in 1894, 1904 and 1910 indicated that that was the case before 1914.

Table 13. Ages of boys in the School.

Year	under 10	10 and u. 11	11 and u. 12	12 and u. 13	13 and u. 14	14 and u. 15	15 and u. 16	16 and u. 17	17 and u. 18	18 and over
1893	0	2	9	14	17	16	7	2	0	0
1904	0	3	11	27	27	30	16	7	3	0
1910	0	4	13	25	40	26	8	12	9	0

The statistics indicated that in these three years there were no boys under ten and, as was pointed out in the 1910 Inspection, very few under the age of eleven. At the other end of the age range there were none aged eighteen, although occasionally a boy did return if there was a delay in taking up a university place. The 1910 Scheme specified once again that no boy was to be admitted under the age of ten or remain "after the end of the School year in which the age of eighteen is attained." The vast majority of the boys were aged between twelve and fourteen. Time and again at Prize Distributions and elsewhere Henry Hobhouse urged parents to keep their sons at school "up to a fairly advanced age. Depend upon it a boy could learn more during the latter years of school life than he could during the earlier years." By 1909 he observed that he had noticed that the majority of the boys were now remaining until they were at least fifteen years old.

The H.M.I. Report of 1920 was to show that this trend continued as in July 1919 out of 148 boys in the School there were sixty-three or 42.6% aged fourteen and over, with twenty-eight or 19% aged fifteen and over. This was perhaps not surprising as the 1910 Report had noted that, "In admitting pupils preference is given to those who show a reasonable prospect of remaining at School until at least the age of 15 or 16. This has had the effect of lengthening the School life, and as the competition for places is severe the number of boys who stay long enough to complete the ordinary School course is considerable." (1)

When the School was being planned and its function debated a considerable emphasis was placed upon it being for the sons of farmers and tradesmen. In April 1892 Hobhouse claimed, "that the scholars came from nearly every class except the wealthy class" and in his article the following year identified the following occupations: "Farmers, 21; tradesmen, 27; professional men, 4; artisans, 11; others, 3." It was possible, however, that Hobhouse, who was so convinced of the importance of education for the sons of farmers as they faced more foreign competition and had to deal with new techniques, was somewhat disappointed by the number of farmers who sent their sons to this new school. In his Prize Day speech in July 1894 he stated that,

> "They did not want to unfit any class for living and work-ing in country districts, which were now suffering somewhat from de-population. In the workshops, in garden and field-work, they endeavoured not to unfit the lads for country life, but rather to fit them to do that work more completely, more intelligently, and more satisfactorily. He was glad to think that many of their farmers recognised the advantages of schools like those. They had a considerable number of boys - though not so many as he would like to see - from the farm-ing class. He was sure that when they recognized the value of such teaching that they would patronize the School more than they did now."

Five years later he reported that some thirty to forty boys who had left the School in the previous three years had gone into farming, compared with sixty into trade, thirty into clerical offices and twenty-three into other schools and colleges. (2)

The statistics compiled for the three Reports indicated that the initial pattern remained substantially the same but that there were some changes emerging as may be seen in Table 14.

Table 14. Occupation of Parents.

Occupation	1894	1904	1910
Farmer	19	31	16
Retail traders	33	34	35
Merchants and Bankers	1	5	0
Professional and Independent	3	9	11
Schoolmasters	3	8	4
Artisans	5	19	9
Clerks	1	18	7
Clergyman	1	0	0
Labourer	1	0	0
Wholesale Traders	0	0	14
Domestic Servants	0	0	2

Knight himself reported in 1911 that, "About 40 or 50 percent of the boys in the School were sons of farmers and tradesmen, a good many were sons of better-class artisans, some were sons of professional men, and a number were the sons of Schoolmasters." (3) Before the First World War the School was established firmly as an overwhelmingly middle-class school. Even with scholarships available most labouring families could not afford to support their sons at such a level and to such an age. The middle classes were increasingly attracted to the School for a number of reasons. Prominent among these was the fact that it was extremely successful in the education it aimed to provide. Even when fees were gradually raised it provided an exceptionally cheap education as a result of the support of the Visitors. In 1894 Inspector Lefroy commented, "Thus a small farmer or tradesman can get a thoroughly practical and scientific education for his son for a sum well within his means." For many boys the location of the School close to two railway stations meant ease of access with cheap daily travel.

Lefroy discovered that, "Special arrangements for cheap season tickets have been made with one of the railway companies." For those from elsewhere in Somerset or from further afield there were boarding possibilities.

The class of boy who attended the new School led the Headmaster of King's School, D.E. Norton, junior, to be absolutely certain that its establishment did not significantly harm his school. In 1894 he reported to his Governors, "Undoubtedly the foundation of 'Sexey's School' has done something to diminish the number of our Day Boys, but so far from complaining of this, I think it is a matter of congratulation that we no longer have a number of boys sent to us, for whom the education provided at this School can be of little or no practical value in advancing them in life."

The expectation in Bruton and its immediate neighbourhood when the proposed School was being discussed and then planned was that it would be of significant value to the sons of local inhabitants. In July 1896 Hobhouse "observed that that School was established primarily as a day school for boys in the Bruton district, and would always direct its first effort to teaching the lads in the immediate neighbourhood. (4) The subsequent admissions indicated that in the beginning that was indeed the case but the very success of the School, along with the availability of County Scholarships which could be held in the School by boys from elsewhere in Somerset, meant that there was a decline in such boys by 1914 as in that year there was just one boy admitted from Bruton itself. It really had become a County School. The pattern of admissions may be seen in Tables 15 and 16.

The phrase 'Rest of Somerset' did of course include towns and villages which were very close to Bruton.

i) Travel to School.

Four of these eight villages and towns were served by the railways and in addition in 1892 the first boy from Frome, where there was

Table 15. Admissions to the School.

Locations	Admitted in 1891	Admitted in 1914	Total in School in 1893	Total in School in 1904	Total in School in 1910
From Bruton	16	1	14	24	10
From rest of Somerset	25	33	50	90	113
From rest of England	0	2	4	4	11
From places outside England	0	3	0	0	3

Table 16. Admissions from neighbouring villages and towns.

Village or town From	Admitted in 1891	Admitted in 1914	Total in School in 1893	Total in School in 1904	Total in School in 1910
Castle Cary	9	4	14	4	4
North & South Brewham	3	0	1	0	1
Shepton Montague	2	1	1	0	0
Milton Clevedon	1	0	2	0	0
Sparkford	3	0	0	0	0
Evercreech	2	0	4	0	0
Wincanton	0	1	3	5	2

no secondary school, joined the School. Thereafter on average three or four new boys came from that town each year before the First World War (and in fact for decades afterwards.) Every school day they caught a train at Frome station at about 7.30 a.m. for the twenty-five minute journey and then walked the mile or so from Bruton Station to the School, past King's School and then down the small lane or path which ran from the Godminster Road behind Berkeley House to Lusty Bridge. The original path crossed the railway lines behind the House before continuing down to join Park Road near the ford. It was judged to be a dangerous crossing especially as the trains became faster and more frequent and so the Parish Council campaigned for either a diversion of the path, a subway or a bridge. For four years the railway company procrastinated but eventually agreed to a diversion in 1904: "The diversion over the GWR at Lusty has been completed and the new path opened. It is a great improvement as besides doing away with the necessity of crossing the railway line, it is itself a very pretty finish to the lane from Plox." At some stage it became known locally as "Lovers' Lane." It made the walk much safer for the boys.

After School each day the boys had to walk back, catching the train to Frome at about 5.15 p.m. Phillips recalled that it was the usual practice of the boys to play a football game all the way. For boys from Frome the return rail fare for eleven months was £3   15s   2d. In 1904 there was some concern expressed that a proposed new secondary school at Frome might provide competition and diminish the quality of the boys who came from there. While this issue was carefully considered it did not seem to have had such an effect.

For boys travelling from the Evercreech Junction direction to Cole Station the trains arrived at 8.35 a.m. and left before 5 p.m. in the afternoon; from the Wincanton direction arrival and departure times were very similar. The eleven month return fare from Evercreech Junction was £1   15s   0d and from Wincanton £2   1s   6d.

In the days when cars were still very rare in Somerset the overwhelming majority of boys walked to School although an increasing number were able to afford bicycles. To cope with these a bicycle shed, "a boon to another section of the school", was built early in 1897 and then replaced by another "capital bicycle house" as part of the additions of 1903. For those cycling or walking to School the weather was an important factor as heavy rain could mean sitting in wet clothes for a long period. When referring to the heating arrangements the Prospectus of 1904 also informed parents that, "Wet clothes and boots may be dried in the cloakroom. It is recommended that boys walking from a distance should keep boots at the School." (5)

ii) Applications.

The success of the School meant that applications for a place increased rapidly. When it came to the sale and letting of local properties the School was often mentioned in the advertisements, such as when Coombe Farm was to be let in April 1896: "Good House and capital School for the Sons of Farmers at very modest cost." All boys had to take an Entrance Examination at the School in June for admission at the start of the new year in August, in which "a minimum standard is exacted according to the age of the candidates." The usual procedure was that about a month before the Entrance Examination a notice would appear in local newspapers, such as one in May 1908: "The Annual Entrance Examination will be held at the School on Friday June 19th 1908. One or more Free Scholarships entitling to Free Tuition and Books will be awarded on the results of the above Examination, if candidates of sufficient merit present themselves." There were exceptions in the early days, for example, in 1892 when the new buildings were ready for occupation, on 29th March Josiah Jackson of Durslade Farm noted, "Mr Knight came & examined Stanley & agreed to take him at 'The Trade School' on Monday next the 4th April." In 1903 Knight stated that, "In selecting candidates for admission, regard was paid to attainments and also to priority of application." One of his constant criticisms was that the level of English was often not as good as he would have wished. In 1907, for example, he commented, "there was no improvement in the qualification of the candidates, especially in the subject of English."

The major problem for the School was not the number or quality of the applicants but the lack of accommodation, as Knight bemoaned in 1906: "We have now reached a stage when the applications are well in advance of the accommodation. Since August last I have had to refuse many applications for admission owing to lack of further accommodation." In the 1910 Report the H.M.I.s commented, "A considerable number of boys are rejected each year so that the standard of admission is kept high." It was a pattern which was to continue after the War when in 1918 Knight reported that he had had to reject fifty boys, including from the locality even though they "were shown by examination to be quite capable of benefitting from a secondary education." Two year later Hobhouse announced that the Governors had had "to draw up rather strict rules as to admission…. they were bound to give preference to those boys who could stay a sufficient time to profit by the excellent education." (6)

The School had become highly selective in its intake which of course helped to explain the considerable success which it achieved. In so doing it had moved away from some of the original ideas at the time of its foundation.

Once a boy had been admitted regular attendance was expected. In July 1895 Knight named seven boys who had not been absent or late during the whole year as an example to others. The following year he named four boys, one of whom, Burrough, who lived three miles from the School, had only been late three times in four years and not at all in the last two. In 1912 Knight reminded parents that, "He was obliged to treat unnecessary absence with severity because of the disruption it caused to their education." By 1920 the abundance of applications allowed him to take a very firm stance. "I would here again remind parents that boys who are not taking proper advantage of what the School offers either from idleness, bad conduct or pressure of other outside interests, are liable to be dismissed in order to make room for boys who are anxious and eager to enter." Unfortunately no documentary evidence has survived to indicate how many, if any, boys were removed as a result of absence or these other activities. (7)

iii) Scholarships.

Although education became free in 1891 in elementary schools that did not apply in other schools and so they charged fees which put them beyond the reach of many parents. An attempt was made to solve this problem by the provision of scholarships, which either offered a free place or a fixed sum for a specific number of years. The Scheme of 1889 allowed the Governors of Sexey's Trade School to offer "Scholarships in the form of free places." They were to be awarded to boys who had been in public elementary schools for at least three years. The number awarded each year depended on the perceived nature of the intake so that in 1893, for example, there were four in the School - three for three years and one for one. The award entitled the recipients to free tuition and books, the latter coming to about 10s.

In the mid-1890s one scholarships seems to have been made available to the Managers of the National School in Bruton for them to award. In practice some of the scholarships were awarded based upon progress and conduct once in the School, which in 1908 Hobhouse considered "as an absolutely reasonable requirement in the case of free scholarships." He went on to state that in a school of their size there should be even larger numbers of such scholarships, "that they ought to be given as far as possible to the boys of parents who could not afford to pay anything substantial for their education, and to boys who were likely to profit by such education."

From the earliest days of the School the East Somerset Agricultural Society, which covered Bruton, Castle Cary and Wincanton, offered three scholarships of £10 a year each for three years. It was not lost upon at least one local newspaper in July 1891 that the three men behind the scheme, Henry Hobhouse, A.J. Goodford and T.O. Bennett, "seem to form a sort of 'happy family party' for directing the fortunes of both the Agricultural Society and the School." Nevertheless it believed, "that the scheme is a good one, and contributed to extend the usefulness of both the school and the Agricultural Society, and to make them more beneficial to the neighbourhood in whose interest they exist." Every year before the First World War three boys a year benefitted. (8)

In the long term of even greater importance for some of the boys was the establishment by Somerset County Council, itself very much under the influence of Hobhouse, of a system of County Scholarships to aid boys from twelve years of age until they completed higher education. There were Junior Scholarships of £15 a year for three years, followed by Intermediate Scholarships of £30 a year for two years. Finally there were a smaller number of Senior Scholarships of £60 a year for three years tenable at a university or technical institution. There is no doubt that before 1914 Sexey's dominated this system aided by the fact that once awarded parents could choose which school their son should attend. In 1893 there were twenty-three boys on Junior and Intermediate Scholarships in the School.

Table 17 gives some indication of the number of Senior and Intermediate Scholarships achieved by the School.

These figures represent 61% of all Senior Scholarships and 65% of all Intermediate Scholarships being awarded to boys in the School. The H.M.I.s in their 1904 Report gave a fairly accurate assessment when they stated that, "About two-thirds of the whole number of Intermediate County Scholarships appear to be normally held in the School." The same pattern continued, for example, in 1913 boys in the School obtained both Senior Scholarships and four out of the seven Intermediate ones. By 1925 the figures stood at thirty-six out of fifty-eight Senior Scholarships and 102 out of 187 Intermediate ones.

Table 17. Senior and Intermediate Scholarships 1895-1908.

| | Senior Scholarships | | | | | | Intermediate Scholarships | | | | | |
	1895-1904	1905	1906	1907	1908	1895-1904	1905	1906	1907	1908	Total
Number awarded by Somerset County Council	20	2	2	2	2	64	4	5	5	6	84
Number gained by School	11	1	2	1	2	41	3	4	2	5	55

One perhaps unforeseen consequence of the success of the School was that it had an adverse effect upon at least one neighbouring school. In December 1912 the Headmaster of Shepton Mallet Grammar School reported that their average number that year had been sixty-two. "There had been keener competition than usual in the neighbourhood for pupils owing to the opening of a higher elementary school at Midsummer Norton and to the enlargement of Sexey's School, Bruton, between which they were unfortunately sandwiched." (9)

The value not only of the Intermediate but also of the Junior Scholarships in allowing some boys to remain in education was incalculable: because of the quality of the education they received and the way it enhanced their chances of achieving the career which they wanted and also the level of success within it. The Senior Scholarship permitted a number of really able boys to enter higher education with the universities of Cambridge, Oxford, London, Reading and Victoria [Manchester] figuring prominently. As a result of the scientific leaning of their education Finsbury Technical College proved attractive with at least fourteen boys having entered residence before 1908.

g) A boarding school.

The Scheme of 1889 sanctioned the Governors establishing a school for day boys which could accommodate fifty scholars. When the Visitors purchased the Cliffe House Estate, the Governors of the School were interested only in obtaining a small piece of land for their buildings and not the main house itself. The intention of the Visitors was that that would continue to be leased to others and in fact Mrs Whalley had such a lease which was due to terminate at the end of 1891 but was extended until Midsummer 1892.

It became apparent immediately that with the rapid rise in numbers, especially of County Scholars from greater distances, that some boarding provision was going to be required. This reason was the justification cited by Hobhouse in July 1896 when he explained that the Governors, "had thought it right to add to that day school a certain amount of boarding accommodation. They had a number of distinguished scholars from various parts of the county, whose presence raised the level of the school, and for whom boarding accommodation must be provided." (1)

While Hobhouse, Bennett and Knight realised at once the potential of Cliffe House for boarding accommodation given its proximity to the School, it was only at their meeting on 13th September 1892 that the Visitors agreed to lease the house to the Governors as a Boarding House at a rent of £60 a year. In fact throughout the spring of that year other potential tenants had been contacting Bennett to obtain information about the property as it had been advertised as available.

When the Visitors had been contemplating purchasing the estate in 1890 Bennett had provided them with a brief description of the house: "a detached modern Building with South aspect and attractive gardens. It is stone built and slated..... in excellent repair and order... The Offices are suitable... and is well supplied with hard and soft Water and Gas. The Stabling, Sheds and outbuildings are well-placed and sufficient." His subsequent replies to potential tenants gave further details: it had a Drawing Room 19 feet 10 inches by 19 feet 6 inches. Dining Room 18 feet 6 inches by 14 feet, Morning Room 13 feet 9 inches by 14 feet and Study 10 feet by 14 feet. The Hall was some 34 feet in length and 4 feet wide. Above were five bedrooms, servants' rooms and W.C. The basement was occupied by the Kitchen and Butler's Pantry. (2) It was in fact a small country house, especially when compared with the present-day building which is the result of several extensions.

Mrs Whalley vacated the premises as agreed and the Visitors even paid her £4 15s 0d "for Garden Crop left at Cliffe House." Not for the first time the House witnessed an influx of boarders when the new ones under the supervision of Knight became established in October 1892. Boarding was therefore essentially a private venture for the benefit of the Headmaster. Although the Governors charged him a rent of just £32 a year for the house, the anticipated comfortable profit from the boarding enterprise which was seen as a method of supplementing his salary, occurred only rarely before 1914.

The house itself, which seems to have varied the spelling of its name thereafter - sometimes including the last 'e' and sometimes not, was equipped with five beds in each of the four large bedrooms and two beds in the smaller one. Other facilities were somewhat limited as even by 1920 there were just two baths, six washbasins and two internal and two external W.C.s. There was no fire escape. Any serious or infectious medical cases were to be transferred from the house to a cottage nearby where rooms were permanently reserved.

The boarder boys were fed with food prepared in the basement kitchen but unfortunately no indication of what was provided has survived. Whatever it was must have been insufficient for some of the growing boys as a former pupil recalled that one boarder, George Walker 1898-1901, had a "propensity for currant buns which he daily bought at the School gate and carried in a pile one above the other to Cliff House at dinner time." One local trader and one boarder had obviously found a ready market.

The boarders had to arrange their own entertainment and soon it became a tradition to stage a Christmas Concert which with so many boys wishing to take part tended to be long but "which reflected great credit on the musical ability and energy of the Cliffe House boarders." In 1902, for example, there were a range of solos, readings, instrumental solos, a short farce, 'Furnished Apartments', and two sessions with a phonograph." (3)

The introduction of boarders into the School was to create two problems. The first one was relatively easy to solve when it emerged in 1908 as a result of the annual inspection of the Board of Education. The Scheme of 1889 allowed the Governors to build a school for fifty day boys and in a Memo in 1908 an official at the Board drew attention to the fact that that permission had not changed in subsequent Schemes. "In the circumstances it appears to be clear that the Govs. had no power to admit boarders into the School." In the sixteen years that boarders had been received no one else appeared to have noticed this fact: not the Governors, the Charity Commissioners, the Board of Education, their Inspectors or H.M.I.s at the time of their inspection in 1904. On 23rd September 1908 the Board of Education decided that the Governors needed to apply to admit boarders, which they did on 19th October. The Board agreed and in the Scheme of 1910, while it was re-iterated that it was a day school, it was added that, "if the Governors think fit a boarding school for boys shall be maintained in or near the Parish of Bruton, in the present school buildings." (4)

The second problem proved to be more intractable and that was the number of applications for boarding places and the lack of boarding accommodation. The H.M.I. Report of 1904 considered that while the Boarding House was "substantially built" it was "not well designed for the purpose" and that "the house should not hold more than 12 boys." The Governors acknowledged that there was a problem and Hobhouse reported in his Prize Distribution speech that it had "engaged the attention of the governing body". While they accepted "that accommodation had not been equal to their desires", a new boarding house would be very expensive.

In 1893 there were eight boys boarded in the town but it was the 1904 Report which was the first one to deal fully with the question of the large number of boys who by then boarded with private families in the town. "A large number of boys (24) board in the Town in lodgings which are recognized by the Head Master. The Governors disclaim all responsibility in respect of these boys, and the Head Master does not profess to be able to ensure anything like efficient supervision of them after leaving school." While the Inspectors would have liked to have seen a new boarding house capable of holding not less than forty boarders, they accepted that the resources were not available for the necessary capital expenditure.

In practical terms, nothing happened until once again the boarding situation was criticized in the 1910 H.M.I. Report. They considered the "Boarding accommodation inadequate and over-crowded" and recommended a new boarding house with provision being made for the Headmaster and his family. The Report also drew attention, as had the previous Report, to the number of boys boarding in the town: at the time of their visit some twenty-two, but added that the demand for admission to the School was "so great that even this number is sometimes exceeded."

This time the Governors did respond, pointing out that the anticipated cost of a new boarding house would be about £4,000 and they "do not think themselves in a sufficiently strong position financially to carry it out at present." Four days later as Chairman of Somerset Education Committee Hobhouse held a meeting with Mr Bruce from the Board of Education in which he re-iterated the Governors' financial concerns. While he accepted "that the accommodation for these boys was not ideal, the matter was perhaps less important because the boys are of a class who are accustomed to the sort of conditions in which they are lodged and they and their parents are content." Perhaps not the most enlightened comment to be uttered by the man who did so much for education in the Bruton area. Class division remained strong in rural areas well into the twentieth century.

Hobhouse went on to point out that the Headmaster inspected the arrangements in the houses and that "no disciplinary trouble has occurred." Bruce did suggest that the Governors could form a Visiting Committee to help the Headmaster but that idea seems to have provoked no response. He also mentioned that he had come across instances elsewhere where such boys were not properly fed and Hobhouse did agree that he would "look further into the question of boys' feeding." Bruce was probably not completely satisfied with the response from Hobhouse as later in April the Governors received a request from the Board that they "be furnished with particulars of the steps that are taken to ensure that the boys who attend the School and are lodged in the town are properly cared for."

In a reply in May 1910 F.W. Hooper gave some details of how their system operated. "The Headmaster keeps a list of persons who are prepared to receive boys. Names are added to this list only after the Headmaster is personally satisfied as to the respectability of the householder and the accommodation of the house." He did concede, perhaps following the lead of Hobhouse, that, "The conditions in these lodgings are not 'ideal' but are probably at least as good as in the house from which the boys come." He pointed out that the boys tended to be there only for sleeping and meals. The sum paid by the parents was a matter of negotiation between them and the householder but was generally between £20 and £24 a year. He did draw attention to the fact that some boarding arrangements were made without consulting the Headmaster, often involving other family members or friends. He included with his letter a copy of their regulations for boarding in the town.

"Sexey's Trade School, Bruton.
Regulation as to boys lodging in the town.

1. The meals and hours of study of the boys will be arranged to correspond with the requirements of the School.

2. All boys are expected to take part in the School games, unless excused by the Head Master on the request of the parent.

3. Boys will not be allowed on any account to loiter in the streets.

4. In case of enforced absence from the School (through illness or other reason) the Head Master must be informed immediately.

5. The rooms occupied by Boarders will be open to occasional visits of the Head Master."

This list was hardly a comprehensive scheme for safeguarding or caring for these boarder boys but it seemed to have satisfied the Board so no further correspondence resulted. (5)

Although the Governors took no other immediate action, the question of a new boarding house remained under detailed consideration. In April 1914 Hooper informed the Board that the Governors had considered mortgaging the School premises to raise £3,000 for a new boarding house. It was proposed that it would have five dormitories, four sleeping ten boarders each and one just six, a Sick Room for two boys, a Dining room for eighty boys, five staff rooms and two servants' rooms.

In July 1914 the Governors sent out a Circular asking for contributions towards the new boarding house which was estimated to be going to cost £3,400. They pointed out that the "position and usefulness [of the School] will be impaired" without such action. They wished to raise £1,000 from public bodies and individuals to reduce the potential mortgage. The Headmaster had already offered to contribute £60 and Hobhouse £250, provided a similar sum was raised. In September however Hobhouse had to confess that the appeal had failed as it had raised just £100. "Then came the War, which of course put an end to all hope of raising more money by voluntary contribution at present." All that he could say at Prize Day 1914 was that, "They hoped that when the war shadow had passed away and prosperity had returned they would be able to carry out that scheme."

In fact by 1920 the situation had deteriorated, as in a confidential part of the H.M.I. Report Knight was reported as saying that, "the war lead the scheme to be dropped for a time and the increased cost at the present time was he understood an effective bar to these plans being put into execution." He went on to state that such was the demand for boarding education that while he could supervise some of the boys boarding in the town, "a greater number had made their own arrangements and occupied lodgings largely without formal supervision." (6) A far from ideal situation but it is impossible to determine if the acceptance of more and more boys, many of whom were boarders, was driven by the desire for a greater revenue from tuition fees to benefit the School, more boarding fees to supplement the income of the Headmaster or the belief that as many boys as possible should be given the opportunity to benefit from the type of education offered at the School.

h) Examinations, Reports and Prizes.

In order to assess the progress of individual boys some form of assessment was essential. The Scheme of 1889 required that, "There shall be once in every year an examination of the scholars by an Examiner or Examiners appointed or approved for that purpose by the Governors but otherwise unconnected with the School." Such an Examiner was required to give a written report to the Governors covering not only the "proficiency of the scholars" but also the instruction given and the discipline. Before 1914 there was some amendment to the system with the involvement of external bodies. "The Lower Forms are examined by an external Examiner appointed every year, the Upper forms enter for various public examinations. The whole School is examined by the Staff three times a year."

In 1893 boys from the School were entered for examinations of the Science and Art Department, a great incentive being that success would lead to an important grant. The decision to be involved was only made after significant discussion: "The connection with the Department of Science and Art was only made by the school authorities after careful deliberation. It was evidently unwise to unduly hamper the staff in their work or to disarrange the curriculum of so young a School... too great stress can easily be laid upon percentages." This was a view echoed by what the H.M.I.s found in 1904, "Examinations are properly regarded as a means and not as an end in themselves." (1)

The boys appeared to take these examinations in the stride: "The old Science and Art examinations, on the result of which nothing hung but honour, gave us excellent practice [for County Scholarship exams], and we took them in the evenings in every sort of subject, from drawing to advanced mathematics." In the first year the School was very successful with over fifty certificates being awarded and as Knight reported at Prize Day, "a very substantial amount of grant." Table 18 gives an indication of the percentages achieved in that year.

Table 18. Percentages of passes in 1893

Subject	Sexey's Trade School %	Whole country %
Geometrical Drawing	94	54
Freehand Drawing	46	42
Model Drawing	46	39
Mathematics	50	24
Theoretical Chemistry	44	43
Practical Chemistry	27	32

The success continued so that in 1906, for example, the boys gained twenty first class certificates and forty-three second class certificates. Some of the subjects entered were particularly useful as Josiah Jackson noted on 8th May 1894 that he went to the School to see an examination on "The Principles of Agriculture." (2)

In 1901 candidates were entered for the Oxford Local Examinations for the first time: three senior boys sat the papers and all passed, two with honours and one with a distinction in Chemistry. Such successes were widely reported in the local press and in 'Lists of Successes' published by the School. Between 1901 and 1908, for example, the School achieved twenty-four Senior passes with honours and forty-seven Junior passes with honours. There were six ordinary passes for Seniors and eighteen for Juniors. Failures were in fact rare such as just one in 1905. In total the Seniors gained sixteen Distinctions and the Juniors twelve - several being placed first or second out of up to 10,000 candidates. Reflecting the leaning of the School there were seven distinctions each in Chemistry and Botany and three in Mathematics, but also four in History and three each in English and French. Such was the success of V.S. Summerhayes in coming first in Junior Geography that he was awarded the Silver Medal of the Royal Geographical Society. (3)

Every year the Examiner appointed by the Governors presented his written Report to them. In many respects those produced in the first few years of the School's existence were crucial as they undoubtedly influenced contemporaries' decisions on sending their sons to the School. Taken together they were extremely favourable. In order to publicize them they were invariably read out at the Prize Distribution by one of the Governors, for many years T.O. Bennett. This procedure meant that key parts of them were reproduced in the local press. "The premises are well-built, well-arranged, & well-warmed, & ventilated. The tone and order are excellent, obedience to orders on the part of the scholars is prompt & exact.... and it is evident that the school is a place for the foundation of good habits as well as a place of instruction." (1893)

"a varied, extensive and practical course of Studies is pursued, and that the boys are taking full advantage of the great opportunities offered to them.... The general discipline of the School seemed to me to be excellent." (1894)

"The curriculum seems to be admirably adapted to the class of boys.... The discipline of the School is excellent. The boys are respectful and yet there is an air of freedom in their manners which is most refreshing." (1895)

"The manliness, honesty, industry, obedience and good manners of the boys are evident at all points.... The writing throughout the School is a strong point." (1899)

"I feel confident that the training given, tends to develop every manly trait in the boys' character and eminently fits them for useful positions in life." (1900)

"There was an air of earnestness and reality in the classrooms; discipline was complete, but not severe; he did not see an idle boy." (1906)

"A quick and willing obedience to authority which spoke volumes for the spirit and discipline of the School." (1907)

When it came to individual subjects there were some variations and suggestions through the years but overall the Reports were very favourable and must have made a very positive impression on any prospective parents. (4)

For boys who had been particularly successful Prize Day could be one of the highlights of the year. The first one occurred in

April 1892 when the School was formally opened and the second exactly one year later. It then moved to late June or early July to be followed by the summer holidays, but in 1897 it was found to be more convenient for it to take place in December and it remained there for the rest of the years before 1914. The main reason for the final move was that it allowed the Headmaster to present the results of any external examinations which had been taken, usually in April or June, and also to give information about any scholarships awarded and entry to institutions of higher education. It was invariably held on a Saturday so that schoolwork was not interrupted and all the boys were required to attend. At the end of the ceremony some of the boys performed songs such as a cantata 'A Merry Christmas' in December 1900 and short recitations. Tea followed.

Once the School was formally established and its name known in places of higher education the tendency was to invite academics to present the prizes and deliver an address: these included Professor Lloyd Morgan, the Principal of University College, Bristol in 1900; Professor Barrell, 1904; Professor Thompson, Principal of Finsbury Technical College, 1905; Professor Sadler, 1908; Professor Pope of Cambridge, 1912; and Professor Dickinson of University College, Reading, 1913. Occasionally a member of Somerset County Council such as J.E. Wakefield in 1911 presented the prizes. In 1902 a Governor, the Earl of Cork and Orrery returned ten years after he had formally opened the School. When the Bishop of Bath and Wells was taken ill in 1903 his stand-in at very short notice was Mrs Henry Hobhouse - the only occasion that a woman presented the prizes before the First World War.

Initially just one prize was awarded in each subject area but that increased as the School grew in numbers. As well as for subjects there was an award for Good Conduct, which took the form of a bronze medal, and later for regular attendance. When Victor Jackson won the Drawing Prize in July 1893 he received, appropriately enough, a box of instruments. In fact the Jackson brothers were very successful: in June 1895 Victor and Edgar were awarded one prize each and Stanley two, and in December 1898 Stanley received three prizes and Willie and Edgar were given a certificate each.

The overwhelming majority of the prizes took the form of books. In 1893, for example, the Junior Religious Knowledge prize was 'Pilgrim's Progress' and for Science, 'First Year of Scientific Knowledge'. For Senior English 'Tennyson', History 'Green's History', Religious Knowledge 'Farrar's Life of Christ'. Perhaps slightly more unusual was the Junior Arithmetic prize, 'Chambers' Dictionary.' Each year a small amount of money was allocated for these prizes from school funds such as £10 in 1897 and £15 in 1913-14.

For those boys who did not receive a prize the internal examination system along with the "somewhat elaborate system of marking" was crucial in placing them in the appropriate teaching group. "Classification is determined by merit only, with a salutary disregard for the sordid financial considerations which are often found to encourage premature promotions." (5)

i) The Curriculum.

i) Subjects for study

The Scheme of 1889 specified that the curriculum was to include Reading, Writing, Arithmetic, Geography, History, English Grammar, Composition and Literature, Geometry, Algebra, Mensuration, Land Surveying, Practical Mechanics, "Such branches of practical science in its application to agriculture or manufactures as the Governors may from time to time fix", Drawing, Drill and Vocal Music. Interestingly the Governors were given a fair amount of discretion over the subjects to be included and it was immediately apparent that the intention was to offer a type of curriculum, and school, which was significantly different from the curriculum available in many of the existing schools for pupils in the age range specified: they tended to be academic whereas this one was much more practical. The first Prospectus made it absolutely clear that some subjects were only to be available for the upper age range: Book-keeping, Mensuration, Land Surveying and one or more of Mechanics, Physics, Chemistry, Animal Physiology, Botany, Natural History and Geology.

Within this Prospectus examples were given of the content of each of these subjects which demonstrated clearly a leaning towards Science as it was applied to agriculture and manufacturing. For Mechanics there was the use of tools and common machines, weights and measures; Chemistry included the constituents of air, water, soils, manures, feeding stuff, milk, butter and cheese; Animal Physiology covered the structure, on-going health and diseases of man and domestic animals; Botany included the growth, cultivation and requirements of common plants and trees; Natural History, the habits and uses of stock, poultry, dogs, birds, worms, destructive insects and other pests. "The scholars should thus on leaving the school be fitted to take their place at once as useful and intelligent assistants in the farm, work-shop, or manufactory." (1)

A Prospectus for June 1904 indicated that, although the School was subject to the Board of Education as a Secondary School, Division A, the curriculum had remained substantially the same. For the lower forms Handwriting and Elementary Science were specifically included and for the upper forms French, which Knight himself had taught for many years. The H.M.I. Report in 1910 found the same curriculum and commented, "The Head Master has preferred quite deliberately to impart a very marked bias to the Curriculum in the direction of Science, Mathematics and Manual work, and undoubtedly his policy has achieved a very remarkable success."

There were those in the early days of the School who strongly criticized Knight's emphasis upon the teaching of Science but gradually attitudes changed. In 1902, for example, the Earl of Cork stressed the importance of Chemistry as, "The Germans had made great advances in this subject, and in consequence were their keen competitors in commerce." Much more fundamental, however, were the principles upon which Knight based his curriculum. They were probably best articulated by Professor John Read when his former headmaster retired in 1927. "The knowledge we acquired at School is the knowledge of 'understanding' rather than the knowledge of 'learning.' It is knowledge that has never worn off.... To think for oneself; to solve one's own problems; to exercise initiative; to check, confirm, and prove one's results; to take wide views; to be prompt, punctual, and punctilious; and to work to the best advantage: these are among the leading virtues inculcated by Mr Knight's methods of training." (2)

As might be expected through the years various subjects attracted comments: some favourable and some less so. Although not initially listed separately practical work was undertaken from the very beginning: first woodwork and then metalwork in the purpose-built workshops. Knight was absolutely clear that in teaching these two practical subjects "there was no attempt made to teach a trade." He believed that, "The work should be educational in its aims, considerations of utility should be subordinated to educational development; no attempt should be made to turn out carpenters or engineers. Knowledge of processes and tools, the manipulation of material, the development of the power of co-ordinating brain, eye and hand should be guiding principles." His stance was supported by Professor Barrell, "there the boys had a double education, working with their hands, eyes and brains at the same time, and that was a very great and good thing for them."

In an Appendix to his evidence to the Acland Committee in 1911 Knight gave details of his two year Woodwork course: it included planeing, gauging, squaring and sawing, grooving, chisels, hammers, different types of trees and their properties, mechanical principles of tools, nature and geographical distribution of different types of trees. A practical example of what was entailed may be found in the surviving Woodwork Exercise Book of A.J. Jennings aged fourteen in 1902. Over four pages were diagrams of a Wooden Plane, Wood graining, Square and a Half Lap Joint. There was also a Table headed 'Wood Seasoning'. (3)

Table 19. Wood Seasoning.

	Advantages	Disadvantages
1. Natural Seasoning	It is very cheap.	It takes a very long time.
2. Boiling and Steaming	It makes the wood hard.	Only small pieces of timber.
3. Floating in river	Large pieces of wood can be used.	

Knight believed that Metalwork should be started after two years of Woodwork which gave the basic training and skills with tools, especially as the former required even greater accuracy. The new metalwork building opened at the beginning of 1894 was fitted with forge, anvil and benches with vice and tools. During the next two decades a regular teacher was usually employed assisted by a local blacksmith. Knight gave a breakdown of the course to the Acland Committee and it included, gauging, cutting, filing, drilling, forging, tempering and bending. The boys made a variety of items from different metals, such as gardener's labels (zinc), set squares (brass), funnel with handle (tin), small bucket (iron sheet), stove rake (iron) and garden trowel (sheet steel). (4)

In 1910 the H.M.I.s were satisfied with the course in Manual Instruction. "The course of Manual Instruction is usually thorough and complete.... the course as a whole may rightly be regarded as a most useful and effective contribution to the educational work of the School." Not all former pupils were so convinced, for example, in 1914 John Read severely criticized some aspects of the course but that however produced a spirited defence from another Old Sexeian, Robert Longman (1894-9), who had become an electrical engineer. He viewed it as "a fine training for the hand and eye." He added that, "It is one of those things which I look back on with the greatest of pleasure and satisfaction." (5)

The Science part of the curriculum was generally very well received by the boys and by various inspectors, such as in 1895,

"The course of general elementary Science taught in the School is admirable." Initially Knight himself taught virtually all of the science lessons but then in 1895 appointed Thomas Hartley to teach both Chemistry and Physics. He remained until 1903 when he was followed by Herbert Crowther who retired in 1937. Teaching Science did in fact attract a significant grant in the 1890s from the Department of Science and Art, a welcome addition to the School's limited budget. In 1898, for example, sixty-three boys were under instruction and earned a grant of £384 which represented some £6 2s 0d per head, which compared with the County average of £3 10s 0d. In fact Sexey's Trade School "enjoys the proud distinction of standing at the head of the list for the average of grants earned" by the 156 schools involved.

The emphasis upon Science did lead to several unusual occurrences. On one occasion a boy who wished to buy a 'gold' watch from another boy showed it to Knight who then explained the effect of chemicals on metals to the class, especially that gold would be unaffected. He then lowered the watch into a chemical solution and all the boys saw the 'gold' dissolve. On another occasion a pungent smell filled one of the rooms. A plumber was called, floorboards lifted but nothing discovered. Eventually some budding chemists admitted their involvement and Knight was apparently so suitably impressed by their initiative that severe punishment was avoided.

For several years a more practical problem arose when G.M. Tincknell reported that starlings had built nests in the ventilators of a fume cupboard and neither ordinary fumes nor fumes of sulphur, phosphorous, hydrogen sulphide, hydrochloric acid etc. could shift them. It was not unusual for a bird to fly down and perch on the apparatus in the glass cupboard itself. (6)

As part of the Science Course offered to the upper classes, Knight introduced Botany. This subject was in fact very, very rare in boys' schools in the 1890s as it was to be thirty years or more before biological subjects became established. In an obituary for one of Knight's pupils in 1965 it was claimed that, "In this respect Sexey's School was unique in the country." In fact an earlier obituary in 1953 for another former pupil considered that Knight "was to prove himself so truly a pioneer of nature study and of science teaching in secondary school." With so vast a rural area on the School's doorstep it was inevitable that advantage was taken of it on a significant scale. In 1910 the H.M.I.s commented that, "Much has been done in the past to encourage boys at the School to take an interest in field Botany."

In general the various Reports on the School were usually favourable for the other subjects available, although inevitably in the decades covered there were bound to be occasional criticisms, for example, in 1894 while handwriting and spelling were judged to be satisfactory, "More attention should be given to Punctuation." In 1910 there was criticism of the way that Literature was linked to History in Form III, "it appears to be too disconnected."

Arithmetic was often praised: "Arithmetic very good both in quantity and quality." (1894) and "Arithmetic is a strong point in the School." (1895). A glimpse of what was involved in the mensuration part of the syllabus comes from a Notebook of A.J. Jennings in his first year in the School in Form III. The work he did included the calculation of the square footage of rooms, the cost of papering rooms, the number of stalks of wheat in a field, number of trees, the calculation of the third side of triangle, multiplication of different lengths using feet, yards and furlongs, and the area of circles. (7) All very practical work.

Drawing was very much encouraged and the Report of 1895 commented that, "Freehand drawing deserves praise." Some of the boys excelled at Art so much so that Frank V. Harvey (1901-6) won a number of prizes such as the King's Prize, Bronze Medal and went on to exhibit a number of pictures at the Royal Academy in 1913. In February 1903 Knight wrote an article entitled "The Value of Drawing" for the "School World" magazine which was illustrated not only with the drawings of Harvey but also of other boys: Leonard Butler (1901-4), Leonard Wansborough (1896-9), and Basil Osborne (1895-1900). (8)

The Scheme of 1889 required religious instruction to be delivered "in accordance with the doctrines of the Church of England." This requirement was re-iterated in the first Prospectus but with the proviso added that, "any boy will be exempted from such instruction on the written request of his parent or guardian." In January 1894 Mr Lefroy found that four or five day boys "claim benefit of conscience clause" and that one boarder, although withdrawn from religious instruction, went to Church. In fact it was the usual practice for Knight to escort his boarders to the Parish Church each Sunday.

In April 1894 the examiner appointed by the Governors commented that, "The passages from the Bible offered for Repetition had been learned with remarkable accuracy." Phillips on the other hand considered that Scripture had a "lowly place in the curriculum", which he attributed to the fact that it played no part in examinations. It was taught therefore by whichever master happened to be available. "Of instruction, in fact, there was almost none: we just read verse by verse, selected books from one or the other Testament, and were then given the customary ten written questions to test attentiveness and capacity to memorise facts." (9)

The most serious criticism of the curriculum as it operated under Knight was that it was very unbalanced, a point made in the 1910 Report, "The Curriculum is certainly open to the charge of being ill-balanced, only some 11 hours out of a week of about 29 hours being devoted to literary subjects (including Scripture)." Given the success of the School, "at least for the cleverest boys", they hesitated to recommend any changes.

One consequence of the curriculum balance was that there could be a lack of attention to some areas. In 1902 the examiner expressed concern about the extent and nature of the reading of some of the boys. It was a point elaborated upon by the Earl of

Cork in his Prize Day Address. "It is a fault which I have found in many schools.... and it is this: an utter want and knowledge of good reading." He went on to criticize the "sort of monotonous reading which I am afraid is too frequently found in the elementary schools of the country." Knight did respond quickly for the following year he was able to report that, "A change in the teaching of English literature has taken place in the direction of inducing boys to appreciate the masterpieces of our language more than they usually did."

From the earliest days of the School the boys had been encouraged to read with the establishment of a small lending library, although clearly it had not always been a success in that objective. In 1894 the Library was reported to have been improved "owing to the generosity of individual governors, and a small reference library for the upper boys had been purchased." The 1904 Prospectus stated that, "Each boy is entitled to borrow from the Lending Library, without extra fee, one volume at a time." In addition there was a small Reference Section in the Museum, which itself also served as a Reading Room. By 1910 the H.M.I.s were still not fully convinced that English received all the attention that it might throughout the School as they reported that, "It may be doubted, however, whether as yet the full value of English had been adequately utilized in the Curriculum of the higher forms". (10)

The time devoted to Science and Manual Instruction meant that some subjects had to be omitted from the timetable altogether. Knight made the unilateral decision that that should be the Classics: an interesting choice given his own education in the Classics at the Grammar School, or perhaps because of it. He believed that a literary training could be derived from other subjects, a point he re-iterated on several occasions, for example in 1901, "He wished to point out that although Latin was not taken in the School, considerable literary training was given in English and French." In the light of some of the comments made about English in the School such a claim may have been over optimistic. Nevertheless in his written evidence to the Acland Committee in 1911 he returned to the same point. "I venture to suggest the desirability of omitting Classics altogether, depending upon English and one Modern Language for the necessary literary training." There was, however, by that time the hint of a modification, "or at least deferring Classics until a comparatively late age." He had possibly come to realise the difficulties the lack of these subjects had created for some of his ablest boys. He had been delighted when London University dropped the compulsory Latin paper in its matriculation examination and in 1902 as a result four candidates from the School all passed in the first division. "At very short notice.... without any special preparation." Their success was a significant endorsement of the teaching within the School.

For boys such as Harold Scott and Hubert Phillips, who both won scholarships to Oxford or Cambridge where Latin and Greek were compulsory, the lack of a basic grounding in them at school was a major problem. Scott managed to obtain just enough private coaching during the summer holidays. Phillips achieved his scholarship when he was just seventeen years old but as he failed the Greek paper his entry to Oxford was delayed for a year and as a result he returned to the School to be the Senior Monitor for a second year. He was fortunate that he too received some private tuition: in Latin for two years from Ernest Alexander, a graduate of Cambridge and the Mathematics Master at Sexey's, and in Greek from Rev. Sydney Cooper, the Vicar of Christ Church, Frome.

As early as 1895 the examiner that year, William Hands of Battersea Training College, had expressed his concern about the lack of Latin as he felt it generally helped boys to understand their own language. Nearly twenty years later John Read supported the inclusion of Latin which he felt the senior boys could largely undertake in their private study time with some assistance. He added that such a course of action would be infinitely preferable to "the time frittered away in 'Drawing Points'." Knight remained unmoved. At the universities, however, limited change was being mooted and even Henry Hobhouse was having doubts about the policy of Greek at Oxford for in 1911 he reported that, "He had recently been to Oxford to record his vote against compulsory Greek.... he thought it an extremely short-sighted policy to close the door against any clever boys because of their want of a knowledge of Greek." (11)

One of the most important features of Knight's own teaching, and which he actively encouraged in his Assistant Masters as the School grew, was the use of practical examples. From the earliest days in 'The Glen' the boys had had to calculate the height of the beech tree at the bottom of the garden and this was extended to other trees. Once the School had moved to its permanent site calculations were made about the area of its own buildings and local fields including the notorious Steed's paddock which was an irregular polygon. On at least one occasion experiments were conducted on falling objects from the top of King Alfred's Tower on Kingsettle Hill near Stourhead.

At the appropriate times of the year some of the older boys visited neighbouring farms for lessons on grafting, hedging, pruning and ditching. In February 1893 Josiah Jackson recorded that hedging and ditching instruction was taking place on his farm and "Mr Knight brought over some of his bigest (sic) boys to watch and assist." There was a different reason for a visit in June of the following year: "Mr Knight & some his Boys came over & measured Swede." The boys also attended external lectures on farming such as in January 1899 when the County Instructor in Agriculture delivered four lectures in Bruton on such topics as improvements to plants by breeding, soils, manures and feeding stuffs. It was reported that about sixty people attended but it was "composed mainly of boys in attendance at Sexey's Trade School. (12)

By 1894 some twenty small plots of land had been given to the boys for gardening purposes and they were encouraged to keep a diary of their gardening activities through the year. How long this practice lasted is impossible to determine as no documentary evidence remains but they probably disappeared during one of the building programmes. It was not until 1917 during the First World War that gardens reappeared when food shortages meant that the lawns around the flagpole in front of the School were dug up and some twenty perches of land used for growing potatoes, yielding some thirteen and a half hundredweight. The land was divided into three plots, one each under the control of Forms IV, V and VI respectively. All the boys were then required to calculate what would have been the total yield of the plots if they had been one acre each. Form VI would have won with just over five and a half tons - another practical exercise. Squads of boys also helped local farmers during these difficult years, gaining some valuable experience along with £2   14s   0d, but it was for a total of 330 hours work. (13)

Initially many of the walks, excursions and outside visits were led by Knight himself but as the number of Masters increased others became involved. Scott recalled that Knight "often led us on our botany walks through the Somerset lanes and woods and inspired us with his own enthusiasm for all natural things." Phillips was particularly taken with the botany walks of Walter Watson, who apparently knew the names of all the flowering plants in the area and was an expert on mosses. After he left the School in 1907 Watson wrote several books on Botany and a large number of articles for the 'Annals of Botany' and 'Journal of Botany." (14)

The walks occurred in the afternoon and usually lasted several hours, for example, one for older boys in May 1904 to Hadspen, via Shepton Montague and Bratton St Maur took five hours, although there was a stop in the grounds of Henry Hobhouse's mansion for tea which was provided by Mrs Knight. Walks to Cogley Wood, Creech Hill, Wyke Champflower and Castle Cary were regular occurrences and many were reported in various editions of the School Magazine. There was always meticulous recording of the flora and fauna observed depending on the time of year, along with anything else of interest. Hedges, ditches, ponds, walls, trees and any natural features were examined, recorded and commented upon. No opportunity was lost for practical work so when the boys on one walk were caught in a thunderstorm they were set an exercise to calculate the distance away of the lightning.

On these walks the usual procedure was for the boys to carry rucksacks in which to place any specimens collected, but also to carry some food and between them a kettle to make tea. At the appropriate time a stream would be found and sticks and dry leaves collected to make a fire.

There were occasional longer walks which occurred on a Saturday. One in February 1897 was to Stourton when some thirty boys, mainly boarders but with some from Frome and Shepton Mallet and accompanied by Masters set out. Once again the opportunity was taken not only to observe the different flora and fauna and some very early butterflies but also to learn the history associated with Alfred's Tower, the nature of falling objects and the geography of the area, aided by Knight's telescope and the fact that at that time few trees blocked the views from the top of the hill. The party toured the gardens of Stourhead House and in the dusk sang the School Hymn in the 'Pantheon'. They then marched back to School in the dark, taking the wrong turning at least once. (15)

A few of the periods out of the classroom were longer, for example, during the summer holidays in 1912 some members of the teaching staff "had organized a delightful walking tour over Exmoor for a party of boys." A photograph of the summer walk in 1914 shows a group of fifteen boys and two Masters. Most wore shorts but nearly half retained their ties. Large rucksacks were the order of the day and there were two wooden poles about four and six feet long made from thin branches, suspended from which by their handles were the expedition's cooking pots and which were rested on the shoulders of the boys as they walked along behind each other.

Sexey's Boys' School Summer Walk 1914.

Other trips had a much more practical basis such as one to the Cheese School of the Bath and West of England Agricultural Society held at Butleigh during the October holidays. A small group of older boys attended under the supervision of Knight. As he taught French he was able in 1903 to arrange for five boys and himself to spend a fortnight in Paris. One of the boys who went was Harold Scott and he later recalled: "Everything was new to us - the language, the customs, the buildings, the steamboats on the Seine and the vegetables and fruit in Les Halles." Knight was taken ill during the trip and so the boys were able to do some sightseeing by bus and Metro on their own. One discovery which they made was that, "Paris was not an altogether friendly city in those days." On a number of occasions they were called "ces sacres Anglais." Although Edward VII had visited Paris in May of that year and had made a very favourable impression, no formal treaty had been signed so the Entente Cordiale was not yet fully in place. The H.M.I.s in their 1904 Report were suitably impressed with the expedition. "It is obvious that the educational value of such an opportunity is by no means limited to its stimulating effect on the School work in French."

One other practical aspect of the boys' education was that they operated a Meteorological Station at the School. Rainfall was measured daily at 9 a.m. and temperature at 9 a.m., 12.30 p.m. and 5 pm. Statistics were published in the School Magazine and from which they were able to demonstrate interesting variations, for example, between 1st June and 31st October in one year the rainfall was 112% of the usual amount, yet within that period from 14th to 27th September only a quarter of an inch of rain fell. On June 28th 1917 the School measured 9.84 inches of rain, which was the heaviest rainfall up to that point ever recorded in a twenty-four hour period in the British Isles. (16)

To ensure that the boys were working hard all lessons were marked and "standardized according to a very careful system." Each boy kept his own record of his marks which was reported to his Form Master at regular intervals and a weekly position worked out. One boy, boarder Harold Chubb (1912-1916) sent a postcard rather than a letter home, so that he could save a penny, to his mother in Martock in his first year at the School when he was eleven years old. "I was forth to top last week I am very sorry the week before I was bottom but all I have are the 2 boys one is 13 years old and the other 16 years and they do not no 2 x 14 the boy of 13 dose not know 2 x 6." Clearly the School had some work to do to help him improve his spelling and punctuation!

The marks recorded were added to those achieved in the examinations and the final total determined prizes and promotions. It was a matter about which Knight reminded the parents from time to time, as in 1912, "He asked parents to show their interest in a boy's progress by examining the mark book regularly." He reminded them that, "Much attention was given in that school to an intricate system of marks, whereby a boy's promotion and prizes depended on steady work throughout the year, rather than on a single examination." His own detailed scrutiny of the marks was one of the methods by which he kept a very close eye on what was happening in his School. (17)

The length of the day into which all the subjects in the curriculum had to be fitted varied slightly through the decades. When the School opened in 1891 the hours were fixed at from 9.30 a.m. to 4 p.m. "with intervals." A detailed timetable prepared by Knight for Lefroy's inspection in 1894 indicted some extension for senior boys as the days ended at 4.30 p.m. During the morning there was a ten minute break between 11.20 and 11.30. The lunchbreak was from 12.30 to 2 p.m. The Prospectus in 1903 showed further amendments with the day lasting from 9.15 a.m. to 4. 15 p.m. with a lunch break of one and a quarter hours from 12.45 until 2 p.m. It is possible that some of the amendments were necessitated by variations in the railway timetables. The amount of teaching time, however, remained fairly constant at around five hours for juniors and five and half hours a day for seniors. In addition for fifteen minutes before lessons began there was an Assembly conducted by Knight. This was un-denominational and ended with the School Hymn. After that any notices were read out. As was customary Religious Instruction lessons were always at the beginning of the day to allow those withdrawn to come later.

For the boarders the day did not end at 4.15 as there were often Games and then at 7.30 p.m. each evening they returned to the large Schoolroom (now the Library) for one and half hours of supervised homework. It has been claimed that the smell of cooking which came through the door which led to the Headmaster's house was often a significant distraction. In 1910 the H.M.I.s reported that, "Homework is as a rule set a week in advance, so that the boys have time to look forward and to make their own plan of study." (18)

Table 20. Breakdown of the Timetable in the 1890s.

Subject	Seniors	Juniors
	Hours per week	Hours per week
English Grammar, Composition	1	3¾
Handwriting and Spelling	½	3¾
Geography, Map Drawing	1	3
Arithmetic (including Bookkeeping)	3	4½
Algebra and Pure Geometry	3	0
Drawing (Freehand and Geometrical)	2½	3
Mechanics and Woodwork	3	0
Mensuration (including Land Measuring)	½	0
Chemistry	5	0
Elementary Science	0	1½
Religious Education	1½	1½
History	1	1
Reading	0	1½
Music	½	½
Metalwork	2	0
Drill	½	½

The school year started near the beginning of August and then consisted of four terms, with two weeks' holiday in October, three weeks at Christmas, one week at Easter and five weeks in the summer, including the whole of July. These holidays were of course supplemented by a number of half-day holidays granted for a variety of reasons. Knight considered that the three-term pattern led to terms of thirteen or fourteen weeks in length and that that was too long a period for productive work. His system also had the added advantage of avoiding half-term holidays. He was all too aware as well that many of his boys came from a farming background and the holidays did coincide with some of the periods when their assistance at home was required. For some families who had other children in different schools this arrangement created a problem if those schools had adopted the three-term pattern and so, for example, summer holidays did not necessarily overlap. It was not until 1929, two years after Knight's retirement and under the headmastership of W.E. Page, that the School changed to the three-term pattern.

In 1911 the School was cited in 'The Times Educational Supplement' as an example of a school which gave manual training but did not specialize for a particular trade, "the aim being to lay a general foundation, suitable for boys entering upon commercial, agricultural, or professional pursuits." The article contained the view of Knight that he did not want to create an 'Agricultural School' as he believed "that specialized and utilitarian teaching can only be given to older boys, *after* they have had their general intelligence trained, and the general principles of knowledge instilled in due proportions." It was a philosophy which clearly worked, especially in the area of science. When Knight retired in 1927 Professor John Read drew attention to the fact that Old Sexeians were teaching in the Universities of Cambridge, Manchester, Bristol, Wales, St. Andrew's, Glasgow and Sydney. These and other former pupils had produced "a long and noteworthy list of original research papers and other publications, mainly in science, and particularly in agriculture, botany and chemistry." They were prominent in agricultural research and he noted their presence in at least eight leading centres including Cambridge, Manchester, Rothampsted and Cannington. (19)

For one small group of pupils there was to be some variation in the curriculum and that was those who wished to become Pupil Teachers. Discussions had started in 1905 and by the beginning of 1906 the approval of the Local Education Authority, whose Chairman was Henry Hobhouse, had been received. The County agreed to pay £7 per annum per pupil teacher, exclusive of books. In February 1906 the Governors formally applied to the Board of

Education for permission to become a Pupil Teacher Centre. Their letter, written by Hooper, noted that there were a small number of boys who wished to become Pupil Teachers and the Governors felt that they would greatly benefit by continuing to be educated in the School. They proposed a two-week cycle: one in the School when they would continue to receive instruction and one in an elementary school. This Centre was to be just for boys who had been educated in the School.

In a lengthy discussion paper two of the Board's inspectors, Dibben and Battiscombe, reviewed the proposals. They considered that the calibre of many of the boys in the School was very high and that if they had to transfer to another school they might not continue and so be lost to the teaching profession, especially if the teaching they received was not of such a high standard. They believed that the two-week plan was a viable proposition as new material in a subject would be introduced in the week when they were attending lessons, and they would also spend Saturday mornings in the School in the weeks when they were in elementary schools. They concluded that, "The experiment is certainly one that deserves encouragement.... we recommend that the Centre be recognised."

In the years which followed there was a steady stream of Pupil Teachers in the School such as John Steeds who went back to the National School in November 1895 and eventually became the headmaster of an Elementary School in Surrey. He was followed by Francis Plenty in February 1895 and by 1910 the Inspectors recorded six Pupil Teachers being trained and each year more were added such as W.H. Westcott and R.H.G. Jones in 1913: the former left in 1915 to attend Reading University and subsequently became a Biology teacher, the latter also left in 1915 and went to Reading and ultimately became the Headmaster of a primary school in Frome, his home town. Although the Centre was just for boys from the School, candidates from other schools could sit their examination there. In 1907, for example, the total entry for the examination that year was sixteen of whom ten passed and six failed. (20)

ii) Physical Activities.

Even though the School possessed a Gymnasium the only form of physical activity which appeared on the timetable was Drill, and that for just half an hour a week for each class. In general this entailed marching around and various arm movements, usually in the open air but if wet in the Gymnasium. Charles Beck, the Examiner in 1900, was suitably impressed as he reported, "the Drill considering the short time at disposal deserves much commendation." Knight was somewhat annoyed in 1903 when he received a letter from the War Office to indicate that the School's military drill was to be inspected by army officers. He was informed that the request to the War Office had come from the Incorporated Association of Head Teachers with a view to encouraging Military Drill in secondary schools - no doubt a sign of the concerns of the time. He was also told, "It rests, naturally however, with the School Authorities to decline such inspection if they choose to do." There does not seem to be any evidence that this School was involved at this stage. (21)

For Games themselves all the organization was undertaken principally by the boys. The 1910 H.M.I. Report found, "Games are fully organized by a committee of boys elected formally by the rest of the School." Masters, however, who were ex-officio members of the committee, were the ones who in turn supervised the games. Two men who taught the junior forms had some responsibility for games: Louis Winter between 1897 and 1908 and John Hart from 1908 to 1914. When the former left it was claimed, "he has steadily developed the Games to their present condition, has been responsible for many improvements in the Sports," and by careful management of finances enabled the Football Club to erect their own pavilion. There was an overall Athletic Club which covered cricket, football and gymnastics and was open to all boys for an annual subscription of 5s. The Prospectus of 1904 informed parents that boys who resided near the School were expected to join in School games.

One problem which the School faced in relation to games was the lack of appropriate playing fields. When the Governors had purchased the original land from the Visitors it was a small area designed primarily for the school buildings. The result as that a reasonably level field had to be found nearby for games and that was Great Down, opposite the School but which entailed a hill-climb to reach it. It was rented from a local farmer for £3 0s 0d a year. One former pupil, Ralph Marsh (1912-17) recalled that, "this provided an acceptable football ground, but in the summer the kindest comment that could be made about a Great Down cricket pitch was that it acted as an excellent bowler's wicket." As early as 1904 the H.M.I.s noted that, "there is not security of tenure" and some concern was raised in 1912 when the Earl of Ilchester sold his Redlynch Estate which included this field, but the arrangement did continue. The matter was finally resolved in 1921 when the Association of Old Sexeians purchased the field as a War Memorial for all the former pupils who had been killed during the Great War. At the same time Henry Hobhouse presented to the School a field at Lisbury to be used for cricket and athletics. (22)

Sexey's Trade School 1st XI, 1895.

The Football Team 1895, with W.A. Knight seated in the centre and to his left W.G. Watson, the first Assistant Master 1891-1895.

– Official activities.

Football was played between October and Easter each year. The School encountered a variety of local teams, some of which came from other schools in neighbouring towns, such as Sherborne, Shaftesbury, Gillingham and Frome; and also town teams, such as Bruton, Frome and Evercreech. With their limited number of boys the School was remarkably successful: some matches were of course lost such as by three goals to nil against Shaftesbury Grammar School in December 1901 but the following season revenge was obtained by seven goals to two. The week before the School had beaten Gillingham Grammar School by twenty-four goals to nil, although it was acknowledged that, "the Gillingham XI were much below their usual strength."

The most successful season seemed to have been 1907-8 when the First Eleven won all the nine matches it played. Year after year reports appeared in the School Magazine but with all their success it did not stop comments being made about the ability of the players. In 1903, for example, of one named player it was said, "he is a trifle slow at present," and of another, "His energy makes up for all his other deficiencies in the game." General advice was also offered, such as, "Never kick without thinking where the ball is going.... Never hesitate in tackling a man... use dash and determination in front of goal." Most matches were also reported in local newspapers which once again provided excellent publicity for the School.

The very location of the football field on the top of a hill did create its own problems. In March 1911 one report stated, "a perfect hurricane was blowing, and the wind on a field situated at such a height as the one played upon rendered the ball almost unplayable, and well-nigh froze the players." The School on this occasion managed to win by four goals to three. Away matches were an experience as Harold Scott recalled, "In horse-drawn brakes we travelled for our matches to schools in the neighbourhood.... In the winter we sat crowded together for warmth, with a horse-cloth over our knees and our collars pulled up round our ears, and at every steep hill we had to get out and walk. We were used to walking and it warmed us up for the rest of the chilly journey. We sang as we went, and no journey was complete unless Sam Vigor, the driver, gave his version of 'My Grandfather's Clock'." (23)

Cricket was played in the summer but was split into two periods as a result of the summer holiday in July. The matches played revealed the same degree of success as with football so in 1908, for example, Knight reported that "not a single cricket match had been lost." In general the opposition teams came from the same schools and places as the football teams. In May 1908, for example, the School beat Foster's School, Sherborne, by forty-eight runs and later in the month Shaftesbury Grammar School by ninety-eight runs. The latter's defeat was nothing when compared with their humiliation in June 1899 when they had been bowled out for just six runs, of which five were extras. At times there seemed to have been excellent bowlers such as Frederick Osborne (1900-3) who in a match against Shepton Mallet Grammar School took ten wickets for just seven runs. One match which the School lost was the first one played against the new Sexey's School, Blackford, "played on neutral ground at Wells" in July 1907 "and proved to be a most exciting one throughout the whole game." (24)

Most years there was a full analysis of the batting and bowling averages: the top batsman receiving a bat and the top bowler a Cricket Bag. What becomes clear from the statistics is that, as was the practice at the time, school teams could include Assistant Masters. In the period 1908-1913 four Masters, Crowther, Jones, Hart and Tunnell were very effective batsmen, with the first three also being competent bowlers. As with football, comments and advice appeared in the relevant School Magazines: in 1913, for example, the Vice Captain "has a good style of batting, but never scores many runs"; another was "splendid field; poor bat." A wicket keeper was advised that he "would be better if he stopped the ball with both hands." One further player was referred to as "erratic" and another "has strange style of batting, which sometimes comes off." (25)

On an afternoon early in each September from 1893 was staged the annual Athletic Sports. This day was a particularly important one as it allowed parents, present and past, former pupils and other members of the public to attend and witness the prowess of the boys and view the general nature of the School. Various preliminary heats were staged in the days before and were not all without incident, such as in September 1907 when one of the Griffith twins fell and broke his collar bone.

Admission to the Sports' Field, which was a field loaned by T. Jennings, was by programme which cost 6d at the Gate. For many years the Bruton Brass Band and then Bruton Excelsior Band played at intervals during the afternoon and visitors were provided with tea. The events seemed to have become increasingly popular with the boys as in 1904, for example, there were over 750 entries by them for twenty-six events, compared with 592 entries the previous year. The day remained popular before the First World War so that in 1911, for example, it was stated that, "There was a large attendance on the field.... A capital programme was arranged and well carried out, the various events being keenly contested, despite the heat." (26)

One more official 'sport' was started later and that was rifle shooting. A Rifle Club was formed on a purely voluntary basis in 1907. Hobhouse considered that, "It was excellent in more than one respect. It was admirable for training the eye and the nerve, and it was certainly useful to many people in after life, entirely apart from its value for military purposes." The heightening tension which was developing in Europe in this period may well have played a part in the formation of such clubs in this and other boys' schools. The following year Knight was able to report that the Club was flourishing and that the Donegall Badge given by the National Rifle Association for the best shot in the School had been awarded to Douglas Sims. He was later to serve as a Captain in the North Somerset Yeomanry in France during the War.

By 1909 the School's Rifle Club was taking part in competitions against other local clubs, although initially not very successfully.

Having lost to the Wincanton Club both at home and away, the boys consoled themselves with the thought that, "taking into consideration the youth of the school club, and the fact that no special sighting device was used, there is no reason to feel disappointed with the results of the matches." The following year saw the Club enter the Junior and Senior sections of the Imperial Challenge Shield Competition, but again with limited success with an average score of 50.9 and 55.9 respectively out of 100. In that year the decision was taken to include the scores on the rifle range as contributing towards the 'Dux Ludorum', with an average score of seventy being awarded twenty-five points.

In July 1912 for the first time ten boys with one Master, Leslie Wright, attended a week's camp at Bisley where there were some 480 boys altogether. The week was spent in Physical Drill and Musketry. For some of the boys the highlight was a field day spent alternately attacking and defending a position against the Scots Guards. On one day there was a Masters' competition in which Wright came second. He later became a Flight Lieutenant in the R.N.A.S. and then a Captain in the R.A.F. until 1919. All ten boys who attended this Camp served in the First World War, with two being killed.

In the School the Masters clearly attempted to keep pace with the boys in shooting but in competitions between them the boys invariably won, such as by 350 points to 316 in September 1912, with Knight achieving the highest score of the eight staff taking part. (27)

The final official form of physical activity centred on the Gymnasium, once one had been opened in 1894. Unfortunately no description seems to have survived of its actual contents. As no provision was made on the timetable for physical activities, except Drill, much of its use must have been restricted to the lunchbreak and after school. Such activities were regarded as 'extras' as there was a Gymnastic Section of the Athletic Club which was open to all boys on payment of their 5s. The first reference to a Gymnastic Class did not appear until 1909 when Frederick Beminster, who was involved in Manual Instruction, started one.

One other physical activity, which occurred rarely and then only for a limited time, did receive official sanction. In the severe winter of 1916-1917, for example, Redlynch Lake froze and the owner of the Estate at that stage, Colonel Pepper who was a Governor, invited the boys to skate on the Lake. Knight agreed to the request for a half holiday and did so again a week later when there had been no thaw. He could not, however, be persuaded to do so for a third time. (28)

– Semi-official activities.

There were several activities of a physical nature that occurred which were permitted but had no, or minimal, involvement of Masters. The most prominent of these was Fives but exactly when it started is unclear. In 1903 Hobhouse referred to the building of "a new fives court" which "he might call a luxury." It proved to be a great success with the boys both at lunchtimes and after School, although only two or four could play at any one time. Phillips (1904-10) recalled that the monitors always had first claim on the Court after School and that its official name was 'Rugby Fives' as it was played with the flat of the hand rather than a bat. "After some years' practice I became quite good at it, on two occasions reaching the final of the school championship." In fact one of his contemporaries, W.H. Chubb (1904-9), stated that, "he was not an opponent to be despised on the fives court." By this time Fives was certainly well-established and organised.

Ralph Marsh, who joined the School in 1912, recalled that by that year most of the court had been demolished so that only the original back wall remained.

"This wall was a square approximately 10 feet high, flanked by two short side walls (each 18 inches long) set at an angle to ensure that a ball would bounce off in a direction roughly parallel to the back wall, thus making an opponent's return difficult. Also, the tops of the walls were overhung about an inch by an inward-facing parapet. A ball hitting the underside of this parapet was directed vertically downward close to the wall and became virtually unplayable. Two or four contestants could play and they stood on or behind a level asphalt floor, about 10 by 12 feet. The players did not wear gloves and used a tennis ball."

A second physical activity in this category was Rounders which was played for five years up until Midsummer 1898 and was described as "scientific, artistic, gymnastic, educational." It was played on the south-western side of the school buildings, in an area bordered by the Headmaster's lawn, a private field and the road to Pitcombe and Cole. If the ball landed in the road the player was out but if it reached the field on the other side of the road it automatically scored two rounders. On the other hand, "if the ball was hit on the lawn or into the private field, we ran the risk of summary jurisdiction.... A reckless stroke might have painful consequences.... The ball had to be fetched! This required caution, a quick eye to detect unsympathetic observers, alertness, audacity, and courage." As always at this School there was a practical element as, "The distance run to score a 'rounder' varied inversely with the size and weight of the hitter" so many of the players carried a pocket book to work out the lengths involved. A claim was made that this game was replaced by 'French Cricket' but a decade later it appeared that rounders was still being played, this time at a safe distance from the Headmaster in the paddock near Cliff House.

Finally, as there was no swimming pool in the School the boys swam in the River Brue. Unlike the boys from King's School, however, they were occasionally accompanied by a Master and went to "Black Hole" which was a pool just about deep enough for swimming at Cole. The surrounding bushes served as the 'changing room'. (29)

– Unofficial physical activities

As well as playing football all along the road from Bruton Railway Station to the School, some boys had improvised games inside the School building. Phillips recorded that the monitors indulged in lecture-room football at lunchtimes with one of the small wooden spheres used in Physics' lessons as the 'ball', and watched by twenty or thirty boys seated in the tiered desks eating their lunch. This activity came to an abrupt end when it was spotted by Knight on one of his patrols and a small pane of glass in a door broken.

Occasional heavy snowfalls paved the way for snow-fights. In April 1908 the snow was about seven inches deep and a half-holiday was declared. A large snow-fight followed in the paddock with some thirty to forty boys on each side and with a neutral zone between them. At this time Phillips was the head monitor and seems to have become "the natural target of almost every member of the opposing side." His face bore the marks for several days afterwards. (30)

j) Aspects of School Life.

Before 1914 there was no official school uniform although all boys were required to possess and to wear a School cap. The decision to impose a cap seems to have been made very early in the life of the new School as in October 1892 Josiah Jackson recorded, "Victor & Stanley brought home some new Caps with Sexeys monogram upon them for themselves." Early photographs picturing boys wearing caps indicate that initially not all of them did carry the monogram and that boys were beginning to wear a cap with a coloured ring on its crown - a design adopted in yellow on all later caps - and in fact that version may be seen at the front of the photograph of the 1914 Summer Walk. It was also clear that in lessons such as Manual Instruction the boys continued to wear their caps. Boys were expected to wear their caps on all occasions when they were in public, whether in Bruton or their journeys to and from School and in their home towns and villages. If a boy passed a Master outside of School he was required to raise his cap.

One photograph taken in the early 1890s showed five boys standing outside of the original Cliff House building before any alterations and extensions and each was wearing a mortar board. Unfortunately there was no explanation of the reason for this but it is possible that they were the most senior boys or the monitors.

The early photographs indicate that all boys wore a jacket, many with a waistcoat underneath and from this some of the older boys displayed a watch chain. The overwhelming majority of boys wore an ordinary tie with just one or two sporting a bow tie. Many of the younger boys wore trousers which reached their knees and which were met by long socks. Older boys wore longer trousers. Ankle boots appeared to have been common. Not all boys arrived at the School appropriately dressed, for example, Scott recalled that when John Read first came he was a "tall, rather gangling figure, fair-haired, ruddy faced with clothes that tried with little success to reach his wrists and ankles, complete with straw hat and ancient bicycle." (1)

While the boarders in Cliff House had their meals prepared for them in its basement kitchen, there was no mid-day meal for day boys and so they had to resort to bringing sandwiches with possibly a pie and cake. Phillips recalled that every morning for six years his mother would get up just after 6 a.m. to prepare his breakfast and pack his sandwiches for lunch. The H.M.I.s noted in 1910 that there were some 80 boys who remained in school each day at lunchtime but added, "The monitorial system is so effective that it is not found necessary for any of the assistant masters to remain on the premises." For those day boys eating their sandwiches cold water was available to drink from a pump and later an outside tap. On wet days the food was eaten in a classroom but on fine days, especially in the summer, many boys would sit on the grass at the top of the steep hill behind the School, looking down on the Great Western Railway. (2)

Discipline had to be maintained and so corporal punishment was regularly administered in pre-1914 schools and Sexey's was no different. Despite his nickname of 'Wacker', which was derived from his initials, Knight did not seem to have been a particular champion of the cane. In fact on one occasion in 1894 he commented, "There had practically been very little punishment, certainly no serious cases during the year and the discipline was quite satisfactory." The cane was of course used in isolated instances, such as one boy bullying or fighting with another and general unruly behaviour which led to accidents. Such incidents, however, seem to have been rare although they undoubtedly did occur. In 1912 Harold Chubb wrote to his mother shortly after he started at the School, "I get pushed about a lot I expected that." As no punishment book from Knight's period has survived it is not possible to ascertain the extent to which the cane was used.

One of Knight's most interesting systems was the 'Conduct Book'. If a boy was doing something in class, or outside of it, with which a Master was dissatisfied, he would say to the Form's conduct monitor, "Take X's name" and the monitor would enter it into his Conduct Book. If a boy's name was taken three times in a day, he faced an interview with Knight after the end of the school day and he would decide at that point if the cane or another punishment was to be given. Only the Headmaster was permitted to administer the cane. The H.M.I.s in 1910 were very impressed with the Conduct Book system and considered that the thoroughness with which Knight examined these provided him with abundant information and was one of the keys to his success in the organisation of the School. In addition each boy also kept his own mark book and this too was regularly submitted to the Headmaster for inspection and again he could take any action he felt necessary if he was dissatisfied with any aspect of it.

With a good understanding of boys' psychology, for lesser offences Knight banned detentions after school, lines, copying sections from literary works and even holiday tasks as he considered that the latter were to be enjoyed or in a rural area freed some of the boys to be available for work on their farms. He realised that some of these punishments risked destroying a boy's interest in literature and did little to improve his handwriting. In their place he operated a system of exclusion, more recently referred to as a withdrawal of privileges. For a clearly defined period a boy could be excluded from the gymnasium, fives court, museum, even their own classrooms at lunchtimes and before or after School. Monitors too were delegated power to impose these exclusions. (3)

To help maintain discipline and ensure the smooth-running of the School outside of lessons, Knight appointed a small group of monitors from amongst the most senior boys. Reflecting on his time as head monitor Phillips commented, "I was ultimately responsible to the headmaster for what went on in the classroom and play-ground, before and after school and in the lunch-hour." He was supported by at least six other monitors who each had a specif-ic responsibility: such as the bell, keys, Playground, Gymnasium, Museum and Library. The monitors met once a week to report boys for minor misdemeanours and the boys summoned to appear before the monitors to explain their actions and if necessary receive a punishment. In 1910 the H.M.I.s stated, "there can be no doubt as to the reality of the influence which they exert in the School." One interesting privilege for the head monitor was that once every term he could ask for a half-holiday for the School. This request was made at the end of morning school and invariably granted: games of football on Great Down or cricket sometimes on a pitch at Godminster, would then be hastily arranged.

There were occasional problems with the system of monitors such as in 1907 when the head monitor, F.K. Makins, decided to increase the authority of the monitors whom he required to enforce a new code of rules which he had drawn up and to set an example. While Knight agreed the rest of the monitors, who had not been consulted, did not and for a number of days refused to co-operate but then peace and harmony was restored. Phillips was later to develop the system and received praise from the Headmaster, "The monitorial system had been further developed under the able guidance of Phillips who had impressed upon the school the influence of his own high standards." Unfortunately no details were given.

Problems still occurred as indicated by a letter written in 1916 which alleged that there was "a considerable amount of ill-feeling growing up in the school between the boys and the monitors.... The foolish bullying manner of certain members of the monitors... has weakened the respect in which they are held." It was signed

'An Observer', but as the monitors continued in office the problems must have been resolved and the system was praised once again in the H.M.I.s Report of 1920. (4)

One of the most remarkable buildings in the School was the one referred to as the Museum. In 1922 the Somerset Year Book published an article by Knight describing it and the editor took the opportunity to comment, "It is not often that a mere school, and a young one at that, is equipped with a Museum that is both laid out on sound scientific principles and yet is extremely interesting to the casual visitor. But Somerset is no ordinary county, and Sexey's Boys' School, Bruton, is no ordinary school." A plan of the Museum was included and showed that one side of the room was devoted to History and Archaeology. It was arranged and items displayed in chronological order, with exhibits from Ancient Egypt to a piece of metal from a Zeppelin destroyed during the Great War. The rest of the Museum, in keeping with the emphasis of the School, was devoted to scientific subjects with large sections on Zoology, Botany and Geology. This vast array of exhibits were in display cases along the other three walls, with two sets of bookshelves some seven feet high at right angles to one wall, thus dividing the large room into three sections. Many of the original exhibits were donated by Henry Hobhouse and the Natural History area arranged by E.W. Swanton, the Curator of the Haselmere Museum.

A photograph taken in 1902 showed the walls above the display cases crowded with pictures and photographs. There were tables and chairs in the room to allow the boys to work and read as the room also served as a reference library for staff and senior boys and a lending library, which by 1904 had some 600 volumes, for all the boys. Each year a small amount of money was allocated from the School funds for the purchase of books for the Library, such as £9 14s 2d in 1897 and £10 in 1913-1914. It was the room in which the oldest boys studied and played bridge. Younger boys were permitted to play chess and draughts in one section but not card games.

Sexey's Trade School Museum 1902.

Hobhouse was very impressed with the Museum and its use as a reading room as he commented in 1905 that it "is quite the best and most intelligently arranged annexe of the kind with which I am acquainted, and .... it would seem to be as keenly appreciated by the scholars as by the visitors to the School." A year earlier the H.M.I.s had reported that they "were struck with the excellence of the School Museum". They were particularly impressed that it was managed "by a committee of boys and the way in which they purchased weekly and daily papers by means of a subscription." (5)

Throughout the winter months a Literary and Debating Society met on a weekly basis. Some of the topics for debate have a remarkably modern feel to them: in November 1908, for example, for one debate the motion was, "A Channel Tunnel would be Advantageous to the Country." This was defeated whereas the following week, "India should be made a Self-governing Colony" was passed. Five years earlier a motion that, "Alien Immigration should be controlled by Law," was carried by twenty votes to nine; whereas, "The House of Lords is useless and should be abolished," was narrowly defeated. Before the horrors of the First World War were fully appreciated, the motion, "War is beneficial to the Human Race" was carried by twenty-nine votes to thirteen.

This Society was also an ideal channel for contemporary information to be delivered and put into context. In November 1914 Knight delivered a lecture on "Belgium", supported by Lantern slides and which fifty-four boys attended. Two weeks later he gave another lecture on a set of war pictures which he had procured. The following year Sydney Bowler, the Geography Master, delivered an evening lecture on "Geographical and Historical causes of the Present War." Such lectures and the availability of newspapers and magazines in the Museum meant that there was no excuse for any of the boys to be ignorant about what was happening in the world around them. (6)

Once a year the boys had the opportunity to enjoy themselves on 5th November when they constructed a large bonfire, which in 1905 was regarded as "higher than usual." There seemed to have been a very liberal attitude towards safety as in that year it was reported, "that two very intimate friends conceived the idea at the same moment of jumping over the fire." (7) The report of events in 1912 was even more alarming on the occasion when the bonfire was reported to be "the biggest on record." Exactly who the persons involved were has become lost in time. "Dan'l did some daring deeds, which left the spectators breathless. The Cary cannon, like the Turkish Artillery [a reference to contemporary events in the Balkans] was not very effective. It is rumoured that a certain well-known chemist, caught by the prevailing enthusiasm, relaxed so far from his usual air of detachment, as to experiment with gun-cotton. The 'Guy Fawkes' gang who tried to burn Cliff House, are reported to have regretted their action." (8)

The small number of boys attending the School, along with the positive relationship between them and the Headmaster and Assistant Masters, meant that for many boys there was a strong desire to remain in contact with the School long after they had left. Many of the boys continued to live and work in the area, for example, an analysis of former pupils who had joined the School by the end of 1914 revealed that 195 were still within a radius of about twenty miles from the School, 34 were in Bristol and 65 in London. A further 63 were in different parts of the Empire, most notably Canada, Australia, Africa and India, while 12 were in the United States of America and 3 in Argentina. Many of the Old Sexeians wrote to Knight detailing their journeys, experiences and thoughts about these parts of the world and extracts from these appeared in edition after edition of the School Magazine.

The number of former pupils working and living in London meant that inevitably they would meet together from time to time. Within a very short while they formed the Association of Old Sexeians to maintain contact with the School. It became customary for them to hold an annual meeting to which the Headmaster was invited and he would give them an update on the year's events, such as in October 1908. In 1912 another branch was formed in Bristol, to which Knight also travelled. In an obituary in 1949 it was recorded that, "only a rare directing personality could have created and upheld so strong a feeling of corporate loyalty among the pupils of a newly founded school." (9) In the decades which followed its creation the Association was to prove to be a strong support to the School, not least financially with a range of gifts and projects and giving freely of their time when they were appointed to the Governing Body.

In the late nineteenth and early twentieth centuries there had been considerable concern about the physical state and health of pupils in elementary schools. For them a system was gradually developed in the years after 1900. Little appeared to have occurred in the secondary stage until later and certainly not in Sexey's Boys' School as it was not until November 1912 that Hooper informed the Board of Education that the Governors had resolved to adopt the scheme of Somerset County Council for medical examination of pupils in secondary schools and to charge a fee of 2s   6d for each new pupil. A month later the Board agreed, with the proviso that any boy who already possessed a Medical Certificate from the Medical Officer of Health on leaving elementary school should not pay the fee.

In 1912 Hobhouse explained, "it was thought right... to obtain the advantages of medical inspection in secondary schools.... so that they might be sure that there was no-one suffering from ill-health in the School." By 1920, however, little had happened, possibly as a result of the impact of the War and the H.M.I.s were not impressed with progress made. "No physical measurements are taken at present nor is there any medical inspection. It is recommended that all boys should be medically inspected on entering the School, and that physical measurements should be taken and recorded once a term and the results sent to the parents of the boys with the terminal reports. (10)

k) Finance and Fees.

Once the School had been established and built it required on-going sources of finance to maintain its day-to-day operations. Much of the original money had been derived from the Visitors of Sexey's Hospital through their Sexey's School Foundation. Their support, as specified in the original Scheme, was to be continued with an annual Endowment of £250, which remained unchanged before 1914. They also provided assistance in other ways, such as paying half of the contributions towards the Headmaster's Pension Fund and allowing him to rent Cliff House at well below the market rate. They made contributions towards building projects, such as £125 for the new Laboratory and other buildings in 1897.

From 1893 another source of income was Somerset County Council. Under the influence of Hobhouse it could be relied upon for contributions towards building projects, such as £450 in 1894 "for buildings and fittings", £125 in 1897, and £300 in 1905 towards the erection of a new Physics Laboratory and Woodwork Shop. Initially much of their money had to be devoted to Science and Technical and Manual Instruction. Specific requirements were that the County Education Committee had to be represented on the Governing Body; that "the School must be open to inspection without previous notice by the Director of Technical Education". By March 1900 the County Council had provided a total of £1,075 towards new buildings and equipment. (1)

The County Council also provided an annual maintenance grant based upon the number of pupils under instruction. This grant was usually paid at the rate of £2 per head for the first 100 pupils and £1 per head thereafter. As the number of boys at Sexey's Trade School generally increased so did the grant, but as the sample of years in Table 21 indicates, there were variations. The amount of money achieved by the School in relation to the total amount granted by the County was significant, for example in 1901-2 out of a total sum granted of £2,544 the School received £239, the largest single sum awarded. (2) Indirectly of course the County also aided the School through the large number of Junior and Intermediate Scholarships awarded to individual boys.

Table 21. Annual grants from Somerset County Council.

Financial Year	Grant in £
1897-1898	228
1898-1899	225
1899-1900	230
1901-1902	239
1906-1907	271
1907-1908	288
1908-1909	287
1913-1914	270

Under the influence once again of Hobhouse the Wincanton District Education Committee made small grants occasionally, such as £25 in 1897 towards the construction of the new laboratory.

A further source of finance was from central government and at first from 1893 this was through the Department of Science and Art as a result of an examination in each science and art subject taught in the School. These examinations were normally held in May of each year between 7 p.m. and 10 p.m., after which the day boys had to travel home by any means which they could arrange or find alternative accommodation. The success of the boys in these examinations was remarkable as may be seen in the increase in grants: in 1893 £57, in 1895 £96, in 1897 £384, in 1898 £355, in 1899 £385 and in 1900 £429. (3) The establishment of the Board of Education in 1900 allowed it to oversee the grants to the School. By 1908 it amounted to £431 and by 1913-14 to £514. Other smaller grants were available, such as £13 10s 6d in 1905 for the Pupil Teacher Classes.

In any single year a significant source of finance was the Tuition Fees: in 1897, for example, these amounted to £374, £585 in 1900, £738 in 1907 and £769 in 1910, to fall back to £700 in 1913-14. They were the largest single source of revenue. The original Scheme of 1889 had envisaged that the tuition fees should be set "at the rate of not less than £3 nor more than £5 a year for any boy." The first Governors made the decision to set the fees at £4 a year, that is, £1 each term: it was a figure described in one advertisement as a "very moderate cost." Nevertheless that figure, to which had to be added about 10s a year for books, and the fact that while at school a boy was not contributing to the family income but still had to be fed and clothed, meant that it was beyond the resources of many of the labouring classes. It was to remain at this figure for over a decade, by which stage it represented, according to Hobhouse, "one third of the cost of the education given." When it was raised to £5 in 1904 he believed that it "did not represent one half the cost of the education."

Hobhouse explained to the parents that the increases in fees had been forced on the School as after the H.M.I. inspection in 1904, "The Board [of Education] had required them to make certain improvements in the school buildings which had involved considerable expenditure." This increase, however, did not prove sufficient to meet the improvements in education which the Board demanded and so from Midsummer 1906 the tuition fees were increased again, this time to £6 a year. (4)

The Scheme of 1910 permitted fees to be set in the range £5 to £8 and it was not long before the Governors had to raise the level to the maximum allowed. Hooper wrote to the Board of Education in November 1912 to inform them that as a result of their financial position the Governors had resolved to increase the tuition fees to £8. Much of the additional cost was attributed to the increase in the number of Assistant Masters. There were then no further increases before the outbreak of the War. (5)

In terms of the collection of the tuition fees, the system was straightforward: while the parents of some boarders might make use of the postal system, the majority of boys simply brought the money in termly instalments to the School and gave it to the Headmaster. In October 1892, for example, Josiah Jackson noted in his Diary, "Stanley took his school fees to Mr Knights (Sexeys school)." (6)

The levels of the various sources of finance meant that for most of the period under consideration the School maintained a surplus each financial year: in December 1897, for example, it was £246   0s   3d and £554 in 1910. Reports from the H.M.I. inspections were favourable as in 1904 they commented, "the School is at present paying its way and showing a fair surplus on the year's working." They went on to recommend that some of this surplus could "be devoted to provision of additional classrooms and boarding accommodation." In 1910 their summary was that the "Financial position flourishing."

Within two years however the situation had changed dramatically and in June 1913 Hobhouse wrote to the Board of Education on behalf of the Governors to inform them that the accounts for 1912-13 had a small balance but that was only the result of a special grant from Somerset County Council. Their estimate for 1913-14 was that there would be a deficit of about £120. Although numbers in the School had remained fairly constant higher prices were clearly having an adverse effect. Hobhouse himself attributed the problem to the number of teachers: increased recently at the request of the Board. It was in fact projected that the salary bill for the Headmaster and his staff was likely to be £1,335 out of a total income of £1,899, which represented some 70% of all expenditure. He reminded them that the tuition fees had been increased several times and had reached £8, "which is as much as the School will bear." The Governors did not wish "to do anything which might interfere with the efficiency of the School" but opposed running it permanently at a loss. It also meant that any boarding development would have to be privately funded.

As the Board replied that the School could continue without a reduction in the number of teachers for another year, no further action was taken before the outbreak of War. By March 1919 rising demand for places, an increase in fees to £10 along with larger grants from both the Board of Education and Somerset County Council meant that the balance was restored to £621. (7)

One final source of income was the fees paid for boarding. These however were in a different category to other forms of income as, although the level of these fees was set by the Governors within the boundaries prescribed by later Schemes and they had overall responsibility for boarding facilities, boarding was a private operation run by Knight for his own benefit. Any Accounts which he may have kept do not appear to have survived, as well as very little other documentary evidence.

By 1894 the Headmaster was charging full boarders £20 a year and weekly boarders £16 and a decade later the figures were £24 and £20 respectively, with payments being made on a termly basis. No change was recorded by 1910, although in that year the amended Scheme did permit the upper figure to be £40. By 1920 the fees had once again increased to £34 for full boarders and £30 for weekly boarders, with the former paying an additional £1 10s 0d for laundry and the latter 15s.

While the capitation fees for boarders in the School increased Knight's salary, the boarding operation apparently added little. In a Memo written after the 1904 H.M.I. inspection an official noted, "The boarding house practically brings him nothing: the increase in the boarding fees only just saves him from an actual loss... he has personally had to do several improvements at his own cost, and he has to provide an Ass. Master with board & lodging, pay Matron &c." (8)

l) Odds and Ends.

As always there are odd items, references and stories which do not fit easily into the general narrative of the history of a school.

i) Aunt Hayne.

In 1893 Lionel Hayne from near Radstock entered the School aged thirteen. He soon had a reputation for being a prankster and within a year or two invented an 'Aunt' who was supposed to live in a cottage at the top of Creech Hill. New boys entering Cliff House would receive an invitation to tea on a Sunday afternoon from Aunt Hayne. They would be taken to the bottom of the Hill and the cottage pointed out in the distance. Their reaction on finding an abandoned building was never recorded. (1)

ii) Captain Scott.

When Captain Scott set out on his expedition to the Antarctic in 1910 Sexey's Boys' School supplied one of the sleeping bags. It was one in which Dr. Edward Wilson died and in which he probably wrote his final letter to his wife: "I leave this life in absolute faith.... All is well. Your little Testament and Prayer Book will be in my hand or in my breast pocket when the end comes." (2)

316

iii) Enlargement of Cliff House (post Knight.)

In 1929 the Governors were authorized to borrow £1,000 for enlarging and improving Cliff House. In the end they borrowed £300 from Henry Hobhouse and £300 from the Derlyn Company Limited, one of whose Directors was W.F. Pepper who was a Governor. The money was repaid in June and July 1932 but in 1948 confirmation of this repayment was required and solicitors Dyne, Hughes and Archer investigated and reported that, "The School Ledgers, in which both the loan and the repayments would have been entered, were lost when the Wincanton Offices of Dyne, Hughes & Archer were destroyed by enemy action on the night of 14th/15th May 1944." The Westminster Bank in Bruton however was able to confirm that the repayments had been made. The effects of "enemy action" does help to explain why so little of the early financial and administrative material relating to the School has survived. (3)

iv) Aeroplanes.

For all his scientific interest, Knight did not foresee the development of aeroplanes. In 1908 Brian Robertson aged eleven from Bristol entered the School. He was very keen on aeroplanes and predicted that one day he would visit the School by plane. In a rash moment Knight promised that if that ever happened he would grant the School a whole day's holiday. On 3rd May 1918 Captain Brian Robertson of the Royal Flying Corps duly landed his plane on Great Down after circling low over the School and 'looping the loop.' By the time that he took off the following morning many budding engineers had examined the plane and discussed its construction.

Knight kept his promise and a holiday was granted. (4)

m) Conclusion.

The foundation of Sexey's Trade School owed a considerable amount to the vision for education propounded by Henry

317

Hobhouse. Time and again he re-iterated what he believed to be the essentials for education in the late nineteenth and early twentieth centuries. "They were endeavouring, to give as large a proportion as possible of practical and scientific teaching. In their workshops the boys learnt the best way in which to use their hands in wood and metal. In the chemical laboratory they were taught some of the most important laws of nature, the quality of various properties, and the effect they had upon different forms of life." More than a decade later he summed up briefly their wishes. "They aimed at giving a good sound general and scientific education to the boys attending the School." (1)

The responsibility for implementing this vision, which he largely shared, rested with the young headmaster, W.A. Knight. He possessed a remarkable degree of energy, determination and conviction, sometimes in the face of contemporary criticism of the teaching of science in secondary schools. In an Appreciation written at the time of his retirement, Professor John Read declared,

"Mr Knight held strongly to the view that every possible facility should be offered for the teaching of scientific subjects in secondary schools.... The whole record of the School has shown that a proper inculcation of scientific knowledge, blended with an appreciation of the spirit and service of science, does not unduly exalt the material at the expense of the spiritual.... the principles of science and with the fundamental laws which prevail in the world around us is not incompatible with a simultaneous development of the artistic and literary faculties."

A clear exposition of Knight's principles underlying his objectives was given by W.C. Moore (1913-1919) in an Obituary for Professor Frederick Brooks (1894-1898). "It was not only a love of nature that was stimulated in him during his schooldays. He, like all his fellow pupils, was taught, among other things, not only to work but also *how* to work, even at unpalatable tasks; to play as well as work with zest; to overcome difficulties and become self-reliant; and to be thorough." (2)

The methods fostered by Knight soon reaped academic success for some of the boys and there is no doubt that that fact proved an irresistible attraction for families with boys far beyond Bruton and its neighbourhood. The availability of County Scholarships enabled parents of academically able boys to choose to have their sons educated at Sexey's Trade School: success bred success. It also led to the development of the boarding side of the School which had never been envisaged under the original Scheme. When considering the proposal to permit the School to become a Pupil Teacher Centre, one official of the Board of Education noted, "The exceptional efficiency of the School.... attracts a class of scholar superior to that which is found in any other of the Somersetshire Schools [which] cannot hope to compete in this respect with Sexey's School which attracts the pick of the County Scholars." (3)

To help to achieve and sustain the success of the School Knight maintained rigid control over all aspects of school life. In 1904 the H.M.I.s noted, "he has sufficient knowledge of the curriculum to exercise an effective control over the whole teaching work." Six years later a similar observation was made, "He keeps a firm hand on every branch of the School curriculum and supervises every department of School activity." (4) How far such a system resulted in the failure to introduce new methods or ideas and how far it discouraged some of the Assistant Masters was never recorded. Certainly under his successor, W.E. Page, the atmosphere became more relaxed, although as Knight was appointed a Governor of the School, moved into a house just along the road from the School and remained very active in the district, that was no easy task.

Such overall control did of course mean that there was little discussion of subjects to be included in the curriculum and it was Knight's decision alone to exclude Latin and Greek, despite the fact, or perhaps because of it, that he himself had received an education in the Classics. For many years this omission did present a significant problem for those boys who wished to enter the traditional universities, especially Oxford and Cambridge which still retained this entry requirement. Fortunately for some of the candidates their own ability and assistance from elsewhere meant that they were able to learn enough of these subjects to meet the entry requirements.

The School which was founded in 1891 was a far cry from the original seventeenth century concepts. The first Trustees of Hugh Sexey in the years after his death in 1619 reached the conclusion that he wished to educate both boys and girls so that they could be apprenticed to trades. Financial constraints, and perhaps some prevailing attitudes, meant that the girls had to wait until 1877. They were then trained for Domestic Service. The surviving documentary evidence indicates that the majority of the boys who were selected to be educated in the Hospital were from families who were poor, predominantly from those who were labourers or semi-skilled.

The Victorian middle classes in Bruton had a different vision and were determined to create a school for their sons in the town. The surviving documentary evidence demonstrates very clearly that it was the sons of middle class families who dominated entry to Sexey's Trade School: very few boys from the families of labourers appeared. In addition the concept of a school for Bruton and its immediate neighbourhood was soon amended as boys either began travelling daily from towns and villages further away or boarded in Cliff House or with local families.

Knight created and maintained an extremely close bond with his pupils, with many joining the Association of Old Sexeians and remained in contact with the School for decades. For him the First World War must have been a dreadful period: some 385 or 45% of all former pupils served in the armed forces between 1914 and 1918 and of these at least sixty-one were killed, along with three Assistant Masters. Many of those who served wrote to their former Headmaster and although the original letters no longer exist, some were reproduced in full or in edited versions in the contemporary School Magazines, while many others were summarized. They gave to the boys of the period a very vivid idea of what was happening. (5)

Above all, the foundation and early years of Sexey's Trade School showed what could be achieved when a small number of determined men with a vision for education, which did not necessarily correspond with some contemporary ideas and practice, were given the freedom, elementary facilities and limited resources to implement their theories. Once established the success of the School ensured that it would continue to attract boys of a high calibre: they in turn fostered the ideas and ideals of the School in their wide range of careers both in this country and abroad.

5

Other Schools.

a) Pre-nineteenth century.

The Free Grammar School catered for a small minority of boys from Bruton, with very few if any coming from a labouring background. (See Vol. I.) The predominant attitude was that those who were going to labour for a living did not need an education as much of what they were going to do could be learned by experience and from parents and other employers. From the early 1660s a small number of boys were fortunate enough to be educated in Sexey's Hospital and then apprenticed. Another group of apprentices were parish orphans or children of the paupers in the parish who were judged to be likely to become a burden to the ratepayers. A small batch of Apprenticeship Indentures issued by the Overseers of the Poor between 1660 and 1832 show that some thirty-eight children, including just two females, and predominantly aged between ten and fourteen, were apprenticed by the Parish. Many more of these Indentures have been lost as the Accounts of the Overseers make reference to a significant number of other children. For them there was no school. (1)

There were some men and women providing some education in Bruton before 1800 but in most cases the surviving references are so brief, sometimes just a name, that it is impossible to determine for certain their clientele. As most of them would have charged a fee it would generally rule out the poorest in the town.

One sixteenth century reference was to John Alscop, schoolmaster of Bruton, Somerset, who was involved in a case in the Court of Star Chamber at some stage during the reign of Queen Elizabeth I. On 30th May 1584 Bartholomew Warner MA was licensed as a schoolmaster in Brewton. As neither of these men seem to have been connected with the Free Grammar School they may well have operated a school at the first stage of education, sometimes referred to as a petty school.

At this first stage in education children from about the age of seven or eight would learn the alphabet and then to read words in English. Most of them in the medieval period and beyond would also have had to master words in Latin, which in a very Christian society would allow them to learn the three most important prayers in Latin: the 'Paternoster' (The Lord's Prayer), the 'Credo' (The Apostles' Creed) and 'Ave Maria' (Hail Mary). While they were taught to recognise the words and pronounce them in Latin they did not necessarily know what they meant unless that was explained to them. Any boys who showed ability had the possibility to move on to a Grammar School and then to university. In the Tudor period some writing must have occurred in a petty school in Bruton as entry to the Free Grammar School required the boys to be able to read and write Latin. In some villages the parish priest would act as the teacher and in others the parish clerk whose role in teaching reading seems to have become very common in the sixteenth century.

In the seventeenth century a number of men and women appear to have been involved in teaching in one form or another in the town. John Turner subscribed to the Articles of Religion for the first time in September 1629 as a Schoolmaster in Bruton and did so again in 1634. In September 1672 Enoch Grey was licensed as a Congregational "teacher or preacher." In May 1693 John Loveless was licensed "to teach an English School and Writing in the pishe [parish] of Brewton." He was probably the same man who was also paid to write out the Overseers' Accounts between 1697 and 1714.

The most comprehensive list was drawn up by Rev. John Randall in 1665 in his capacity as the Minister of Bruton. He identified six people who taught in the town, two men and four women: William Allan, Grace Wilton, widow, Henry Evans and his wife, and Mary Judde. He regarded all of these as, "teachers of Children all frequenters of the publicke assembly & of civill conversation", which indicated that they belonged to the Protestant Church. Between them they probably operated four small schools. One, Rebeka Dringe, "who teacheth many Children", did not meet with his approval as she was "a separatist & ill affected", in other words, she belonged to a Non-conformist congregation. For much of the seventeenth century there had been a strong non-conformist presence in Bruton, including a Lecturer funded under the terms of the Will of Maurice Berkeley in 1617. When Enoch Grey received his licence in 1672 some six Meeting places received licences: they were for Congregationalists although two of them were also referred to as for Presbyterians. (2)

In the eighteenth century there were a limited number of references to teachers. Richard Balthazar subscribed to the Articles of Religion in July 1705 on his appointment as a Schoolmaster in Brewton. In 1746 Thomas Moore, who was also the Parish Clerk, subscribed to the necessary oath to be "licensed to hold and teach a School in Brewton." He was clearly well-regarded locally as from 1753 he was employed to teach reading and writing to several of the younger children of Lord Ilchester at Redlynch: "to teach Master Fox to read." In a 1794 Directory two schoolmasters were listed: the first was John Penny who was given the same title in 1796 when he was left £50 in a Will and again three years later when he leased Roper's Tenement in the High Street from John Dampier. In his capacity as a teacher he occasionally taught the boys in Sexey's Hospital in the absence of the Master. He was a prominent inhabitant, serving as a Churchwarden between 1805 and 1807, having previously been an Overseer of the Poor in 1792-3. The second schoolmaster listed was John Sims, junior, but no other details about him have emerged, except that he was Surveyor of the Highways in 1801. (3)

b) For the Middle Classes.

By the early years of the nineteenth century attitudes towards education were beginning to change which led to the spread of Sunday Schools and then the monitorial schools of the British and Foreign Schools' Society and the National Society. (See Chapters 2 and 3) While these schools included children from the labouring and middle classes, others developed which with their higher fees were aimed much more at the middle classes.

i) An Academy.

'English and Commercial Academies' were founded as a cheaper alternative to grammar schools. They tended to concentrate on local children but a few welcomed boarders as well. The parents of many of the pupils were farmers, shopkeepers, clerks and apothecaries and hence the curriculum was more vocational. One such Academy made a brief appearance in Bruton as an advertisement appeared in a local newspaper on 3rd January 1814.

"Bruton, Somerset, Mr Oram and Son, gratefully acknowledge the very flattering patronage with which they have been favoured, and hope to secure its continuance by an unremitted and affectionate regard to the health, comfort, improvement, and best interests of their pupils. The course of instruction includes Classical English, Mathematics and several departments of a Commercial Education.

The Terms (which are moderate) and particulars may be made known on application. The business of the Academy will be resumed on Monday the 10th of January, 1814.

Dated December 27 1813."

The wording of the advertisement indicated that this Academy was already in existence before 1814, although it was not listed in the 1794 Directory, but it may not have survived for long for while it was still operating in June 1816 it was not included in a Directory for 1822.

One example of its work has survived and is headed, "Specimens of Penmanship For Midsummer 1816." It continues:

"Descriptive Poetical Selections
Written
by Richard White at Mr Oram's
Academy
Bruton Somerset
June 18th 1816"

Four short poems were then written: 'Praise of Egypt', 'Personification of British Rivers', 'Love of God', and 'Praise of Britain'. Each one was in a standard clear hand but the titles were in varying styles with upright and sloping letters which were in different thicknesses and with flourishes around the words. (4)

ii) 'Proprietorial Schools.'

These were schools established by one or two proprietors, often founded in the 1820s and 1830s. Some were for day pupils only but others offered boarding and initially many tended to be exclusively for boys but times changed. Once again they attempted to be a cheaper alternative to the grammar schools, although with boarding fees that was not always the case, and they stressed the favourable living conditions which may have attracted some parents. Most offered a curriculum more in keeping with the demands of the nineteenth century. A number of these schools were established in Bruton and the surrounding area.

One of the earliest recorded was that of Rev. C.N. Michell who in June 1807 announced that, "for some years has confined his attentions to the Education of FOUR YOUNG GENTLEMEN" and that he had two vacancies after Michaelmas. "Each pupil is accommodated within a separate and airey Lodging Room, and in every instance treated with liberality." He did not specify his curriculum but expected a very large fee of one hundred guineas. Rev. Charles Nosworthy Michell, born in 1770, was in fact the son of the Master of the Free Grammar School, Rev. Edward Michell. A much cheaper alternative was the school operated by Stephen Penny, the son of John Penny, who accommodated ten boarders and charged £25 a head per year for tuition and board, but once again there was no indication of the subjects covered. He too was a prominent inhabitant, being a Churchwarden in 1829-1830 and an Overseer of the Poor in 1830-1831. Like his father, he also supervised and taught in the Hospital at times.

Such schools existed in the villages around Bruton and provided an ideal way for a clergyman to supplement his income. In 1827 Rev. James Sidney of Milton Clevedon, advertised that he received six pupils under twelve in his Vicarage. For forty guineas a year and two guineas entrance fee, he would instruct them in English, Latin, Greek, French, Writing, Arithmetic, Geography and History. Books of course were an extra. He stressed that he was married and that, "The Pupils live entirely with the Family, and each have a separate bed." Seven years later he was taking nine pupils, was not offering French, had amended the age range and had a more refined fee structure: thirty-four guineas a year for pupils under eight; forty guineas for those aged between eight and fourteen; and forty-five guineas for those over fourteen. (5)

As the decades passed it was not uncommon for proprietors to offer day and boarding facilities for both middle class boys and girls. In 1837 the name of John Sparks appeared in the Baptism Register of St. Mary's Church as a schoolmaster and in 1840 a Directory listed John and Jane Sparkes as owning a Boys' and Girls' Boarding School in Patwell Street in Bruton but no details were given. They did not appear to be there at the time of the Census the following year.

When Daniel and Elizabeth Byles ceased to be the Master and Mistress of the National School in 1864 they established a "Middle Class Boarding and Day School", also in Patwell Street. As "Trained Certified Teachers" they advertised, "that these schools are conducted according to the Modern System of Education, and are especially intended for the sons and daughters of Farmers, Tradesmen, and others, who desire to obtain for the children a Sound and Useful Education." Day pupils were charged 10s 6d a quarter and boarders under eight four guineas a quarter, between eight and twelve years old four and a half guineas and over twelve five guineas. At the end of the Christmas Term they staged "their break-up party" with a large Christmas Tree "covered with articles made by the young ladies of the school." Parents and friends were invited and heard recitations and songs. In September 1866 the Byles' gave notice that they were about to give up the school so "are desirous of meeting with a purchaser." They claimed there was "a good opening for an energetic Master and Mistress, especially if able to teach French and Music." There is, however, no evidence that a school continued there. Byles became the Master of the Shepton Mallet Workhouse and his wife the Schoolmistress there. (6)

The middle class school which survived the longest was that owned by John Jelley. He himself had entered the Grammar School aged nine in 1817 under Rev. Cosens where his progress was so good that he was awarded a special prize in October 1819 of a book valued at 10s 6d "as a stimulus to future industry." He maintained a link with the School as he taught elementary subjects to some of the boys there. He may have started his own school in Coombe Street but by the time of the 1841 Census with his wife, two daughters and a son he was in the High Street, two houses to the west of Sexey's Hospital, and he remained there for the rest of his life. A decade later one daughter, then aged eighteen, was an assistant in the school where there was one female boarder. Age compelled him to give up the school in September 1881 after nearly fifty years and he died in 1888 aged seventy-nine. The year before William Muller commented that Jelley carried on the school, "with very great success - and some of the most promising young men in the town - and some of the old ones too - had to thank him for the thoroughly good, sound, practical education he inculcated." (7) Some of his former pupils erected a Tablet to his memory in St. Mary's Church and referred to him as, "a wise and successful Schoolmaster" and acknowledged "his worth and their obligations. His Body rests in God's Acre around these walls."

c) For the Working Classes.

Education for the working classes also expanded in the nineteenth century, predominantly in the Sunday Schools and in the Monitorial Schools and with these Bruton was no exception. In addition the town had the Blue Coat School in Sexey's Hospital to provide some education for a small number of poor boys before they were apprenticed. (See Chapter 1a) There were also other schools available, almost exclusively patronised by the working classes.

i) Dame Schools.

In a small room in a cottage children would gather for what in some cases was little more than a child-minding service while their parents worked. At their best they could offer very elementary reading and writing using limited resources, and sometimes, and more often than not the most useful, some practical instruction such as sewing or knitting which would be beneficial for their future. The school was often run by an elderly woman, occasionally an elderly man, who was poor and had no other way of earning a living. For them its great advantage was that it kept them away from the dreaded Poor Law. Many parents were grateful for the child-minding aspect for one or two pence a week which allowed them to work. They also appreciated the fact that they were flexible and informal with no Attendance Register religiously kept so a child could be kept at home to do a job or run an errand. As so many of the National and British Schools were large, noisy and rigidly disciplined, some children preferred the small numbers in a quiet cottage room. These positive aspects have led some historians to suggest that the role of the Dame Schools has been underestimated.

> "Where a deaf, poor, patient widow sits,
> And awes some thirty infants as she knits......
> Her room is small, they cannot widely stray, -
> Her threshold high, they cannot run away." (George Crabbe)

Two Parliamentary Returns gave some indication of the extent of such schools in Bruton in the early nineteenth century. In 1818 there were three un-endowed day schools catering for about 120 children, which when added to the ninety children who attended a Sunday School, led to the comment, "The poorer classes are not without sufficient means of education." As the population in 1811 had been recorded as 1,667 that may have been an over-optimistic observation. Another Return in 1833 found eight schools for which the parents paid, one started in 1819, another in 1822 and a third in 1827: the remaining five were for very young children. In total some 97 boys and 108 females were attending these schools but as one of them was just for females it is possible that only the five for very young children were actually Dame Schools. In that case there were 52 males and 42 females attending.

Nineteenth century Census Returns gave some indication of those involved in education who were not linked with either the National or Sunday School. In the Bruton Returns they were usually referred to as 'schoolmistress'.

Table 22 indicates that no men ran such schools in Bruton and that the majority of those involved were aged fifty and over, with the eldest being seventy-four. The number declined dramatically by 1861 probably as a result of the success of the new National School. (8)

One other woman, Mrs Ann White, kept a Day School, first in the High Street and then in Quaperlake Street for at least ten years as she first appeared in a Directory in 1866 but was not included after 1878. As no other details were given it has proved impossible to determine if she was operating a Dame School or a Middle Class Day School.

ii) Workhouse Schools.

For a very small number of the poorest children from Bruton there was some education if they were sent to the Poor Law Union

Table 22. Schoolmistresses based upon Census Returns.

Year	Name	Age	Status	Location	Other details
1841	Mary Dunn	50		High Street	15 year old daughter
1841	Elizabeth Giles	65		High Street	Lived alone
1851	Jemima Ackerman	35	unmarried	High Street	Lived with unmarried sister, a milliner
1851	Grace Green	56	married	High Street	Husband Charles
1851	Hannah White	57	widow	High Street	Lived alone
1851	Catharine Chamberlain	74	unmarried	Tolbury	Lodged with William Isgrove and his wife
1851	Mary Hunt	59	widow	West End	10 year old daughter
1851	Elizabeth Lucas	35	married	West End	Husband John, 4 sons and 1 daughter
1861	Daughter of John Indemaur	15	unmarried	Quaperlake Street	

Workhouse in Wincanton after 1836. Bruton had had its own Poorhouse since 1734 but education did not seem to have taken place there: the priority was to apprentice parish orphans as soon as possible to avoid any costs.

Two sample periods give an indication of the number of children involved. Between August 1836 and December 1838 some twenty-three children aged ten years and under entered the Workhouse from Bruton, most with one or both of their parents. Between January 1870 and November 1873 the number was twenty-eight. By the terms of the Poor Law Amendment Act 1834 these children had to be educated, if only to try and steer them away from reliance upon the Poor Law and so each Workhouse employed at least one schoolmaster or schoolmistress, and often both. The quality of these teachers varied considerably and life inside the Workhouse was not conducive for some of them with its rigid rules and regulations. Many of them tried to move as soon as possible to a better paid and less restrictive job in a National or British School.

One Government Commissioner reflected very much the contemporary attitude that social advancement for the poor was to be avoided when he considered that, "The condition of the workhouse school very nearly approximated the ideal of what elementary education in the country ought to be - perfectly unassuming, and perfectly in keeping with what the children's future career is likely to be." An H.M.I., who inspected workhouse schools in the West County in the 1860s, was more balanced in his judgement for while he found that some Guardians did not want to spend money on teachers: "The notion is not yet eradicated that a person fit for nothing else may still be fit to teach pauper children." Yet at their best these schools were very successful as "there are very few pauper children who become adult inmates of the workhouse." (9)

In one sense the pauper children in the Workhouse were in a superior position to the children of the working classes outside of the House: for the former education was compulsory for some fifty years before that for the latter. They were compelled to attend on a regular basis and their numbers were small which allowed each one to receive plenty of attention in lessons, although the areas covered were very limited, consisting of the 3Rs, religious instruction and occasionally a little geography and history.

d) For Females.

i) The nature of education for girls

For centuries the education of girls was not viewed as a priority: it was perceived to be very much a family concern. For upper class girls there was often a governess who would teach reading and writing along with some general knowledge. The necessary social attributes would be included and which usually consisted of a little French, singing and needlework. In 1626, for example, Dame Elizabeth Berkeley of Bruton Abbey bequeathed to her daughter Margaret, "a Neddlework Carpett of my owne making and all the Needleworke stooles in my Closett not yet finished." For many years in the late eighteenth and early nineteenth centuries Agnes Porter was employed as the Governess for the daughters of Lord Ilchester at Redlynch. In one letter in 1813 she included some observations on the roles and attributes of two young ladies who were cousins within a wealthy family in Bruton. "Miss Letitia Goldesbrough is a very sensible, good young lady. She frequently declines going to a gay juvenile party to stay at home alone with the old admiral, her father to play cribbage with him for his amusement.... Miss Mary Goldesbrough, who is very pretty and good-natured, and so charming a Musician that she has melody in her throat and harmony at her finger-ends. She is indeed compleat mistress of her instrument, and gives high gratification to her hearers." (10)

From a very young age working class girls were required to assist their mothers in the house so from them they learnt what was expected of a wife and mother. In rural areas they often went into the fields with their mothers as well to help at various times of the year - planting potatoes, haymaking, gleaning at harvest time and collecting fruit in the autumn. As first the cloth industry and then the silk industry developed in Bruton girls were to be found either helping with spinning yarn in their cottages or in the mills themselves.

In the nineteenth century these girls had the opportunity of attending both the Sunday Schools and then the National School. There they received almost the same education as working class boys, although as has been seen, their curriculum in Bruton National School had some differences from that of the boys to suit what was perceived as their future roles in life.

The major development for middle class girls came in the nineteenth century and was typified in 1850 when Miss Buss became Headmistress of the North London Collegiate School and from 1858 with Miss Beale as Headmistress of Cheltenham Ladies College. The pattern of education which they established was followed by many other girls' schools later in the century.

ii) Fee-paying schools

Bruton boasted at least two female fee-paying schools before the middle of the nineteenth century. Miss Mary Alford was listed in 1794 as running a Ladies' Boarding School and it was still in operation in the High Street in the early 1820s. Unfortunately no other details seem to have survived. In July 1837 an announcement appeared in a local newspaper that, "The Duties of Mrs Cann's School will commence on Monday, the 31st instant." This was a Ladies' Boarding and Day School based in Cliff House. It was listed in a Directory in 1840 but not thereafter. Once again no details have survived.

In the 1860s Cliff House was again being used for educational purposes as in February 1864 Miss Gale advertised that she was a "Linguist and Pianist" based there. In a series of advertisements from 1869 she referred to herself as the Principal of the Ladies' College, Bruton. Such advertisements usually announced when the studies would re-commence but again without providing any further details. (11)

The most successful and certainly the longest-lasting of the fee paying schools for girls in the nineteenth century was that operated by the daughters of Rev. William Skinner, the Minister of the Congregational Chapel. In the 1850s the school was based in the High Street but then moved to Grove House in Quaperlake Street where it was referred to as a Ladies' School. It was run by Anne and Emma Skinner until the early 1890s when Anne appeared as the sole owner. Although it was a school for girls, in the 1890s it did take young boys as well, for example, in May 1893 Josiah Jackson recorded, "Called at Miss Skinner's & agreed all being well for Willie to go to her school for half term to go in about 6 weeks from now." Willie would have been seven years old at that time.

This Ladies' School remained fully involved in the community and often gave concerts and entertainments, for example, in April 1894, "An Entertainment was given by Miss Skinner's pupils in the Congregational Schoolroom on Thursday.... the room being crowded" A range of subjects were covered in the school, for example, in July 1899 it was reported that in the recent Department of Science and Art examinations four girls had passed in Drawing, two in Needlework and two in Writing. Two years later Irene Gass passed the Local Cambridge Junior Examination. (12)

In February 1901 Anne Skinner was presented with a time-piece in gratitude for her work in the Congregational Chapel for fifty years, especially the Sunday School. The following year she retired from the Grove House School, then being referred to as the Principal for nearly fifty years, and was presented with a cheque for £35.

The new Principal was one of the existing teachers there, Mrs M.A. Jones, who immediately advertised it as a Boarding and Day School for Girls and promised a "Thorough Education" with "Pupils prepared for Local Examinations." She continued the musical tradition with, for example, an end of term concert in December 1904. "The various items were well rendered and the way in which they were carried out reflects great credit on the governesses." The Report added that, "The fancy needlework and painting done by the pupils during the term were on view and were greatly admired."

In January 1904 the School had opened in new premises in the High Street, "a more central position." It was in the house formerly occupied by Dr. Carsburg, whose patients were informed that in future he was to be found "a few yards further up the street at the Old Bank House" (Hamilton House) which in turn necessitated Land Agent T.O. Bennett moving his offices into Bank

Cottage. A new advertisement specified that the School was still a "Boarding and Day School for girls", but in addition, "Boys under Ten also Taken." Two years later Miss Jones was presented with a silver hot water jug "as a farewell gift from her pupils on her giving up the school." The wording of this Report suggested that the School closed, possibly suffering from the success of Sunny Hill Girls' School. (13)

Just before the First World War another fee-paying school for girls appeared in the High Street, this time operated by Miss Paynter. It is possible that it took over the same premises as those used by Miss Jones as in December 1910 it was clearly well-established when reference was made to an annual concert. "This concert was of such high excellence and was so well carried out that it gave great pleasure to the full audience." Such was the number of people attending that each year it was staged in the Wesleyan Schoolroom at West End. In 1913 it was referred to as a Collegiate School and was still presenting its annual concert in December 1914. (14)

iii) Sunny Hill Girls' School.

The importance of this School in the education of girls during the twentieth century and the beginning of the twenty-first century has been considerable. It is therefore appropriate that some, although not a full, discussion of its early history should be included in this study, especially as a number of its instigators came from Bruton. It did receive girls from the town but its emphasis was upon those from elsewhere in Somerset and boarders, so as a percentage the number from Bruton was small. In addition it is of course not in the parish of Bruton, which is the main focus of this book, but rather in that of Pitcombe.

– The beginning.

By the 1890s it was possible to argue that some educational facilities were in place for girls in Bruton. The Reports produced by Inspectors after their visits to the National School indicated that it was generally fulfilling the requirements of an elementary education for both boys and girls up to the appropriate school-leaving age. For a limited number of girls training leading to Domestic Service was then available in Sexey's Hospital. The existence of small fee-paying private schools for girls in the town meant that for more middle class families additional educational opportunities were available.

Nevertheless the remarkable success of Sexey's Trade School for Boys in the 1890s stimulated discussion about the desirability of a separate school for girls. What was perhaps surprising was that the construction of such a school was so long delayed, possibly as a result of the depression in agriculture which limited the amount of money available but also may have been a reflection of the general conservativism of the area. It was once again the same men who spearheaded the campaign for girls' education, most notably Henry Hobhouse and T.O. Bennett, now ably supported by W.A. Knight from Sexey's Trade School.

For all his persuasive skills, however, Hobhouse was unable to convince the male Visitors of Sexey's Hospital, through their Sexey's School Foundation, to finance the sort of school for girls which he envisaged. The result was that as there were no endowments such an undertaking had to be financed through private capital raised from individuals. The school exhibited, therefore, "the nature of a private adventure school", as Hobhouse was to call it in 1902. Those investing would expect a return on their capital even if they were motivated by philanthropic considerations.

The initial private company was established by the "Memorandum and Articles of Association of the Bruton Girls' School Company Limited", incorporated 17th February 1894. Its stated objective was, "To establish and maintain in or near Bruton, Somerset, a Boarding or Day School for Girls, and to supply efficient instruction in secondary and technical subjects together with moral and religious training." To achieve this objective the

Company needed to purchase or acquire land and erect a building. Initially the Company aimed to raise £800 through 160 shares of £5 each and three of the first subscribers were Hobhouse, Bennett and Knight with one share each.

It was then to be five more years before practical discernible action followed. During that time much more detailed consideration was given to the proposals, discussions took place, potential sites visited and costings received. The Memorandum of Association was re-issued and was substantially the same but the School was now described as Boarding and Day rather than "or". It was interesting that in both cases the word 'boarding' preceded 'day', which might suggest the thinking of the instigators, possibly as a result of the success of the boarding aspect of the recently founded boys' school. The other significant development was that much more finance had to be raised so that there was to be a nominal capital of £4,000 achieved through 160 shares of £25 each. (15) Interestingly the word "technical" was retained, most probably under the influence of Hobhouse but now with the practical experience of Knight. Once the School was opened, if it had followed a curriculum along the lines of Sexey's Trade School it would have been a remarkable pioneer in girls' technical education but it seemed to become more limited in its outlook.

James Golledge, the new school's Honorary Secretary, was later to claim that the share capital was "subscribed entirely by private persons, who desired to do a public service", although he did add, "while getting a limited and modest rate of interest from their money." This philanthropic nature was re-iterated by H.M.I.s in their Inspection Report of 1906: it "represents a public spirited attempt to meet the well-felt need of a secondary school for girls in Bruton." (16)

In July 1899 advertisements appeared in local newspapers requesting Tenders to build the new school, with plans having been drawn up by A.J. Pictor of Bruton. The contract to build was awarded to Thomas Hobbs of Bruton. There had been what was described as "Considerable difficulty" in obtaining a suitable site but eventually Mrs T.O. Bennett sold to the Directors of the Company some three acres of a field, "on an open elevated site", which she owned in the Parish of Pitcombe. Its position was to allow the finished building to "command extensive views of the surrounding countryside."

The School itself was built with local stone "of a warm buff colour" with Bath stone dressing, the roof was covered with plain red tiles and the windows and doors painted creamy white, "the whole combining to form a very pleasing and effective, if simple group of buildings." There was a large schoolroom forty-four feet by twenty feet which could be divided into two by a moveable partition and two other smaller classrooms for cooking and laundry work. There was a dining hall which could seat fifty girls and linked to a kitchen, scullery and pantry. There were two separate rooms for the teachers. On the upper floor was a large room for science and art and three dormitories with twenty to thirty beds. In addition there were staff bedrooms, bathrooms, lavatories and a small sanatorium. By December 1901 the total cost of the land and buildings had reached £3,662 3s 7d. (17)

Sunny Hill Girls' School c. 1904.

In 1900 advertisements appeared in local newspapers to inform parents that the School for girls aged nine to seventeen would open on 2nd October, with fees of two guineas a term for day pupils and eight guineas a term for boarders, there being four terms. It was to be called Sunny Hill Girls' School but was occasionally referred to as the High School for Girls. The following year another advertisement promised a "Modern Practical Education" in new buildings with beautiful country surroundings. At the opening of the School it was stated that, "The aim of the School is to provide at a moderate cost a thoroughly good modern literary and practical education for the daughters of professional and business men and farmers in the neighbourhood." (18)

– The Governors.

As the School was founded by the Directors of a private company they became the first Governors. Initially there were seven of them, which included one woman, Mrs Margaret Hobhouse, and was under the chairmanship of Henry Hobhouse. Amongst them were T.O. Bennett, W.A. Knight and R.T.A. Hughes, a Bruton solicitor. By the time of the 1906 H.M.I. inspection the number had been increased by one and they were stated to "display the liveliest interest in the School; the meetings are well attended and there is no difficulty as to a quorum." When the School was placed under a Scheme of Management in January 1912 it became necessary to reconstitute the Governing Body so that there were eleven Managers: an ex-officio chairman who was the chairman of the Governors of Sexey's School Foundation, seven Representative Managers of whom four including one woman were appointed by Somerset County Council, two including one woman by Bruton Parish Council and one by the Governors of the Sexey's School Foundation. There were also to be three Co-optative Managers. By 1915 the H.M.I.s found that four of the eleven Managers were women. Once again the Inspectors reported that, "The Managers take a very keen interest in the fortunes of the School." At the time of both Inspections it was the case that the Head Mistress was regularly invited to their meetings and was fully consulted by them. In this period the Head Mistress had no automatic right to attend the meetings of Governors.

– The Teaching Staff.

Miss Edith Radford so impressed the interviewing panel that she was offered the position of Head Mistress on the spot. She had followed the traditional pattern of so many teachers at that period: a pupil teacher, in her case for four years in Burton-on-Trent, then to a Training College, for her Whitelands in Chelsea where she obtained a first class certificate. After a short time in Peterborough she taught girls in Carmarthen for the next eight years.

She maintained a very firm grip on "every department of School activity, and makes her influence felt in all the details of organization....The Head Mistress plans all the courses in consultation with the Assistants." That was the view of the Inspectors in 1906. They considered that, "Her tenure has been marked by a steady increase in the number both of boarders and of day scholars, and the present prosperity of the School is due largely to her unremitting energy and personal influence." It was an opinion re-iterated by the Inspectors nearly a decade later, "The growth of the School and the very successful management of the boarding arrangements are very largely due to her untiring energy and constant supervision."

In her Prize Day Address in December 1913 Miss Radford summed up her fundamental aims for the School:

"A very real feeling of the responsibility of the individual to the community and of the community to the individual.......
It is our constant endeavour to teach the girls proportions in which lie the true beauties of life: that in all matters of manners and customs, of conscience and personal pleasure, the community is more important than the individual, and in connection with such matters, the individual must give way to the general good and convenience of the community; but that in all questions of honour and principle, the individual and the community are equally affected - what dishonours one dishonours all." (19)

She was undoubtedly a very formidable woman and leader, held in "respectful awe" by both pupils and teachers alike.

As the number of girls in the School increased so did the number of Assistant Mistresses: in the first year Miss Radford was joined by one other Mistress, a figure which had risen to six by 1906, six full-time and one part-time in 1910 and seven full-time and one part-time in February 1915. As a result of this the salary bill increased from, for example, a total, including the Head Mistress, of £200 in 1901 to £395 10s 4d in 1904. There was no actual salary scale initially and the payments were considered "not large in themselves" in 1906 but they were supplemented by board and lodging at the School. In a confidential meeting with the Managers in 1915 the H.M.I.s did express the view that the salary of the Head Mistress remained low, even though it had just been increased by £25 a year and the Managers contributed £15 a year towards a pension for her.

In 1914 each Assistant Mistress had responsibility for a Form which varied from ten to twenty-two girls and taught Monday to Friday, after an Assembly and roll call, from 9.30 a.m. to 12.30 and from 1.30 p.m. to 3.30 p.m. In addition each Mistress undertook up to two hours a week of teaching outside of these hours, the exceptions were the Drill Mistress with six hours and the Music Mistress with fifteen hours. Music was, of course, an extra with a charge of two guineas a year for Elementary and three guineas for Advanced, each charge increased by one guinea by 1915. In addition the Mistresses supervised the evening homework session of the boarders for one and half hours and one for day girls who waited at the School to catch their trains.

There was clearly some variation in the quality of the teaching, for example, in 1906 the English teacher was referred to as "a zealous and capable teacher," and, "The greater part of the science teaching is of a praiseworthy character." On the other hand some teaching was regarded as unsatisfactory: "French is not very satisfactory at present" was the verdict in that year, although it was noted that the French teacher was to take a holiday in France in the summer "in order to improve her French and get acquainted with some new aspects of teaching languages." History teaching was severely criticized in 1910 as the teacher just read a book to the class and gave "a running commentary upon the incidents as they arise."

Part of the reason for the variation in quality must rest with the low salaries paid but the H.M.I.s also noted that, "The average duration of service is short. Conditions of residence tend to restrict the field of applicants." In addition once there some teachers found a school in a rural area too limiting, "the majority of teachers prefer the attractions of town life." The Report in 1915, however, did stress the positives: "Forms are small, corrections light... and discipline is easy. The conditions of life are very pleasant for the Mistresses." Miss Radford was all too aware of the importance of the support of her teachers. In her Prize Day Address in 1913 she stated, "I wish publicly to acknowledge my appreciation of the delightful way in which all members of my staff had thrown themselves into every school activity... No school can prosper without an enthusiastic and self-sacrificing staff. (20)

– Pupils.

In the years after 1900 the number of girls in the School rose steadily as may be seen in Table 23. The number of boarders was limited by the availability of dormitory space. In some years such as 1902 there were nearly twice as many boarders as day girls but in 1905 there were slightly more day girls than boarders and the latter tended to be the pattern before 1915, excluding Pupil Teachers, some of whom boarded.

As girls joined and left the School quite regularly during the year, the actual numbers in different months within a year varied. The School, for example, actually opened with fifteen girls. Within a decade the number of girls in the School had tripled compared with its 1901 maximum, a fact which must reflect highly on the work and determination of Miss Radford.

Table 23. Pupil numbers, excluding Pupil Teachers.

Year	Numbers
1900	21
1901	29
1902	41
1903	47
1904	53
1905	55
1910	66
1911	70
1912	71
1913	73
1914	83
1915	90

The H.M.I. Reports of 1906 and 1915 presented statistics on the "Class in Life" from which the girls came. See Table 24. Direct comparison cannot be made as in the 1906 Report Pupil Teachers were also included. It was clear, however, that with fees being charge it generally excluded girls from the labouring classes.

The areas from which the girls were drawn indicated that the School was not designed to serve exclusively Bruton or its immediate vicinity. By 1914 some 11% of girls came from the town, 85% from the rest of Somerset and 4% from elsewhere in England. Of the fifty-two day girls in that year thirty-one travelled to school by train every morning, with twenty of them coming from Frome. The location of the School close to two railways stations at Cole and Bruton was of considerable importance in its development. Some irritation was expressed by Henry Hobhouse in 1902 as the Directors had failed to persuade the Somerset and Dorset Railway Company to run an earlier train from Templecombe. "A responsible prefect is appointed in every case to supervise day girls who travel by train." (21) Local girls often cycled to school and

Table 24. Class in Life of Parents.

Class in Life	1906, including Pupil Teachers			1915, excluding Pupil Teachers
	Boarders	Day	Total	Total
Professional, Independent, &c	6	8	14	12
Merchants, Manufacturers, &c	1	2	3	8
Retail Traders	6	9	15	27
Farmers	12	13	25	20
Commercial Managers, Clerks, &c	14	12	26	8
Domestic/Public Service, Artisans	4	5	9	20
Unknown				1

the necessary bicycle shed was available. While boarder girls were provided with lunch, day girls usually brought their own, although they were required to eat it in the dining hall, "where a separate table with plates, knives, water &c are provided for them."

Although the School admitted girls from the age of nine, with the occasional one under that age, there were in fact very few girls aged eleven or under: in 1906 for example, there were just four and in 1910 eight. The 1906 Report noted that, "very few enter before 13." In 1912-13 just one girl entered the School aged under eleven and in 1913-14 five. The availability of County Scholarships for Elementary Pupils who wished to become Pupil Teachers explained much of this as it was necessary for them to remain in education until at least seventeen years of age. As a result the average age of admission to this School tended to be higher than that to many other schools.

One of the biggest problems which the School faced was not in attracting girls but in retaining them. This issue was highlighted

by the Head Mistress in her Prize Day Address in October 1902:
"Progressive work has however been much injured by the fact that
so many of the girls have remained at school for such a short time.
It frequently happens that girls are sent to school for one year or
less, their parents apparently expecting them to receive a thorough
education in that time." She went on to give some statistics: of
the sixteen girls who had already left the School only seven had
attended for a full year; of the forty-four girls in the School only
thirteen had been there more than a year.

By 1915 the H.M.I.s were able to report that progress had been
made as the average length of stay was over three years, although
they noted that some girls still remained less than two years. As a
result of this observation the Managers discussed the notion of a
"minimum School-life" and W.A. Knight suggested that a notice
of the period of stay should be printed in the Prospectus, as he did
for his School. (22)

As well as the day girls and the boarders the other group of
girls within the School were the Pupil Teachers. They had first been
admitted in 1904, many with a County Scholarship which was
valid for two years from the age of fourteen. There was an initial
influx of thirty-three in 1905 and twenty-seven the following year
but then there was some decrease as between1910 and 1915 their
numbers averaged nineteen a year, with in some years up to half
of them boarding. In some respects it was a mixed blessing for the
School: it certainly added to the number of girls on the premises
and each one of them brought a welcome annual grant of £7 a year
from the County.

There were, however, problems, such as in 1905 when the Head
Mistress had to confess to Inspectors, "that there has been a little
social friction between the Pupil Teachers & the ordinary scholars."
She did, however, feel that it was disappearing, although she may
have been over-optimistic. Fee-paying girls from a particular class
background came face to face with girls from a different background
and an elementary school. Nevertheless formal recognition of the
system was given on 10th April 1905.

Far more serious was the organisational problem as the Pupil Teachers were in the School one week in every two - the other week was spent in an elementary school assisting the teachers. As many of these girls had no secondary education as they came straight from an elementary school, they had to be taught in separate groups which became an administrative nightmare, a problem highlighted in the 1906 H.M.I. Report and dealt with in detail in the one in 1915 when only seven out of the twenty girls admitted had attended a secondary school. In a confidential meeting with an Inspector the Managers expressed their concern "that the School had suffered in many ways by the admission of Pupil Teachers" and it was believed that, "it is not improbable that the prejudice would tend to disappear if Pupil Teachers with <u>no</u> secondary training ceased to be admitted." In their main Report the H.M.I.s stressed that it was extremely difficult to prepare girls for Senior Local Examinations in two years when they had not attended a secondary school. (23)

– The Curriculum.

The curriculum introduced in 1900, and which was largely unchanged before 1914, was the standard one for that period: Religious Instruction, English Language and Literature, History, Geography, French, Mathematics, Science, Art, Domestic Economy which included housewifery, cooking, laundry work and needle-work, Music and Physical Exercises. Latin was later taught as an additional subject to a few girls outside of normal school hours.

Physical exercises seemed to have attracted considerable attention, possibly as the Head Mistress was keen on fresh air, a fact she re-iterated in a number of her Prize Day Addresses. For much of this period there was a separate Drill Mistress and she appeared to have been very through according to the Inspectors. One problem was that before 1914 the gymnasium shared a room with cookery so that there was little room for equipment.

The games played were hockey in winter and tennis and netball in summer: by 1914 the School possessed two hockey pitches, six tennis and three netball courts. Originally the area they covered was some two acres but this was increased on the initiative of Hobhouse by the purchase of land opposite the School when it was sold in 1912 by the Earl of Ilchester. Games were in fact initially voluntary but proved to be very popular, so much so that in summer some of the day girls who travelled by train would catch a later one home so that they could be involved. The School was divided in four 'Houses' and each one had a games captain and a selection committee to choose members of the various teams. The system was overseen by the Drill Mistress. House matches appear to have been very keenly contested.

Just before the outbreak of the war in 1914 the School was experiencing some success in sport. In the summer of 1912, for example, the School won the Inter School Tennis Cup and during the winter season 1912-13 played fifteen hockey matches against other schools and ladies' clubs, won eleven, lost three and drew one. (24)

– Additional Building.

While the original building provided sufficient accommodation for the girls in the short term, increased numbers and the development of the School as a Pupil Teacher Centre meant that consideration soon had to be given to some alterations and additional space. In his Annual Report to the Directors in March 1904 Hobhouse declared that, "the need of further accommodation has become manifest." The following year he reported that, "New music-rooms, cloak-rooms, and a bicycle-shed have been added, and the Science and Cookery rooms have been doubled in size." The cost of the work was some £616 5s 9d with a further £197 5s 4d for new furniture and equipment. One feature of the four music rooms was that they were all sound-proofed, which might have been much appreciated by some of the residents. In addition a new house which had been built near the School had been rented to provide dormitory accommodation for weekly boarders and an original dormitory converted into a classroom. The H.M.I. Report in 1906, however, believed that still more classrooms and a new dining hall were required.

The Inspectors were proved correct as the continued growth of the School meant that these additions did not provide enough space. Eventually late in December 1911 the original architect, A.J. Pictor of Bruton, drew up plans for a new wing to be built on the south side of the existing building: included were six new classrooms accommodating 112 girls with six dormitories above to accommodate twenty-eight girls, amended in February 1912 to accommodate thirty-three girls; bedrooms for the Head Mistress, seven other teaching staff and some of the domestic staff; a new Science room for twenty-four girls and Dining Room capable of holding eighty girls. The Tender was won by Messrs Hobbs and Hill of Bruton for £1,595   14s   10d and the extension was formally opened on 11th April 1913. It was built with Ham Stone with Bath Stone dressing and a tiled roof.

The H.M.I.s were suitably impressed: "the Managers are to be congratulated on the improvement effected." They did, however, draw attention to the fact that the cloakroom accommodation for the day girls was very cramped and the offices unsatisfactory: "they are badly ventilated and the roofing is not weather-proof. In appearance and suitability they are much below the standard of the rest of the school building." (25)

– Finance and Fees.

When the private company to establish the School was founded there was the expectation by the shareholders that they would achieve a return, albeit small, on their capital investment. One of the requirements of the Scheme of Administration of 1912 was that the investors should be paid back their initial investment. The first three years were a struggle and each of these years witnessed a deficit which in total was about £230   10s   8d. Thereafter as numbers increased, each year produced an operating profit, such as £135   19s   2d in 1903 rising to some £596 in March 1914.

The Inspectors in 1915 noted that the School was "working at a substantial profit and there is a balance of nearly £900 in hand" Particularly worrying however was their next observation, "Governors did not appear to have realised the size of balance." Such a comment may well have raised questions about their degree of close scrutiny. At least when it came to building their proposed new Sanatorium they did not have to take out a mortgage.

In most years the two largest items of expenditure were payments for supplies to tradesmen and the salaries of the teachers, being £921 19s 7d in 1904, for example, out of total expenditure of £1551 13s 2d. Each year small sums were paid for repairs to buildings and furniture. When extensions occurred as in 1904 it was necessary to arrange loans to cover part of the expenditure, for example, the Governors borrowed £330 in that year.

When the School was being proposed in 1899 the County Education Committee under Hobhouse's influence had agreed that they would be prepared to make an annual grant and the School was formally placed on the necessary list in April 1902. Initially these grants were in the region of £100 to £120 but had risen to £196 by 1914 and then accounted for some 8% of the School's income. When the School was accepted as part of the Sexey's School Foundation in 1911 it received an annual grant from it of £200. After 1912 the Board of Education provided an annual grant which amounted to £401 in 1914, some 17% of total income. The overwhelming majority of the income therefore was derived from fees.

In 1900 tuition fees were fixed at eight guineas a year and they had increased to nine guineas by 1910. Weekly boarding fees were initially twenty guineas in 1900 and were raised to twenty-one guineas by 1910 whereas full boarding fees started at twenty-four guineas and remained constant before 1914. Laundry, of course, was three guineas extra. Together these fees produced a total income of £453 1s 4d in 1901, rising to £1,411 3s 3d in 1904 as numbers increased. Although there were some fluctuations the fees still raised over £1,600 in 1914. The year before Hobhouse had commented that the boarding fee just covered costs but the tuition fee did not as the true cost was £14 a year.

For a number of the girls no tuition fees were involved as they managed to obtain a County Scholarship which paid them. By 1915 there were thirty such girls or nearly one third of the total number in the School. At that stage there was still some concern amongst fee-paying parents about their impact on the School, especially as so many of them came from elementary schools and once again class divisions were evident. They were however reassured by Hobhouse that they were selected for their special attainments and that they very soon adapted themselves to the high tone which prevailed in the School. (26)

– Status.

In the years between 1900 and 1914 the status of the School changed. It was initially conducted by the Directors of a Private Company under the terms of various Companies Acts. In 1904 the Directors decided to enquire if it could apply to be re-organised as a Secondary School. The Hon. Secretary, James Golledge, approached the Board of Education in June but in October was advised that it was ineligible unless the Company was wound up and its property vested in Trustees. Golledge responded the following month by stating that the shareholders had received no interest whatsoever and that all surplus profits had been devoted to the School. He pointed out that it was already "treated on the same footing as the Public Endowed Secondary Schools of the County" and received grants.

The Board did send an Inspector to the School who produced a very favourable Report. "The School appears to be quite equal to and even above the average of girls' boarding schools and on the grounds of efficiency of blds [*buildings*] and staff merits recognition." At that point however the application was withdrawn. In his 1905 Report to the Directors Hobhouse explained that it had become impossible for "the Company to comply with the new conditions imposed by the Treasury on Grants made to Company Schools", although he gave no written details.

A different route was then investigated as early in 1905 discussions took place between the Directors and a Senior Examiner of the Board of Education, Ellis, which concerned a change of status to that of an Endowed School eligible to receive grants. Such an approach was agreed in March and the following month the School was recognised as a Pupil Teacher Centre. (27)

The final change in status before 1914 came in 1911 when, under the influence of Henry Hobhouse, the Visitors of Sexey's Hospital agreed to bring the School under the Sexey's School Foundation. In order to achieve this the original company was to be wound up and the Foundation would purchase the School and the site of three acres one rod twenty seven perches for a sum of up to £2,500 of which £1,650 was to be paid to the shareholders. The Foundation would give the School a grant of £200 a year. The Board of Education agreed in principle. This change paved the way for the School to be placed upon the list of Secondary Schools recognised for grants and for a new Scheme of Administration to be agreed and implemented. (28)

– Discipline

In 1906 the Inspectors commented that, "There is practically no punishment except the repetition of returned lessons.... There is no detention in School." Time and again the behaviour of the girls was reported to be good. Much of the credit for this situation rested with the character of the Head Mistress and the example which she set that generated considerable success.

To assist the teachers a number of monitors were appointed. In 1906 it was stated, "The monitorial system is well organised and is utilized for developing in the girls a sense of responsibility and for encouraging habits of neatness and orderliness." There were monitors for the supervision of games, the library, the arrangement of flowers and the classrooms. One girl was in charge of each dormitory and responsible for the discipline and tidiness of it. "Throughout the School there was abundant evidence of the effectiveness of these arrangements, and the disciplinary value of the training thus afforded can hardly be over-estimated." In 1915 the Form Monitors, or prefects as they had become known, were chosen by the Head Mistress. "They are responsible for the honour and behaviour of the girls in the absence of Mistresses, and are empowered to inflict small penalties.... It is reported that the girls look up to them and respect their authority." The Report concluded that, "The general behaviour of the pupils is very good, discipline is easy and the conditions of life at the School are exceedingly pleasant." (29)

One indication of the positive impression created and the impact on the girls by the School may be found in the flourishing Old Girls' Association which existed before 1914. In 1913 Miss Radford reported that some 150 former pupils were members and that they held two meetings a year. In fact she informed the Prize Day audience that she was expecting sixty of these Old Girls to be in the School the next day in order to view the new buildings and to take part in a hockey match against the School team. (30)

– Success.

As was customary at this period the Directors appointed an Examiner to come into the School to examine all or some of the girls and present a written Report. Such Reports tended to be very favourable, such as that of Miss Birch, the Headmistress of Whiteland College in 1904. There was, however, an increasing tendency to undertake external examinations, particularly those set by the Oxford Local Examination Board: in 1902 four girls entered and all passed; in 1903 eight girls entered and passed; in 1904 twelve girls entered, all of whom passed, four with Honours. In 1913 twelve girls passed at the Senior level and six at the Junior level - at least nine in all received Honours. Such results were widely publicized in the local press and provided excellent publicity for the School. As Music was available as an extra, girls were entered for examinations of the Associated Board of the Royal College and Royal Academy, for example, four girls entered in June 1902 and all gained certificates.

In relation to external examinations an interesting remark appeared in the 1910 H.M.I. Report: "The School has done creditably in external Examinations, but it is necessary to utter a warning against attaching too great a value to results. Examinations should be taken naturally as the close of a complete course of study, but if care is not exercised there is a danger that the individual initiative of a pupil may be sacrificed to the supposed needs of special preparation." (31) It was a sentiment with which one Manager, and Headmaster, W.A. Knight would have agreed wholeheartedly.

– The Girls' Futures.

As a role model for the girls the Head Mistress was an outstanding example of what could be achieved and she was ably supported by the very small number of females who served as Directors/Managers, such as Mrs Hobhouse and Mrs Cash. When the girls were examined it became customary to approach a woman, such as Head Mistress, Miss Birch. Another opportunity arose with Prize Day and in most cases the principal guest was a woman, such as Hon. Mrs Hamilton Russell of Yarlington in December 1913. Mrs Horner of Mells in 1902 emphasized that what the girls needed was "stimulus and discipline." In April 1913 the prizes were distributed by the Dowager Lady O'Hagan who spent much of her Address stressing the importance of "manual instruction and domestic economy" as she was convinced that upon a woman and "her able management of the home that the future of the country and nation depended."

At the end of each Prize Day, as was customary, the work of the girls was on display, such as their needlework in 1902, along with some girls performing with musical instruments and their cookery skills being put to the test with the cakes which they had made for the refreshments. By 1913 they were much more ambitious with a lengthy programme of music and vocal items, some of which were accompanied by the school orchestra, with the performance ending with the school song, "Follow the Gleam", before the National Anthem. As usual, however, the cakes for tea were made by the girls. (32)

The School was undoubtedly providing a good education for the girls before 1914. In December 1913 W.A. Knight observed, "that the education of girls tended to approximate to the education of boys.... he also knew that the conduct of the school was excellent and that the character-making was sound." It was also the case that Miss Radford highlighted each year at Prize Day the increasing number of girls who were being entered for, and very successful in, external examinations.

In keeping with the prevailing attitudes of the time, however, the horizons of many of the girls were limited. In 1906 the H.M.I.s reported that, "The great majority of girls are prepared for home life or Elementary School teaching." In 1910 they found that the "two upper Classes of the School consist almost entirely of girls who intend to become teachers." In the light of the number of Pupil Teachers who attended the School before 1914 that was a significant career path.

A major weakness in this School's system before 1914 was that it did not provide leaving exhibitions which would have helped to finance girls' future education. As the Inspectors discovered in 1915 the Managers tended to argue that they did not have the necessary funds. The result was that while a good number of girls progressed to colleges for teacher training, very few attended a university. By 1913 a handful of girls did achieve an Inter Award, such as Mildred Longman, Mary Wood and Gertrude Moody in Science and Kitty Makins and Maggie Burton in Arts, with the latter progressing to an Honours Botany Course at Bristol University. It was not until 1913 that the School was able to boast of its first full university degree when a B.Sc. was awarded to Mildred Longman.

Such a situation represented not only a limited level of aspiration within the School but also was a reflection of the prevailing attitudes within society. Hobhouse tried to be more positive but he too was deeply imbued with these sentiments. He observed in 1902, "The greatness of our country depended as much or more on cultured women as on cultured men; and by making the curriculum attractive by the study of natural objects, botany etc. he contended that the School contributed to that end."

No other speech or document reflected the limited futures of so many of the girls who attended the School in its early years as that delivered by the Head Mistress herself in April 1913. "Many have finished their College course and have become successful teachers in various parts of the country and some abroad. Some are training as nurses, some are doing secretarial work, others are at home, several have married, and Sunny Hill has now several grandchildren." (33)

e) In the surrounding villages.

As well as the various schools in Bruton itself and Sunny Hill Girls' School in the Parish of Pitcombe, there were a number of schools in the surrounding parishes, especially in the nineteenth century and mainly for children from labouring families. There were of course exceptions, for example, there were no schools at all in Milton Clevedon or North Brewham in 1833. In 1818 Pitcombe and North and South Brewham had just a Sunday School each, the former of which was used to instruct "46 apprentice girls belonging to a silk manufactory" and the latter a joint one for 146 children. It was noted, "The poorer classes have not the means of education, and are desirous of possessing them." In the same year Shepton Montague had two small day schools, each of which was attended by twelve children. (34)

By 1833 the education situation had improved as South Brewham had two day schools, one supported by voluntary contributions along with some small payment from parents, and the other required parents to pay all the cost. Together they educated ninety-two boys and seventy-six girls. Pitcombe, with Hadspen and Cole, had three day schools financed by parents but the total attending was just twenty-four boys and girls. Shepton Montague still had two day schools again financed by parents and which contained thirteen males and seventeen females. It was the only one of these three villages which had more girls in their schools than boys. The small number of children in these schools would indict that they were predominantly, if not exclusively, Dame Schools. Just over forty years later in 1875 it was reported that there was still a mixed school in Pitcombe but that in Shepton Montague there was a National School for boys. (35)

A Sunday School existed in Redlynch before 1816 under the patronage of Lady Ilchester as in that year Elizabeth Cook, "Mistress of Sunday School", was paid a salary of £2   12   0d and then the same amount the following year. Lady Ilchester sent a yearly subscription of £2. With such a small population the numbers within it were not considerable: in 1833 for example there were eight boys and ten girls.

Of far greater significance was that a Charity School for Girls was founded in Redlynch on 31st January 1712 by Sir Stephen Fox and was under the direction of Mary Wilmott, who was "to take care and teach & to maintain on Diet Working and Lodging eight Girls for which she is to be allowed ten shillings pr Week..... Widd Wilmot's Salary £6   0s   0d and for Cloathing the eight Girls at 15 shill each £6   0s   0d." It was then agreed that her own daughter should be added to the number of girls to make the total nine. The School, which cost £239   19s   1½d to build, was "always to be kept in good repair, and the furniture to be kept clean, & Supplyed, the charge of their Sickness and Burial was to be likewise defrayed." Any shortfall was to be made good by the Steward of the Redlynch Estate.

The girls were to work on wool, probably mainly combing and spinning, which was supplied by Richard Moor and he also paid them for their work. The girls were "to be admitted at 10 years of age unless objects of very great Compassion, and then at 8 or 9, they are to be kept to their Work, Reading &c and those of 14 and upwards to do all the Household work by turns Weekly."

The girls left the School aged seventeen with a sum of £2, presumably after up to seven years training at least able to read and certainly well qualified for domestic service or work in the cloth industry. How long the girls actually remained in the school is unknown but a list of the names of the nine girls in the School in July 1716 contained those of just two girls, Ann Gill and Mary Coleman who were on the original list from two years earlier.

Priority was given to girls from Redlynch, then Shepton Montague and Kilmington, which reflected the location of the majority of the land in the local estate of Fox, and "in failure of these places from Brewton." In fact two of the first nine girls admitted were from Bruton, Philadelphia Burgess aged nine and Anne Gill aged seven. Of the original nine girls admitted to the School one was aged thirteen, three aged eleven and one each aged ten, nine, eight and seven, along with Martha Wilmot aged sixteen. The School remained in operation until at least the middle of the eighteenth century. (36)

f) Evening to Continuation Classes.

Even with the provision of the National School and other schools in Bruton in the nineteenth century two major problems were evident: one was irregular attendance, if at all, until education became compulsory in 1880; and the other was the unfortunate situation that children had to leave school after a very short time or at an early age because of the desperate need of some families for them to work and earn money. One solution was for limited instruction to be given in the evenings and hence through much of that century references were made to 'Evening School', 'Evening Classes' and occasionally 'Night School'. In the 1890s the title 'Continuation School' became the accepted terminology. These classes fell into two broad categories: those under the direction of the National School Master and those run by other organisations and groups.

i) Evening Classes.

Classes were held in the evening from at least the time when the new National School opened in 1851. In a Return in 1852 Rev. James White recorded such classes on Monday, Wednesday and Friday evenings for one and a half hours each time: an "Evening School in connection with the Day School." When Mr and Mrs Daniel Byles were appointed to the School in 1854 it was specified that the Evening School would be on the same evenings between 7 p.m. and 8.30 p.m. It was stated that of their joint salary of £70 some £10 was for them conducting the Evening School. They were often aided by voluntary teachers especially in more specialist subjects. In 1868 one local newspaper commented, "We are pleased to hear that so many voluntary teachers have come forward to help in the good work." Evening classes in general were stimulated after 1855 when it became possible for those pupils who 'passed' the examination in the 3Rs to be awarded a grant just like pupils in the elementary day schools.

For the first thirty years or so of the life of the Evening Classes, which operated through the winter months usually from October to April, when the demands of agriculture were far less, they focussed on those pupils whose previous education had been limited. There were however no age restrictions ever specified and all ages seemed to have been welcomed, including married women such as Mrs Cox and Mrs R. Parsons in 1908. There was therefore a tendency to concentrate upon the basic subjects, especially reading, writing and arithmetic, along with other subjects such as geography and drawing. These sessions initially occurred in the National School itself but once the Infant Schoolroom was opened in the High Street they transferred there. When more pupils were remaining at school for longer, the curriculum broadened in the last two decades of the nineteenth century so that in 1893, for example, the following were also available: mensuration and wood-carving. By 1898 once the School had been split into male and female departments, the girls were able to study Domestic Economy, Dress-cutting and Dressmaking, and Needlework, as well as more Geography. The following year Shorthand was added. (37) The level achieved in the work could be very good as in 1896, for example, the results of the Drawing examination of the Department of Science and Art led to the highest grant being awarded.

Attendance at these classes is difficult to ascertain as phrases such as "well attended" were often used. It has been suggested that there was a decline in attendance in the 1860s after the introduction of the Revised Code as a pupil attending classes in a subject such as cookery had to be presented for the examination in the standard elementary subjects as well. In October 1868 some sixty names were recorded but when Josiah Jackson, as one of the Managers of the Continuation School visited the Art Class in February 1893 he found six students in attendance. There were clearly fluctuations, even within the same winter session, for example in April 1899 F. Wood, who had taken over the boys' department and also taught Manual Instruction at Sexey's Trade School from 1896 to 1902, noted that while the total number of girls had increased that of the boys "had somewhat fallen off towards the end of the session." In 1898-9 the average attendance of males was ten and females eleven. The following year the overall average was thirty. There were clearly regular attenders so that in April 1900 eleven females and ten males were awarded Attendance Certificates and three girls certificates for three years attendance.

The Evening classes did charge a small fee for the courses provided but unfortunately no details have survived: elsewhere in Somerset fees ranged from 1d a month for two sessions a week to 3d a week for three evenings. In Bruton the charge was felt to be so low that it would not discourage attendance. The School was financed by a number of subscribers who gave regular donations, such as the Visitors of Sexey's Hospital with an annual donation of £1 1s 0d and individuals, such as J.F. Jones from the Brewery.

On one occasion he stated that, "he was highly pleased with the work of the school," and, "he assured the boys they could never learn too much." In addition grants were available from organisations, such as the Science and Art Department, subject to the performance in their examination.

To encourage attendance all stationery was provided free of charge and fees were returned at the end of the session if attendance had been regular. In addition there were occasional social events which by the late 1890s had become an annual supper, "a sumptuous supper" as it was called in April 1899, to which prominent supporters and subscribers were invited and in which the past session was reviewed and certificates awarded. Such events were widely reported in local newspapers and provided considerable publicity. In 1908 there was an evening with refreshments followed by dancing and games. In October 1913 the opening of the winter session was marked with a social evening which was reported to have been well attended and exhortations given for even more to attend, "it is hoped that many more will take advantage of this opportunity for improvement during the winter months." The award of Attendance Certificates was another method of encouraging regular attendance. In 1908, for example, twenty-six pupils were awarded Certificates by the County Education Committee and in February 1910 there were actual prizes for attendance and conduct. To encourage attendance by the boys a football team was formed at some stage before November 1910 when they played a team from Queen Camel which they lost by four goals to two. Such matches continued to be played each year so that in January 1912, for example, they played the Castle Cary Boys' Brigade. (38)

In the late nineteenth and early twentieth centuries when Inspectors visited the Continuation School, as it had become known, their Reports tended to be favourable. In May 1895, for example, it was stated that, "The School has again been carried on with much success", and the following year, "The School has been a greater success than ever." This particular Inspector praised the singing and book-keeping and "some exceedingly good wood-carving." By 1900 "considerable progress has been made in all subjects." There were occasional criticisms, such as in the same year when the school had been split into male and female departments and for the latter under Miss L.A. Birt it was felt that, "The discipline might be a little firmer."

Such schools clearly had a place in local communities for as late as 1899 Rev. Hayward, the Vicar of Bruton, considered it was important "to continue their education where it was left off at the National School.... as children were allowed to leave school much too early. A noble and great work may therefore be done at these school...... theirs was a very successful school, and he urged the scholars not to get tired of it." (39)

ii) Miscellaneous instruction.

The second category of instruction occurred as a result of the actions of external agencies and did not come under the auspices of the National School. Much of its emphasis was upon practical work and advice on subjects particularly suitable for a rural area and was to be found mainly at the end of the nineteenth century. Developments which had occurred as a result of the application of science and much greater understanding through the work of institutions such as the Rothampsted Experimental Station and a similar one at Cannington, had to be communicated to a wider audience.

The major impetus for this expansion of information came with the creation of County Councils in 1888 as the following year the Technical Instruction Act gave local authorities the power to raise a penny rate in order to "supply & aid in supplying technical or manual instruction." Under the influence once again of men like Henry Hobhouse Somerset was not slow to establish a Technical Instruction Committee which was to oversee so many of the new courses.

Table 25 gives an indication of some of the instruction available in Bruton in 1890s. It shows that there was a combination of

Table 25. Courses available in Bruton in the 1890s.

Year	Course	Details	Organiser
Various years in 1890s	Elementary Science	W.A. Knight at Sexey's Trade School	Somerset Co. Co.
	Chemistry	Ditto	Ditto
	Woodwork	W.G. Watson " "	Ditto
1892	Cookery	Miss Kate Hodges in Infant Schoolroom	Wincanton District Ed. Com.
1893	Cookery	Miss Hodges and Miss Wright	Somerset Co. Co.
	Drawing Class	W. Collins of Frome Sch. of Art	Ditto
	Dressmaking	Miss Ross of Liverpool	Ditto
	Butter School	Miss Benjafield and Miss Williams in Assembly Rooms. 10 maximum	Ditto
1895	Cookery	Miss Collingdon in Infant Schoolroom	Wincanton District Ed. Com.
	Demonstration on allotments at Prospect followed by evening lecture on "The cropping of gardens."	Mr W. Iggulden	Ditto

(continued)

Table 25. Courses available in Bruton in the 1890s. *(continued)*

Year	Course	Details	Organiser
1896	Grafting Lessons	2 days in orchards of T.O. Bennett and in those of Mr Jeffery in Gants Lane	
1897	Hedging	Finished with competition at Gilcombe	
1898-9	Poultry Keeping	2 lessons by Mr Snell with average attendance 37	Wincanton District Ed. Com.
		6 lessons with av. attendance 16	Ditto
	Nursing Lectures	1 lesson with attendance of 20	Ditto
	Rick Thatching and Spar-making	4 lectures by Mr Muir with average attendance 60	Somerset Co. Co.
	Lectures on various Agricultural subjects		
1899-1900	Farriery School	10 days, attendance 2	Somerset Co. Co.
	"The Physiology of Farm Animals"	Lectures by Mr Muir at Sexey's T.S.	Ditto
	Orchard Management	1 lesson by Mr Little, attendance 11	Ditto
	Pruning Orchard Trees (demo)	1 lesson by Mr Little, attendance 16	Ditto
1902	Course on Plant Life	C.E. Moss at Sexey's Trade School	Somerset Co. Co.

theoretical and practical work and that in virtually every instance it was organised directly or indirectly by Somerset County Council through its Technical Instruction Committee. (40)

g) Self-help.

The acquisition of information and knowledge could be achieved though self-help. As early as 1833 the Independent Chapel had established a lending library attached to its Sunday School, presumably for the benefit of its own scholars and in October 1851 formed a Reading Society, "for the Reading and circulation of useful and constructive Books" which by the following month had twenty-three members. The lack of any other documentary evidence makes it impossible to determine how far such a library aided education in Bruton. Similarly a Directory of 1861 referred to a Reading Room but gave no indication of its location. It may have been associated with a Mechanics or Working Men's Institute which was formed early in September 1859 with fifty members each subscribing one penny a week. This money was used to purchase newspapers and periodicals which were supplemented by those donated by various benefactors, "to supply the reading room with a number of the leading papers and periodicals." There was also a scheme by the Institute to create a Penny Bank and the two were well-received by one local newspaper which enthused, "We are really gratified at seeing intellectual progress and prudent economy thus advancing hand-in-hand." The Institute however did not appear to have survived for very long. (41)

A more organised situation existed by 1875 when a subsequent Directory recorded, "There is a subscription Reading Room in the High Street, in connection with the Bruton Mutual Improvement Society." That it was based upon a subscription would have placed it beyond the reach of most labouring families. This Society was essentially middle class as it drew its membership from local doctors, solicitors, headteachers, farmers and tradesmen. Through the winter months in the years after its formation in 1871 it met regularly to hear lectures, stage debates as well as hold musical evenings. For those who were already literate it was an excellent opportunity to gain additional knowledge and understanding, and possibly to advance their prospects in the town. In 1891 its Library was reported to contain nearly 250 books and in that year Henry Hobhouse presented it with fourteen volumes of the centenary edition of Walter Scott's novels. In 1893 discussions were underway, and committee formed, to establish a Reading Room for the town in a separate house and Josiah Jackson attended a series of meetings for that purpose. By the end of the year one was in existence but once again a subscription had to be paid and so it was less likely to be patronized by the labouring classes in significant numbers. (42)

The prospect of a free public library, however, had been raised in 1891 under the terms of the Will of Miss Frances Jane Ward who died in June of that year. It was to be in memory of her father Daniel and her uncle John Sharrer Ward, the mill owners. After various bequests she left the residue of her estate in trust for her two brothers with the instruction that on the death of the last of them the fund should be allowed to accumulate for twenty years and then handed over to five trustees, including the Vicar and the two churchwardens, to create a public library in Bruton. When her last brother died in 1894 some inhabitants attempted to have the twenty year period set aside but after a lengthy court case they lost. It was not until July 1914 that the Ward Library on the site of the old Wellington Inn at the junction of Quaperlake Street and Patwell Street was finally opened. It was reported that in relation to the lending section, "A large number of books are on the shelves and well-selected and can be had free, according to the rules." (43)

6

Conclusion.

D ocumentary evidence for education in Bruton before the nineteenth century is very limited with the exception of the Free Grammar School. (see vol. I) Sexey's Hospital continued to provide some schooling for a small number of boys before they were apprenticed from c.1660 to 1877. The names of a few other men and women have appeared in relation to education but exactly what they did has not.

It was clear that education required a significant and sustained philanthropic effort. Subscriptions had to be sought in the nineteenth century to build, for example, the three Sunday Schools, the National School and Sexey's Trade School. Being able to make such subscriptions, either on a single occasion or preferably regularly, was a statement that a particular person or family had entered the ranks of the elite in the town. Once such schools were in place parents were required to pay a contribution but vast fund-raising activities occurred as well to ensure that they continued. Grants could be obtained, often at different times, from outside organisations such as the National Society, the Science and Art Department, the Board of Education and Somerset County Council. Such grants were well received as long as local independence was not threatened with some unwanted solution imposed by a central body.

Of major importance in Bruton was the emergence in the nineteenth century of an articulate and active middle class, particularly men, who had a pronounced view on how their town should be managed and run. They were greatly stimulated in the early nineteenth century when Sir Richard Colt Hoare, the Lord of the Manor, sold most of the houses and other properties within Bruton which he owned, while he retained the surrounding landed estate. Within a very short time former tenants became property owners in their own right, paying all the necessary rates and taxes and hence displaying a much greater interest in how their money was spent and the general direction of the town. These were the men behind the establishment of the Church of England Sunday School and then the National School. Others such as George Amor had a religious fervour which led to the foundation of the Sunday Schools of the Non-Conformists. As the century advanced a small group of men became instrumental in all the most significant developments. Foremost amongst them was Henry Hobhouse, (see Appendix for an outline of his career), supported by men such as Thomas Oatley Bennett and William Muller. Without their collective vision, enthusiasm and determination the history of Bruton would have been very different.

Motivation for all this philanthropic activity in education was complex. Undoubtedly in a rural community there was a continuation of the concept of charity, evident in the medieval period in the monastery of Bruton with its distribution of alms, and after its dissolution discernible in the bequests in Tudor and Stuart Wills. There was the expectation that a wealthy local inhabitant would make a bequest in his or her Will to aid the poor, as may be seen in the case of Hugh Sexey. The involvement of the Berkeley family as the Lords of the Manor for over two centuries in Bruton, such as support for the erection of the Market Hall, was indicative of the same belief, with a pronounced degree of paternalism. Such paternalism lingered into the nineteenth century.

With philanthropy, of course, came an element of social control. The comments made by the various instigators of education in Bruton made it absolutely clear that they were educating local children to fulfil their allotted role in society - there was no attempt being made to raise them above their 'station in life'. The spread of education in terms of the numbers involved, compulsion and the gradual raising of the school leaving age did mean, however, that in the nineteenth century it became possible for an able pupil, especially a boy, to achieve far more than their parents or grandparents had done.

It did not escape the attention of the middle classes in Bruton that it was essential to ensure that there was an identity of interests in the town so that it would prosper. The establishment of Sunday Schools and a National School would ensure that the appropriate values were taught and fostered. There was huge gulf between many of the middle classes and the labouring poor so that the hope existed that by funding these schools, and other philanthropic projects, the former could justify the inequalities and elicit some degree of loyalty.

The middle classes themselves could send their children to the National School but for the payment of fees other options were available, such as the Grammar School, an Academy and a number of 'proprietorial' schools at different times. Sexey's Trade School and then Sunny Hill Girls' School were specifically designed for boys and girls from that sort of background. It could therefore be argued that there was the possibility by 1914 of a secondary education for middle class boys and girls but only an elementary one for working class children.

Significant developments did occur in the education of children in Bruton in the nineteenth century. The fact that education became compulsory, with the school leaving age gradually raised, and then became free meant that through the decades after 1880 hundreds more children had the opportunity of an education in the town. Increased literacy meant that they did have the possibility of a different type of job and access to far greater amounts of information, especially with the availability of newspapers and magazines in Reading Rooms and much later the free Ward Library. For the 40% or so of men who qualified for the vote in parliamentary elections before 1918 that had important implications.

While the instigators of a number of the developments in the nineteenth century were men, the role of females was also of crucial importance. For a small number of girls there was the possibility of an education in a day or boarding school run by females, such as Mrs Byles, Miss Skinner, Miss Jones and Miss Paynter. The foundation of Sunny Hill Girls' School in 1900 increased the chances of an education for a number of middle class girls from Bruton, although before 1914 its horizons reflected very much the expectations of that period.

For girls from labouring families there was first the Sunday Schools with many of the teachers being female volunteers, usually selected from within the school itself or the appropriate church. The importance of role models must not be overlooked. There were also the Dame Schools, again usually with a female in charge. While the education received may not have been of a high standard, their importance within working class life must not be underestimated. They often taught practical skills such as sewing and knitting and by making only a small charge allowed more members of the child's family to be employed elsewhere and so increased the money brought into the home each week.

Within the National School there were once again the role models for the girls: primarily the Schoolmistress, but also Assistant Mistresses, pupil teachers and monitors. A career path could open up for a talented girl. In addition, while there were some differences, the curriculum for the boys and the girls was substantially the same, particularly in the 3 Rs. Before 1914 however the horizons for most of the girls in the National School remained restricted.

Most of the influence and power within education in the period under consideration rested with men. The Governors and Managers were predominantly male and the Headteachers likewise, with the exception of the Headmistress of Sunny Hill Girls' School. As far as the Headmaster of Sexey's Trade School was concerned women should not teach boys: until the circumstances of the First World War forced him to employ them.

Indirectly females played another significant role in education, for as well as being Subscribers, they were involved in a wide range of fund-raising activities, attended and took part in concerts and entertainments, such as performances by Miss Beatrice Heginbothom and her all-female orchestra, and provided the refreshments at a host of events. Without their input the outcomes of such activities may have been very different.

There was also remarkable dedication by some of the men involved. Governors and Managers served for periods of twenty years or more; both E.R. Hayter and W.A. Knight headed their respective schools for nearly forty years each and George Amor acted as the Superintendent of the Wesleyan Sunday School for fifty years.

The examination of education in just one small market town over a long period of time has revealed what was achieved by its residents, for much of it predominantly on their own, with minimal outside assistance, or interference. From virtually no provision in 1400, by 1914 all children under fourteen were compelled to attend a school. For all of them it was at least up to an elementary level, but for more and more a secondary level was available which could lead on to a college or university place for a tiny minority. Those men and women who had instigated and championed the spread of schools in Bruton, of whatever type and for whatever reasons, or had actually taught the children of its inhabitants, had delivered a remarkable amount. However, as the remainder of the twentieth century was to reveal there was scope for much more to be undertaken.

Appendix.

The Right Honourable Henry Hobhouse.

Born 1 March 1854, son of Henry Hobhouse of Hadspen House and his wife Hon. Charlotte, 3rd daughter of Lord Talbot of Malahide
Educated Eton and then Balliol College, Oxford
1880 called to the Bar at Lincoln's Inn, London
1885-1906 Liberal M.P. for East Somerset
 -1937 Justice of the Peace for Somerset
1889-1925 Member of Somerset County Council
1890-1937 Ecclesiastical Commissioner
1890-1937 Visitor of Sexey's Hospital, Bruton
1894-1895 Member of the Royal Commission on Secondary Education
1900-1910 Member of the Consultative Committee of the Board of Education and worked on the Education Act 1902
1900-1913 Chairman of Somerset Education Committee
1901-1906 Recorder of Wells
1902 appointed a Privy Councillor
1905-1925 Chairman of Somerset County Council
Died 25 June 1937.

The Right Honourable Henry Hobhouse.

Notes and References.

BM   Bruton Museum
H.M.I. Her (or His) Majesty's Inspector
S.H.C Somerset Heritage Centre
T.N.A. The National Archives
W.H.C.Wiltshire Heritage Centre

Introduction: setting the scene.

1. J. Leland, Itinerary, vol. II , London, 1710, p. 74; J. Vanes, ed., The Ledger of John Smythe 1538-1550, Historical Manuscript Commission, J.P. 19, London, 1994, pp. 4, 82-3, 166-7, 201; Wiltshire Heritage Centre, Hoare Papers 383/142, Return of Querys to the Society of Antiquaries, pt. I, No. 30 (mid 1750s); Report of the Select Committee on the Silk Trade, P.P. 1831-2, XIX, Minutes of Evidence of John S. Ward, p. 209.
2. For more detailed consideration of Bruton's population growth see P.W. Randell, Death Comes to Bruton: a market town in Somerset c1400-c1900, Guildford, 2014, esp. pp. 12-14.
3. S.H.C. D/P/brut 13/6/1, Apprenticeship Papers 1660-1832; D/P/brut 13/2/5, Overseers' Accounts 1726-1748.

1. Within Sexey's Hospital.

1. S.H.C. DD/SE 81, Deed of Conveyance 14 June 1616; T.N.A. PROB 11/134, Will of Hugh Sexey 19 August 1619; W.K. Jordan, Philanthropy in England 1480-1660, London, 1959, esp. pp. 241-250, 252, 261. For details of Hugh Sexey see P.W. Randell, The Life and Times of Hugh Sexey of Bruton: Auditor to James I, Guildford, 2015.
2. S.H.C. DD/SE 39/2, Reply of Sir Lawrence Hyde et al, 1623.

3. S.H.C. DD/SE 39/19, Letter from Edward Bisse to Edward Wyckes, Esq 17 June 1642. Thomas Banks claimed that his wife Ann was Sexey's rightful heir and entitled to the whole estate but the Trustees did not accept the claim, pointing out that he had made limited provision for her in his Will. It seems however that they were prepared to help her children.

4. S.H.C. DD/SE 38/8, Deed of Incorporation 10 December 1638.

5. H. Hobhouse, A Short History of Hugh Sexey's Hospital, Taunton, 1951, p. 9; R.C. Hoare, Monastic Remains of the Religious Houses of Witham, Bruton and Stavordale, privately printed, 1824, p. 76; S.H.C. DD/HI/218, Case for Opinion of Counsel 1793.

6. S.H.C. DD/SE 43/15, Mr Cheekes Accompte May 1662.

7. S.H.C. DD/SE 44, Queries submitted to Feoffees 1790; DD/HI/218, Case for Opinion of Counsel, 1793; 'Bath Chronicle', 15 April 1852; S.H.C. DD/SE 44, Visitors' Meeting 3 June 1691; Hoare, op.cit., p. 76; S.H.C. DD/DN 4/4/206, List of Candidates 1856; 4/4/16 List of Candidates 1853.

8. S.H.C. D/P/brut 13/3/8, Examinations re Settlement 1741-1796: Examination of Moses Lumber September 1747.

9. Hoare, op.cit., p. 79; Further Report of the Commission to Inquire Concerning Charities, 1824, PP 1824, XIV, p. 375; Hobhouse, op.cit., Visitors' Minute Book 1839.

10. S.H.C. DD/BT 7/2, Small Account Books, vol. I, 6 June 1794, vol. 4, 12 May 1804; DD/SE 47/2, A Schedule of Goods belonging to the Hospital of Brewton... February 9 1703; DD/BT 7/1, Hospital Account Book 1846-7; DD/BT 7/12, Annual Account 1874.

11. S.H.C. D/P/brut 13/2/1, Overseers' Accounts 1653-1669, 13/2/2 Overseers' Accounts 1669-1678; DD/SE 45/1, Petitions to the ffeoffees of Sexey's Hospital, No 16; 45/2, No 20.

12. Mr Cheekes Accompte, op.cit.; S.H.C. DD/SE 43/17, Accounts of Robert Ludwell 1666-1676; Annual Account 1874, op.cit.; Hoare, op.cit., p. 79.

13. Bruton Museum, Box 51, Bruton Sunday School and Infant School Minute Book; 'Shepton Mallet Journal'. 30 August

1867, 3 September 1869; BM, Box 51, Bruton National School Log Book 1870-1900, 14 September 1875.

14. S.H.C. DD/SAS/S/2528/1, Letter from James W. Parfitt to the Earl of Ilchester 7 October 1852; Annual Accounts 1874, op.cit.; S.H.C. DD/BT 7/1, Bruton Hospital Rental and Account Book 1836-79; DD/DN 4/4/65, Notes made by F.H. Dickinson in Meeting in 1850s; Schools' Enquiry Commission (Taunton Commission) 1868, vol. XIV, p. 189.

15. S.H.C. DD/SE 47/2, A Schedule of Goods 1703, op.cit.; SE 47/4, List of goods Left by Mrs Elliott... 1712.

16. Castle Cary Visitor, vol. IX, 1912-13; S.H.C. T/PH/vch/87, Diocesan Registry Papers: Answers of John Randall 20th September 1665/6; J. Walker, An Attempt toward recovering an Account of the Number and Suffering of the Clergy.... in the late Rebellion, London, 1714, p. 207; Small Account Books, op.cit., vol. 1, 1791-8; vol. 2, 1797-1800, vol. 5, 1805-11, vol. 7, 1819-35.

17. Letter from John Parfitt to Earl of Ilchester, op.cit., containing enclosure headed "Daily Prayers"; Charity Commission 1824, op.cit., p. 379.

18. S.H.C. DD/SE 47/2, A Schedule of Goods, 1703, op.cit.; SE 43/17, Accounts of Robert Ludwell 1675-6, op.cit.; Hoare op.cit., p. 79; S.H.C. DD/DN 4/4/98, Notes made at a Meeting 6 September 1853 by F.H. Dickinson.

19. Letter from John Parfitt to the Earl of Ilchester, op.cit., containing enclosure "Hospital Dietary 1852"; S.H.C. DD/SE 43/2/2, Account Book headed 'Cost of Maintenance of Boys' 1857-1871.

20. Mr Cheekes Accompte 1662, op.cit.; Small Account Books, op.cit., vol. 7, 1819-1835; 'Shepton Mallet Journal', 7 November 1873; 'Bath Chronicle', 22 September 1831; 'Sherborne Mercury', 9 September 1856.

21. S.H.C. DD/SE 46/1-12, Apprenticeship Indentures 1663-1793; Hobhouse, op.cit., p.9; S.H.C. DD/DN 4/4/117, Application for Apprentices 9 September 1856; DD/BT 7/9, Apprenticeships 1842-1874: Certificates and Testimonials; DD/SE 46/13, Apprenticeship Indenture.

22. 'Sherborne & Yeovil Mercury', 15 April 1799; S.H.C. DD/BT 7/9, Apprenticeships 1842-1874: Letter of T. Thornhill 1867; DD/SE 46/1, Apprenticeship Indentures 1663-1670; DD/ BT 7/9, Certificate of Samuel Bord, 24 October 1871; Small Account Books, op.cit., vol. 7, 1819-1835; DD/DN 4/4/148, Letter from Henry Hobhouse to H. Dickinson 22 August 1860.

23. Mr Cheekes Accompte, 1662, op.cit.; Accounts of Robert Ludwell 1666-1676, op.cit.; Charity Commission 1824, op.cit., p, 376; Small Account Books, vol. 1, 1791-1798.

24. S.H.C. DD/SE 43/1, Accounts of Valentine Trim 1636-1639; SE 44/5, Mr Albyns Book of Disbursements 1652-5; Mr Cheekes Accompte, op.cit.; Account of Robert Ludwell, 1666-76. op.cit.; 'Sherborne and Yeovil Mercury', 15 April 1799; Hoare, op.cit., p. 78; Taunton Commission Report, 1868, op.cit., vol. XIV, p. 189; 'Salisbury and Winchester Journal', 15 August 1863; Small Account Books, op.cit., vol. 7, 1819-1835.

25. ibid. vol. 1, 1791-1798, vol. 5, 1805-1811; 'Western Gazette', 26 November 1880: Inquiry into the Charity called Hugh Sexey's Hospital.

26. 'Sherborne Mercury', 22 October 1798; S.H.C. A/ACI/1, Letters relating to James Whitaker, 1809-1828; DD/BT 7/9, Apprenticeships: Letters of H. Mabbett and Rev. F.E. Hutchinson, 1867.

27. S.H.C. DD/AH 11/16/6, Bruton Hospital 1842; Taunton Commission Report, op.cit., vol. XIV, p. 189; S.H.C. DD/SE 43/20, Account Book 1784-1787.

28. Taunton Commission Report, 1868, op.cit., vol. XIV, pp. 188-9; S.H.C. DD/BT 25/29, Letter Book 1886-1889: Letter from T.O. Bennett to Charity Commissioners 19 September 1888; 'Western Gazette', 9 February 1877; Sexey's School, Bruton, Magazine, No. 25, Easter 1903: Speech of Earl of Cork and Orrery at Prize Day 1902; 'Western Gazette', 22 April 1892.

29. 'Western Gazette', 26 November 1880; S.H.C. DD/DN 4/4/105, Letter from James Parfitt to H.M. Dickinson 31 July 1854; Report of the Royal Commission on the Employment

of Children, Young Persons and Women in Agriculture, 2nd Report 1869, PP 1868-9, XIII, Evidence of Mr Amor, occupier, Bruton.

30. S.H.C. DD/BT 27/3, Bruton Hospital Girls' School Minute Book, 24 February and 7 April 1883, (hereafter Girls' School Minute Book); 'Western Gazette', 19 September 1890; S.H.C. DD/SE 72, Hugh Sexey's Hospital Bruton Minute Book 1888-1906, 12 September 1893, (hereafter Minute Book); ' Western Gazette', 18 December 1903; Minute Book, op.cit., 2 March 1895; 'Western Gazette', 26 November 1880; T.N.A. ED 27/4094 Report of Inspector Bruce, 7 November 1887.

31. Minute Book, op.cit., 17 September 1889; Girls' School Minute Book, op.cit., 5 July 1884.

32. S.H.C. DD/SE 73, Sexey's Hospital Minute Book 1906-21, 6 November 1909; T.N.A. ED 35/2178, Sexey's Girls' School: Board of Education internal Minute 10 May 1909; S.H.C. DD/BT 2/2/7, Sexey's Girls' School Accounts 1882-1886: Year ending 31 August 1882; Minute Book op.cit., 2 January 1894; 'Western Gazette', 26 November 1880.

33. Minute Book, op.cit., 7 September 1889; S.H.C. DD/JO/44, Ironmongery Accounts 1878-9.

34. Report of the Select Committee on Education: Science and Art July 1884, p. 32; T.N.A. ED 27/4084, Report of Inspector Bruce, 7 November 1887; 'Western Gazette', 26 November 1880; S.H.C. DD/BT 2/2/7, Sexey's Girls' School Accounts 1882-86; T.N.A. 35/2178, Accounts of Girls' School 1908; ibid., internal Minute 10 May 1909; Minute Book, op.cit., 14 September 1899.

35. Girls' School Accounts, op.cit., 1883-4; Minute Book, op.cit., Monthly Meeting 8 October 1898; S.H.C. DD/BT 27/3, Advertisement for Mistress 11 September 1884; Girls' School Accounts, op.cit., 1884-5; DD/BT 26/29, Visitors' Account Book 1889-1898; DD/BT 25/91, Sexey's Hospital Letter Book 1883-1886: advertisement April 1884.

36. T.N.A. ED 35/2178, Sexey's Girls' School: internal Minute 10 May 1909.

37. Girls' School Minute Book, op.cit., 7 October 1882; Girls' School Accounts, op.cit., 1882-3; Minute Book, op.cit., Monthly Meeting 3 August 1889; Girls' School Accounts, 1882-3, 1883-4, 1885-6; S.H.C. DD/BT 26/29, Visitors' Account Book 1889-1898, 18 July 1892.

38. S.H.C. DD/BT 25/85, Sexey's Hospital Letter Book 1880-1: Monthly Meeting 1 April 1880; Girls' School Minute Book, op.cit., 7 October 1882, 8 October 1881, 7 October and 11 November 1882, 13 January 1883; Girls' School Accounts, op.cit., 31 August 1883, 31 August 1884, 31 August 1882; S.H.C. DD/SE 73, Sexey's Hospital Minute Book 1906-21, entries for 6 February, 3 July and 18 September 1909.

39. S.H.C. DD/BT 25/90, Visitors' Letter Book 1881-3: Letters from T.O. Bennett to Charity Commissioners 28 March 1882, 12 September 1882, 23 January and 9 April 1883. Insurance was taken out with the Phoenix Fire Office of London (Bruton Agency).

40. T.N.A. ED 35/2178, internal Minute 10 May 1909.

41. Visitors' Letter Book 1881-3, op.cit., Meeting 1 April 1880; Girls' School Minute Book, op.cit., 1 December 1883; Minute Book, op.cit., 4 October 1890, 15 September 1891; Girls' School Minute Book, op.cit., 11 November 1882; DD/BT 25/98, Sexey's Hospital Letter Book, 1896-1899, Letter from, T.O. Bennett to Miss Maitland, Bath, 8 June 1899; T.N.A. 27/4084, Report of Inspector Bruce November 1887, op.cit.; Minute Book, op.cit., 7 April 1894.

42. T.N.A. ED 35/2178, internal Minute, op.cit.; Girls' School Minute Book, op.cit., 13 January 1883, 3 February 1883, 5 July 1884, 6 November 1886; Sexey's Hospital Letter Book 1893-6, 8 September 1894.

43. T.N.A. ED 35/2178, internal Minute, op.cit.; ED 35/2175, Letter from A. Cardew at Board of Education to the Visitors 15 April 1910.

44. T.N.A. ED 35/2157, Letter from Henry Hobhouse to Board of Education 10 May 1910; ibid., Report of Conference at Sexey's Hospital 11 June 1910.

45. Ibid., Minute of W. Galbraith 31 August 1910; Letter from Board of Education to Visitors 24 September 1910; 'Western Gazette', 4 November 1910.

46. T.N.A. ED 35/2179, Sexey's Foundation Scheme 16 December 1911.

47. T.N.A. ED 27/8358, Plans for alterations 27 September 1911; ED 27/8360, Letters between F.W. Hooper, Clerk of the Sexey's Foundation, and Board of Education 8 January, 11 October and 19 November 1912.

48. 'Taunton Courier', 2 August 1911; 'Western Gazette', 27 June 1913.

49. T.N.A. ED 70/2066, Note of Board of Education official J.S.H.

50. BM, Box 51, Bruton National School Log Book 1900-1932: Copy of 1913 Board of Education Report; T.N.A. ED 70/2066 Interview Memorandum 27 February 1920.

51. 'Sherborne Journal', 25 January 1877.

52. 'Dorset County Chronicle', 1 February 1877; 'Western Gazette', 9 February 1877.

53. 'Western Flying Post', 18 January 1878.

54. 'Wells Journal', 1 March 1871.

55. 'Shepton Mallet Journal', 26 November 1880.

56. T.N.A. ED 27/4083, Scheme 15 July 1881.

57. 'Western Chronicle', 24 December 1886, 18 February and 1 July 1887.

58. T.N.A. ED 27/4094, Inspector Bruce's Report, 7 November 1887; 'Shepton Mallet Journal', 7 July 1899.

2. Sunday Schools.

1. T.N.A. PROB 11/130/1, Will of Sir Maurice Berkeley, 20 April 1617 with Codicil 28 April 1617.

2. F.M. Eden, The State of the Poor, vol. I, London, 1797, pp. 444-450; R. Brinley-Jones, ed., The Letters of Hannah More, London, 1925, p. 183.

3. BM, Box 52, Bruton Sunday School Notebook, Letter from Captain George Henderson to Rev. Dalby of the National Society, 22 July 1837.

4. S.H.C. D/D/Rm1, Protestant Dissenter Meeting Houses 1736-1792 and D/D/Rm2, 1792-1799.
5. The Evangelical Magazine, vol. VIII, 1800, London, p. 218; The Evangelical Magazine, vol. X, 1802, London, p. 334; S.H.C. D/D/Rm3 Protestant Dissenter Meeting Houses 1800-1807, 22 June 1802; S.H.C. D/N/Scu 4/2/7, Church Record Book of the Transactions of the Church of Christ of the Independent Denomination at Bruton. In 1802 it was noted in the 'Evangelical Magazine' p. 509, that another place of worship should be purchased or built. It is not clear from the surviving documentary evidence if the 1803 Chapel in the High Street was a new purchase or an extension/adaption of the one they occupied in 1802. Returns of the Select Committee on Education of the Poor, 1818, PP 1819, IX, pt. II, p. 776.
6. T.N.A. H.O. 64/4/114, fols. 237, 239.
7. Abstract of Education Returns, 1833, PP 1835, XLII, p. 776; Abstract of Answers and Returns, 1841, PP 1843, XXII, p. 299.
8. BM, Box 52, 2007.111.13, Establishment of Sunday School.
9. BM, Box 52, Bruton Sunday School Notebook, Letter from Captain Henderson to Rev. Dalby, op.cit.
10. S.H.C. D/P/brut 18/6/1, Bruton Church Sunday School Meeting, 18 December 1835; W.H.C. Hoare Papers 383/947, Printed Statement of Receipts and Expenses (undated but 1840).
11. S.H.C. DD/JO/26, Bruton Parish Accounts, Minutes of Vestry Meeting 29 July 1836; BM, Box 52, 2007.110.12, Indenture 8 March 1837; 2007.111.10, Account of Edward Dyne for Conveyance Work.
12. 'Sherborne Journal', 5 July 1838; BM, Box 52, 2007.112.19.1-6, Accounts 1835-1841.
13. R. Brinley-Jones, op.cit., p. 184.
14. S.H.C D/P/brut 4/1/3, Churchwardens' Accounts 1831-1874.
15. Lambeth Palace Library, I.C.B.S. file 3025, cited in Victoria County History of Somerset, vol. VII, p. 41; Bristol Post Office Directory and Gazetteer with Gloucestershire and Somerset, 1859, p. 714; Bath and Wells Diocesan Kalendar, 1888, p. 41.

16. For details of Friendly Societies and their celebrations see P.W. Randell, Alcohol, Violence, Feasts and Fairs: Leisure Pursuits in Bruton, Somersetshire, c1500-c1900, Brighton, 2012, esp. pp. 175-6, 202-207.
17. 'Shepton Mallet Journal', 18 June 1875; 'Western Gazette', 31 December 1864; 'Shepton Mallet Journal', 8 February 1867; Monthly Review, September 1893; S.H.C. DD/JO/45, East Somerset Savings Bank Ledger, Account of Mrs E. Ridley, Trustee of Bruton Church Sunday School.
18. 'Dorset County Chronicle', 15 June 1837; Sweetman's Monthly Illustrated Journal, July 1872.
19. East Somerset Savings Bank Ledger, op.cit., Account of William Muller, Esq, Bruton Treasurer of the Sunday School Penny Club. It has not proved possible to identify these last two teachers with certainty. Assuming that they were resident in Bruton itself, the 1841 Census listed two men with the name Thomas Rawlings: one was a painter aged 25 who lived with his wife in Grove Alley and the other was a 65 year old inmate of Sexey's Hospital. One Lydia Fish was listed and she was a washerwoman aged 60 who lived in Coombe Street.
20. S.H.C. DD/DN 4/4/39/14, Testimonial of George Perrott from the Committee of the Management of the Bruton Sunday and National Schools (undated but Nov/Dec 1851).
21. P.W. Randell, Death Comes to Bruton, a market town in Somerset c1400-c1900, Guildford, 2014.
22. Select Committee on the State of Children employed in Manufactures, 1816, PP 1816, XIII, Evidence of John Sharrer Ward 6 May 1816, p. 74.
23. The Evangelical Magazine and Missionary Chronicle, New Series, vol. XIV, December 1836, p. 565; A General Directory for the County of Somerset, published by the Somerset County Gazette, Taunton, 1840, p. 79; S.H.C. D/N/Scu 4/2/7, Church Record Book, op.cit., Meeting 30 June 1859.
24. 'Western Gazette', 21 May 1864; Church Record Book, op.cit., entry for 26 April 1869.
25. ibid. 13 April 1871; S.H.C. D/N/Scu 4/2/46, Congregational Church Committee Minute Book Meetings 5 July 1880, 28 March 1881.

26. 'Western Chronicle', 26 July 1907.
27. 'Shepton Mallet Journal', 23 August 1867; 'Western Gazette', 23 July 1882, 15 May 1891, 3 November 1882.
28. 'Shepton Mallet Journal', 18 June 1858, 29 May 1863; The Castle Cary, Wincanton and Bruton Monthly Review, July 1893.
29. 'Shepton Mallet Journal', 20 June 1862.
30. Church Record Book, op.cit., 11 January 1889; 'Western Flying Post', 7 June 1841; 'Shepton Mallet Journal', 19 November 1880; The Evangelical Magazine and Missionary Chronicle, 1831, New Series, vol. IX, London, p. 42; ibid., 1855, New Series, vol. XXXIII, London, p. 301
31. S.H.C. D/N/frc, Frome Wesley Circuit Minutes of Local Preachers' Meetings 1835-1854, 26 September 1836; SHC D/D/Rm9, Dissenter Meeting Houses 1842-1852: 3 May 1844; D/N/smc 4/3/58, Methodist Chapel Account Book 1844-1882; 'Western Gazette', 12 October 1888.
32. ibid. 28 May 1886, 24 February 1888, 11 January 1889.
33. C. Clark, Tales from Old Bruton, Charldon Publications, 1998, Poster p. 30; 'Western Gazette', 11 January 1889.
34. S.H.C. D/N/smc 4/3/58, Account Book, op.cit., 17 September 1852; Monthly Review, August 1893; C. Clark, The Diary of a Wessex Farmer: Josiah Jackson 1882-1904, Charldon Publications, 1996, p. 278, 21 August 1902.
35. 'Western Chronicle', 10 July 1896.
36. C. Clark, The Diary, op.cit., p. 306, 1 August 1904; 'Somerset and Wilts Journal', 25 September 1858; 'Western Gazette', 21 January 1887.
37. 'Somerset and Wilts Journal', 10 March 1860.
38. 'Western Chronicle', 23 August 1895; C. Clark, Diary, op.cit., p. 152, 16 March 1895, p. 156, 22 and 24 May 1895, p. 195, 20 May 1897 passim, p. 200, 25 August 1897.
39. C. Clark, Tales from Old Bruton, op.cit., p. 29.
40. 'Wells Journal', 24 June 1897; Castle Cary Visitor, vol. I, 1896-7, p. 187.
41. Castle Cary Visitor, vol. VIII, 1910-1911, p. 187; 'Western Chronicle', 20 December 1912, 4 October 1912; ibid., 14 August and 4 September 1914.

42. 'Western Gazette', 13 January 1888; ibid. 21 January 1887; C. Clark, The Diary, op.cit., p. 163, 24 October 1895, p. 199, 19 August 1897, p. 192, 16 March 1897, p. 200, 27 August 1897.

43. Royal Commission to Inquire into the Present State of Popular Education, 1861, PP 1861, XXI, pt. I, p. 623; Digest of Returns on Education 1818, op.cit., pp. 793, 795, 798; Abstract of Education Returns, 1833, PP 1835, XLII, pp. 795, 818, 821; W.H.C. 415/438, Pocket Book of John Goldesbrough 1814, entry for 3 February; S.H.C. DD/X/KR, Pocket Ledger of J. Goldesbrough, 1817, entry for 14 April.

44. Castle Cary Visitor, vol. VII, 1908-1909, pp. 141, 71.

3. The National School.

1. 'Western Flying Post', 20 August 1842; T.N.A. MH 32/85, Correspondence of Assistant Poor Law Commissioners: Robert Weale, 19 September 1837.

2. BM, Box 52, op.cit., Bruton Sunday School House, Letter from Captain Henderson to Rev. Dalby, 22 July 1837; Report of Meeting November 1839, Meetings 16 and 23 March 1840.

3. BM, Box 52, op.cit., 2007.112.19.5, Statement of Accounts 1840; 2007.112.16, Draft of Letter from George Henderson June 1840.

4. Ibid., Bruton Sunday School House, Letter from Col. Coles to Capt. Henderson, April 1840; Meeting 6 April 1840 which prepared Address; Notes of G.H. April 1840; Meeting 27 April 1840; Rules and Instructions 6 April 1840.

5. Owen & Co., Directory for Wiltshire, Somerset, Bristol & Bath, Leicester, 1878, p. 5; 'Wells Journal', 17 July 1903; 'Somerset and Wilts Journal', 26 February 1859; 'Western Chronicle', 22 September 1893, 30 November 1900; 'Wells Journal', 8 June 1906; S.Villiers, Village Schooling in Somerset, Wellington, 2012, pp. 131-3.

6. 'Morning Post', 20 November 1848.

7. T.N.A. ED 103/117, Building Application for a National School, 8 March 1851, pp. 315-323.

8. 'Bath Chronicle', 10 July 1851. Just over a year after the new School was opened Ross was declared bankrupt, 'Wells Journal', 16 July 1853.
9. 'Bath Chronicle', 27 May 1852.
10. S.H.C. DD/EDS/1, Bruton, Plan of Proposed School, 13 June 1851.
11. BM, Box 52, op.cit., 2007.112.1.2, Letter from Council on Education to Rev. James White containing a summary of the Inspector's Report, 12 August 1859.
12. T.N.A. R.G.9,320/4, Census Returns 1861, p. 45.
13. Return of the Number of Children who shall be Chargeable, 1 July 1853, PP 1854, LV, pp. 2 and 5; T.N.A. MH 12/10570, 45290/62, Letter from Robert Clarke to the Poor Law Board, 3 December 1862.
14. Royal Commission to Inquire into the Present State of Popular Education, 1861: Report of Rev. James Fraser, Assistant Commissioner for Dorset, Devon and Somerset, PP 1861, XXI pt. II, pp. 26, 46, 69, 79; W.H. Hudson, A Shepherd's Life, London, 1910, p. 4; Report of the Royal Commission on the Employment of Children, Young Persons and Women in Agriculture, 2nd Report, 1869, PP 1868-9, XIII, Evidence of Mr Amor, occupier, Bruton, p. 494; Select Committee on the State of Children employed in Manufactures, 1816, PP 1816, XIII, Evidence of J.S. Ward, pp. 74-6; Reports from Assistant Commissioners on Handloom Weavers, 1840, Report of A. Austin on the South West of England, PP 1840, XXIII, p. 438.
15. BM, Box 52, op.cit., 2007.112.5, Return for Bruton National School, Silver Street, undated but c.1849-1851.
16. Average Attendance statistics 1882-1898 based upon Annual Reports of the Committee of the Council on Education which listed elementary schools aided from the Parliamentary Grant. Statistics for 1900-1914 compiled by Board of Education, T.N.A. ED 21/15072, Bruton National School.
17. Bath and Wells Diocesan Kalendar, 1888, p. 41, and 1891, p. 40.
18. BM, Box 51, Log Book, Bruton National School 1870-1900; Log Book, Bruton National School 1900-1932.

19. S.H.C. D/G/WN 8a/12, Appointment of School Attendance Committee, 18 April 1877; Appointment of Relieving Officers as Inquiry Officers, 9 May 1877.

20. T.N.A. ED 6/58, School Attendance File (Wincanton).

21. S.H.C. D/PS/winc 1/11, Magistrates' Entry Book 1878, winc 1/12 Register of Court of Summary Justice January 1880-August 1882; S.H.C. A/BRI 1/2, Shepton Mallet Register 1886-1890; 'Western Gazette', 3 January 1902; 'Wells Journal', 4 December 1891, 10 October 1909, 11 March 1910, 3 June 1910; S.H.C. A/BRI 1/2, Register, op.cit.; 'Western Gazette', 3 January 1902; 'Wells Journal', 6 March 1914.

22. 'Wells Journal', 12 April 1912, 26 February 1909, 26 March 1909, 22 October 1909, 27 May 1914.

23. BM, Box 52, 2007.112.5, Return c.1850; 2007.111.15, Appointment of Master and Mistress, 28 March 1854. The Hullah System named after John Hullah was class singing which started with very simple melodies and progressed to more difficult ones. Sunday School House, op.cit., Books to be used.

24. S.H.C. DD/SAS c/795, Sweetman Papers, vol. 7, pp. 102-3.

25. BM, Box 52, op.cit., 2007.112.1.2, Letter with summary of 1859 Report, op.cit.

26. 'Western Gazette', 14 July 1865; 'Shepton Mallet Journal', 12 July 1867 and 30 July 1869.

27. Extracts for various subjects are taken from the two surviving Log Books, BM, Boxes 51 and 52.

28. S.H.C. C/E/4 380, Schools' Enquiry Forms 1902: Bruton National School.

29. 'Shepton Mallet Journal', 27 April 1877; 'Western Gazette', 9 November 1888, 13 May 1892; 'Wells Journal', 2 August 1907; 'Western Gazette', 21 June 1878.

30. Hunt and Co's Directory and Topography, 1850, p. 18; S.H.C. DD/DN 4/4/39/12, Letter from George Perrott to F.H. Dickinson, 5 December 1851; 4/4/39/14, Testimonial of George Perrott.

31. BM, Box 52, op.cit., 2007.111.15, Meeting to confirm the appointment of Mr and Mrs Byles, 28 March 1854.

32. 'Salisbury and Winchester Journal', 22 October 1859; 'Shepton Mallet Journal', 19 April 1861; 'Bath Chronicle', 13 March 1856; Shepton Mallet Journal', 23 December 1859.

33. T.N.A. ED 27/4074, Letters from John Grove Bord, Revs. White, Aitkens and Randolph and Henry Dyne, May 1864; 'Western Flying Post', 25 September 1866; 'Bath Chronicle', 12 May 1887.

34. 'Western Gazette', 15 November 1867 and 1 May 1868; 'Shepton Mallet Journal', 28 June 1867; 'Western Gazette', 27 March 1868 and 12 July 1867; 'Shepton Mallet Journal', 17 July 1868 and 18 February 1870.

35. S.H.C. C/E/4381, Particulars of Teachers 1902; T.N.A. RG 10/2127, Census Returns 1871; 'Western Gazette', 2 September 1870 and 1 September 1871.

36. 'Shepton Mallet Journal', 5 March 1886, 28 February 1879, 28 January 1859.

37. Castle Cary Visitor, vol. VII, 1908-9, p. 35; 'Bristol Mercury', 7 November 1893; 'Western Gazette', 29 August 1880.

38. 'Western Gazette', 4 April 1890; Castle Cary Visitor, vol. VII, op.cit., p. 35.

39. E.R. Kelly, Post Office Directory for Somerset 1875, London, 1875, p. 342; 'Wells Journal', 27 July 1888, 13 January 1888; Castle Cary Visitor, vol. VII, op.cit., p. 35.

40. 'Wells Journal', 20 November 1896.

41. 'Western Gazette', 6 April 1883, 18 March 1898; 'Shepton Mallet Journal'. 14 April 1899; S.H.C. Q/RSM/1, Members of the Royal Clarence Lodge of Freemasons, Bruton, 1865-1891.

42. For details of Friendly Societies in Bruton, see P.W. Randell, Stones We Cannot Eat: Poverty, the Poor Law, Philanthropy and Self Help in Bruton, Somerset, c1500-c1900, Brighton, 2009, pp. 396-409. 'Western Gazette', 22 July 1887; The Wincanton, Castle Cary & Bruton Monthly Review, September 1893. For reports of the Blue Ball Friendly Society dinners see, for example, 'Western Gazette', 10 June 1881 and 25 May 1888.

43. For details of Bruton Mutual Improvement Society, see P.W. Randell, Alcohol, Violence, Feasts and Fairs: Leisure Pursuits

in Bruton, Somerset, c1500-c1900, Brighton, 2012, pp. 85-87; 'Western Gazette', 2 March 1888, 10 February 1888.

44. 'Frome Times', 13 September 1882; 'Western Gazette', 2 May 1890, 12 April 1889.

45. 'Western Gazette', 2 March 1888; 'Shepton Mallet Journal', 21 April 1899; 'Western Chronicle', 20 March 1896.

46. ibid. 14 November 1913.

47. BM, Box 52, op.cit., 2007.112.5, Return for Bruton National School by George Perrott undated but c1849/50; T.N.A. ED 7/104 No 52, Preliminary Statement respecting Income and Expenditure ending Christmas 1852; BM, Box 52, op.cit., 2007.112.8, Letter from Secretary of the Committee of the Council on Education to Rev. James White, 28 December 1854 containing handwritten note on reverse; 2007.110.9, Letter 4 January 1855; 2007.110.2.1, Letter 11 December 1856.

48. BM, Box 52, op.cit., 2007.110.5, Indenture for Pupil Teacher Elizabeth Freeman, 1 December 1857; 2007.111.3.1, similar Indenture for Elizabeth James from Penrith in Cumberland dated 1 June 1860.

49. BM, Box 52, op.cit., 2007.110.2.1, Comments of H.M.I., December 1856; 'Shepton Mallet Journal', 10 February 1865; 'Western Gazette', 9 December 1881.

50. S.H.C. C/E/4 380, Schools' Enquiry Form 1902, op.cit.

51. Return of Each Public Elementary School 1893, PP 1894, LXV, pp. 518-9.

52. BM, Box 52, op.cit., School House Rules & Instructions; 2007.111.15, Appointment of Mr and Mrs Byles 25 March 1854.

53. The Poetical Works of George Crabbe, vol. IV, London, 1834, p. 77; T.N.A. ED 7/104 No 52, Preliminary Statement op.cit.; S.H.C. D/G/WN 8a/13, 29 June 1881; 8a/15, 23 February 1887.

54. S.H.C. DD/EDS/1, Bruton Plan, op.cit.; BM, Box 52, op.cit., 2007.112.12, Bruton National School Subscriptions for Desks; 2007.112.3, Letter from Secretary of Committee of Council on Education to Rev. James White, 8 June 1853; T.N.A. ED 21/10572, Bruton National School: Report of Inspector Millard, 29 January 1909.

55. BM, Box 52, op.cit., 2007.112.1.2, op.cit., Summary of Inspector's Report 1859; T.N.A. ED 21/10572, op.cit., Memo to Mr Tillard, 23 January 1914.

56. ibid. Copy of Letter stamped R.Walrond to Local Education Authority, undated; Memo to Mr Tillard, 23 January 1914.

57. ibid. School Premises - Blacklist: Summary of Defects March 1909; Internal Minute Paper, 21 June 1909; Letter to Board of Education from Managers, 20 August 1909; Letter to Board of Education from Managers, 25 May 1911.

58. 'Western Gazette', 9 July 1864.

59. For details of Shrove Tuesday celebrations and Bruton Feast, see P.W. Randell, Alcohol, Violence, etc. op.cit., pp. 173-4, 36-39.

60. 'Western Flying Post', 2 January 1855; 'Salisbury and Winchester Journal', 22 October 1859; 'Western Gazette', 20 May 1881.

61. For details of deaths in Bruton, see P.W. Randell, Death Comes to Bruton, a market town in Somerset c1400-c1900, Guildford, 2014; 'Shepton Mallet Journal', 7 November 1873; 'Western Gazette', 1 April 1887; 'Wells Journal', 29 June 1905.

62. ibid. 15 May 1908.

63. ibid. 6 March and 31 July 1914.

64. Statistics cited in J. Lawson and H. Silver, A Social History of Education in England, London, 1973, pp. 383-4.

65. 'Western Gazette', 20 January 1882, 18 May 1888, 25 May 1888, 8 June 1888, 24 October 1890.

66. 'Salisbury and Winchester Journal', 22 October 1859; 'Western Gazette', 2 March 1888; 'Western Chronicle', 29 July 1910; 'Western Gazette', 2 March 1883.

67. 'Somerset and Wilts Journal', 4 August 1855; Shepton Mallet Journal', 7 August 1863, 14 July 1865, 30 July 1869; 'Frome Times', 29 August 1860.

68. 'Shepton Mallet Journal', 20 March 1863; 'Western Chronicle', 1 July 1887; 'Sherborne Mercury', 9 September 1856; 'Shepton Mallet Journal', 20 May 1870; 'Wells Journal', 28 January 1910.

69. 'Shepton Mallet Journal', 30 August 1867, 3 September 1869.

70. H.W. Hillier, ed., Sexey's School, Bruton, Register 1891-1952, privately printed, 1953, p. 12.

71. T.N.A. ED 21/10572, Bruton National School Inspector's Report, 22 December 1871; S.H.C. DD/BT 25/1, Letter Book of T.O. Bennett, April-November 1873; T.N.A. ED 21/10572, op.cit., Copy of newspaper advertisement, 10 March 1873; Letter from Education Department to Managers, 12 August 1874.

72. 'Western Gazette', 5 February, 19 February and 5 March 1875; T.N.A. ED 21/10572, op.cit., Letter to Secretary of the Education Department from T.O. Bennett, 14 August 1876.

73. BM, Box 52, op.cit., 2007.111.4, Indenture, 12 September 1876 with attached Plan.

74. 'Western Gazette', 9 November 1888, 29 August 1890; 'Wells Journal', 13 October 1899, 29 June 1900, 4 September 1891; The Wincanton, Castle Cary & Bruton Monthly Review, September 1893.

75. T.N.A. ED 21/10572, op.cit., Draft of Inspector Millard's Report, 24 June 1913.

76. S.H.C. DD/BT 25/90, Letter Book of Visitors of Sexey's Hospital 1881-3, Letter to Charity Commissioners from T.O. Bennett, 28 January 1882.

77. T.N.A. ED 21/10572, op.cit., Letter to the Secretary of the Education Department from T.O. Bennett, 28 June 1895; 'Wells Journal', 24 January 1896.

78. BM, Box 52, op.cit., 2007.112.6, Letter from the Committee of Council on Education to Rev. James White, 29 May 1851; 2007.112.1.2, op.cit., Summary of Inspector's Report 1859; S. Villiers, Village Schooling, op.cit., p.99.

79. For the state of public health in Bruton in the period after 1870 and opposition to improvements, see P.W. Randell, 'Public Health in Bruton 1872-1898' in Notes and Queries for Somerset and Dorset, vol. XXXIII, September 1992, pp. 157-164.

80. T.N.A. ED 21/10572, op.cit., Report of Inspector Millard 26 January 1909; Internal Minute Paper, 21 June 1909; Letter from R.T.A. Hughes, 15 October 1909; Statement of the Managers of the Bruton Church of England Schools, 25 May 1911; Letter to Inspector Tillard from H. Hobhouse, 4 June 1911; Internal Memo to H.M.I. Tillard, 18 July 1911.

81. S.H.C. C/E/21/380, Schools' Enquiry Form 1902; T.N.A. ED 21/10572, op.cit., Internal Report to H.M.I. Tillard, 18 July 1911.

82. T.N.A. ED 21/10572, op.cit., Letter from R.T.A. Hughes to Board of Education, 20 August 1909; Statement of Managers, op.cit., 25 May 1911.

83. 'Western Gazette', 9 August 1889; T.N.A. ED 21/10572, op.cit., Report of Inspector Millard, 29 January 1909; Statement of Managers, op.cit., 7 June 1911; Report of Inspector Millard, 24 June 1913.

84. ibid. Statement of Managers, op.cit., 25 May 1911.

85. ibid. Internal Memo to Inspector Tillard from Felix Clay, 18 July 1911.

86. BM, Box 52, op.cit., 2007.112.3, Statistics for School c1850; 2007.110.7, School Building Form, 8 March 1851; T.N.A. ED 7/104 No 52, Preliminary Statement of Income and Expenditure for year ending Christmas 1852.

87. BM, Box 52, op.cit., (uncatalogued) Letter from Committee of Council on Education to Rev. James White, 5 August 1851; 2007.110.14, Balance Sheet of Building Account of Bruton National School; S. Villiers, Village Schooling, op.cit., pp. 70-1.

88. BM, Box 52, op.cit., 2007.112.8 and 2007.112.7, Printed letters from Secretary of Committee of Council on Education to Rev. James White, 28 December 1854 and 6 March 1856; Return for Each Public Elementary School, 1893, PP 1894, LXV, pp. 518-9; S.H.C. C/E/4/380, op.cit., Schools' Enquiry Form 1902.

89. BM, Box 52, op.cit., 2007.113.1 and 2007.110.2.1, Letters from the Committee of Council on Education, 16 January 1851 and 11 December 1856.

90. 'Bath Chronicle', 27 May 1852; 'Western Gazette', 12 September 1863; 'Western Flying Post', 18 March 1856; 'Bath Chronicle', 27 May 1852; 'Shepton Mallet Journal', 11 May 1860; 'Frome Times', 11 January 1865; 'Western Gazette', 2 August 1889.

91. Report of Inspectors of Factories: T.J. Howell, List of Schools to which grants have been made, 8 December 1846; BM, Box 52, op.cit., 2007.112.24, Letter from J. Howell of the Factory Office to Rev. James White, 10 March 1852; S.H.C. DD/BT/7/1, Bruton Hospital Rental and Account Book 1836-1879; S.H.C. DD/SE 72, Sexey's Hospital Minute Book, Meeting 18 September 1892.

92. C. Clarke, The Diary, op.cit., 18 July 1901 p. 263, 20 September 1901 p. 266, 23 December 1901 p. 270.

93. 'Shepton Mallet Journal', 2 December 1870, 19 February 1875; 'Western Gazette', 12 March and 19 March 1875; 'Western Chronicle', 24 May 1895.

94. J. Skinner, Brewton, printed in Castle Cary, 1861, p. 26; 'Western Chronicle', 16 April 1858, 11 May 1860; 'Western Gazette', 6 May 1881; Shepton Mallet Journal', 25 November 1887; 'Western Daily Press', 25 March 1899; 'Salisbury and Winchester Journal', 26 November 1864; 'Shepton Mallet Journal', 29 January 1886.

95. 'Shepton Mallet Journal', 11 September 1865, 20 April 1866, 4 January 1867. For further examples of such entertainments, see P.W. Randell, Alcohol, Violence, etc. op.cit., esp. pp. 90-98.

96. See for example 'Frome Times', 20 February 1861; 'Shepton Mallet Journal', 22 February 1867.

97. 'Western Flying Post', 19 February, 18 March and 13 May 1856; 'Shepton Mallet Journal', 17 May 1867, 7 October 1870.

98. ibid. 8 December 1865, 20 January 1871.

99. 'Western Gazette', 23 March 1863; 'Shepton Mallet Journal', 15 October 1886; 'Western Gazette', 2 August 1888.

100. 'Frome Times', 23 April 1873; 'Western Gazette', 27 January and 26 May 1882, 28 February 1863, 16 September 1870;

'Shepton Mallet Journal', 24 March 1882; 'Western Gazette', 25 January 1889, 'Bath Chronicle', 31 December 1885.

101. For details of the Mutual Improvement Society, see P.W. Randell, Alcohol, Violence, etc. op.cit., esp. pp. 85-7. 'Western Gazette', 20 January, 27 January, and 3 February 1888, 12 April 1899; 'Wells Journal', 20 November 1896, 20 October 1899; The Wincanton, Castle Cary and Bruton Monthly Review, March 1893.

102. ibid. 9 February 1894.

4.   Sexey's Trade School.

a)   Introduction.

1.   P. Keane, 'An English County and Education, 1889-1902', in English Historical Review, vol. 88, No. 347 (1973), p. 286.

2.   H. Hobhouse, 'Country Technical Schools', in The Record of Technical and Secondary Education, May 1893, 11 pages reprinted as a pamphlet; Sexey's School Magazine, Easter 1908, p. 12: Speech of Professor Sadler at Prize Day, 7 December 1907.

3.   T.N.A. ED 27/4083, Scheme 15 July 1881; Letter to the Charity Commissioners from a Committee of Parishioners in Lyncombe and Widcombe; Letter from Rev. F.W. Weaver, 13 December 1880; Reply of W. Richmond, Secretary of the Charity Commissioners, 15 February 1881.

b)   Establishing a new School.

1.   S.H.C. DD/BT 25/92, Hugh Sexey's Hospital, Bruton, Letter Book 1886-1889: Minute of Special General Meeting 5 April 1887.

2.   T.N.A. ED 27/4084, Report of Assistant Commissioner W.N. Bruce, 7 November 1887.

3.   S.H.C. DD/BT 25/92, Letter Book, op.cit., Letter from T.O. Bennett to Charity Commissioners, 19 September 1888; 'Western Chronicle', 14 December 1888.

4. T.N.A. ED 27/4086, Scheme for the Management of Sexey's Trade School, 28 November 1889. A copy may also be found in S.H.C. DD/BRU 3/2.

5. T.N.A. ED 27/4086, Letters from T.O. Bennett to Charity Commissioners, 29 April and 11 July 1890.

6. Report of Assistant Commissioner Bruce, op.cit., No. 10; C. Clark, ed., The Diary, op.cit., p. 75, 6 June 1890.

7. S.H.C. DD/SE 72, Hugh Sexey's Hospital Minute Book 1888-1906, Monthly Meeting 2 August 1890, Annual General Meeting September 1890, Monthly Meeting 6 December 1890; S.H.C. DD/BT 7/6, Hugh Sexey's Hospital Cash Account Book 1886-1895, December 1890, deposit paid to Dyne & Muller, solicitors.

8. T.N.A. ED 27/4086, Sexey's Trade School, Letter from T.O. Bennett to Charity Commissioners, 3 November 1890; Letter from Henry Hobhouse to the Visitors of Sexey's Hospital, 8 September 1890; Letter from T.O. Bennett to Charity Commissioners, 8 November 1890; S.H.C. DD/BT 7/6, Cash Account Book, op.cit., 7 and 12 February 1891.

The Skipper brothers were born in Norfolk and after training as an Architect in London, George returned to Norwich to work in his father's building firm. In 1879 at the age of 23 he started his own architect's practice, in which he was subsequently joined by his younger brother Frederick. In the early to mid-1890s they were credited with helping to shape Cromer by building the Town Hall and several large hotels. In the late 1890s and early 1900s they undertook major projects in Norwich, including the Royal Arcade and the Norwich Union's Head Office. They built in a range of styles, often very flamboyantly, including Classical Palladian, French Chateau, Arts and Crafts and then Edwardian Baroque. John Betjeman, the poet laureate and campaigner to preserve buildings was later to say of George, "He is altogether remarkable and original. He is to Norwich rather what Gaudi was to Barcelona." It was a view endorsed by Nikolaus Pevsner, the architectural historian.

9. 'Western Chronicle' 24 April 1891; T.N.A. ED 27/4086, Sexey's Trade School, Letter from William Pearce, Clerk of the Governors, to Charity Commissioners, 19 May 1891; Sexey's Trade School, Bruton, Building Account, May 1893; Letter from William Pearce to Charity Commissioners, 26 March 1892.

10. T.N.A. ED 27/4086, Sexey's Trade School: Advertisement November 1890; Prospectuses, late 1890 and January 1891; 'Western Chronicle', 20 March 1891.

11. Sexey's School Magazine, No. 1, 1897: School Chronicles, Early History, pp. 4-5; T.N.A. ED 35/2175, Sexey's School Foundation Accounts; ED 27/4087, Sexey's Trade School: Letter from William Pearce to Charity Commissioners, 19 May 1891.

12. Sexey's School Magazine, No. 3, 1897: School Chronicles, New Premises, pp. 4-5; 'Western Gazette', Letter from T.O. Bennett, 31 July 1891; T.N.A. ED 35/2175, Letter from F.W. Hooper to Board of Education, 19 October 1908; ED 35/2176, Scheme of Government, 15 June 1910.

13. Sexey's School Magazine, No. 3, 1897, op.cit., p. 5; C. Clark, Diary, op.cit., p. 103, 19 April 1892; 'Western Chronicle', 22 April 1892.

14. T.N.A. ED 109/5096, Board of Education Report of First Inspection, November 1904, p. 5; ED 35/2175, Letter from T.O. Bennett to Charity Commissioners, 29 April 1890; Sexey's School Magazine, No. 3, 1897, op.cit., pp. 4-5. Unfortunately no details were given about the desks but they may have been individual ones with the seat joined to the desk - a folding seat and a sloping top being the type still in use in the 1950s and 1960s in the Lecture Rooms.

15. Sexey's School Magazine, No. 4, Midsummer 1898: School Chronicles IV, p. 4; T.N.A. ED 27/4086, Account of William Pearce, 3 July 1894 for cost of erecting additional Classroom &c; Letters between Charity Commissioners and W. Pearce, 12 July, 21 July and 9 August 1894.

16. T.N.A. ED 27/4086, Letters of William Pearce to Charity Commissioners, 9 January and 12 January 1897, 5 January

1898; S.H.C. DD/BT 25/98, Letter Book, op.cit., Letter from
T.O. Bennett to Charity Commissioners, 12 January 1897;
DD/SE 72, Hospital Minute Book, op.cit., Monthly Meeting,
6 March 1897; T.N.A. ED 27/4086, Sexey's Trade School
Summary Statement of Account Year ending December 1897;
ED 109/5096, Inspection Report 1904, op.cit., p. 5. In the
mid-twentieth century when the Gymnasium was converted
into a large classroom an iron stove was inserted for heating.
For those fortunate enough to sit near it the heat was excellent,
for the rest of the room.....

17. T.N.A. ED 109/5096, Inspection Report 1904, op.cit., pp. 3-4;
'Western Chronicle', 10 December 1905; T.N.A. ED 35/2175,
General Report, 2 August 1906; Inspector's Report for year
ending July 1907; Correspondence between F.W. Hooper and
Board of Education, 17 June, 8 July 1910 and 4 January 1911;
'Western Chronicle', 21 May 1895.

c) The Governors.

1. T.N.A. ED 27/4084, Report of Assistant Commissioner Bruce,
7 November 1887, op.cit.; ED 27/4086, Sexey's Trade School,
Letter from T.O. Bennett to Charity Commissioners, 29 April
1890.

2. T.N.A. ED 27/4086, Sexey's Trade School, Scheme of
Management, 28 November 1889; Letter from T.O. Bennett
to Charity Commissioners, 29 April 1890 containing a list
of the names of the Governors appointed; ED 27/4088,
Mr Lefroy's Report, 11 October 1894, p. 5.

3. T.N.A. ED 35/2176, Scheme of Government, 15 June 1910.

4. Sexey's School Magazine, Easter 1917, p. 10; 'Western Daily
Press', 14 December 1901.

5. 'Western Chronicle', 5 July 1895, 24 December 1909.

d) The Headmaster.

1. During one year Knight senior filled the traditional post of
village Constable. In that capacity he was reputedly the last

man to imprison someone in the Round House in Castle Cary. As he was unsure that he had the authority to do so he did not lock the door. The prisoner was so drunk that he did not notice or try to escape.

2. Details of W.A. Knight's career taken from T.N.A. ED 27/4088, Mr Lefroy's Report 1894: List of Teaching Staff, and "Staff Register" in the possession of Sexey's School, Bruton; 'Workington Star', 8 September 1888; H. Phillips, Journey to Nowhere, London, 1960, pp. 47-8.

3. P. Richards, 'Memories of my grandfather, W.A. Knight' in Centenary Sexeian, 1991, pp. 80-1. [Sexey's School Magazine changed its name to 'Sexeian' in Autumn 1979].

4. H. Scott, Your Obedient Servant, London, 1959, p. 14; H. Phillips, op.cit., pp. 48-9.

5. T.N.A. ED 109/5096, Inspection 1904, op.cit., p. 17; 'Times Educational Supplement', 5 September 1911; Report of the Consultative Committee on Practical Work in Secondary Schools (Acland Committee): Evidence of Mr W.A. Knight, 5 November 1911, p. 248; Sexey's School Magazine, Easter 1919, p. 12; Michaelmas 1927: Mr Knight and Sexey's School, an Appreciation by Professor John Read, p. 104.

6. T.N.A. ED 109/5096, Inspection Report 1904, op.cit., pp. 6-7; ED 109/5097, Board of Education Report of Second Inspection, February 1910, pp. 8 and 11.

7. 'Taunton Courier', 21 March 1923.

8. H. Phillips, op,cit., p. 54; Sexeian, 1995, p. 57, Letter from Cyril E. Baker.

9. Acland Committee 1911, op.cit., Memorandum from Mr Knight, p. 253.

10. T.N.A. 109/5096, Inspection Report 1904, op.cit., p. 6; Letter from H. Hobhouse to Board of Education, 29 April 1905 and Note attached written by Mr Ellis; ED 27/4087, Headmaster's Pension Fund: Resolution 7 October 1893; ED 35/2176, Financial Statement 1908-9.

11. T.N.A. ED 109/5098, Board of Education Report of Inspection May 1920: H.M.I. Battiscombe's Report of Conference with Governors; 'Western Chronicle', 19 February 1893 and

26 February 1892; 'Taunton Courier', 9 January 1924; Sexey's School Magazine, Easter 1912, p. 11.

12. 'Western Chronicle', 1 March 1895, 11 December 1896; The Wincanton, Castle Cary and Bruton Monthly Review, February 1893; Sexey's School Magazine, Easter 1917, p. 20; 'Western Chronicle', 20 November 1896; C. Clark, The Diary, op.cit., p. 185, 17 November 1896; Sexeian, 1991, p. 83.

13. T.N.A. COPY 1/424/876-880 and 920. In the mid-1960s W.A. Knight's daughter, Mrs Makins, recalled that it was not unusual for local doctors from time to time to send a patient to him for an X-ray.

14. J. Read, 'A Great Headmaster and Educationalist', in The Somerset Year Book, No. XXVI, 1927, p. 98; Sexey's School Magazine, Easter 1911.

15. H. Phillips, op.cit., pp. 62-3; Sexey's School Magazine, Michaelmas 1927, p. 102; Centenary Sexeian, 1991, p. 87; Sexeian, 1995, p. 60: Obituary of Mrs E.G. Taylor (nee Knight) reprinted from 'The Veterinary Record'.

16. Sexey's School Magazine, Michaelmas 1927, pp. 110-113. Knight lived in retirement near the School at 'Cole Crest' for 27 years, dying in April 1949 aged 83 years, some 13 years after his wife. In his retirement there was a constant stream Old Boy visitors, some of whom stayed for weekends and others who visited just for the day. After his death he was cremated and his ashes interred in his wife's grave in the cemetery of his home town of Castle Cary. For the fiftieth anniversary of his death the grave was tracked down by a later Deputy Headmaster of the School, Rex Waller, with the help of a 90-year-old former pupil of Knight's, Vic Strickland (1921-5). The grave was in a poor state of repair with the headstone badly worn. Raising money from Old Sexeians and with the agreement of Knight's descendants, Waller arranged for the grave to be refurbished and a short service was held, conducted by Old Sexeian, Rev. Dan Olive (1941-5) on 3rd September 1999. (Sexeian, 1999, p. 70)

17. H.W.Hillier, ed. Sexey's School Register 1891-1952, p. 2.

e) Assistant Masters.

1. Numbers and details taken from H.W. Hillier, ed., op.cit., pp. 4-8; ' Western Daily Press', 6 February 1905; 'Western Chronicle', 21 April 1893; Castle Cary Visitor, vol. II, 1898-9, p. 3.

2. T.N.A. ED 27/4088, Mr Lefroy's Report 1894, op.cit., p. 7; ED 35/2175, Inspection Report 1904, op.cit., pp. 7-8; ED 109/5097, Inspection Report 1910, op.cit., p. 9.

3. H. Phillips, op.cit., p. 60; T.N.A. ED 35/2175, Letter from William Pearce to Science and Art Department, 27 September 1898; Inspection Report 1904, op.cit., p. 7; Inspection Report 1910, op.cit., pp. 8-9.

4. G.M. Tincknell, ed., Directory of Old Sexeians 1891-1920; Staff Register, op.cit.; Sexey' School Magazine, Easter 1917, p. 9, Easter 1919, p. 13; T.N.A. ED 109/5098, Inspection Report 1920, op.cit., p. 7; H.W. Hillier, Register, op.cit., pp. 8-9.

f) The Pupils

1. T.N.A. ED 27/4088, Mr Lefroy's Report, 1894, op.cit.: List of Scholars 1903; ED 109/5096, Inspection Report 1904, op.cit., p. 2; ED 109/5097, Inspection Report 1910, op.cit., pp. 3-4; ED 35/2176, Scheme 1910, op.cit., p. 76; 'Western Chronicle', 23 December 1909.

2. Ibid., 2 April 1892; H. Hobhouse, Country Technical Schools, op.cit., p. 5; 'Western Chronicle', 6 July 1894, 22 December 1899.

3. Acland Commission, op.cit., p. 248.

4. T.N.A. ED 27/4088, Mr Lefroy's Report, op.cit., p. 6; S.H.C. DD/BRU 4/1/1, Headmaster's Report, 23 May 1894; 'Western Chronicle', 3 July 1896.

5. Ibid., 10 June 1904; H. Phillips, op.cit., pp. 55-6; Sexey's School Magazine, Easter 1897, p. 9, Easter 1904, p. 7; S.H.C. DD/CGS, Sexey's Trade School Prospectus, June 1904.

6. 'Western Gazette', 10 April 1896; T.N.A. ED 108/5097, Inspection Report 1910, op.cit., p. 24; C. Clark, Diary, op.cit.,

p. 102, 29 March 1892; Sexey's School Magazine, Easter 1904, p. 8; 'Western Gazette', 1 May 1898; Sexey's School Magazine, Easter 1908, p. 9, Easter 1903, p. 9, Easter 1919, p. 13, Easter 1921, pp. 14-15.

7. 'Western Chronicle', 5 July 1895, 3 July 1896; Sexey's School Magazine, Easter 1913, p. 12, Easter 1921, p. 18.

8. 'Western Chronicle', 5 July 1895; 'Western Daily Press', 14 December 1908 and 'Western Gazette', 18 December 1908; 'Western Chronicle', 24 July 1891.

9. S.H.C. DD/CGS 10/19, Sexey's Trade School List of Successes 1903; T.N.A. ED 35/2176, Sexey's School List of Successes 1908; ED 109/5096, Inspection Report 1904, p. 17; Sexey's School Magazine, Michaelmas 1913, p. 85; H.W. Hillier, Register, op.cit., p. x; 'Wells Journal', 20 December 1912.

g) A boarding school.

1. 'Western Chronicle', 1896.

2. S.H.C. DD/SE 72, Hospital Minute Book, op.cit., 13 September 1892; DD/BT 25/93 Sexey's Hospital Letter Book 1889-1893: Letter from T.O. Bennett to solicitors Powell and Powell, 14 September 1892; Letters of T.O. Bennett to J. Eland 28 March 1892, and to Mrs Cockle, 7 April 1892; Letter from T.O. Bennett to Charity Commissioners, 3 November 1890.

3. Sexey's School Magazine, Spring 1960, p. 26: Recollections of A.E. Green (1898-1901), p. 26; Easter 1903, p. 20.

4. T.N.A. ED 35/2175, Internal Memo added to Inspection Report, June 1908; Letter from Board of Education to the Governors, 3 September 1908; Letter from F. Hooper to Board of Education, 19 October 1908; ED 35/2176, Scheme of Government, 15 June 1910.

5. T.N.A. ED 109/5096, Inspection Report 1904, op.cit., pp. 5-6; 'Western Daily Press', 6 February 1905; T.N.A. ED 35/2175, Inspection Report 1910, op.cit., p. 8; Letter from F. Hooper to Board of Education, 5 April 1910; Record of Meeting between Henry Hobhouse and Mr Bruce 9 April 1910; Letter from Board of Education to Governors, 21 April 1910; Letter from

F. Hooper to Board of Education, 11 May 1910, including copy of 'Regulations as to boys lodging in the town', undated; Letter from Board of Education to Governors, 26 May 1910.

6. T.N.A. ED 35/2175, Letter from F. Hooper to Board of Education, 2 April 1914; Sexey's Boys' School Circular, July 1914; Letter from H.Hobhouse to F.W. Battiscombe at Board of Education, 19 September 1914; Sexey's School Magazine, Easter 1915, p. 11; T.N.A. ED 109/5098, Inspection Report 1920, op.cit.: Confidential Report.

h) Examinations, Reports and Prizes.

1. T.N.A. ED 27/4085, Scheme 1889, op.cit.; ED 35/2176, Inspection Report 1910, op.cit., p. 24; Sexey's School Magazine, Christmas 1897, pp. 4-5; T.N.A. ED 109/5096, Inspection Report 1904, op.cit., p. 10.
2. H. Scott, op. cit., p. 14; 'Western Chronicle', 6 July 1894; Sexey's School Magazine, Michaelmas 1906, p. 83; C. Clark, The Diary, op.cit., p. 138, 8 May 1894.
3. 'Western Daily Press', 14 December 1901; T.N.A. ED 35/2176, List of Successes: Summary of results 1901-1908; Sexey's School Magazine, Easter 1914, p. 12.
4. T.N.A. ED 27/4088, Mr Lefroy's Report, op.cit., including Report of Examiner H Walker for 1893; ED 27/4089, Reports for Sexey's Trade School 1894-1900; Sexey's School Magazine, Easter 1907, p. 7, Easter 1908, p. 9, Easter 1913, p. 12.
5. C. Clark, Diary, op.cit., p. 125, 1 July 1893, p. 158, 29 June 1895, p. 223, 17 December 1898; Monthly Review, op.cit., August 1893: Sexey's Trade School, Distribution of Prizes; T.N.A. ED 109/5096, Inspection Report 1904, op.cit., p. 9.

i) Curriculum.

1. T.N.A. ED 27/4085, Scheme 1889, op.cit.; ED 27/4086, Sexey's Trade School Prospectus, op.cit.
2. S.H.C. DD/CGS 10/19, Sexey's Trade School Prospectus June 1904; T.N.A. ED 35/2176, Inspection Report 1910,

op.cit., p, 10; Sexey's School Magazine, Easter 1903, p. 11; Professor John Read (1896-1901) in Sexey's School Magazine, Michaelmas 1927, p. 105.

3. 'Western Chronicle', 6 June 1894; Acland Committee, 1911, op.cit., Evidence of W.A. Knight, p. 250; Sexey's School Magazine, Easter 1905, p.10; Acland Committee, 1911, op.cit.: Appendix A to Evidence of Mr W.A. Knight, pp. 89-92; S.H.C. A/BVZ/12, Manual Instruction: Woodwork Exercise Book August to October 1902, A.J. Jennings, Form III, Age 14.

4. Acland Committee, op.cit.: Evidence of Mr W.A.Knight, p. 249; 'Western Chronicle', 16 February 1894; Sexey's School Magazine, Midsummer 1898: School Chronicles, p. 4; Acland Committee, op.cit., Appendix B, p. 92.

5. T.N.A. ED 35/2176, Inspection Report 1910, op.cit., pp. 22-3; Sexey's School Magazine, Easter 1915, pp. 36-7.

6. T.N.A. ED 27/4089, Report for 1895 by W.B. Hands; Castle Cary Visitor, vol. II, 1898-9, p. 84; Sexeian, 1991, p. 81; Letter from G.M. Tincknell to 'Countryside Monthly', reprinted in 'Shepton Mallet Journal', 7 July 1911.

7. 'Jack Brimble: An Appreciation' published in 'Nature' vol. 208, No. 5013, 27 November 1965, reprinted in Sexey's School Magazine, Easter 1966, pp. 30-1; Professor Frederick Brooks in 'Obituary Notices of Fellows of the Royal Society', vol. 8, No. 22, 1953, p. 341; T.N.A. ED 35/2176, Inspection Report 1910, op.cit., pp. 18-19; ED 27/4089, Report April 1894; Inspection Report, 1910, op.cit., p. 13; Report for 1895; S.H.C. A/BVZ 13, Notebook of A.J. Jennings, Form III, Age 14.

8. T.N.A. ED 27/4089, Report for 1895, op.cit.; The Somerset Year Book 1922: Some Somerset Artists, p. 40 with Harvey's picture facing; Sexey's School Magazine, Easter 1903, p. 20.

9. T.N.A. ED 27/4085, Scheme 1889, op.cit.; ED 27/4086, Sexey's Trade School Prospectus, op.cit.; ED 27/4088, Mr Lefroy's Report, op.cit.; ED 27/4089, Report of Charles Bickmore April 1894; H. Phillips, op.cit., pp. 59-60.

10. T.N.A. ED 109/5097, Inspection Report 1910, op.cit., p. 10; Sexey' School Magazine, Easter 1903, pp. 8 and 10, Easter 1904, p. 8; 'Western Chronicle', 6 July 1894; S.H.C. CGS 10/19, Prospectus 1904, op.cit.; Inspection Report 1910, op.cit., p. 14.

11. 'Shepton Mallet Journal', 20 December 1901; Acland Committee, op.cit., Addendum A, p. 253; Sexey's School Magazine, Easter 1903, p. 8; H. Scott, op.cit., pp. 15-16; H. Phillips, op.cit., pp. 61, 65, 97; T.N.A. ED 27/4089, Report of William Hands, 1895; Sexey's School Magazine, Michaelmas 1914, p. 106, Easter 1912, p. 9.

12. C. Clark, The Diary, op.cit., p. 119, 23 February 1893, p. 140, 15 June 1894; 'Taunton Courier and Western Advertizer', 11 January 1899.

13. 'Western Chronicle', 6 July 1894; Sexey's School Magazine, Easter 1917, p. 39, Christmas 1917, p. 113.

14. H. Scott, op.cit., p. 14; H. Phillips, op.cit., p. 69; H. Hillier, ed., Register, op.cit., p. 8.

15. See, for example, Sexey's School Magazine, Midsummer 1904, pp. 32-3 (Hadspen), Easter 1911, pp. 46-7 (Cogley Wood), Midsummer 1904, p. 35 (Cogley Wood), Easter 1911, pp. 46-7, Cogley Wood and another to Wyke Champflower), May 1897, Tour to Stourton, re-produced in Sexeian 1999, p. 68.

16. Sexey's School Magazine, Easter 1913, p. 12; Photograph of 1914 Summer Walk in possession of Sexey's School; Sexey's School Magazine, Midsummer 1898, p. 4: School Chronicles IV; H. Scott, op.cit., pp. 14-15; T.N.A. ED 109/5096, H.M.I. Report 1904, op.cit., p. 13; Sexey's School Magazine, Christmas 1905, p. 92.

17. H. Phillips, op.cit., pp. 49-50; T.N.A. 35/2176, H.M.I. Report 1910, op.cit., p.10; Sexey's School Magazine, Easter 1913, pp. 12-13.

18. 'Shepton Mallet Journal', 20 March 1891; T.N.A. ED 27/4088, Mr Lefroy's Report, op.cit.: 1894 Timetable; S.H.C. DD/CGS, Prospectus 1903, op.cit.: School Hours and Holidays; Sexeian 1991, op.cit., p. 78; T.N.A. ED 35/2176, H.M.I. Report 1910, op.cit., p. 24.

19. 'The Times Educational Supplement', 5 September 1911; Somerset Year Book 1927, op.cit., p. 97.
20. 'Western Chronicle', 9 February 1906; T.N.A. ED 35/2175, Letter from F. Hooper to Board of Education, 7 February 1906; Memo from H. Dibben and E. Battiscombe, 21 May 1906; 'Western Chronicle', 2 August 1907.
21. T.N.A. ED 27/4089, op.cit., Report of Charles Beck, Midsummer 1900; ED 35/2175, Sexey's Trade School: Letter from W.A. Knight to Board of Education, 1 July 1903 and Reply of Board, 23 July 1903.
22. Sexey's School Magazine, Michaelmas 1908, p. 78; S.H.C. DD/CGS 10/19, Sexey's Trade School Prospectus, June 1904; Sexeian 1991, p. 78; T.N.A. ED 109/5096, H.M.I. Report 1904, op.cit., p. 5; H. Hillier, Register, op.cit., p. xi.
23. 'Western Gazette', 6 December 1901; 'Shepton Mallet Journal', 7 November 1902, 31 October 1902; Sexey's School Magazine, Easter 1908, Christmas 1903, pp. 76-7; 'Shepton Mallet Journal', 31 March 1911; H. Scott, op.cit., p. 14.
24. Sexey's School Magazine, Christmas 1908, p. 105; 'Western Gazette', 29 May 1908; 'Shepton Mallet Journal', 16 June 1899, 5 September 1902; 'Wells Journal', 6 July 1907.
25. Sexey's School Magazine, Michaelmas 1910, p. 77, Michaelmas 1913, pp. 84, 85.
26. 'Western Chronicle', 13 September 1907; Sexey's School Magazine, Michaelmas 1904, p. 47; Castle Cary Visitor, vol. VIII, 1910-11, p. 175.
27. Sexey's School Magazine, Easter 1908, pp. 8-9; 'Western Chronicle', 24 December 1909; Sexey's School Magazine, Michaelmas 1909, p. 51. Easter 1911, p. 47, Michaelmas 1912, pp. 102-3.
28. S.H.C. DD/CGS 10/19, Prospectus 1904, op.cit.; Sexey's School Magazine, Easter 1909, p. 18, Easter 1917, p. 20, Centenary Sexeian, 1991, p. 79.
29. Sexey's School Magazine, Easter 1904, p. 7; H. Phillips, op.cit., pp. 51, 58; Sexey's School Magazine, Easter 1964, p. 26; Centenary Sexeian, 1991, p. 78; Sexey's School Magazine,

Midsummer 1898 and Midsummer 1908; Centenary Sexeian, 1991, pp. 78-9.

30. H. Phillips, op.cit., pp. 52-3; Sexey's School Magazine, Midsummer 1908, p. 47, Easter 1964, pp. 26-7.

j) Aspects of School Life.

1. C. Clark, The Diary, op.cit., p. 112, 24 October 1892. For early pictures of boys wearing caps, see J. Lello, Centenary History of Sexey's School, privately printed, 1991, p. 8 and Centenary Sexeian, 1991, p 75, and for clothes in general p. 76; Sexey's School Magazine, Spring 1963, p. 24.

2. H. Phillips, op.cit., p. 55; T.N.A. ED 109/5097, H.M.I. Report 1910, op.cit., p. 24; Sexeian 1992, p. 61.

3. 'Western Chronicle', 6 July 1894; Centenary Sexeian, 1991, pp. 79-80, 78; Sexeian, 1992, p. 61; H. Phillips, op. cit., pp. 58-9; T.N.A. ED 109/5097, H.M.I. Report 1910, op.cit., p. 24; H. Hillier, op.cit., pp. 1-2.

4. H. Phillips, op.cit., pp. 97-8; T.N.A. ED 109/5097, H.M.I. Report 1910, op.cit., p. 24; H. Phillips, op.cit., pp. 50-1; 'Shepton Mallet Journal', 23 December 1910; Sexey's School Magazine, Xmas 1916, pp. 113-4; T.N.A. ED 109/5098, Report of Inspection May 1920, op.cit., p. 10.

5. The Somerset Year Book, 1922, pp. 42-3, - the Editor was Douglas Macmillan, himself an Old Sexeian, 1894-1897; Centenary Sexeian, 1991, p. 78; H. Phillips, op.cit., pp. 70, 52; Sexeian, 1992, p. 61; Sexey's School Magazine, Easter 1905, p. 8; T.N.A. ED 109/5096, H.M.I. Report, 1904, op.cit., p. 5.

6. Sexey's School Magazine, Easter 1909, p. 19, Michaelmas 1903, Christmas 1914, p. 118, Easter 1915, p. 23.

7. Sexey's School Magazine, Christmas 1905, p. 80.

8. Gun-cotton was a highly explosive cellulose nitrate made from clean cotton dissolved in a mixture of one part nitric acid and three parts sulphuric acid. Sexey's School Magazine, Christmas 1912, p. 116.

9. G.M. Tincknell, Directory of Old Sexeians 1891-1920; Sexey's School Magazine, Christmas 1908, p. 105, Easter 1914, p. 3; 'Taunton Courier, 23 April 1949.

10. T.N.A. ED 35/2175, Letter from F.W. Hooper to Board of Education, 11 November 1912, Letter from Board of Education to Hooper, 9 December 1912 and acceptance of Governors 11 December 1912; Sexey's School Magazine, Easter 1913, p. 10; T.N.A. ED 35/2175, Report of Inspection, May 1920, op.cit., p. 10.

k) Finance and Fees.

1. Local Taxation Returns made to the Department of Science and Art, 1894, p. 42: Somerset County Council, Sexey's Trade School; T.N.A. ED 27/4086, Summary Statement of Accounts for 13 Months ending 31st December 1897; Local Taxation Returns... 1895, p. 64; Report of Somerset Education Committee 1899-1900, p. 37, Table A Showing Capital Expenditure during the 9 years ending 31 March 1900.

2. The annual grants were generally published in Somerset County Council Education Committee Annual Reports and often then reported in local newspapers, see, for example,'Shepton Mallet Journal', 29 August 1902.

3. The statistics for Sexey's Trade School may be found in Appendix B of the Annual Reports of the Department of Science and Art.

4. T.N.A. ED 20/4086, Summary Statement 1897, op.cit.; ED 35/2175, Receipts and Payments 1913-1914; ED 27/4085, Scheme of Administration, December 1889, p. 7; 'Western Gazette', 10 April 1896; Sexey's School Magazine, Easter 1904, p. 7, Easter 1905, p. 7; 'Western Chronicle' , 10 December 1905; Sexey's School Magazine, Easter 1907, p. 7.

5. T.N.A. ED 35/2176, Scheme 1910, p. 6; ED 35/2175, Letter from F.W. Hooper to Board of Education, 11 November 1912 and Reply of Board, 9 December 1912; Letter from Henry Hobhouse to Board of Education 28 June 1913.

6. C. Clark, The Diary, op.cit., p. 112, 19 October 1892.

7. T.N.A. ED 20/4086, Summary Statement 1897, op.cit.; ED 109/5096, Report of Inspection, 1904, op.cit., p. 3; ED 109/5097, Report of Inspection, 1910, op.cit.: Synopsis; ED 35/2175,

Letter from Henry Hobhouse to Board of Education, 28 June 1913 with 'Estimate of Receipts and Payments' attached; ED 109/5098, Report of Inspection, 1920, op.cit., pp. 1,3.

8. T.N.A. ED 27/4088, Mr Lefroy's Report, op.cit., No 8; ED 109/5096, Report of Inspection, 1904, op.cit., p. 9; ED 109/5097, Report of Inspection, 1910, op.cit., p. 2; ED 37/2176, Revised Scheme, 1910, op.cit., p. 6; ED 35/2175, Internal Memo by Mr Eddis attached to H.M.I. Report 1904.

l) Odds and Ends.

1. Sexey's School Magazine, Christmas 1922, pp. 145-6.
2. Cited in A. Mee, ed., The King's England, London, p. 82.
3. S.H.C. DD/SE 90, Bruton, Sexey's Boys' School: Charge to Henry Hobhouse and Derlyn Company Limited.
4. Sexey's School Magazine, Midsummer 1918, p. 51.

m) Conclusion.

1. 'Western Chronicle', 3 July 1896, 24 December 1909.
2. Sexey's School Magazine, Michaelmas 1927, pp. 103-4; 'Frederick Tom Brooks 1882-1952' by W.C. Moore in Obituary Notices of Fellows of the Royal Society, vol. 8, No. 22 (1953), p. 34.
3. T.N.A. ED 35/2175, Proposed Pupil Teachers' Centre, 1906.
4. T.N.A. ED 109/5096, Report of Inspection, 1904, op.cit., p. 7; ED 109/5097, Report of Inspection, 1910, op.cit., p. 8.
5. P.W. Randell, ed., 'Danger and Duty Nobly and Simply faced'. The Great War 1914-1918 as recorded in the School Magazines of Sexey's School, Bruton, privately printed, 2006.

5. Other Schools.

1. S.H.C. D/P/brut 13/6/1, Apprenticeship Papers 1660-1832.
2. T.N.A. STAC 10/4/106, Court of Star Chamber 1558-1601; S.H.C. D/D/ol 8, Licensing Book 30 May 1584; D/D/vc 58, Subscription Book 18 September 1626; T.H.Peak, 'The Somerset Clergy and the Church in the diocese of Bath and

Wells, 1625-1642', M. Litt. Dissertation for the University of Bristol 1978, p. 394; G. Lyon Turner, Original Records of Early Nonconformity under Persecution and Indulgence, vol. 2, London, 1911, p. 1119; S.H.C. D/D/Bs 42, Subscription Book 1672-1694; D/D/Whs, Box 2, Diocesan Registry: Answers of Clergy of the deanery of Cary; G. Lyon Turner, op.cit., pp. 1088 and 1119.

3. S.H.C. D/D/BS/43, Subscription Book, 18 July 1705; D/D/Rn 1, Licences to Teach 1746; J. Martin, Wives and Daughters: Women and Children in the Georgian Country House. London, 2004, p. 217; The Universal British Directory, vol. II, London, c.1794, p, 391; S.H.C. DD/DN/13, Will of Robert Pavy 19 November 1796; DD/BR/iw/1, Indenture of John Dampier, Esq., to John Penny, Schoolmaster, 1799;

4. 'Sherborne Mercury', 3 January 1814; S.H.C. DD/BRU 10/14, Mr Oram's Academy: Specimens of Penmanship, 1816.

5. 'Morning Chronicle', 9 July 1807; Castle Cary Visitor, vol. IX, 1912-13, p. 75; Pigot's London and Provincial Commercial Directory: Somerset 1822-3, London, 1823, p. 438; 'Sherborne Mercury', 7 July 1827; 'Dorset Country Chronicle', 27 March 1834.

6. Bragg's Directory: Bruton Academies 1840; 'Shepton Mallet Journal', 29 April 1864; 'Western Gazette', 31 December 1864; 'Shepton Mallet Journal', 21 September 1866.

7. A.D. Fox, King's School, Bruton, Register, 3rd edition, 1911; 'Western Gazette', 24 February 1888; 'Western Chronicle', 18 February 1887.

8. For the role of Dame Schools, see for example, M. Gorsky, Patterns of Philanthropy, Woodbridge, 1999, p. 238; The Poetical Works of George Crabbe, vol. IV, London, 1834, p. 77; Digest of Returns to the Select Committee on Education of the Poor 1818, PP 1819, IX, Pt II, pp. 776, 806; Abstract of Education Returns 1833, PP 1835, XLII, p. 797; T.N.A. HO 107 934/3, Census 1841; HO 107 1931, Census 1851; HO 9 320/4, Census 1861.

9. S.H.C. D/G/WN 60/1 and 60/2, Admission and Discharge Books 1836-8; WN 60/3, Admission and Discharge Book 1869-1874; Royal Commission on Popular Education: Report

of Rev. James Fraser, Assistant Commissioner, PP 1861, XXI, pt. II, p. 89; T.N.A. MH 32/108, Reports of Inspectors: Report of T.B. Browne, January 1864 and 1870.

10. T.N.A. PROB 11/149/156, Will of Dame Elizabeth Berkeley, 1626; J. Martin ed., A Governess in the Age of Jane Austen: the Journals and Letters of Agnes Porter, London, 1999, p. 324.

11. Universal British Directory, op.cit., p. 390; Pigot's Directory, op.cit., p. 438; 'Dorset County Chronicle', 27 January 1837; Bragg's Directory, 1840, op.cit.; ' Frome Times', 17 February 1864; 'Western Gazette', 13 August 1869, 17 January 1871.

12. Information on the Misses Skinners' School taken from various editions of Kelly's Directory in the period 1850-1900; C. Clark, The Diary, op.cit., p. 112, 2 May 1893; 'Western Chronicle', 13 April 1894, 4 August 1899, 1 March 1901.

13. 'Western Chronicle', 22 February 1901, 7 November 1902; 'Western Gazette', 22 August 1902; 'Western Chronicle', 23 December 1904, 22 January 1904, 11 April 1906.

14. ibid., 16 December 1910, 3 August 1913, 18 December 1914.

15. 'Shepton Mallet Journal', 31 August 1902; S.H.C. DD/Su 19, Memorandum and Articles of Association, 17 February 1894; T.N.A. ED 35/2180, Sunny Hill Girls' School, Memorandum and Articles of Association, January 1899.

16. ibid., Letter from James Golledge to Board of Education, 28 June 1904; T.N.A. ED 109/5100, Report of Inspection by H.M.I.s, November 1906.

17. 'Western Chronicle', 14 July 1899; 'Western Daily Press', 27 October 1900.

18. ibid., 15 September 1900; 'Western Gazette', 5 July 1901; 'Western Daily Press', 27 October 1900.

19. T.N.A. ED 109/5100, Report of Inspection 1906, op.cit.; ED 109/5102, Report of Inspection by H.M.I.s March 1915; 'Western Chronicle', 12 December 1913.

20. Inspection Reports 1906 and 1915, op.cit.; T.N.A. ED 109/5101, Report of Inspection by H.M.I.s 1910; 'Western Chronicle', 11 April 1913.

21. T.N.A. ED 35/2180, Report of Bruton Girls' Company, February 1902.

22. 'Shepton Mallet Journal', 31 October 1902; Inspection Report 1915, op.cit.
23. T.N.A. ED 35/2180, Report of Inspectors to Board of Education: Bruton Pupil Teacher Centre, 17 February 1905; Inspection Report 1915, op.cit.
24. 'Western Chronicle', 1 April 1913, 16 October 1914.
25. T.N.A. ED 35/2180, Report of Bruton Girls' School Company, 19 March 1904 and 4 March 1905; Architect's Report, 22 December 1911, Amended Plans, 22 February 1912; Inspection Report 1915, op.cit.
26. T.N.A. ED 35/2180, Annual Reports of School Company, op cit.; 'Shepton Mallet Journal', 24 March 1899, 13 April 1902; 'Western Chronicle', 11 April 1913.
27. T.N.A. ED 35/2180, Letters from James Golledge to Board of Education, 18 June and 2 November 1904; Reply of Board of Education, 13 October 1904; Report on Suitability for Recognition, 3 December 1904; Report to Directors, March 1905; Report of Meeting between Directors and Mr Ellis, February 1905.
28. T.N.A. 35/2180, Letter from Henry Hobhouse to Board of Education, 16 June 1911 and Reply for Board, 26 June 1911; Letter from Board of Education confirming School on List of Secondary Schools, 5 February 1912.
29. Inspection Report 1906 and Inspection Report 1915, op.cit.
30. 'Western Chronicle', 11 April 1913.
31. 'Shepton Mallet Journal', 31 October 1902; Castle Cary Visitor, vol. IV, 1902-3, p. 168; 'Western Chronicle', 11 April 1913; Inspection Report 1910, op.cit.
32. 'Shepton Mallet Journal' 31 October 1902; 'Western Chronicle', 11 April 1913, and 12 December 1913.
33. ibid., 12 December 1913; Inspection Report 1906, op.cit.; 'Western Chronicle', 11 April 1913 and 12 December 1913; 'Shepton Mallet Journal', 31 October 1902.
34. Digest of Returns, 1818, op.cit., pp. 775, 793, 798.
35. Abstract of Education Returns, 1833, op.cit., pp. 795, 818, 821; F.R. Kelly, County Topographies: Somerset, London, 1875, pp. 386, 426.

36. S.H.C. DD/X/KR, Pocket Ledger of J. Goldesbrough, Discove, 11 March 1816, 14 April 1817; Dorset Record Office, D/FSI, Box 258: Charity's at Redlinch & in Sommersetshire, pp. 1-5. Until at least 1810 there was a building in Dropping Lane referred to as 'the charity house'. This was most likely the house which subsequently became known as 'The Hollies' and in the late twentieth century as 'Monkshead'. See Victoria County History of Somerset, vol. VII, 1999, p. 41.

37. T.N.A. ED 7/104 No 52, Preliminary Statement of Income and Expenditure, Bruton Mixed School 1852; BM, Box 52, 2007.111.15, Appointment of Mr and Mrs Byles, 28 March 1854; 'Western Gazette', 31 January 1908; 'The Wincanton, Bruton and Castle Cary Monthly Review', November 1893; Somerset Education Committee Reports, 1898-1899, p. 13, 1899-1900, p. 14; 'Western Chronicle', 17 July 1896.

38. C. Clark, The Diary of a Wessex Farmer, op. cit., p. 119, 8 February 1893; 'Shepton Mallet Journal', 23 October 1868, 14 April 1899; 'Western Chronicle', 27 April 1900; 'Shepton Mallet Journal', 14 April 1899; 'Western Gazette', 31 January 1908; 'Western Chronicle', 3 October 1913; 25 November 1910, January 1912.

39. 'Western Chronicle', 13 May 1895, 17 July 1896, 25 May 1900; 'Shepton Mallet Journal', 18 April 1899.

40. The information in this Table is taken from Somerset County Council Annual Reports in the 1890s and announcements which appeared in local newspapers.

41. Abstract of Education Returns, 1833, op.cit., p. 797; S.H.C. D/N/Scu 4/2/7, Church Record Book.... of the Independent Denomination of Bruton, 13 November 1859; F. Kelly, ed., Directory for Somerset 1861, London, 1861, p. 300; 'Shepton Mallet Journal', 9 September 1859, 23 September 1859.

42. F. Kelly, County Topographies 1875, op.cit., p. 120; 'Western Gazette', 22 October 1871, 20 March 1891; C. Clark, The Diary, op.cit., p. 129, 6 October 1893, p. 130, 2, 18 and 20 November 1893, p. 131, 14 December 1893.

43. 'Wells Journal', 5 August 1897: Case of Ward; ibid. 10 April and 24 July 1914.

www.ingramcontent.com/pod-product-compliance
Lightning Source LLC
Chambersburg PA
CBHW022112080426
42734CB00006B/97